GW01395993

Praise for
STRUGGLE AND MUTUAL AID

"A scholarly take on the development and influence of the mid-nineteenth-century international workers' movement...a persuasive reinterpretation of a period of labor activism often viewed as 'chaotic, conflictual, and contradictory.'"
—*Publishers Weekly*

"A fascinating book about globalization, internationalism, and wealth redistribution between 1870 and 1914, with lots of lessons for the twenty-first century. When trade and capital flows go global, worker solidarity and political mobilization need to do the same and invent new forms of transnational organizations. A must-read."
—**Thomas Piketty, international bestselling author of** *Capital in the Twenty-First Century*

"An indispensable history of working-class internationalism—this book is a must-read for anybody interested in building solidarity across borders today."
—**Eric Blanc, author of** *Revolutionary Social Democracy* **and** *Red State Revolt*

"*Struggle and Mutual Aid* recovers the history of workers' organizations as an essential component of nineteenth-century globalization. It is a brilliant study of the financing, politics, and practice of labor internationalism, and a counter-example to the apparently inexorable expansion of international capital in the twenty-first century."
—**Emma Rothschild, author of** *An Infinite History: The Story of a Family in France over Three Centuries*

row around the word 'solidarity' today without understand-
ts history or even its meaning. Delalande has provided us
 a much-needed guide to the history of solidarity. This criti-
y important history of international solidarity efforts reminds
that we must know the past to be effective activists today. The
anslation of this book into English should be celebrated on the
eft. Everyone interested in the history of the workers' struggle
must read this book."

—**Erik Loomis, author of**
A History of America in Ten Strikes

"Nicolas Delalande's fresh account of nineteenth- and twentieth-century labor internationalism captures its evolving aspirations, successes, failures, and resiliency amid defeats, reminding us of the pivotal role it has played in world history. Through its captivating survey of cross-border working-class solidarity initiatives, this volume helps us imagine how a revived labor internationalism might challenge the forces presently plunging us deeper into social, political, and ecological crisis. Delalande's vivid history inspires hope—just when we need it."

—**Joseph A. McCartin, coeditor of** *Purple Power:*
The History and Global Impact of SEIU

"In the wake of the destructive coronavirus pandemic, this book provides an extraordinary resource for workers seeking to build new cross-border solidarities to prevent the pervasive globalization phenomenon 'from benefiting only the rich and powerful.'"

—**Joe William Trotter Jr., author of** *Workers on Arrival:*
Black Labor in the Making of America

STRUGGLE AND
Mutual Aid

ALSO BY NICOLAS DELALANDE

A World of Public Debts: A Political History
(coeditor, with Nicolas Barreyre)

France in the World: A New Global History
(coeditor, with Patrick Boucheron et al.)

STRUGGLE AND MUTUAL AID

The Age of Worker Solidarity

Nicolas Delalande

TRANSLATED FROM THE FRENCH BY ANTHONY ROBERTS

OTHER PRESS | NEW YORK

Originally published in French as *La Lutte et l'entraide:*
L'Âge des solidarités ouvrières in 2019 by Éditions du Seuil, Paris.
Copyright © Éditions du Seuil, 2019
English translation copyright © Other Press, 2023
Preface © Nicolas Delalande, 2023

Production editor: Yvonne E. Cárdenas
Text designer: Julie Fry
This book was set in Miller and Knockout by
Alpha Design & Composition of Pittsfield, NH

10 9 8 7 6 5 4 3 2 1

All rights reserved. No part of this publication may be reproduced or
transmitted in any form or by any means, electronic or mechanical,
including photocopying, recording, or by any information storage and
retrieval system, without written permission from Other Press LLC,
except in the case of brief quotations in reviews for inclusion in a
magazine, newspaper, or broadcast. Printed in the United States of
America on acid-free paper. For information write to Other Press LLC,
267 Fifth Avenue, 6th Floor, New York, NY 10016. Or visit our Web
site: www.otherpress.com

Library of Congress Cataloging-In-Publication Data
Names: Delalande, Nicolas, author.
Title: Struggle and mutual aid : the age of worker solidarity /
    Nicolas Delalande ; Translated from French by Anthony Roberts.
Other titles: Lutte et l'entraide. English
Description: New York : Other Press, [2023] | "Originally published
    in French as La Lutte et l'entraide: L'Âge des solidarités ouvrières
    in 2019 by Éditions du Seuil, Paris" — Title page verso. | Includes
    bibliographical references and index.
Identifiers: LCCN 2022027363 (print) | LCCN 2022027364 (ebook) |
    ISBN 9781635420104 (hardcover) | ISBN 9781635420111 (ebook)
Subjects: LCSH: Working class — History. | Labor movement — History. |
    International cooperation — History. | Solidarity — Political aspects.
Classification: LCC HD4851 .D45 2023 (print) | LCC HD4851 (ebook) |
    DDC 331.8809 — dc23/eng/20221014
LC record available at https://lccn.loc.gov/2022027363
LC ebook record available at https://lccn.loc.gov/2022027364

For Léonore,
for Esther & Lucile

Contents

Preface to the English-Language Edition   xi

Introduction   1

    The Nineteenth-Century Globalization   2

    The Making of Solidarity   5

    In Quest of Autonomy   10

    Moral Economy and Money   12

    Rediscovering Worker Internationalism   15

PART ONE: THE YEARS OF EXPERIMENT

1 | **A Workers' State?**   21

    The Credit of the IWA   23

    An Indebted, Secretive Organization   30

    The Hunt for Funds   37

    Reputation, Confidence, and Suspicion   46

2 | **Workers' Money** 59

The Emancipatory Power of Credit 60

Accumulating Funds In "Resistance Societies" 72

The Age of Subscriptions 87

3 | **Struggle and Mutual Aid** 98

The Early Strikes 99

Years of Apprenticeship 114

The Geography of Solidarity 124

4 | **The Pitfalls of Compassion** 145

Forms of Donation 147

The Ordeal of the Commune 159

Refugees Fending for themselves 173

PART TWO: THE YEARS OF CONSOLIDATION

5 | **The Revival of Internationalism** 191

The Strength of Weak Ties 192

The New Working Worlds 207

6 | **Solidarity and the Masses** 228

An International of Trades 230

A Blueprint For Pan-European Syndicalism 242

The Deployment of Solidarity 254

7 | **A Revolutionary Weapon?** 267

The Primacy of National Organizations 268

The Spread of Socialism Worldwide 271

Support for the Russian Revolution 275

The General Strike: A Burning Issue 279

Revolutionary Syndicalism in the USA   **285**
The Rout of Anti-Militarism   **288**

8 | **Footprints and Legacies**   **293**

Competing Benefits   **294**
Blurred Boundaries   **299**
Global Struggle   **303**
Bipolar Solidarities   **309**

Conclusion   **317**

Acknowledgments   **325**
List of Acronyms   **327**
Notes   **329**
Archives and Sources   **395**
Select Bibliography   **397**
Index of Names   **405**

Preface to the English-Language Edition

Can the workers of the world ever join forces to defend their rights, improve their condition, and break the monopoly of capital? Just a few years ago, at the dawn of the twenty-first century, the very suggestion might have seemed absurd, with the words "worker," "solidarity," and "internationalism" sounding at best like whispers from a distant past.

But times have changed. Today, the social and economic turmoil of the COVID-19 pandemic, as well as the return of global inflation, have upended everything.

Never before did frontline health-care workers prove so critical to society than during the months of COVID confinement from 2020 to 2021. As productive activity faltered across the board, governments began to spend colossal sums to stop the spread of the virus, and this in turn radically modified the *rapport de force* between workers and employers. By the fall of 2021, twenty million American workers had quit their jobs in what came to be known as the "Great Resignation." This fleeting phenomenon made headlines; it looked like ordinary workers really were determined to withdraw from the job market for as long as the wages and conditions on offer failed to meet their expectations. For a while, this new, mute brand of strike action disrupted the supply chains of many industrial sectors, forcing salaries upward and fueling inflation. For the first time in decades the balance of macroeconomic forces appeared to be tilting toward work — and away from capital.

This was a serious setback for the kind of unbridled capitalism that had dominated the previous thirty years. In addition, there came a reawakening that was as sudden as it was unexpected. Union and strike action broke out within a political context that had been made more favorable by the election of a Democratic U.S. president, Joe Biden, in November 2020. American workers, whose recent militant tradition was negligible, rediscovered the virtues of collective action. Conflicts broke out in Starbucks coffee shops and Amazon warehouses in 2021 and early 2022, in sectors hitherto bereft of collective solidarity. Alarmed, the managements of these companies spent plenty of effort and money to stamp out their workers' attempts to organize, which they saw as threats to employer omnipotence and worker subordination. With the economic recovery and the glaringly unequal apportioning of gains that followed, not only workers in publishing and mass-market retailing but also young university graduates formed unions and resorted to strike action to obtain better wages and a fairer appreciation of their status.

Although they were fragile and limited, these mobilizations marked a fresh drive for collective solidarity and mutual aid among workers of widely differing social origins, qualifications, types, and ethnicities. This was all the more necessary inasmuch as the voices of nationalist populism had persisted in stigmatizing refugees, immigrants, and foreign workers ever since the crisis of 2008, accusing them of provoking a fall in salaries, finagling welfare benefits, and perverting the cultural homogeneity of societies in Europe and the United States. Among the middle and working classes, frustration with unequal globalization fueled an increasing sense of distrust toward democratic values and institutions.

For all these reasons, there is an urgent need to look back on the long history of past efforts to unite and defend the workers, over and above their differences and divisions. We need to rediscover exactly what the promises and difficulties of collective action really are. For a century, from the 1860s to the 1970s, socialist, anarchist, communist, and otherwise unionized workers, each with their own sets of beliefs, carried forward an internationalist project of colossal power. Their objective was not to close frontiers and restrict exchanges, but to build a globalized system of worker solidarity overarching any national or linguistic differences.

In the past, it was understood that the defense of the popular classes could not be achieved by withdrawing into isolation, building walls, or rejecting others. It could succeed only if the struggles and demands of all could be channeled into a single titanic effort. This vast project, in which few people believed at its outset, was often chaotic, conflictual, and contradictory. It had its own failures, dark sides, divisions, and antagonisms. But it left an indelible mark on the last years of the nineteenth century and on the century that followed. In the United States as in Europe, workers and ordinary people obtained new rights, better protections, and decent wages as a result of mobilizations supported by mass organizations and the internationalist structures that gave them sense and meaning.

The history of all this was *absolutely not* one of an enchanted world of sovereign nations and social progress, followed by a lawless interlude beginning in the 1970s of financial globalization, mass unemployment, and deregulation. On the contrary, from its origins in the 1860s, the workers' movement sought to act within and through globalization, precisely in order to prevent globalization from benefiting only the rich and powerful.

In their confrontation with the global circulation of capital, the workers will always be on the losing side if they cannot join forces. To build a fairer, more supportive, and inclusive world based on struggle and mutual aid: the formula has never been more relevant and necessary. This book is dedicated to rediscovering the grandeur of this ideal and its troubled history, in the certainty that the fervent hopes of the past are still useful resources in planning the struggles of tomorrow. For neither the workers of America, nor the citizens of Europe, nor the people of China will ever improve their respective conditions — or the state of the planet — by degrading the lives of others and barricading themselves behind national borders.

Introduction

The ambition to unite workers across national frontiers emerged in the 1860s at a time when exchanges, migrations, and political cultures were starting to spread across the world. Revolutions in humankind's means of transportation and communication were leading to the growth of a globalized market in which goods, people, and information could circulate at a hitherto undreamed-of rate. The expansion of the telegraph, the growth of the great merchant shipping companies, and the emergence of London as a world center of finance and free markets, inaugurated the first phase of globalization as we know it.[1] Thereafter, powered by technological and economic innovation, the creation of new links between different parts of the world led to even wider consequences, transforming political organizations and cultures everywhere. The globalization of the nineteenth century, like the one of the late twentieth century, changed power balances as well as human aspirations. Its converts and opponents were agreed on one thing only: that they were all living in a completely new era, one — paradoxically — in which nations were becoming more like one another, and at the same time more protectionist.

THE NINETEENTH-CENTURY GLOBALIZATION

The globalization process of the nineteenth century went hand in hand with the growth of capitalism and European imperialism, and within this context the International Workingmen's Association (IWA) was founded in London in September 1864. The IWA, which later came to be known as the "First International," was born as a result of contacts made in London between French and British workers. The occasion was the 1862 Universal Exhibition, organized to celebrate the triumph of progress and industrial capitalism; but this event, perhaps unwittingly, also offered a golden opportunity for the enemies of capitalism to exchange views and build projects. Two years later, French and British workers were reunited at a meeting in support of an uprising in Poland, which was being brutally suppressed by the Russian Empire. From this second encounter grew a project with the far broader ambition of setting up an international workers' association, whose goal was to unite the workers of the world under a single banner.

London, the capital of the British Empire, was both a temple of liberalism and a haven for thousands of European political exiles fleeing the persecutions and censorship of tsarist Russia, Bismarck's Prussia, and Napoleon III's Second Empire. The Chartist effort for greater democracy in Britain had run out of steam in the aftermath of 1848, the "year of revolutions"; for the time being the country's parliamentary system considered itself secure in London. In consequence large numbers of republicans, democrats, socialists, and anarchists flocked to the British metropolis, all of them militants of one kind or another — Poles, Irish Nationalists, the 1867 partisans of Garibaldi in Italy, among many others — who roundly rejected authoritarian politics. Yet the defense of oppressed nations was not the only goal of radical protest and action. Socialist and anarchist ideas had been gaining ground since 1848, despite severe repression. There was a general outcry against the ravages of industrialization: inequality, wretched living conditions, exhausting labor. More and more workers dreamed of changing this economic system for the better, though it was praised to the skies by the liberal establishment.

Karl Marx, himself an exile in London, had not yet completed the first volume of *Das Kapital*. But already many like him were denouncing the profound inequalities engendered by the commercial reach and internationalization of capital: with the lowering of transportation costs and the intensification of migrations, workers found themselves caught in a competitive spiral that the captains of industry and manufacture exploited for profit. The more the globalization of capital forged ahead, the farther the globalization of work fell behind. Although they were physically involved in markets that were ever more closely connected, the workers coordinated very little beyond the frontiers of their own countries. This fact weakened the collective defense of their interests.[2] Clearly the globalization of working conditions was far from tempered by a globalization of the struggle for social justice. The militants who gathered in London at the end of September 1864 were determined to do something about this, despite the differences in their ideological affiliations.

The general council of the association, which was held every week between 1864 and 1872, brought together militants of all stripes and nationalities. Their attitudes to capitalism and bourgeois democracy ranged from extreme radical to moderate. Their divisions, which were real and deep, did not stop them from reaching a first unanimous agreement that it was vital for the workers of Europe and the United States to join forces across the frontiers that separated them. In the United States, the Civil War was raging; the North was fighting for the principle that freed slaves should be able to work in freedom just like everybody else. At the same time, immigrant workers from European countries like Germany, Sweden, and Ireland were beginning to mobilize for the betterment of working-class conditions. A first union, the National Labour Union, was created in the United States in 1866, at the very moment when, for the first time, European workers were also resorting to strike action and unionization. In 1869, the IWA finally took root on American soil among immigrant workers and local radical militants. Within a year it had attracted some four thousand adherents.[3]

What was at stake was the construction of authentic international worker solidarity, so that economic and financial globalization could benefit everybody, not just those who had capital. The famous call to arms that Karl Marx and Friedrich Engels had issued to proletarians of all nations in the *Manifesto of the Communist Party*, published in the beginning of 1848, was still largely unanswered. Even if there had been projects for international worker unity before, the experience of the IWA was something new on account of its sheer ambition, breadth, and durability, so much so that, within a few years, new sections of the association had been opened in England, France, Germany, Austria, Hungary, Belgium, Switzerland, Italy, Spain, the United States, and Argentina. Roughly 150,000 workers were said to have joined up, a figure to be treated with caution given that contemporary estimates tended to be wildly exaggerated.[4] In London, Marx and Engels sat side by side on the general council with English radicals and unionists; French and Belgian disciples of Proudhon; Swiss, Polish, and German emigrants; and libertarians thrilled by the ideas of Bakunin. Very soon the IWA became known for the strikes it supported, its appeals for solidarity, and its numerous sections in different countries. Its aura reached a zenith during the Paris Commune in 1871, which its opponents accused it of having plotted. Even though the association was not directly involved at the start, the damage was done: after the early 1870s, governments perceived the IWA as a worldwide revolutionary threat.

The shared ambition of the founders of the IWA was more modest but ultimately more ambitious. Their plan was to bring the workers of Europe and America together under a single banner. Some of them dreamed of world revolution, but the main priority was to develop capacities for concerted organization and struggle against the globalizing of capital. The IWA was by no means opposed to the mechanics of globalization — far from it. More rapid exchanges of information, cheaper travel between countries and continents, and simpler ways of transferring funds were welcomed by its members, who sought to enable workers to compete successfully with the bourgeoisie, the workers being, if anything, more thoroughly imbued with the values of freedom, mobility, and emancipation than the bourgeoisie. Obviously such values fed the logic of abolishing national frontiers. The seeds of workers' internationalism sown by the IWA were neither the opposite nor the negation of globalization; rather, they pressed globalization into the service of those men and women who were busy creating it. The IWA was not an anti-globalization movement. It was globalization in an early, alternative form, and today the history of its aspirations, uncertainties, accomplishments, and failures can help us to understand what the world might have been and why it has become what it is.

THE MAKING OF SOLIDARITY

The IWA was not the first organization to call upon worker solidarity. It was original in other ways: it preached that solidarity, fraternity, and self-help — all words that were interchangeable at that time — should not to be confined to the register of emotional window dressing but, instead, should generate concrete action that actually improved workers' lives. This program was laid out in the instructions of the association's general council in 1866, which were written by Marx: "It is one of the great purposes of the Association to make the workmen of different countries not only *feel* but *act* as brethren and comrades in the army of emancipation."[5] Understood in this way, solidarity is as much an end as a means, the prospect of a struggle as well as the instrument to achieve it. The need to anchor solidarity in the daily experience of struggle and cooperation was shared by the Russian activist Mikhail Bakunin, when he called on Swiss workers to establish "in their own groups, and after that in other groups, a genuine fraternal solidarity of theory and action, not just for times of crisis ... but also as a feature of daily life. Every member of the International should be able to feel, and should in practice be convinced, that every other member is his brother."[6]

The makings of solidarity are not so simple, however. They can be proclaimed, but putting them into practice is more difficult because the lives of working people tend to separate people, not bring them together. Marx and his contemporaries were well aware of this: the objective conditions of the economic process created a solidarity of *position*, but this did not imply the existence of solidarities of *demand* and *action*. This was what supplied the raison d'être of the IWA: it had to make European workers aware of their common destiny, while convincing them that collective action could be used for their emancipation. Militant engagement was indispensable in forging these links of solidarity, which involved exchanges of information and support, the holding of congresses and meetings, the dispatching of money and assistance, and collective participation in social and political struggle.

As I will show in this book, solidarity is more than a demand or some kind of watchword. It is above all a lived experience, as defined by the historian E. P. Thompson in his masterwork on the English working class.[7] Socioeconomic interdependence is not enough to generate solidarity: it also demands engagement, struggle, and practice, which in turn affect the group that has been formed and its way of thinking.[8] This is what the anthropologist David Featherstone calls the "transformative dimension" of solidarity: instead of reflecting a preexisting objective link, it weaves new interdependencies while transforming old ones.[9]

For the purposes of this inquiry, I have tried to track the intellectual history of the notion of solidarity, along with the practices and arrangements by which it manifests itself.[10] It is one thing to imagine solidarity, its makings, and its inspiration; it is quite another to put solidarity into action. What is interesting about the First International experience is that its militants did both at the same time. They exchanged views, debated with one another, and tried to imagine what a world of greater solidarity would look like, all the while experimenting in a practical way with the social forms and political actions that would bring it to pass. For this reason I have examined speeches, acts, theories, and experiences in tandem with emotions and transactions, with a view to understanding the scale of the task undertaken by the internationalist militants. Nothing is more futile than an appeal to strong feelings reduced to impotent rage, save perhaps an appeal for solidarity that falls flat. There is a price to pay for solidarity: one is expected to make sacrifices and subordinate one's immediate, personal interest to a higher cause that transcends it. One is also expected to share one's resources with other people who may be struggling or otherwise in need. To embrace the ethos of solidarity is to accept a form of interdependence that includes rights and duties, just as the term's juridical origin would imply.[11]

Everything depends on the capacity of the workers — whatever their qualifications, their wage, their sex, their race, or their nationality — to focus on the things that unite them rather than the things that divide them. The IWA, which was founded in the 1860s, inherited a world in which people's local and national professional identities as shoemakers, tailors, typographers, cigar makers, and the like, were more important to them than any class identity.[12] Their world was the workshop rather than the huge factory, and this remained true until the end of the century, even though the progress made by heavy industry, the distribution of a Marxist vulgate, and the creation of powerful social democratic parties contributed to homogenize the representation of the world of the worker, just as they broadened the parameters of various solidarities. This tendency for worker cooperation steadily to broaden should not lead us to underestimate the originality of the work done by the IWA: it was mostly the thoroughly homogenous professions that fought to build links of reciprocity, outstripping the rest. In this book, my goal has been to unearth a series of practices and projects that for now may seem exotic, but which have power to inspire us as we plan the struggles of the future.

As always, in the matter of solidarity there is one frontier that is more difficult to negotiate than the others, and this is nationality. Why on earth would a Frenchman come to the aid of a German? Why would an Englishman help a Frenchman, or an American bother with the problems of a Mexican? The originality of the IWA, in the field of solidarity, lies in its determination to persuade the workers of many different professions to help one another — and in doing so to transcend borders, by rating universal social and professional demands more highly than nationality. Meanwhile the obstacles to the expansion of these cross-border relationships are manifold: the multiplicity of languages, the tangle of judicial and political systems, different standards of living, and different worker cultures were and remain perpetual sources of disagreements and misunderstandings.

But worker internationalism is not without allies in this Herculean task. It is part of a wider movement, that of "suffering remotely," which has been closely analyzed by the sociologist Luc Boltanski. It was in the nineteenth century, through a mixture of the abolition of slavery in the Atlantic world, European philhellenism in the 1820s, the international volunteers in 1848, the "year of revolutions," support for the Polish cause, and even the birth of humanitarian action in the Mediterranean basin, that a new repertoire for transnational social action was invented, whereby cross-border cooperative relationships began to build.[13] Worker internationalism was at once inspired by these phenomena and set apart from them; unlike the humanitarian movement, which justified its solidarity in terms of an irreducible gulf between the receivers and the givers of alms, the workers' movement made clear its will to produce a world of equals in which those who gave help maintained a relationship of equality and reciprocity with the people who received it.[14]

This ideal of equality does not eliminate hierarchies, tensions, or conflicts. Solidarity is at once inclusive and exclusive: it nourishes the links and obligations that are shared between certain groups, while it excludes others. This was true in the past, and it is still true today. In spite of their broadly universalist rhetoric, internationalist militants do not yet imagine that the project of emancipation can benefit everyone. From the very start, women, workers in heavy industry, black and colonized peoples, foreign workers, and agricultural laborers are not viewed or treated in the same way as the white male elites of the best organized professions. The "politics of justice," as Luc Boltanski calls it, could live very well with the "politics of pity," as they did when English workers pitched in to help their Belgian counterparts, to whom they considered themselves immeasurably superior; or when political refugees such as the communards were helped, in spite of the fact that many were at odds with their behaviors. As I will show, worker solidarity borrowed some of the methods of the charitable fraternity, such as collections, concerts, or raffles, in raising money for fellow workers subjected to persecution or injustice. Worker solidarity need not always aim to soften differences and disagreements; on the contrary it may even exacerbate them. These are exactly the kinds of tensions that I wish to examine here, so as to understand under what conditions a new form of internationalism might be possible.

IN QUEST OF AUTONOMY

While it may be useful to listen to the echoes running through this narrative, we should remember that the ideas of nineteenth-century workers were unlike our own. The early internationalist militants' brand of internationalism was very different from the one favored by the left in the twentieth century, which saw the state as the principal instrument of social progress. In fact the nineteenth-century objective was to build networks of solidarity above, beyond, and around the edges of the "bourgeois state," steadily bringing the resources gathered and shared by groups of workers to bear against the power of capital. The achievement of worker autonomy presupposed the creation of circuits of accumulation and redistribution of resources, alongside the much more powerful ones built by state policies of taxation and public credit. The question was, could internationalist workers actually *do without* an international organization per se? Could solidarity be attained by virtue of free will, federation, and reciprocity alone, without recourse to any kind of obligation, coercion, or collective pressure? My inquiry concerns just such an alternative solidarity, conceived at once against, beside, and in the image of the state. Clearly the terms *cooperation* and *solidarity* were long entangled with one another, before they came asunder at the end of the nineteenth century. The former harks back to spontaneous, instinctive, and natural forms of cooperation while the latter relies on the principle of obligation and the ways it can be institutionalized.[15] While the feelings that drive the two are close, their expression differs.

To devote a part of my work to the institutionalization of solidarity occurring within unions or international organizations might appear to go against recent research that favors a "de-unionization" of the history of workers' worlds, the better to examine the practices of insubordination and informal politicization on the fringes of vertical structures.[16] Today, in the age of 2.0 militancy and social networks, anything to do with hierarchical organizations, perennial institutions, political parties, and trade unions could seem way out of date. But during the era that concerns us, from the 1860s to the start of the First World War, knowing to what point worker solidarity should be organized and institutionalized lay at the very heart of modern thinking and discourse.[17] During the 1860s the shape of the trade union was still embryonic: the English trades unionists, convinced of the superiority of their model, moved to export it abroad through relationships of solidarity. Later, especially at the turn of the twentieth century, the model was denounced for bureaucratizing and fossilizing international worker cooperation.

The ambivalent relationships between experience and organization were especially on display during strike action. Strikes offered opportunities to appeal to international worker solidarity. They provoked fierce debates about the nature and scope of the help to be provided, about practical questions linked to the conduct of collective movements, and about the use made of funds received. Strikes also offered a chance to mobilize words and emotions stirred by the links and obligations binding workers across borders. The worker internationalism of the second half of the nineteenth century was inseparable from the innumerable strikes and lockouts (lockouts being work stoppages imposed by employers) that proliferated throughout Europe and the United States and reached their climax in the years preceding the First World War.[18] In the course of such conflicts, solidarity could best be activated by sending help in the form of men or funds, the declaring of strikes in sympathy, and by the organization of protests against violence committed against militant workers. Although unions were not always at the root of them, strikes were a powerful catalyst for union action, since through them the workers gained the experiences of collective decision-making and sorting out what they really needed.[19] Among other things, in this book I will try to demonstrate the creative, integrating quality of conflicts: the moment when workers decide to fight back, which is often depicted today as economically damaging and counterproductive, is a moment of political engagement, exchange, and the airing of opposing views. All of these things are indispensable today, in our own time, if we are to keep democracy alive.

MORAL ECONOMY AND MONEY

Leftist militants, unionists, and socialists have always denounced the injustices of capitalism and its unequal distribution of economic resources. Money corrupts.[20] Yet how can we fight against capital if we have no money? The moral and strategic dilemma is colossal. In more practical terms, it raises awkward questions during strikes: how to collect, manage, spend, and distribute the money pooled by the workers? Is it possible to accumulate and transfer funds without resorting to banks, the core institutions of bourgeois capitalism? Are workers' organizations (their unions, mutual funds, cooperatives, parties, and associations) really capable of managing their resources in a more effective and democratic way than businesses, banks, and public authorities? Can worker solidarity finesse the principles that regulate capitalist economies and liberal societies when, in many ways, it is the creation of those principles?

Such questions invite us to dig further into the "moral economies" of workers' money. The notion of moral economy was popularized by the historian E. P. Thompson in his study of food riots in England in the eighteenth century; it was subsequently broadened in the following decades, becoming diluted almost to the point of dissolving altogether.[21] Nevertheless the term *moral economy* helps us understand why money is at once an economically, socially, and morally charged question, precisely because militant workers roundly — and rightly — reject the idea that the so-called *cash nexus* should be the sole criterion for understanding human relationships. Countless gestures of solidarity between workers of different countries have shown how commercial logic is far from the sole motivation driving people. Yet money is never a neutral quantity, as has been clearly shown by the sociologist Viviana A. Zelizer: the truth of this is clear when one considers the uses made of it by early militants, who were convinced of the need to resist the power of the market, but who were unable to free themselves entirely from the strictures that money imposed upon them.[22]

To find my bearings in the old workers' world, I have turned to economic sociology, which examines the nature of social relationships forged by the exchange of money or services in kind. Viviana A. Zelizer points out three types of monetary transfers that have different and specific meanings. The first of these is payment of compensation by way of a directly negotiated exchange at a fixed price; the second involves social entitlements that more or less acknowledge the autonomy of the person who receives them (though such autonomy may remain open to denial or dispute); and the third is achieved by straightforward gift, which establishes a relationship of subordination between giver and receiver.[23] All three financial procedures imply distinct social relationships that lay at the heart of the nineteenth-century working environment. Producer and consumer cooperatives offered exchanges of goods and services; mutual assistance societies and unions gave access to certain rights, in the form of help and entitlements, in exchange for the payment of regular dues; subscriptions and appeals, finally, were organized to help militants, strikers, and their families who might fall victim to violent repression, poverty, or famine.

In the course of my research in labor archives and the workers' press, I uncovered a number of social practices that intrigued me. To begin with it was very difficult to understand exactly what these practices meant to those directly involved. In the nineteenth century, the actions of solidarity were mostly distinguished by the ways in which they were based on the charitable impulse to offer a *donation*, out of a sense of duty. It meant showing immediate solidarity, without waiting for any formal action in return. Or else it could be based on the idea of an interest-free loan, with the more or less fictional prospect of repayment, or at least of some kind of reciprocity in the future. Both were descended from the project of free credit devised by Proudhon and his disciples after 1848, and in them we can see the outlines of two forms of moral economy, forms that worker groups were eager to distinguish one from the other according to their own relative status and autonomy.[24] Workers in the oldest and most qualified professions were proud of their capacity to live on their own resources; or rather, when circumstances required it, to borrow from other trade unions without resorting to public appeals or generous donors. Loans were thought to be the best fit with the ideal of worker self-sufficiency, more especially since he who accepts a donation faces the stigma of inferiority and in all likelihood a bitter dose of bourgeois moralizing. For this reason the recipients of a militant donation were eager to affirm their hope of eventually being able to help out their own benefactors, the idea of the counter-donation softening the reality of indebtedness. The existence of these two registers explains the close attention paid by militants to the habit of "marking" various categories of money according to the degree of moral economy behind them.[25]

Numerous other social and symbolic forms established themselves through money: power relationships, practical modes of organization, and moral ideals were also very much a part of the equation. For example, the wealthiest trade unions made the help they gave to foreign strikers conditional on making their practices more professional. The quid pro quo might also be a pledge that assisted workers would stay strictly idle for the duration of the strike, exerting no competitive pressure on the wider job market. The dizzy growth of migration in quest of employment was clearly understood as a driving force for worker solidarity, as well as an element that might at any moment blow it to pieces.

REDISCOVERING WORKER INTERNATIONALISM

Broadly speaking, my goal in this book is to rekindle the project of the early internationalist workers and examine the many contradictions and difficulties they came up against. This is very necessary today, in 2023; it has to be acknowledged that social history and worker history have been moribund for the last forty years. Indeed the slow decay of the physical working world since the 1970s has purged all memory of the vigor that created it in the first place. The fact that this history has been so utterly forsaken plays into the hands of today's populists and nationalists, who know nothing and care less about the episodes of struggle and solidarity that shaped the European and American working classes.

As for historians, legitimately enough they have turned to the other aspects of study, neglected hitherto, that are offered by world and transnational history. Many areas of the history of internationalism have been powerfully reinforced and renewed in the last fifteen years, the worker element being studiously left aside. Scientific, liberal, administrative, religious, and sporting "Internationales" have been unearthed or reexamined in the light of the circulations, translations, and appropriations that made them possible in the 1860s and 1870s.[26] It is significant that the term *Internationale*, which was first used to designate international worker organizations, was later used metaphorically to describe more informal transnational communities that had no real institutionalizing project behind them. *Worker internationalism* lost its glittering aura during this process and began to seem banal, even obsolete.[27] Its endless ideological debates, its intractable contradictions, its utter failure to raise European workers against nationalism and imperialism prior to 1914, and the subsequent propensity of the USSR to confuse internationalism with the subjugation of its satellite countries, finally dumped the project among the redundant antiquities of the nineteenth century.[28]

At the same time, this period of relative marginalization has proved fortunate, because now we can see the old project in the light of fresh facts. At last we can disentangle worker internationalism from the sterile debates that have plagued it for so long.[29] It is not because some people have announced, prematurely, that the working class no longer exists, that the history of the working class is also dead and gone. On the contrary: amid the turmoil of social inequality, dread of globalization, and suspicion of foreigners in which we live today, it is more than ever necessary to know more about this history — not to bewail a lost golden age but to envision the rich variety of worlds our predecessors imagined for us.

The worker experience of transnational solidarity was by no means disconnected from broader debates covering other areas it sought to contest. Indeed, the history of globalization actually compels us to reflect on the way in which worker internationalism was intimately lodged within the economic and technological transformations of its time. There is no doubt that it offered a workable alternative to the domination of capital — namely, a project of worker emancipation on a transnational scale.[30] As this project moves back into the mainstream, its borrowings and its specificities become easier to understand in terms of the market, the state, and philanthropy. The act of denouncing capitalism did not release worker movements from the duty of explaining themselves to their members or from managing funds with precision and openness. The history of anti-capitalism is therefore not the exact reverse of the history of capitalism itself; indeed the former fed freely upon the latter. Likewise, even though their rejection of the state and its bureaucracies colored the work done by the internationals and the unions, both were constantly tempted to replicate state methods, albeit with much more modest human and financial resources. The same was true of charitable organizations: notwithstanding their talk of opposition and rupture, philanthropy and worker solidarity used many of the same practices, by turns playing on the registers of militancy, unionism, humanitarian empathy, and revolutionary messianism. The IWA was born at the same time as the International Red Cross and a host of other organizations based on international cooperation. All together, these made the 1860s a key decade, half a century before the creation of the League of Nations in 1919.[31]

The internationalism of the First International, and to a lesser extent that of the Second, are examined here in their centers of action, meaning the spheres of western Europe and the North Atlantic. Inspired by the history of transnational solidarity, my research relies on correspondence, archives, and workers' newspapers that survive in Germany, Belgium, France, the Netherlands, and the United Kingdom. While connections with the United States were easy to take into account because of the abundant secondary literature associated with them, southern and eastern Europe are less copiously represented here. This west European and Atlantic approach may look provincial compared to the long reach of the global anarchist movement, whose origins lay in the eastern Mediterranean, the Philippines, or Cuba.[32] Yet the drive for material solidarity was at its strongest and most intense in the western regions, confronted as they were with the dilemma of institutionalization. It was only in the years between the world wars — with the affirmation of American power, the expansion of communism, and the growth of bitter rivalries between the different worker organizations — that the various forms of international socialism shed their exclusively European identities. Only after they had done so could they endorse the anti-imperialist and anti-colonialist struggles that were taking place elsewhere in the world. This in turn explains why this narrative that begins in the 1860s is prolonged well into the 1920s, at which time the many procedures tested at the end of the nineteenth century finally yielded a codified and routinely operational repertoire of cooperative actions that could be exported to other areas of conflict. It was not until the deindustrialization of the 1970s and 1980s, the erosion of trade union power, and the end of the Cold War that the workers ceased to be in the forefront of initiatives for international solidarity.

The world described in this book has passed away, yet its dreams and dilemmas were no different from our own. London in the early autumn of 1864 was the first staging post on a journey that will bring us back to the world of today, oppressed as it is by the revival of nationalist passions, staggering inequality, and the crisis of the liberal international order. After all, we are not the first of our kind to seek a way to fight against inequalities, whereby we can avoid in the pitfalls of retreat, division, and the culture of everyone for themselves.

PART ONE

The Years of Experiment

1 | A WORKERS' STATE?

T he founding of the International Workingmen's Association
(IWA) marked a turning point in the history of socialism and
international organizations. The meeting that took place in London in September 1864 gave birth to a new institution whose goal
was to defy the globalization of capital and to struggle against
the power of the bourgeois state. The meeting was the result of
an ideological development that began in the 1840s among the
various socialist and worker movements of Europe. The political
environment was favorable; it followed a decade dominated by
the restoration of authoritarian governments in the France of the
Second Empire, as well as in Austria and Russia, since the "year
of revolutions," 1848. Despite the proliferation of wars of independence, national struggles, and imperial rivalries, all over Europe
the 1860s saw liberal reforms that facilitated free speech, notably
among the working classes. The first French militants to arrive in
London in 1862 did so with the consent of the French authorities.
In 1863, a savage Russian repression of the rebellion in Poland led
to a wave of protest that spread well beyond socialist and democratic circles. Although their movements were carefully moni-
tored Belgian, French, and Swiss militants were given freedom of
movement in London, which allowed them to mingle with political

exiles from all over the rest of Europe as well as with representatives of the powerful British trade unions, which had engaged in multiple strike actions and protests since 1859. The Civil War in the United States came to an end in 1865, whereupon four million enslaved people were freed and a flood of immigrants from Europe and Asia flowed in to supply the manual labor needed for the nation's industrial development.

The challenges faced by the IWA's founders were matched by their ambition. There was nothing spontaneous about the universal fraternity of working men: the role of this new organization was precisely to build and expand it, by gathering under a single roof workers from many different countries, professions, languages, and political cultures. The task was immense, and it is easy in hindsight to conclude that the IWA was sure to fail. Its problems were both theoretical and practical. The militants of the general council in London, whose goal was to promote the association's expansion, increase its membership, and build its resources across the European continent and (to a lesser extent) the United States, disagreed about their institution's structure and the missions it should undertake. Should they opt for a decentralized federation, rejecting any principle of authority or verticality? Or should they concentrate its resources and decisions within a central hierarchy, the better to coordinate the fervor and struggle of solidarity? Should their priorities be union action and industrial conflict or participation in traditional politics and the conquest of power at the ballot box?

In general, the association's militants genuinely loathed the bourgeois state system and its bureaucracy; it was natural that they should question the ways in which power and resources were distributed within their own worker-governed bodies. In the fullness of time, the practical issues that arose during these years and the solutions found for them were to play a decisive part not only in the ideological gestation of socialism in Europe but also in the relative suspicion with which it was greeted in the United States, where it was viewed as an imported, thoroughly foreign article.[1] It was no longer a matter of talking about revolution. The task was to build a transnational institution that was good for the long haul. The goal was to shake off the yoke of capitalism altogether.

THE CREDIT OF THE IWA

The fight against capital could not be sustained without abundant means and meticulous preparation. In 1864 revolutionary spontaneity was no less vulnerable to physical repression than it had been in 1848. Its energy could quickly subside. To make their project credible, the founders of the First International were careful to recruit new members, assemble resources, and develop a real capacity to act. At their weekly meetings, which began in October 1864, the members of the general council spent most of their time discussing the association's strategy of expansion. Their determination, coupled with the objectives clearly laid out in the "Inaugural Address," sent the authorities into a panic. Before it was even organized and structured, the IWA provoked, by the simple fact of its existence, ideas and rumors about itself that were very different from the reality. This in turn lent credence to a project that at the time was fragile and uncertain.

The Power of Fantasy

By the end of the 1860s, many observers were convinced that IWA was a rich and potent institution, busily brewing revolutions and financing strikes all over Europe. Its tentacles were said to have penetrated America and even Russia. Police reports — many of them pure fantasy — gave an aura of the exotic and sinister to an institution whose behavior none could fathom. The simplest response was to depict it as a vast international conspiracy, thus taking seriously its call for an international union of workers to fight the forces of capitalism. Informers who managed to infiltrate sections of the IWA regaled their contemporaries with alarmist reports of an omnipotent new threat: "If we supplement these sources of revenue with the sums of money it procures for political purposes, we will easily understand the sheer power of an association whose activities extend throughout Europe and even as far as America...because of its colossal influence and the funds available to it, the association can furnish striking workers with the means to struggle successfully against employers and capitalists."[2]

The thinking of the police authorities was outdated, rooted in an era (1820–1840) when secret societies provided the only means available to liberal, democratic, or socialist opponents of government to unite for political purposes.[3] As a result every clue picked up during an arrest or a police search was seen as further evidence of undercover activities involving a huge universal fraternity of workers, orchestrated from London. In fact the world in which the IWA was engaged had changed completely since 1848, the year the European masses entered politics.[4] In the 1860s its militants had to be on their guard and alert to the traps set for them by informers, but their goal from the start was to act and engage international public opinion in the full light of day. When some of them were arrested and taken to court, as were the members of the Parisian section of the IWA in 1868, their defense consisted in showing that at no time had they ever sought to conceal either their intentions or their operations.

For as long as the association was in existence, investigators searched in vain for its supposed "treasure" that several informers claimed against all reason to have located. The proliferation of strikes between 1867 and 1872 (a phenomenon to which we will return later on) gave credence to the idea that somewhere, somehow, there existed a giant fund by which they were financed. Police reports and the press were full of groundless information that at the same time revealed how nervous the authorities were.

Worker militants mocked the endless official bungling—in 1870, for example, when the Belgian police, believing itself on the point of seizing the "treasure" of the association, unearthed a box full of coal instead.[5] One newspaper even went so far as to announce, a year after the Commune, the arrest in Denmark of the "grand master" and the "treasurer" of the International and the impounding of its "treasure chest."[6] Shortly afterward, an informer of the Paris police claimed to have vital information on the secrets of the International. One of the documents he produced, entitled "L'Internationale, ses banquiers et son personnel en Angleterre et en France," suggested that "the archives, treasury, and accounting office" of the International were now established in Newcastle, adding that "when there are strikes anywhere in France, help is always sent from Newcastle, the metropolis of coal."[7] In reality, the writer was confusing a one-off gift sent by English workers with the much more complicated circuits used to finance strikes at the time. Fabrications like this, which the police had to sort out from hundreds of letters and reports, also show how the authorities manipulated people's imaginations in their onslaught against the IWA: the idea was to strike at its leadership and funding, as though its power and resources were centrally controlled from a single location.

Except that nothing of the sort existed. The informers, whether they were attracted by the prospect of reward or were victims of their own exaggeration, imagined the IWA to be a powerful group shadowing the state—complete with a budget, an organizational structure, and records of its own. What was more, they claimed it was capable of using banking systems and modern means of communication to further its subversive projects. Thus the struggle against capitalism was supposed to be usurping the identity of capital itself, replicating its capacities of organization and projection. The IWA was perceived as a kind of strike action multinational, thoroughly professional and determined, and beliefs of this kind lingered on among investigators long after the official dissolution of the association in 1876. In the early 1880s, all eyes turned to the United States, whence reports sent across to the Paris préfecture de police suggested that International funds that were being set up in Boston, Chicago, and other American cities were to help European militant anarchists. "They seem to have an abundance of money and weapons," wrote an investigator in 1883, describing the "Knights of Labor."[8] The battle against "the anarchist International" reactivated rumors that were already rife at the time of the IWA.[9] Yet it was not until 1920 that the Third International managed to confirm longtime police suspicions by creating a serious centralized structure. This structure was indeed capable of recruiting and training agents to dispatch around the world and of providing financial help to Communist groups in preparation for the revolution; but before the Third International, no cross-border worker organization ever had the power or the effectiveness attributed to it by its capitalist adversaries.

Conspiracy theories such as these reveal much more than the fear gripping the capitalist elites or their desire to manipulate public opinion. They also stem from a fundamental uncertainty surrounding the IWA project ever since its inception, an uncertainty to which even its originators were not immune. For there was no agreement, nor even any clear idea, as to the objective being pursued or the nature of the organization they were building. Should they give form to the dream of international solidarity by building a workers' state with a high degree of coordination and a minimum of collective obligation? Or, conversely, should they oppose on principle any form of organization capable of reasserting state oppression? Was it possible to federate worker associations on a completely autonomous, decentralized basis, or was the need for control and centralization inescapable? These tensions were already present in embryonic form within the First International. In the absence of a clear definition of their respective contours, some participants whose ideas were largely attuned to those of Marx and Engels argued that a central directorate would be the most efficient outcome. Others, more libertarian and more attached to individual emancipation, felt that priority should be given to local, decentralized action, independent of any hierarchical, pyramid-like structure.[10] These two tendencies existed side by side as best they could, until the conflict between them became polarized in the 1870s.[11] They make the study of the early disputes highly interesting inasmuch as the militants of the era were themselves discovering for the first time the conflicts and disagreements that were to bedevil the left for a century to come. Today, advocates of "libertarian municipalism" are reviving the decentralizing traditions of the nineteenth century in a critique of the failed bureaucratic centralized politics of socialist and social democratic parties of the late twentieth century. The fault lines of yesterday are the fault lines of today, even though their contexts have changed.

The deadly tensions within the IWA produced two currents, anarchist and socialist, whose relations were permanently fraught. The earliest figures involved had no clear idea of what they were trying to build. Bakunin himself, who is seen by posterity as the high priest of libertarian anarchism, admitted when he joined the IWA in 1868–1869 that it needed "a serious international organization of workers' associations of all lands, capable of replacing this departing world of states."[12] At the Basel Congress in September 1869, in the course of a discussion about property, Bakunin demanded "the destruction of all the national and territorial States and, on their ruins, the founding of the international State of the workers."[13]

In any event, the IWA was an attempt to institutionalize worker internationalism and make it professional and coherent. At the end of the 1870s there was a showdown between the two distinct forms of internationalist aspiration, the one convinced of the need for a strong central authority after the state was overturned (as set out in the 1848 Manifesto of the Communist Party) and the other defending the autonomy of local sections and an entirely spontaneous approach to revolution (which we may find, for example, in Bakunin's *Statism and Anarchy*, written in Russian). This settling of accounts was the direct result of the International's internal debates. As long as uncertainties of this kind remained, nobody really knew whether the general council in London was simply a liaison office, busily harvesting information and redeploying it on the continent, or whether it had the actual power to control local sections of the IWA.[14]

The Usefulness of Myths

Despite the frequently fantastical nature of contemporary press cuttings and government declarations, the militants of the IWA gleefully encouraged the spread of its legend. They knew that the chorus of nonsense might prove useful in building the institution's credibility, both among potential recruits to the cause and among its adversaries. Misunderstandings and exaggerations were welcome if they made it possible for the association to become better known among European workers, who might be favorably impressed by the power it seemed to wield. The misguided efforts of policemen would result in more people looking to London — and the reputation of the IWA would be strengthened in consequence.

The members of the general council were well aware that the myths were preposterous, but they preferred to use them rather than deny them. During the last month of 1867, Marx complained in a letter to Engels that "what our party really lacks, is *money*." In August 1869, speaking to the general council, he made fun of an article in the London newssheet of the French police, *L'International*, which accused the IWA of preparing a "universal dictatorship" and of being "currently occupied with filling its coffers. When it has done so, it will set about governing by decree."[15] In a report Marx wrote a few weeks later for the Basel Congress, he cited a rumor according to which the Swiss authorities had sent to London "a messenger on the fantastic errand of ascertaining of the International general 'treasury-box.'" He added, "if they had lived at the time of the nascent Christianity, they would, above all things, have spied into St Paul's banking accounts at Rome."[16] Marx knew very well that the strength of the general council lay not in its financial or administrative muscle but in the legitimacy conferred upon it by the members of the association: "The General Council has no army and no budget. Moral authority is its only weapon. It will be powerless if it cannot depend upon the support of the entire association," he conceded at one point, during the angry debates that finally split the organization in September 1872.[17]

Cultivating the myth of the IWA's omnipotence involved a certain risk, especially if the paucity of its resources should be exposed to the light of day. Constant appeals for subscriptions, which were seen as the best way to build up membership and encourage solidarity, might also have the reverse effect of demonstrating that the association had no resources of its own and utterly lacked the means to match its ambitions. Strategic questions of this kind were regularly debated within the general council, which was ever attentive to the image its decisions relayed to the world outside. Its members would rather the council were feared, than shown to be short of funds. When, in November 1866, the council's French correspondent Eugène Dupont requested a Europe-wide subscription to assist some militants in Lyons who had lost their jobs, the London committee preferred to abstain on the grounds that to do so would threaten its prestige.[18]

Similar reservations were expressed four years later when the association was too strapped to print the first address Karl Marx wrote on the subject of the Franco-Prussian war, in which he laid the blame for the conflict squarely on the expansionist policies of Napoleon III's regime and called for fraternization between German and French workers. Johann Eccarius, the German secretary of the council from 1867 to 1871, was a worker exiled to London and a former member of the League of the Just and the Communist League; he opposed the opening of a subscription for a printing fund on the grounds that "it would tell the outside public that we were short of funds which would reduce our importance which greatly depended on the belief that we had large sums at our disposal, and it would not bring any money. It would be the worst thing that could be done to tell the outside public and the governments that we were poor."[19]

The reputation of the IWA and the authorities' dread of it were indeed a question of belief. Hermann Jung, responsible for finances, added: "If we exposed our poverty the press would not respect us as it did: it was because they thought we had plenty [of] money that they considered us powerful."[20] The same prudence was applied to the matter of membership numbers and whether to publish them. Marx preferred not to make known the real strength of the movement, because "the outside public always thought the active members much more numerous than they really were."[21] For this reason, it is hard to form an accurate estimate of the resources and membership of the IWA even today. Lacking reliable information, the authorities pumped up the numbers to justify their active repression. But the cold fact remains that the IWA never benefited from the pools of money that its enemies and even some of its members believed it did. For our part, we need to put aside the myth and penetrate the mechanism as it really was.

AN INDEBTED, SECRETIVE ORGANIZATION

Although we can understand why informers and policemen had a hard time understanding how the IWA worked, it is more surprising to discover that its own members acted in a thoroughly opaque manner. Building an organization implies that there should at least be some kind of minimal transparency concerning its rules, members, and finances. Yet on not one of these points did the members of the general council have any reliable information. Whether this was due to ideological disagreements or an incapacity to follow the evolution of a growing enterprise is by the way; what we must acknowledge is the enormity of their task, which was to unite in a single association vast numbers of workers, living all over Europe, who had never met and whose cultures and political practices were extraordinarily diverse.

Financial Fragilities

The omnipresence of money problems in the correspondence and minutes of the association is inversely proportional to its financial standing. Engels admitted this twenty years later, when he ironically referred to the gulf between the rumors of an IWA "treasury" and the everyday difficulties encountered by the general council in paying its printing bills, its secretary, and its London rent.[22] Not till the enfeeblement and eventual disappearance of the association did the myth of its financial clout deflate. During the hearings in France that followed the repression of the Commune, former members of the International like Ernest Édouard Fribourg admitted that the speculations on the number of militants and the sums of money collected by the IWA had nothing to do with reality: "They said we had vast riches, when in Geneva we couldn't even pay for our delegates' third class tickets."[23] In a long note on the worker societies in Britain at the close of the 1870s, an agent of the Paris préfecture de police concluded that "we were curiously mistaken... as to the financial strength of the International."[24] The minutes of the general council in London confirm this: the IWA was so permanently mired in debt that its actions were limited. There was an awkward contradiction: designed as it was to struggle against capital and the bourgeoisie, how could it go on ignoring the principles of management and openness that were being applied by them, all around it? How could it pursue its high mission, if its members were incapable of rigor, honesty, and good management?

Because the general council was based in London, members of the British trade unions were overrepresented in its deliberations. These individuals, who were strangers to the revolutionary rhetoric of Marx and his fellow continental socialists, were strongly attached to the idea that the association's management should be irreproachable, just as they themselves were compelled to be in their own unions. Accounting transparency at the time was a sine qua non for all companies, associations, or academic societies in the United Kingdom.[25] Militant British workers knew themselves to be under close observation by the authorities as well as by their employers, who wanted nothing more than proofs of their financial incompetence or dishonesty. A royal inquiry was set up in London in 1867, before which a large number of unionists were meticulously interrogated about the finances of their organizations, the way they spent their funds, and the money they allocated to support strike action.[26] In Victorian Britain, people's respectability was judged by the measure of their capacity to apply the virtues of self-help and financial rigor.[27] For this reason the British unionists involved with the IWA, even though they shared its objectives, were adamant that it should act transparently and responsibly, applying accounting practices as impeccable as those of ordinary companies and commercial enterprises. The publication of accounts was, according to them, an indispensable condition for militant credibility and efficiency. British trade unionists seemed weirdly conservative to Karl Marx; but he badly needed them and their resources as ballast for the association. Between the organizational savoir faire of the trade unions and Marx's ideological ambitions, there was a clear convergence of interest. It depended as much on strategic compromise as on profound misunderstandings and ulterior motives.[28]

We can only imagine the consternation with which the trade unionists examined the finances of the association, which was incapable of paying its debts or producing proper accounts. The general council's expenditure far exceeded its income over the period 1865–1866. The association owed money to its landlord, its printers, to several individual lenders, and above all, to the members of the general council themselves, most of whom did not hesitate to advance their own private funds when they felt it to be necessary. Debts would not have been a problem had the general council been in any position to repay them. But not one single debt was paid between the years 1867 and 1870. In July 1869, George Milner, an English member, insisted that funds should be dedicated to debt repayment as an absolute priority. A certain amount of progress was made, which allowed Hermann Jung to boast in July 1870 that the council had begun to pay back its creditors, which "was more than some of the middle-class movements did."[29]

During the Hague Congress, in September 1872, the association still owed more than £25 to members of the general council. Karl Marx saw this as proof that its members were fully engaged in their mission and with the association, including on a financial level; but it also showed that there was a severe lack of regular income. Then there was disagreement about the need to get rid of debts altogether. As the English trade union leader John Hales pointed out repeatedly, "the council ought to be honest, the liabilities ought to be paid and the services rewarded according to our capacity."[30] Like many of his fellow trade unionists, he felt strongly that ordinary debts should be a priority. Others saw no harm in accumulating late payments. The communard Léo Frankel, for example, was convinced of this: "We must live on credit to kill capital" was his mantra.[31] There were two lines of thinking: the first believed capital could be transformed and improved from within without breaking its rules, the second called on the workers to free themselves entirely of those rules and embrace full-on revolution.

As a result the accounts of the general council were as vague and chaotic as it was possible to be: its debts were inaccurately listed, and its credits (basically the money that local sections owed to it) were even worse. A decision to act was taken in the spring of 1870 when a finance committee was formed within the general council and chaired by three Englishmen, Thomas Mottershead, Benjamin Lucraft, and George Harris. They ran into a storm of criticism and defended themselves by condemning the total lack of rigor and professionalism in the association's accounting. They were staggered that an association as ambitious as the IWA could countenance such appalling methods. Mottershead claimed that "the books were in such a state that nobody knew what to make of them," while Harris considered that they were "not kept in a business-like manner, they would condemn it in a court of law." But Hermann Jung pleaded that the secretary general, Johann Eccarius, should be treated leniently: "They did not know," he said, "how poor we had been and not any of those who had advanced money now made a claim for payment." Examination of the accounts by a second committee was scarcely more conclusive: J. Hales noted that there were no written records of receipts or outgoings. Trust alone made it possible to validate the accounts, in contravention of the basic principles of commercial management.[32]

The need to make the organization's management more professional, by the nomination of a finance secretary, was no longer in doubt. Nevertheless it came up against a core value of the IWA, which was founded on the idea that workers themselves were best able to decide their own destiny.[33] This sociological postulate lay at the heart of the organization's setbacks, given that several members of the council believed that finances were too serious a matter to be left to unqualified people. The designation, in October 1870, of a financial secretary illustrates this ambiguity: Marx and Friedrich Lessner proposed that Engels, a recent arrival on the council in 1870, should occupy this function, but Engels declined to do so on the grounds that "none but working men ought to be appointed to have anything to do [with] finances." Marx, ever practical, thought the exact opposite: "An ex-commercial man [is] the best for the office," he said.[34] The organization was torn between worker principles and professional competence, but in the end the London Conference of September 1871 drafted a compromise whereby the accounts were entrusted to a specialist, with an oversight committee of workers to keep an eye on the figures.

Transparency and Credibility

Opaque accounting may have been exasperating at the time for the members of the association, but it is far worse for a historian after an interval of a hundred and fifty years. The documents that survive are few and far between and very difficult to decipher; records of incomings and outgoings are incomplete, to say the least. There are some entries, though, that allow one to form a vague idea of what happened in the period between March 1865 and April 1867, during the association's first years of activity.[35] These financial statements, imprecise and disparate though they are, make a point of presenting balanced accounts. This could only be done via loans from various individuals and advances made by the members of the council themselves. Debts, which were noted separately, amounted to £21 in 1866 and £30 in April 1867, about half the current expenses of the period under consideration, not counting the expenses of the congress. The general council, like the various sections of the IWA, owed money to printers for the publication of addresses and cards. The landlord of the office premises, who was either not paid at all or paid very little, finally agreed to cancel the outstanding rent.[36] This chronic imbalance also affected local sections of the IWA, whose main costs were printing newssheets, postal charges, and travel expenses. Finding enough money for these three outlays was a perpetual concern, in the first age of internationalism.

The salary of the secretary-general of the association, another heavy burden on the budget, was the subject of lively debate. There were some astonishing exchanges as to exactly how much Johann Eccarius, who occupied the post from 1867 to 1871, should be paid. The issue was not only to lighten the burden on the budget but also to define the meaning of militant engagement in an institution of international status. The council was divided between those for whom the association ought to be managed as a model of benevolent militancy (for Hales, "there [are] thousands who spend a lifetime in a movement without expecting any pay") and those for whom the association's ambition and international scale required specific skills that fully justified a fair remuneration.[37] The proposal to reduce the secretary's salary from fifteen to ten shillings per week was given a mixed reception. George Milner was disgusted by this "cheese-paring policy of the Manchester school." In his view, competence had a price: "the work of the secretary [has] no right to be measured by an ordinary trade rule. The Secretary of the association must be a man of capacity a man that was known in Europe and America; to get such a one [is] alone worth the money." Finally, John Hales was elected secretary-general in the place of Eccarius and agreed to take a salary cut. Some approved this gesture, but others thought it sent the wrong signal, lowering the ambitions of the association. One speaker thought it deplorable that an institution normally so prompt to condemn salary reductions was in this case opting for underpaid work.[38] This shows that one could be an internationalist, revolutionary, and anti-capitalist militant, while at the same time seeking to reduce the organizational costs of mobilization.

Rigorous accounting and the publication of same were not just concessions to liberal reasoning and business respectability. They were vital to the good name of the institution, which had to be open to scrutiny by militants if they were to entrust it with their money. There were constant complaints about funds from local sections of the association, which took a dim view of "the council's primitive accounting methods" when they were asked at the annual congresses to validate its statements.[39] Indeed Marx and the general council found themselves more and more frequently under fire as the ideological rifts hardened within the association. Some pro-Bakunin dissident sections even denounced the "dictatorial drift" of the institution. During the London Conference in September 1871, the committee named to inspect the finances of the council was severely critical and demanded the adoption of more rigorous practices. Marx and Engels, as subtle tacticians, threw their weight behind these proposals, the better to evade responsibility and ultimately win approval of the accounts.[40] A year later, Engels personally took charge of the general council's financial report at the Hague Conference, finessing any further objections.[41]

Checking accounts at local section level was an easier matter, though there were numerous run-ins. The newssheets of the International contributed all the minutes of the workers' associations and the debates they had, to help clean up financial bookkeeping. Even so, the general council's chronic incapacity to produce decent accounts was all the more shocking because it went against one of the basic principles of contemporary worker democracy. When the Parisian internationalists prosecuted in 1868 were accused by the *avocat général* of failing to surrender their account registers, their defense — an effective one — was that the documents had remained fully available for anyone to examine until the day they were impounded by the police: "The accounts were always at the disposition of all members, and we never refused to show them, or allow them to be checked down to the smallest detail."[42] Accounts open for all to see were crucial to winning the trust of militants.

THE HUNT FOR FUNDS

"No Rights Without Duties, No Duties Without Rights" was the IWA's motto, enshrined in the Provisional Rules of 1864. It summarized the association's ambitions as well as its difficulties. Defending these rights meant doing one's duty vis-à-vis the international workers' movement, but what exactly was the nature of that solidarity? In the sections as well as at general council level, the first obligation of militants was to pay their dues, without which "solidarity" was meaningless. Money was needed to print texts and newssheets, to pay travel expenses, and to give aid to strikers who needed it. But how to make certain that every section, and every militant, accomplished that duty? Moral obligation and voluntary engagement were not enough. Should the association try to force the issue by threatening exclusion and the imposition of bureaucratic procedures, given that the entire ideological project of the IWA consisted in denouncing the repressive power of the bourgeois state? The practical experience of internationalists obliged them to face an array of deep contradictions.

The Obligation to Subscribe

The existence of the IWA implied a number of entirely new obligations for militant workers. Not only were they expected to contribute immediate help to workers in other countries confronted by conflicts and catastrophes, they were also obliged to pay yearly subscriptions demonstrating their membership and the participation of their sections in an embryonic international organization. The workers of Britain and the continent of Europe were, country by country, accustomed to subscribing regularly to mutual aid societies that were often based on groups and communities of professions with a high degree of familiarity with one another. But the IWA brought change on a spectacular scale: from now on workers were expected to subscribe to a far distant organization based in London, whose leaders were scarcely known to them and whose management lacked transparency. There was still not enough trust to ensure that members would subscribe annually without question. Decades later, Karl Kautsky, a major figure in the German social democratic movement, remembered that the securing of automatic contributions from members was among the greatest challenges met by the First International.[43]

Adherence to the IWA functioned on two levels: workers had to subsidize the sections of which they were members (the sums involved varied case by case) as well as the general council, which required a contribution to its budget. The latter was something very new that imposed an extra sacrifice on the sections and their militants. The principle of it had been established at the Geneva Congress in 1866: belonging to the IWA meant the payment of "a yearly single contribution that every member of the Association must accept" — namely, the sum of one or two pennies given to the general council budget.[44] This dual contribution coupled the principle of an attachment to a local worker community with belonging to an international federation of worker associations headquartered in London. The sections created out of nothing had fewer difficulties than those already in existence that, having decided to join the association, had to convince their members to increase their subscriptions before they could do so.

Every federal structure has to face the problem of how best to divide resources between local needs and supranational ones. In August 1871 Marx wrote that the general council was having trouble taking control because "local dues" were too high. On his copy of the statutes of the International Alliance of Socialist Democracy, founded by his rival Bakunin, he noted his anxiety about the subscriptions required by this section as "ever more taxes to swallow up our contributions!"[45] The ideological differences grew deeper as a power struggle developed for the control of the association and its resources, a classic dynamic in any form of collective organization.

Collecting subscriptions was no small task, either locally or internationally. Reports sent by the sections confirm this. At the Lausanne Congress in 1867, the Paris section claimed that only half its subscriptions due for 1866–1867 had been settled, resulting in a shortfall of funds for current expenses and printing costs.[46] In an attempt to straighten out their finances, the sections (like other worker associations at the time) began opening their meetings with collections of cash (sometimes with an appeal to each member by name), casting each contribution as a vital proof of sincere militant engagement.[47] Money obtained like this not only highlighted the motivation of the people who joined the association; it also showed that the goal of the association itself was not so much to galvanize crowds as to be able to count on the regular contributions of its members. The English, who had the most money, sometimes had difficulty in understanding the complaints of their continental comrades, who found the subscriptions more than a little onerous. George Milner found it hard to believe that the association was having such horrendous financial difficulties; he was astonished that any member might have trouble paying an annual contribution "that amounted to little more than the price of a beer."[48]

Punish or Compromise

The association's reputation clearly depended on its power to attract and enthuse militants all across Europe; but a surge in its membership without a corresponding increase in its funds would alienate not a few. Therefore, regardless of its principles, the general council acted very carefully when its financial and strategic interests were at issue. It was tacitly understood that the rise of the IWA as a force in new regions might at times justify a certain level of compromise with its rules, provided no one was given to believe that membership of the IWA could be obtained scot-free.

IWA relations with the British trade unions were particularly delicate.[49] On 20 November 1865, "Citizen H. Jung made an appeal to the British members to be up and doing to collect money for the Congress and declared that the dolce far niente of the British members paralyzed his efforts among his own countrymen in London and Switzerland."[50] The IWA, as the historians Henry Collins and Chimen Abramsky have noted, represented one of the earliest attempts in the United Kingdom to integrate the British trade unions into some kind of wider political structure.[51] Its quandary was the gigantic imbalance, numerical and financial, that existed at the time between the British trade union movement and movements in other countries, where such structures were barely tolerated by governments or even forbidden altogether. In the year 1866–1867, the British sections contributed a total of £56 to the IWA's budget, almost twice as much as the French (£30) and seven times more than the Swiss (£8). No other countries were mentioned as contributors.[52] Of course, these figures bore no relationship to real membership numbers, and although the English unions were happy to join the association they were unwilling to provide figures as to their own revenues.

The sums raised by individual and collective subscriptions were the focus of many debates. Discussions were held on several occasions as to whether to offer equal subscriptions per member for groups that might wish to join the association collectively; or whether it might be possible in function of their size, their relative wealth, or their professional singularity to have different levels of subscription. Yet the total annual subscription to the general council, which was eventually fixed at one penny, remained entirely theoretical. There was a fierce scuffle about this during the Geneva Congress in 1866. When the London representative Matthew Lawrence called for flexibility in order to attract the English unions, his French opposite numbers took an obstinately egalitarian line, fearing that the English unions, the richest in Europe, might gain special privileges. Fribourg, recalling the association's provisional statutes, claimed that this would lead to "an inequality of rights because there would be an inequality of duties. All members should pay equal charges."[53] Another French delegate, Félix Chemalé, was more accommodating: he suggested that the English unions could have their subscription costs halved. In short, the general council, whose idea was to enlarge the association substantially by including the British, was confronted with a dilemma: on the one hand, if it insisted too much on the necessity for contributions, it might scare off the more impoverished unions. On the other, to accept nonpaying or less-paying unions might weaken the organization as a whole, since membership numbers might outstrip the funds to support them.

In the end, the general council showed considerable pragmatism in agreeing to negotiate the cost of membership at a time when its strategic development was at stake. The admission of a union with thousands of members might well open the door to an agreement to reduce the price of individual dues for everyone else. This solution seemed better than adopting a hard line, which could deter the trade unions from joining an organization whose usefulness was not always quite clear to them. In August 1866 Karl Marx himself opined that the secretary of the association should at least have the possibility of reaching agreement with the poorer unions. Two years later, when the eighteen-hundred-member Geneva-based Deutscher Arbeiterbildungsverein announced its intention to rejoin the association, its representatives proposed to pay two pounds sterling a year to the general council, amounting to four times less than the sum set by the statutes of the association.

The general council, like the local sections, refused to remain passive when its members balked at paying their subscriptions. Although participation in the IWA was a voluntary choice, the general council needed control mechanisms, even sanctions, to guarantee the minimum of collective discipline that was vital to its internationalist project. In London, the will to keep firm control of defaulting sections produced a new set of practices. Reminders were sent out, and a proposal was made to keep an open list of late payers on a blackboard in the council's meeting hall. The conciliatory approach of the early days was replaced by firmness, notably in the case of Marx, who was worried about the growing influence of the International Alliance of Socialist Democracy founded by Bakunin. By 1871–1872, the time for accommodation with sections whose ideological positions contravened the official line of the general council was well and truly over. The Spanish delegates at the Hague Congress in September 1872 were given a bitter taste of this when they were told they would have to pay their dues in full before they would be allowed to take part in the conference. The militant Raphael Farga i Pellicer finally did so, but this did not prevent the meeting from ending with the exclusion of Bakunin's supporters — a proof, if any were needed, that questions of money were still being used as pretexts for settling ideological differences.[54]

The improvement of collection methods led to the adoption of more bureaucratic arrangements. From its earliest beginnings, joining the association had included a membership card signed by the correspondents of every country in the council. These cards allowed members to recognize one another, notably when they traveled abroad and were entertained by a section other than their own. Some even suggested the cards should be numbered, so the council could keep track of its members, but on this issue prudence prevailed; obviously, if the cards were seized by the authorities a system of numbers would make it easy for the authorities to identify other association members. The cards made it possible to identify militants as members of the association; but there was no indication as to whether they were up to date with their dues. At the London Conference of September 1871, a complementary system was devised by a committee tasked with finding ways of obtaining funds.[55] It was decided that every year members would have to stick a one-penny stamp on their cards, the equivalent of their yearly subscription. Apart from its financial interest, this move made it possible to separate the grain from the chaff by setting the most engaged militants apart from those who avoided their obligations. Cards, stamps, and certified statuses were so many tricks used to manage the association and control its members. Even so, many denounced them as bureaucratic drift: one of Karl Marx's Belgian correspondents, Édouard Glaser de Willebrord, even warned him against adopting procedures that he thought would be impossible to apply.[56]

The IWA appealed to universal fraternity, but like any other organization it had to deal with clandestine "free riders," in a context wherein financial bad faith was compounded by profound ideological disagreements. Worker solidarity could not survive without measures of sanction, and exclusion, given that unions were pledged to supply aid and services to their members. In principle a militant worker who failed to pay his dues to his section forfeited the right to attend its meetings and express his views in its debates.[57] Engels himself adopted the firmest possible position on this at the London Conference of September 1871: as far as he was concerned, militants whose cards showed their payments were not up to date were automatically barred from the association's congress.

Competitive Philanthropy

A tightening of rules and oversights was only one option among many, all of which grew more important as control of the association became the focus of a struggle for power. In the early years of its existence, the general council sought ways of generating funds without recourse to pressure or coercion. Its British members, notably, were aware of the awesome fundraising skills of contemporary philanthropic groups and their success in raising money. The British therefore suggested there was no reason that an appeal to the goodwill and generosity of potential donors might not do the same for the association.

Several council members mentioned the ease with which religious associations were able to extract funds from their numerous members. Here the emphasis was not on the goodwill of a few wealthy donors but on small contributions from thousands of individuals — at a time when the press made it easy to launch large-scale fundraising campaigns. William Randal Cremer, a reformist trade unionist and member of the general council from 1864 to 1866, declared that, "as it was by collecting pence that the religious bodies raised the greater part of the money for propagandism, he thought that in this instance we might with benefit borrow their plan of action. There were hundreds who would give one penny but would not give a shilling."[58] Cremer proposed a fixed contribution for a limited sum, whatever the donor's income level.

The IWA's project, which involved collecting funds on a transnational scale, was indeed comparable to what the churches and philanthropic associations were doing at the time. It was even quite important to compete with these movements, to show that the cause of worker solidarity was as good as any other charitable endeavor in terms of its breadth and efficiency. Transnational movements of all kinds were proliferating in the 1860s: for example European Catholics assisted the besieged papacy by way of parish contributions, which compensated up to a point for the loss of revenue engendered by the swallowing up of Vatican territories by the new Kingdom of Italy.[59] Likewise in 1860 a number of personalities belonging to the Jewish bourgeoisie in Paris founded a new organization, the Alliance Israelite Universelle, to collect funds to build schools and hospitals for Jewish people in central Europe and the Ottoman Empire;[60] and in 1863 the International Committee of the Red Cross inaugurated a new age of humanitarian mobilization. More impressive still was the capacity of another Catholic institution, L'Oeuvre de la Sainte-Enfance, to procure colossal sums from the faithful on behalf of Chinese infants "abandoned by their families."[61] Even the children of France and elsewhere were encouraged to save small sums for this initiative; the goal was to establish long-distance emotional and financial links with the Chinese population, which in the aftermath of the Opium Wars (1856–1860) was subject to an intense effort of evangelization by Catholic and Protestant churches.

A number of militants were against the use of techniques from the charitable or philanthropic repertoire to galvanize the working masses. At the London Conference of September 1865, when the association was still less than a year old, some speakers suggested that commemorative medals should be struck and put on sale: these might tighten the bonds of friendship between members of the association, which could appear as part of a new material culture (a declaration of enrollment "varnished and mounted on canvas and roller" was promised to the English unions that joined in 1865).[62] Several British members cited the example of Robert Owen's socialist movement, which had thrived thanks to practices such as these. But in general — because of the dim view of it taken by Marx and Engels — the "prescientific" era of socialism was sidelined by an organization bent on obtaining the long-term determined commitment of its members to a serious union of workers.

REPUTATION, CONFIDENCE, AND SUSPICION

The task that the IWA set for itself was all the heavier in that it aimed to bring together workers and militants of different countries who did not know or trust each other. Within a few years, thousands of European workers had joined the new association, mostly through the local societies and professional associations to which they belonged, whose only contact in London was the member of the general council assigned to the supervision of correspondence with their respective countries. For example, Marx was assigned to Germany, Jung to Switzerland, Dupont to France, and Engels to Italy and later Spain.

If solidarity was to make any kind of difference, the militants had to be able to recognize, identify, and utilize means of communication that made long-range dialogue possible.[63] Nothing could be more difficult in a world where the contours of worker organizations had barely begun to emerge, and in which police agents, informers, and ill-intentioned individuals found it easy to create doubt and stir up trouble. While trust is "an invisible institution," it is nevertheless indispensable to any form of organization, especially one that operates internationally.[64] The main challenge for the leaders of the IWA lay in working out how they could build a united, inclusive organization in a world of such diversity, in which the crucial elements of friendship and personal acquaintance alone were no longer sufficient to handle huge numbers of adherents.

Identifying Militants

Just like the states it fought against and the police forces that watched its every move, the IWA needed to know its members, where they came from, and what their reputations were. Compiling lists of names was out of the question, given the risk that government security services might get hold of them. There were legions of investigators compiling just such lists, by sifting through subscription registers, intercepting letters, and researching names mentioned in the militant press. When ordered to produce these documents, militants protested their good faith and claimed that no single register existed. In principle every member was a membership-card carrier, but only the members of the general council knew more or less how many cards had been printed and sent, and to whom.

Cards, letters of recommendation, and proxies allowed militants to rely on the support of their local communities or of well-known influential figures within the network of European socialism. In this way a militant could earn himself a good reputation, by way of the contacts he managed to make and the names he was able to cite as his supporters and acquaintances. Letters between members of the IWA were filled with remarks on the morality of various militants, their career paths, their gray areas, and the confidence or otherwise they deserved. A "militant reputation" would emerge from a mist of encounters and recommendations, rumors and misunderstandings.

At the time London was a magnet for workers, revolutionaries, journalists, messengers, and informers from all over Europe, and anyone wishing for access to the London general council and the deliberations of the English trade unions had to have serious backup. According to Marx, a man should have "a reputation before he was elected to the Council."[65] People appearing out of nowhere, with nothing more to recommend them than revolutionary fervor, were treated with great caution, especially if their way of life aroused any kind of suspicion. The sincerity and probity of militants coming from outside tight-knit local communities were subject to requests for information from correspondents in the countries from which they came. The sudden arrival of hundreds of French refugees after the Commune uprising in Paris made this process even more delicate, with police infiltration growing more frequent.

This is illustrated by the drastic rules adopted in January 1872 by a "political and mutual solidarity society" based in London and known as the Cercle Revolutionnaire. The admission of a new member could only be allowed if he was recommended by three existing "morally responsible" other members and supported by detailed information as to the candidate's profession, his domicile in London, and the stages of his journey there after the defeat of the Commune. All this information would then be displayed for two weeks at the group's HQ, so that anyone who had misgivings about the candidacy could come forward and testify against it. This period of "novitiate," as it was called in some of the sections of the International, endowed the networks of "acquaintanceship" — as well as the community itself — with considerable influence in the procedure of evaluating people's militant integrity.[66] A majority of three-quarters of the members of the Cercle then had to vote in favor of the new member's admission. This extremely rigorous procedure was designed to guarantee "the private and political honesty" of applicants.[67]

The circulation of militants from one country to another, and from one culture to another, did not always allow for a free exchange of information. A Belgian militant complained in July 1872 that an individual who had been in trouble with his comrades in Belgium had gone on to take part in worker demonstrations on the other side of the Atlantic. Identity documents seemed to him entirely necessary to keep tabs on the good character of members of the association: "It is high time that all members of the International carried a stamp or card which would be the same for all sections....[C]ould we not create a hard-to-fake passport for members of the International, which would guarantee the bearer to be an honest man who happens to have left his home country?"[68]

Nor were the emissaries sent from London to the continent exempt from these documents, especially when they were supposed to carry aid money. In the general council, Martin Boon expressed his anxiety about the trustworthiness of certain intermediaries being used to extend the association's sphere of influence. He did not want "men who knew nothing of labor questions [to be able] to say they represented the International." The council was conferring official powers on people that they could later abuse. A trip to Belgium in the summer of 1871 made by the English delegate James Cohn (a cigar maker) provoked the fury of Karl Marx and other members of the general council, who thought that he had failed to respect the mandate given to him. He was accused of taking advantage of his seat in the council to visit a foreign country with the real intention of defending the interests of striking engineers in Newcastle rather than those of the association. Mottershead was more indulgent: "Men do the bidding of the people who pay them; no doubt James Cohn saw himself as the employee of the engineers, and no doubt the engineers themselves considered him responsible to them more than to anyone else."[69]

Problems of communication and mutual understanding were rife. Many exiled militants, in London or elsewhere, used several European languages in their conversations and correspondence: Marx, Jung, Eccarius, and Lessner were all cases in point. It was no coincidence that in 1865 the presidency of the London Conference was given to Jung: his mastery of three languages (German, French, and English) was much appreciated.[70] But this was not the case for workers whose experience of traveling from country to country was more limited. British workers may have been the most numerous and the most powerful, but often they spoke no language but their own. The members of the Belgian general council complained of difficulties in understanding and translating texts sent to them from London, many having been lifted from newspapers originally published in English. This problem was evident when they were visited by James Cohn in the summer of 1871. César De Paepe, one of the leading figures of the International in Belgium, expressed his disappointment: "We shook his hand in a fraternal manner and he was immediately given a chance to express his mission: but the language difficulty — not one of us spoke English — prevented us from chatting with him more intimately, as we would very much liked to have done. That's all."[71]

The importance of these issues explains why, on several occasions, the congresses of the International talked of ways to improve communications between peoples. This was not a marginal matter: worker internationalism, like any other internationalism, cannot hope to prosper unless the language barrier is at least partially overcome. The 1867 Lausanne Congress threw up a host of propositions, including the use of phonographs, the creation of an international language (Esperanto was invented twenty years later in the late 1880s), and ways of simplifying writing. All this was crucial for figures like the Swiss militant James Guillaume, who was convinced that the emancipation of the masses would come about through a revolution in education and teaching, along with a significant reduction in the time spent on rules of spelling and grammar that were as complicated as they were useless.[72] The congress concluded that a universal language was much to be desired and that a reform of orthography "would benefit everyone by offering a powerful contribution to the unity of peoples and the brotherhood of nations."[73] In the United States, meanwhile, the members of Section 12, who were more closely connected to local radical traditions, agitated for the adoption of universal workers' languages or monetary reforms, which as far as Marx and his circle were concerned were "matters of peripheral importance."[74]

Moving Money

Knowing how to evaluate the reputation and integrity of its members was a key matter for an association that needed to circulate the funds of solidarity around its different sections. The probity of the people who actually handled money (section treasurers, subscription officials, correspondent members sitting on the general council, couriers despatched to strike localities) was carefully scrutinized. Intermediaries were nearly always brought in when cash (membership subscriptions, donations, etc.) had to be moved from one place to another. In 1869 for example the French correspondent Jules Johannard traveled in person from London to Paris, and then from Paris to Rouen, to deliver to striking workers a sum of money that had been initially lent by the English unions. The police were usually hot on the trail of the International's couriers, whose pockets they imagined to be stuffed with banknotes to finance subversive activities. Money could also be sent by mail, but in this case the militants preferred to send it in small doses so as to avert major losses and police interceptions. Cash transfers were made strictly by hand, for example during the annual congresses when the continental sections settled their membership dues to the IWA.

These material obstacles severely limited the speed with which the association could act, since it was obliged only to use agents in whom it could have complete confidence. A return trip from the continent to London, or vice versa, could take several days, at the time when strikes never lasted longer than a few days or weeks. In other words there was an unavoidable delay when it came to moving solidarity funds to where they were needed. Dematerialized, paperless transfers were already possible, but their use by militants of an association that was fundamentally hostile to capitalist banking institutions remained limited. International funds were very seldom placed in banks or savings institutions. Even so, the treasurer of the general council announced in February 1871 that, on the recommendation of Engels and Boon, he had deposited £35 in an account at the Birkbeck Bank, at an interest rate of 4 percent.[75] Inevitably, the growing professionalism of the association's financial management obliged it to take occasional liberties with certain declared dogmas, such as rejection of all interest and remuneration from capital.

The association's roundabout arrangements, whereby its meandering funds reached their destinations by mail or in the luggage of traveling militants, sometimes led to their vanishing altogether. One of the principal functions of the newsletters and correspondence exchanged by the members of the association was to sign off receipts for sums of money that militants were constantly sending them — usually to cover membership fees, subscriptions, and bills for association cards and copies of statutes ordered at the general council. Every missive contained passages referring to money received or sent (the other great subject of letters being the reputations of other association members). These passages served as rough accounts, in the absence of formal registers. When a dispatch had been announced but was slow in coming, correspondents grew furiously anxious, for fear that the money might prove to be lost — or infinitely worse, that they might be suspected of stealing it. In early 1869 the treasurer of the Belgian council, Alphonse Vandenhouten, warned its correspondent, to whom he had written several times without getting an answer: "Tomorrow evening I shall have to read your letter to the Belgian General Council; they will find it strange that you have sent no confirmation that you have received the money. Please use your next moment of leisure to deal with this." A similar anxiety arose a few months later, this time in reverse, when the London correspondent chided De Paepe for not having acknowledged reception of cash sent by English workers to help Belgian strikers: "What surprises me most is that *L'Internationale* [the newspaper] has given no sign that it has received the subscriptions: the English, my dear De Paepe, are especially punctilious when it comes to money, and I must say in that they have my full approval." The following autumn, the Belgian correspondent seems to have vanished completely; the Belgian militants had no further news of him and complained that they had never received the English subscription money.[76]

The thousands of letters written and exchanged during these years were the principal vector of communication and money transfer for the association. So it is hardly surprising that the question of postal charges attracted the attention of the members of the Geneva Congress in 1866, who were mostly in favor of the standardization of international postal relations. It didn't matter that this idea was also supported by governments and private companies: the postal network was definitely one of the mechanisms of internationalism that transcended ideological differences. Thus Cremer invited the members of the association to pressure their governments to obtain a reduction of postal charges and even to adopt a single postal tax to facilitate the flow of letters from one country to another. Militants also attempted to limit the customs fees that burdened the international circulation of newspapers and printed documents. Belgians and Swiss tried to negotiate with their respective authorities to keep costs down.[77] Here too, far from being protectionist, militants joined forces with liberals in their will to eliminate the physical and customs-weighted frontiers that restrained the circulation of men and printed words.

The Threat of Corruption

Trust played a vital role in maintaining the credibility of the IWA. Its leaders knew very well that they were under intense scrutiny, not only by their own adherents but also by state authorities eager to discredit an international organization that they found deeply disturbing.

Militants were also aware that corruption and scandal were serious dangers to the cause. An 1870 almanac, published in Liège by Belgian internationalists, featured an imaginary dialogue between a group of villagers concerning the role and initiative of the IWA. A local priest and a coal-mine accountant warned the workers against the association, saying it talked about solidarity and progress but its real goal was to get its hands on their money: "They go all over the place holding meetings on behalf of the workers, but instead of preaching economy and sobriety they convince them to pay money each month into a fund which can be used to support them if ever they go on strike." One of the workers asks: "Who knows? When I've paid my money, it might go straight to London or Brussels, and that's the last I'll see of it." A militant from the International then responds to these misgivings by enumerating in detail all the procedures used to keep track of funds, with the assurance that every penny remains fully at the disposal of local sections, according to the principle of subsidiarity, whereby decisions are devolved to the lowest practical level.[78]

These reassuring words were highly topical. The Belgian authorities had only recently been able to create a major fuss about a matter that was embarrassing for the International, to say the least. The treasurer of the Fayt section in the province of Hainaut, a man named Godeau, had abruptly vanished with the section's money box. The government seized on this theft to paint the entire association as a criminal enterprise, guilty of the worst kind of embezzlement. A brochure published by the Belgian International acknowledged that it was difficult, at a time when its membership was heavily on the increase, to be fully confident about the honesty of every newcomer despite the most rigorous procedures: "The delegates arrive in a place where few of them are acquainted with anyone at all; the members of the committee chosen by the assembly introduce themselves, and right away you expect them to guess who's honest and who isn't?" But the matter was serious enough for the Belgian general council to print several thousand tracts to counter a government propaganda onslaught targeting industrial workers. It was not unusual for swindlers and crooks to slip into the ranks of the association, given that it was impossible to carry out full background checks en every one of its thousands of members.[79]

These scandals tarnished the reputation of the entire institution, which was trying to convince workers to entrust it with their money instead of putting it in a bank or a savings account. The IWA's financial affairs had to be impeccably honest, so internal commissions of inquiry were quickly nominated before problems of this kind became common knowledge. In Spain, for example, the Barcelona Federation investigated a member of the marble workers' section who was suspected of misappropriating funds allocated to the printing and distribution of copies of the statutes. The commission returned a devastating report, deploring the fact that the militant in question had refused to explain himself publicly. Elsewhere, Engels — who supervised correspondence between the Italian section and the general council — reported that doubts had arisen about the Neapolitan militant Stefano Caporusso, who was suspected of removing 300 francs from the local section's reserve without the express authorization of his general council. Even though this sum had been earmarked as compensation for

Caporusso's earlier arrest by the police, he was expelled from the association. The reputation of the entire structure hinged on the capacity of its members to respect the procedures and rules of transparency it had imposed upon itself.[80]

■ ■ ■

The IWA was clearly not a workers' state; very few of its members wanted it to become so, and its financial resources were nothing short of laughable by comparison with those of the bourgeois states against which it was fighting. There was a fundamental contradiction at its heart: the voluntary engagement of its members would never alone suffice to create a universal federation of workers. A work of institutionalization was necessary to broaden the scope of the association, to generate the trust without which no long-distance connection was possible, and to collect the funds it required for the practice of solidarity. These constraints made it important to clarify the ideological concepts that were supposed to justify and rationalize militant action. Hence the nature of its relationship with the state became one of the stumbling blocks in debates between representatives of the various allegiances within the European workers' movement, who could never agree on what kind of state should be built after the destruction of the bourgeois regimes. At the 1867 Lausanne Congress, the committee appointed to study the question reached the conclusion that "the State is not a power and an authority in itself; instead it is the representative of *social power* and *social authority*," which did nothing to resolve the question of how power could legitimately be exercised. Bakunin's stance on this remained nebulous until he formulated his anti-statism more explicitly in the early 1870s. Otherwise, from the British trade unionists, who advocated worker responsibility and the virtues of self-help, to the disciples of the German socialist Ferdinand Lassalle, who were prepared to recognize the Prussian state provided it endorsed universal suffrage and the implementation of social policies, the IWA offered an umbrella for every ideological position imaginable — from individualist anarchism to revolutionary collectivism, by way of moderate reformism.[81]

Classic histories of the IWA have often blamed its failure on its toleration of ideological diversity. For years afterward, the Marxists who took part in its deliberations bitterly regretted not having crushed the various dissident "sects," whose amateurishness and unscientific approach to socialism fatally weakened the internationalist project. It is my own belief that the First International left a rich political legacy through the sheer inventiveness of its ideas, its political strategy, and its practice of solidarity. And this inventiveness makes it worthy of study today, for the debates that took place among its militants freed them to imagine the world in new and different ways. In short, the IWA was a vehicle of the kind of hope we ourselves need so badly, a hundred and fifty years on.

The IWA, babel of worker internationalism that it was, largely failed to overcome the tensions surrounding it. From 1869 onward, the conflict between Marx and Bakunin grew sharper. More and more militants — especially in Switzerland, Italy, France, Spain, and the United States — were worried about the project for centralization proposed by the author of *Das Kapital*, who was increasingly seen as a champion of authoritarianism. Bakunin stood for a much more federalist and decentralized model, less concerned with seizing political power and taking control of the state. Disagreements between the two were amplified by the chaotic events of 1870–1871: the war between Napoleon III's France and Bismarck's Prussia made the reconciliation of patriotism and internationalism well-nigh impossible for militants in either country, and above all, the Paris Commune, which lasted from March to May 1871, created deep divisions within the International itself. While a majority of IWA members supported the Commune, others were more reserved (as were the British trade unionists) or even frankly hostile. The fragile institutional structure built up since 1864 was shaken to its foundations when the English militants began slowly distancing themselves from the association, severely weakening Marx's position against the attacks of the federalists. Their disagreements came to a head during the London Conference in September 1871, but it was not until the Hague Conference the following year that a clean break was made when Marx and Engels contrived to exclude their adversaries once and for all. Bakunin and his supporters departed to perpetuate their ideas and their aspirations with the Jurassian Federation, which was based in Switzerland; but, rather than lose control of the London general council, they called a vote to transfer it lock, stock, and barrel to New York, in the hope that German workers who had emigrated to the United States could be relied upon to further their ideas.[82] In America too, the movement was divided between centralizers, who were supported by German-language sections, and federalists, who were strongest in the English- and French-language groups. The association could not survive this bitter infighting for long, and its official dissolution was announced in 1876.

The acrimonious end of the First International should not, however, obscure the enormous breadth of its achievement. It built up a wealth of contacts between communities in Europe and the United States, it left behind it rules and procedures so effective that they became common practice around the world and it created transnational relationships of trust and good repute. The battles within its general council at the end were dwarfed by the sheer richness of this experience: outside these institutions the IWA was "nothing but the international bond between the most advanced working men in the various countries and civilised world," wrote Karl Marx in his conclusion to *The Civil War in France*.[83]

This institutional legacy was only one benefit among many pioneered by the association. Let us now examine some of the other projects and aspirations that were formulated by its members.

2 | WORKERS' MONEY

Debates on the nature of the IWA, its hierarchical and vertical organization, and the London nerve center's relations with its continental periphery, preoccupied contemporary militants and have continued to fascinate the historians of later generations. Yet they represent no more than the most visible aspect of a much wider experience, which camouflaged a host of less obvious and more durable elements. To examine the economic and moral perspectives of working communities in the 1860s is to vault over the great conflicts that separate us from the aspirational richness and teeming ideas of the time. The best sources for it are the workers' press, surviving private correspondence, and the minutes of the general assemblies of the various associations, all of which present a picture of the moral economies of workers' funds when they were first being debated and tried out. Some of these ideas were crowned with success, others had little effect or failed miserably. But on the whole they demonstrate an intellectual dynamism and overwhelming energy that produced a new crop of utopian, revolutionary workers.

More than taxation, gifts, or confiscation, it was the realm of credit, free or reciprocal, on which most of the IWA's militants placed their hopes. For them, solidarity mainly consisted in repossessing the resources that capital was hogging for itself to the detriment of workers. This didn't necessarily mean they had to reject every one of the values promoted by the capitalist ethic of the time, such as the moral duty to pay one's debts or take care of business in a responsible, self-sufficient way. This effort began at a local level, with the establishment of funds managed by the workers themselves, "resistance" societies (as contemporary unions defined themselves) to prepare for strike action, and consumer and producer cooperatives. From the start, these local practices were conceived within an international framework: worker solidarity had to rely on cross-border worker credit, the relationship being more horizontal than vertical and inspired by thinking that was more federalist than centralizing.

The First International was created to restore to workers the control and use of their own money — the sole condition whereby the "non-solidarity" in which workers were trapped would be supplanted by a solidarity that was both more real and more effective.[1] This utopia was embodied in the places, gestures, and social relationships that transformed worker interactions and provided them with new instruments for struggle and emancipation. The chapter that follows is an invitation to delve into a forgotten mental landscape that is sometimes disconcerting, because so radically different from what later became (and remains) the dominant culture of the reforming leftists and revolutionaries of the twentieth century, at a crossroads in the history of ideas and practical sociology.

THE EMANCIPATORY POWER OF CREDIT

Despite the looming presence on the IWA's general council of Marx and Engels, who were deeply suspicious of any move that might distract their militants from the holy grail of political power, the prevailing theories among European workers in the 1860s were profoundly influenced by the idea that salvation and emancipation depended on the increasing use of credit. The international struggle against capital depended on the easy movement of funds across national frontiers, with as much if not more emphasis on the lender/borrower relationship as upon simple compassion and generosity. Where Karl Marx and Friedrich Engels saw the irreconcilable nature of capital and work as the bedrock of class struggle, many other militants and theorists, now forgotten, believed fervently in the democratization of credit and the opening of workers' access to capital.[2]

The discussions that took place at the meetings of the International were powerfully influenced by theories on the nature of credit, which had been fashionable since the 1830s among the proponents of Saint-Simon and various other socialist schools of thought.[3] Many believed in the "miracle" of credit, which they saw as a civilized economic practice that could help people bring their projects to fruition. Well before the liberal capitalists of the twentieth century used the idea to promise social advancement and prosperity to the American middle class, it was utopian thinkers and self-taught workers who promoted the merits of free credit, on condition that it allowed workers to purchase capital and not the other way around.[4] Proudhon recommended it explicitly, in 1848 and after, when he suggested free credit and the establishment of a people's bank as peaceful solutions to the social dilemma. The organization of free credit for workers was expected to bring about the elimination of interest (seen basically as the theft of work by ownership), thereby circumventing the state, which was criticized for its power to levy taxes. Despite the failure of his People's Bank project after 1849, Proudhon continued to defend these ideas until his death in 1865.[5] For him, mutual credit was the future for the economic emancipation of producers, rather than electoral politics or the formation of coalitions, as described in his last work, *De la capacité politique des classes ouvrières* (1865).[6] Free credit united all the objectives of the social utopia imagined by Proudhon: equal exchanges, reciprocity among producers, the disappearance of conflict between work and capital, access to capital for all, freely consented contracts replacing the coercive authority of the state. Proudhon's messianic theorizing particularly infuriated Karl Marx, who saw the People's Bank as pure illusion; Proudhon was also attacked by the liberal economist Frédéric Bastiat, for whom the idea that one could eliminate interest without destroying not only the currency but also all other forms of economic activity was frankly preposterous.[7]

Nevertheless, Proudhon's ideas found a strong echo among the workers of Paris. The signatories of the famous *Manifeste des Soixante*, published in 1864, among whom were several future members of the International (Henri Tolain, Zéphirin Camélinat, and Charles Limousin), were effusive in their praise of credit and mutualism, distancing themselves from measures associated with collectivist socialism such as agrarian laws or the redistribution of wealth. "Freedom of work, credit, solidarity, of these we dream. The day they come into being, for the greater glory and prosperity of the country that is so dear to us, there will be no more bourgeois, no more proletarians, no bosses, no workers. All citizens will be equal under the law."[8]

For Proudhon and his supporters, free credit heralded nothing less than the dissolution of social classes and the coming of genuine economic solidarity, based on the principle of reciprocity. Despite the violent opposition of Karl Marx to Proudhonist ideas, the question of credit was regularly on the agenda of the first congresses of the IWA, where such projects could be discussed conveniently by an international attendance.[9] The French and Belgian militants took the initiative in this, because they in particular had high expectations of it. The role of worker credit — meaning money that workers might lend directly to one another without resort to financial institutions — was debated in Geneva in 1866, Lausanne in 1867, and Brussels in 1868. A special committee was nominated in Brussels to study "means of using worker credit wisely."[10] True emancipation was felt to be only achievable if the workers managed to place their resources in a common pool, circumventing the banking and financial establishments controlled by the bourgeoisie. Free credit represented the highest form of reciprocity and equal exchange: it would abolish the perennial economic inferiority of the workers and thereafter give them easy access to capital. Mutual credit establishments such as production cooperatives were the mainstays of worker self-sufficiency.[11]

Broad agreement was reached on the goal of diverting workers' savings away from the institutions of bourgeois capitalism. In their report to the congress of 1867, the Belgian militants of the International represented by César De Paepe warned against the development of publicly subscribed state loans, which had been general currency since the 1850s. Public debt, which increased hugely with the wars waged by European states between 1850 and 1860 and the administrative and military modernizations they provoked, was vigorously condemned by the internationalists, who saw it as a straightforward embezzlement of popular savings that served only to compound the fiscal burdens placed upon the workers.[12] For this reason many called for their abolition and advised workers to steer well clear of public loans:

> This new system of small subscriptions is all the more favorable to the consecration of the tyrannical privileges of capital and the state, in that it gives many more people an interest in preserving the present status quo. . . . Working people need to understand that every penny they deposit in a savings bank and every penny they give to a banker or invest in some financial operation . . . serves to strengthen the chain that holds them in slavery. . . . What can be done to break this chain of wretchedness, which grows longer and stronger every day? Instead of extending credit to the bourgeoisie and their governments, the working classes must finance themselves.[13]

Worker participation in company profits, by the purchase of bonds or dividend-yielding shares, was another idea suggested from time to time. It was firmly resisted, as a deliberate deception. Popular or worker shareholdings were promoted in the twentieth century, especially in Europe and the USA after 1945; designed to democratize capitalism and avert the peril of revolution, they could have no liberating effect unless they were accompanied by direct worker control of the means of production. Thus a cardinal issue in the struggle against the bourgeois capitalist state was how to corral workers' savings.

Despite their caution, the members of the general council involved in these discussions approved the project of placing savings at the service of the workers. Eccarius and Lessner denounced the harmful effects of savings banks, which they accused of stripping the workers of an essential weapon in the fight against capital. The English workers, who were in the vanguard of social conflict at the time, were also more exposed than others to Victorian theories about the just rewards for hard graft, frugality, and saving money.[14] Eccarius estimated that there were about £25 million of workers' money deposited in bourgeois banks; Lessner added that the promotion of savings banks by the Victorian elite, led by Mr. Gladstone, was deliberately intended to nudge the workers toward conservative attitudes by chaining them to "the wheel of the government cart."[15] The promotion of savings banks, which was taking place in every European country, was thought to be strengthening the supervisory bourgeois hold over workers under the humanitarian cover of "protecting the working class from drunkenness and destitution."[16]

The shift from non-solidarity to solidarity implied a modification in the economic practices of the workers as well as a change of direction in the flow of credit. For its supporters, free credit forestalled the creation of new means of payment to replace state currencies guaranteed by gold and/or silver. This link between credit and currency was already present in Proudhon's idea of a People's

Bank. Likewise, the Belgian militants of the International wished to invent new means of exchange, which they projected as dematerialized and guaranteed by simple trust between worker cooperatives. Here the emancipation of the workers would change the course of a possible generalization of the practices of commercial exchange between producer and consumer societies. Thereafter, the perfecting of a circular paper exchange would eventually liberate production workers from the capitalist chains that bound them.[17] As formulated by Tolain at the Brussels Congress, this form of exchange would be based on common interest and a shared sincerity of internationalist engagement, and hence would make possible an alternative economic system entirely free of state sovereignty and material guarantees.[18] The vertical centralization of resources coercively obtained through taxation would be replaced by a regime of incessant horizontal loans and funds for assistance, managed and supervised by the workers themselves. As for the dream of free credit (meaning credit without remuneration of lent capital by interest payments or risk premiums), it would be saturated by constant fluxes, circulations, and exchanges, thus creating a network of shared reciprocity.

The hopes invested in the virtues of free credit went well beyond economics. The aim was to render the state superfluous, to make exchange among equals the basis for working relations, supplanting the ties of domination/subjection that characterized the bourgeois economy. Within this culture of worker self-sufficiency, which was so prevalent in the period 1850–1860, the state offered nothing in the way of progress for the future. So the objective was to promote a republic of small producers, united by the mechanisms of credit and exchange, with no dependance on any vertical, centralizing institution that would prolong the existence of hierarchical relationships between individuals. For the Proudhonian militant Félix Chemalé, the moment credit was based on trust, "trust not being centralized," "the state would have nothing else to do but make sure people stick to their contracts." "The state itself is a contract," he added darkly.[19] This hoped-for dissolution of public authority was far from unanimously approved by the First International, many of whose members favored the principal of collective property or the achievement of universal suffrage, which implied an implicit recognition of the legitimacy of the authorities. For this reason even those who shared the goal of keeping workers' savings out of danger recommended that not much should be expected of promises of free credit. Eccarius, in the same debate, reminded his colleagues that these free credit theories were largely confined to France and Belgium. The real struggle, which Marx's circle were awaiting with such fervor, would take place in the political arena, not the economic one.

Other dissenting voices were raised, notably that of Cohn, the leader of the English cigar makers' union, who expressed anxiety about proposals to suppress the remuneration of capital. Probably his speech was an accurate reflection of the way English workers felt, being well aware of the huge capital funds required for the development of industrial activities. At that time these activities were far more advanced on the other side of the Channel than on the continent. "What would you do at the present time to pay for colossal enterprises like the transatlantic telegraph?" said Cohn. "How could you possibly find the necessary capital in the form of an interest-free loan? When people lend money it is only because they want to make a profit. So I don't believe your reform can possibly be carried out, and I will not vote in favor of your resolutions."[20] All in all, there was no agreement on the question of free credit, whose presence was more muted in post-1868 theoretical debates after Proudhon's French supporters had been marginalized within the International.[21]

An International Lending Federation

The IWA did much more than provide a forum for squabbles about free credit. For many who attended its meetings, it offered an opportunity to start projects, root them in reality, and generally set them on an international footing. Worker credit should observe no frontiers: worker unity stemmed from the interests and values workers shared, and there was no reason why it should be stuck within the borders of nation states. If free, untrammeled credit opened the possibility of dissolving public authorities and circumventing sovereignties, then international worker credit could become the invisible thread joining the various sections of the International itself.

Credit should no longer just link communities of knowledge; it should go well beyond them, vaulting across frontiers. For some outside observers this was the true calling of the IWA, founded as it was on bringing local credit into contact with production cooperatives. The possibility of creating a personalized form of credit section by section, with an extension of the same practices into a broader and more formal framework, was seriously considered.[22] Joseph Collet, a French refugee in London and, after 1864, the editor of the *International Courier* (a bilingual English and French newspaper that echoed the ideas of the International), saw the organization of credit as a godsend for the autonomy of workers. The tailors of Geneva appealed to workers to contribute "the smallest obol" they could spare to the collective fund: "No more effective means is available to us than that of organizing credits, exchanges and a Mutual Council Bank, for ourselves and by ourselves." These mutualist cooperative views made themselves heard right up to the general council. In 1871, Boon, a disciple of the Chartist James Bronterre O'Brien, called for the creation of

> an international bureau and depositery wherein the Internationals may deposit their worked-up products and receive for the same an International Note or Exchange Medium; such notes to be exchangeable among all the members of the International (and the public if they will accept them). Such a system of International Exchange

based upon positive and exchangeable wealth (such as boots, clothing, watches, etc.) would be the means of cementing the International in one mighty bond of brotherhood and be the means of inaugurating a system of exchange enabling the working classes of all countries to exchange their products on the principle of cost, the limit of price, without the assistance or control of traders in all countries.[23]

Thus the workingmen's International was designed as an institution whereby cross-frontier economic practices of exchange and reciprocity could be fully deployed. The militant side of its activity was perhaps less important than the construction, on an international basis, of an alternative economic model capable of taking root in several countries at a time. The solidarity it generated was derived from direct economic exchanges, carried out independently of bourgeois institutions. From this point of view the International was not so much a secret organization, workers' state, or propaganda hub, as it was an international lending network for workers, able to collect and circulate their savings via a free form of credit that bypassed the usual financial institutions.[24] The funds placed in the International were constantly on loan to the groups or sections that needed them, with no risk that they would be immobilized or trapped. This capital, amassed and loaned, would serve the cause of worker self-sufficiency rather than contribute to worker alienation.

But concrete results were few and far between. Most took the form of loans that workers granted to themselves, as did, for example, the bronze workers of Lyon who in July 1869 organized a loan of 40,000 francs for their own cooperative activities; or the Marseille craftsmen's federation, which guaranteed a loan of 1,500 francs (in bonds of one franc) for the local polishers' union.[25] The Belgian militants of the International were notably enthusiastic about the principle of free exchange and the links binding them to other sections in Belgium and abroad. It was common for a section to subscribe to a foreign newspaper in exchange for a foreign subscription to one of their own. In Germany, credit and loan institutions for workers had grown fairly widespread in the wake of a movement launched in the 1850s by Hermann Schulze-Delitzsch, which had recruited more than 135,000 members through cooperatives linking producers and consumers with savings institutions and lending funds. Some of these were related to bourgeois milieux, which made them suspect in the eyes of IWA militants.[26]

Such practices of mutual assistance and reciprocity had another, less evident objective, that of enabling militant movements. The statutes of the IWA and its sections included a reference to the existence of "international credit," a link — independent of the general council — that existed between its members.[27] The idea was a simple one: a militant of a given section — provided that it was up-to-date with its subscriptions — could expect to be welcomed and protected by any foreign section, whatever the reason for his visit (search for employment, political exile, mission assignment on behalf of the association). The existence of a network of sections, linked to each other by shared objectives and statutes, was a great support for the mobility of workers. This network refreshed the idea of a form of transnational assistance, which would derive not from mere charity but from active participation in a single organization.[28] The duty of mutual assistance was rooted in traditions of companionship linked to corporate identity and also to those of masonic secret societies.[29] Article 10 of the general rules of the IWA provides that "each member of the International Association, on removing his domicile from one country to the other, will receive the fraternal support of the Associated Working Men."[30] The Brussels marble workers' union even imagined that workers could travel and be welcomed abroad by other professional communities, on simple presentation of a card proving their membership in the International Association.[31]

But it was in the special circumstances of strike action that free credit and mutual assistance really came into their own.

"Cash assets which in ordinary times are used for cooperative purposes, should become resistance funds when workers are on strike," declared the Geneva sections.[32] To support social struggle and prepare for strikes, it was suggested that "resistance societies" (another name for trade unions) could be federated: thus, at this time, the IWA was already working on an embryonic project for bringing trade unions together under a single banner, with the Spanish and Belgian members in the forefront. Within the IWA itself, the issues of a central headquarters and a governing body were being overtaken by a rising tide of transnational mutual assistance and shared interest. Reciprocity, it was felt, should be applicable as much in daily economic relationships as in the more exceptional circumstances of political struggle and active resistance to lockouts. In this sense, militant action was indistinguishable from the more mundane forms of economic organization that the militants themselves were trying out.

The Ethics of Reciprocity

These multiple reflections on the nature of free credit and an international federation of loans to workers demonstrated the pervasiveness among contemporary skilled workers of a moral economy based on a desire for self-sufficiency and reciprocity. The instrument of this ideal was not the *gift* but the *loan*. Emancipation would never be generated by goodwill and generosity; it had to feed on the capacity of everyone to be at once borrowers and lenders, within an uninterrupted cycle — and perpetual redeployment — of debts and loans. The idea behind international solidarity was to create an economic, moral, and political link between people that, instead of enslaving some for the benefit of others, would contribute to a collective emancipation of workers, whatever their origin or nationality. In this sense, the political and economic dreams that energized most of the militants of the time expressed a desire on the part of ordinary workers to embrace the promise of extended, generalized credit. To do so, they had to regain control of their own resources, stop putting up with liberal bourgeois moralizing, and refuse the exactions of governments and employers.

The moral and political grandeur ascribed to credit was directly related to the much more depreciative vision of charitable giving. Workers engaged in the struggle were highly sensitive to this distinction, and they dwelled on it at length in their exchanges and correspondence. The most qualified among them made it a point of honor not to beg: if they asked for help, it would take the form of a loan that they felt honor bound to repay, through their capacity to accumulate resources of their own. The loan functioned as a gesture recognizing the superiority of the best-organized professions, which saw themselves as the vanguard of the workers' movement.[33] The close attention paid by these professions to the "earmarking" of monetary transfers — whereby loans and gifts, solidarity and charity, were carefully distinguished from one another — was a mark of their status and dignity. In 1864 the French signatories of the *Manifeste des soixante* were determined to stay as far away as possible from commercial lenders and charities alike: "We don't want to be clients; we don't want to be on the dole. We want to become equals. We reject charity. Justice is what we want."[34]

This culture of worker autonomy rested squarely on what might be called an ethic of reciprocity. The militants of the IWA, who hated the coercive power of the bourgeois state, strongly objected to relationships of obligation and subordination. For them, solidarity was above all a horizontal link, nourished by voluntary and freely consented exchanges between the various workers' associations of Europe and elsewhere. But this edifice could only stand if everyone involved considered himself morally bound to give back that which had been lent to him, thus maintaining solidarity and strengthening the links to whose emergence he had contributed. The workers of the International would agree to lend money because they themselves had already received money, or because they hoped one day to receive it, should a strike or a lockout place them in a difficult position.

ACCUMULATING FUNDS IN "RESISTANCE SOCIETIES"

These ideas about credit and mutual assistance assumed that there were actual funds available to be shared. The circulatory internationalist dream meant putting in place practices of collection and management of money in locally based funds, in which stocks of workers' contributions would steadily accumulate. The flow of this money could hardly be diverted away from the local institutions and social groups from which it came. At the time, the groups expected to implement all this were known on the continent as *sociétés de résistance* ("resistance societies," the term being preferred to *syndicat* as a translation of the very English *trade union*). In context, the word *resistance* had a double meaning. The first meaning implied struggle and the demands that the money was expected to underpin; the second signified — in a broader sense — the formation of an alternative workers' economy, whereby economic emancipation through credit, cooperation, and mutualism would lead naturally to political resistance. The solidarity workers needed for their stand against capitalist exploitation came straight from the daily experience of pooling resources.

The emergence of the International coincided with a massive push to organize worker communities throughout Europe and America. The two phenomena, although they seemed disjointed because the worker associations appeared independently of the International Association, were soon feeding off each other. Without always being entirely legalized, unions, associations, and professional guilds came into being in most western and northern European countries. In the United States, a first union organization was founded in 1866. Led by William H. Sylvis, the National Labor Union made contact with the IWA in 1868, though it did not join. The year 1869 saw the creation of the Knights of Labor, whose role was to be crucial in the 1880s, notably from the standpoint of worker internationalism (see chapter 5). Eventually the support of immigrants flowing into America from Europe, Germany, Ireland, and Sweden proved decisive. With time, the newspapers and congresses of the IWA grew more adept at facilitating comparisons of experiences and expertise, as a professional understanding of militant practices became another condition for joining the International. The proliferation of strike action between 1866 and 1872, along with the forms of solidarity it generated, encouraged local societies to adopt the forms and practices the IWA had found to be the most effective — that is, those of the English unions. For all these reasons, the very existence of the IWA accelerated the formation of closer relationships between worker communities, leading to ever more practical exchanges and reciprocal observations. Its role as a platform for lively discussion was fundamental, proving much more important than any project for building a centralized institution.

For the militants of the International, the work of building worker solidarity began at the base, with experience of what happens when the workers themselves take collective responsibility for managing the funds they manage to set aside. Money, as ever, was the driving force: the emancipation of the workers hinged on their ability to regain control of the monetary resources that employers were diverting for their own profit. The exercise of individual and collective autonomy had a cost nonetheless. The short-term cash sacrifices the workers had to make could obscure the collective benefits that might be expected in the long term. Hence the classic dilemma of collective action: How might workers be persuaded that their best interest lay in uniting their strength and resources when, to them, their very survival seemed — in the short term — to depend on paternalistic institutions put in place by the bourgeoisie?

The Control of Provident Funds

The most favored model for all this was the resistance society. The first stage of worker emancipation began with the creation of collective forms for the mutualizing of resources, whereby workers could find out at first hand how collective decision-making worked and could comprehend the obligations imposed by solidarity along with the benefits it yielded in return. The mutualizing of resources meant financial sacrifice from the workers and hence a risk of organizational conflict; but the building of working capital was unquestionably the first stage of resistance to bourgeois capital.

This issue was highly sensitive in the 1860s, at a time when workers were often invited — and sometimes even constrained — to put money aside in savings banks founded by state authorities and liberal elites or in provident funds set up by employers. There was no lack of money in the skilled professions that formed the bulk of the International's membership (typographers, bronze workers, weavers, cigar makers, and so on), but its collection and use were not spontaneously geared to benefit the workers. For this reason almost everywhere in western Europe the strikes that occurred in the late 1860s were about the recognition of the workers' right to manage their own money and form aid associations and mutualized credit organisms that were independent of their employers. In the United States the main emphasis was on the eight-hour day.

A case in point was that of the Paris bronze workers in 1867. The employers of this industry refused to recognize the legitimacy of the bronze workers' Société de crédit et de solidarité, founded after a first successful bout of industrial action in 1865. Instead, they promised assistance and employment to those workers who remained independent and abstained from "contributing money in support of actions that threatened the dignities and interests of all." Thus the subsequent lockout was not applied to workers who opted out of the bronze workers' solidarity and credit association, which at the time had upward of three thousand members. The struggle initiated by the roughly five thousand Parisian bronze workers won the support of the International precisely because the issue was one of freedom and dignity. The strike, far from weakening the bronze workers' ability to mobilize, generated gigantic meetings at which thousands of participants debated slogans, strategies, and ways of financing their action. The virtues of the association triumphed in the month of April 1867.[35]

Other industrial conflicts in other parts of Europe provoked similar discussions, most notably on the subject of provident funds, which were of vital importance to the system of patronage set up by the industrial elites between 1850 and 1860. To stabilize the workforce and minimize conflicts, employers organized housing for workers and schools for their children, offering lines of credit and creating funds for their welfare. The workers themselves, who were denied any role in the management of these services, were expected to be thankful to their bosses for such generosity: this was, after all, the golden age of the "industrial paternalism" so accurately described by Charles Dickens in his 1854 novel *Hard Times*. Its scope included the United States, where it was exemplified by such figures as George Pullman, the railroad magnate. Pullman's omnipotence was to remain unchallenged until the great strike of 1894, which shook the world.[36] The tutelary relationship was denounced during the strikes, as was the employers' claim to an exclusive right to decide how workers' money should be spent or saved.[37] Bitter conflict resulted from the determination of bourgeois paternalists to supervise all this and the equal determination of workers looking for genuine autonomy; it crystallized over the issue of contingency funds, their management, and the sources of their cash. In a relationship of patronage, workers' obligation to contribute was decided over their heads, with a view to raising their moral standards and generally managing their lives. By contrast, according to the cooperative, mutualist model then in the ascendant, such decisions were supposed to come from the workers themselves, who might prefer to allocate their own resources in function of their own personal and collective needs.

The affirmation of this right and its embedding in practice were among the main talking points of the 1869 Belgian congress of the International, which called upon "all sections ... to create provident funds and find legal ways to regain control of the workers' funds presently in the hands of employers."[38] In January of the same year at Verviers, the weavers' union had gone on strike to protest a local employer's decision to deduct money from his workers' wages to build a mutual aid fund. A government minister, Alexandre Jamar, had recently recommended that industrialists should initiate aid funds, consumer associations, and crèches. This was exactly what the workers themselves were calling for, but they meant to go about it on their own, without reference to their employers.[39] The protest was also aimed at bosses who had unilaterally subtracted money from the wages of employees who had dared to join strikes.

One might imagine that this issue only concerned a minority of organized, prosperous professions, whose workers had ample margins for maneuver and negotiation with their employers. Yet it was also a problem for relatively new industrial sectors like mining and metallurgy. The Belgian strike actions of 1869 at Charleroi and the coalfields of the Borinage — where there were nearly twenty-seven thousand active workers in 1870 — targeted the coal companies, which maintained the right to control their contingency funds.[40] This debate hugely mobilized the militants of the International when, on 1 January 1871, the mine workers' contingency fund established by the government came to term. This was the moment to show that worker resistance societies, organized on the scale of whole industrial areas, could take charge of the fund and resist state intervention. Likewise in France, the management of mine workers' contingency funds sparked conflicts that were passed on to posterity. For example, in the 1869 dispute at Saint-Étienne, a strike broke out after miners demanded the creation of a mutual assistance fund independent of management, which they wanted to see filled by deductions from wages and payments imposed on companies. These demands were brutally repressed: fourteen civilians were killed at La Ricamarie on 16 June 1869, a massacre at the end of the Second Empire that galvanized Napoleon III's Republican and Liberal opponents. At the end of the same year, in Prussian Silesia at the other end of Europe, eight thousand mine workers at Waldenburg downed tools after their employers tried to confiscate the sickness relief fund they had built up.[41] Thereafter, similar conflicts continued to occur over the same bone of contention.

Patronage and the Le Creusot Strikes

The Le Creusot strikes of January and April 1870 offer the most emblematic example of these feuds over workers' funds. Le Creusot, a small town in central France that was barely known in the 1830s, suddenly emerged as a symbol of the European industrial revolution like Manchester, England, or Essen, Germany. By 1860, the Schneider family had transformed this town, insignificant until the turn of the nineteenth century, into a hub of the European steel industry employing more than ten thousand workers. Above all, Le Creusot was the showcase of the political and social power of the Schneiders, who epitomized industrial paternalism and the close links between business and politics under the July Monarchy and the Second Empire.

Everything began at the end of 1869, with a dispute between steelworkers and their employer over the management of the factory's contingency fund. This fund, which had been created on the Schneiders' initiative in 1838, provided medical and pharmaceutical help to staff, distributed pensions and allowances, and organized primary schooling for children. It was financed by a 2 percent deduction from workers' pay, increased to 2.5 percent in 1861, without their having any say about the sums taken or how they were to be used.[42] Beginning in the summer of 1869, there were strong demands for worker control of the fund, stemming notably from the Cercle d'études sociales founded by a group of republicans that included the worker, unionist, and politician Jean-Baptiste Dumay.[43]

Convinced despite all this that he could count on his workers' unwavering support, Eugène Schneider organized a plebiscite on 15 and 16 January 1870. To his astonishment, the majority voted for worker control, in spite of a sizable abstention. The patronage he had espoused following the ideas of Frédéric Le Play, for whom the factory was one big family under the patriarchal authority of its employer, was directly opposed by the workers' demands for autonomy. Company schools, housing estates, food and supply stores were not enough to guarantee the tranquility and loyalty of the working class. Many workers were flatly refusing to owe their lives to the company and to go into debt for mere food and lodging. Conversely, the factory management was alarmed by the potential consequences of giving any degree of participation to the workers who, they believed, would divert the funds intended for assistance and contingency use to help pay for strike action.

The result of the plebiscite comforted Schneider's workers in their determination to manage their own contingency fund. On 19 January, a delegation led by Adolphe Assi, a worker in the company's railways department and a former partisan who had fought with Garibaldi in Italy, met with Henri Schneider, the company head and son of the patriarch (who did not arrive in person till the following day). The group demanded the right to manage the fund and the possibility for worker contributors to retain their rights even if they left the company and moved away from Le Creusot: in other words such rights would cease to be tied to local residence and instead be fully attached to the people themselves.[44] The firm's management, which accepted neither the results of the vote nor the legitimacy of the worker delegation, called in the army to reestablish order. The strike, which lasted for five days, ended with Assi's arrest and the dismissal of nearly seventy workers, but not before it had attracted national and international attention. At the time Eugène Schneider was president of the Corps Législatif, the Second Empire's lower house of parliament elected by universal male suffrage. There, the republican opposition led by Léon Gambetta and Alphonse Esquiros challenged Schneider about the disturbances in his "fiefdom," as his opponents called Le Creusot.[45] For the *Figaro* newspaper, this episode bore the imprint of the International, even though no link whatever existed between the IWA and the strikers.[46]

A second strike was not long in coming, on 21 March 1870 — but this time it was called by mine workers. Here the role of the International was clear, because a section of it had been created at Le Creusot after the arrival of Eugène Varlin on 18 March, three days earlier. Benoît Malon, a correspondent of the *Marseillaise* newspaper and a delegate of the French section of the IWA, joined Varlin at the beginning of April.[47] Like the steelworkers, the miners demanded the right to manage their contingency fund themselves, along with a ten-hour day. This time around, the organization of assistance to the strikers turned into a major issue: to break the strike and recover the trust of their workers, the Schneiders made a succession of philanthropic gestures, distributing coupons and other largesse through their charity and through the town's curé, in exchange for going back to work. Malon denounced these crude maneuvers in the *Marseillaise:* "Offers of free bread and lard will not be enough to split the strikers," he wrote. Above all, the management of the factory, supported by the *Figaro*'s editorialists, tried to cast doubt on the strike committee and the way it was sharing out the cash subscriptions it was receiving from all over the world. Malon defended the committee tooth and nail, commending its integrity and efficiency. The *Marseillaise* reminded its readers of the inviolable nature of the funds collected by the strikers; these funds could not be confiscated, despite the fact that the society collecting them might have been judged illegitimate.[48]

The striking miners received sympathy and financial aid from France and abroad. French, Belgian, Swiss, and British militants were enthusiastic in their support: for them, this conflict between one of Europe's best-known employers and its workers exemplified a string of other battles to defend worker autonomy against bourgeois patronage. The issue was focused not so much on improving worker conditions as on obtaining the right of workers to start their own contingency funds and to decide how they should be used. This, according to the *Marseillaise*, was "a question of dignity." The Belgian internationalists welcomed the Le Creusot workers' struggle against Eugène Schneider, who in their view personified the limitless arrogance of industrial employers: "He alone decides wages; he alone decrees what taxes will be paid; he alone supplies workers with bed and board and lays out the streets and roads they must use." The Geneva sections exhorted the strikers to recover "control of the cash docked from their wages." The issue was control of workers' money, as the Rouen section said in its expression of support: "Persevere in your demand to manage your own savings, which this millionaire refuses to return to you." The strikes involving the Schneiders' "capitalist fiefdom" quickly became legendary in the European workers' movement, as one of the symbols of socialism's struggle against the "tyrannical organization" of employers.[49]

Despite the funds flowing in from France and abroad, the Le Creusot strike collapsed within three weeks and the workers were defeated. The local reputation of the Schneiders was temporarily tarnished, as was shown by the wider events of 1870–1871 and the short-lived proclamation of an autonomous Commune by Jean-Baptiste Dumay and other members of the International on 26 March 1871. After the Commune was crushed and order had been restored, the Schneiders resolved to get rid of their contingency fund altogether, paying pensions and benefits directly instead. In their view it was better to set up a purely philanthropic and vertical relationship with their workers than to grapple with funds subtracted from wages that might expose them to demands for participation and control.[50]

Schools of Democracy and Industrial Action

The miscellaneous aspect of resistance societies, in a world that was still relatively random and unspecialized, gifted the authorities with a powerful instrument to discredit them. The associations were accused of mixing up their economic purposes with strike actions, whereas the workers they were supposed to represent saw the two as complementary. Critics of the authorities set particular store by the way in which the societies managed the funds they collected from their adherents. Even in England, the birthplace of trade unionism, trade unions were faulted for not placing strong enough accounting distinctions between money meant for welfare benefits and money used to underwrite strikes and subsidize professional (trade) matters. The royal commission nominated in 1867 to investigate union organizations warned them to observe a clear distinction between these two aspects of funding, in such a way that cash distributed as sickness, accident, or retirement benefit should not be threatened by sudden and drastic expenditure on strike action. The issue was also a legal one, inasmuch as the English unionists were actively working to obtain the same kind of protection under English law as the "friendly societies." They went on to achieve this in the 1870s.[51]

In addition to collecting resources to support the economic and social emancipation of workers, resistance societies offered apprenticeship and professional training in militant action. Building this up was vital to the local and institutional effectiveness of worker mobilization. The necessity for militants to get together, deliberate, and take collective decisions on what to do with the funds they shared was viewed as excellent practice for future solidarity. Resistance societies were thus more broadly conceived as "schools for strikers," platforms for education and training that might strengthen the links between workers as well as their capacity to resist the pressure of employers. For Eugène Dupont, a French delegate at the general council, they made it possible for workers to understand better "the exercise of social and political rights." It must be remembered that at the time there were no major national political parties; Marx himself viewed trade unions as "schools for socialism."[52]

The main objective of the resistance societies was to professionalize the workers' recourse to strike action — and above all to stop them getting into conflicts they were bound to lose. First of all, they had to be sure they could rely on a treasury in reasonable proportion to the gravity of the dispute to come, in view of the numbers of workers likely to be involved and the period of time they could expect to be on strike. Complete openness and respect for clearly stated procedures, as much in terms of decision-making as of the management of available funds, were a guarantee of effectiveness; these principles had been pioneered by the English trade unions, whose successes were acknowledged all over Europe. A "good" strike by English standards was one whose demands were precise and believable, whose backup resources were assured and mostly adequate, and whose means of action were both legal and appropriate. These conditions were essential; moreover, respect for them made possible an appeal to the solidarity of other members of the International, who would more readily agree to lend their resources should a dispute go on longer than expected. Loans of cash represented more than mere financial support: they were a mark of recognition for the serious and well-thought-out organization of those workers who applied for them.

At the very least this was a theoretical model according to which concrete situations (detailed in the next chapter) might be handled.

At the time, trade union action in Europe was in its infancy; all too often workers found themselves faced for the first time with the specific needs and constraints of organizing a strike only when they were already committed to it. Issues like this caused bitter disagreements between militants, as the events at Le Creusot showed. The militant Jean-Baptiste Dumay, an internationalist and a communard, spent the 1870s in exile in Switzerland before being elected as a republican parliamentary *deputé* on his return to France; in his memoirs, written several decades later, he was highly critical of Assi's role as head of the delegation to the factory management in January 1870. He reproached Assi with a failure to understand how important it was to form a strike commission made up of representative workers who could credibly guarantee proper management and fair distribution of the funds collected to support the strike. Dumay, who at the time was recovering from serious illness, was unable to accompany the group of workers that met with the Schneider family. According to him, his absence left the field dangerously open for the amateurism and unprepared-ness of Assi, whom he tried to warn:

> I added that 7,000 workers couldn't remain unemployed for long without badly needing help, that contributions would very likely be called for by the opposition press, and that some kind of organism would be required to receive, distribute, and keep records of the money flowing in. Assi serenely replied: "My friend, I'm here to take care of all that! If M. Schneider asks for somebody to negotiate with, I'll go and work it all out with him. If people send money, I will per-sonally receive it and pass it around, I don't need anyone's help with that." I was devastated to see a man so brash and pleased with him-self carried by events to the pinnacle of such a movement. I told Assi, and the other comrades of our republican group who were going with him, that their strike was stillborn, it couldn't last more than eight days.[53]

A few weeks later, during the conflict started by the miners in March–April 1870, a proper strike committee was formed and put in place with the help of the internationalist Malon, who came straight from Paris to give his advice. The number of delegates on the committee was doubled, from six to twelve, "in the hope of reducing to nothing the calumnies to which they were exposed," in particular regarding the use of the many contributions sent from France and abroad.[54] The professionalism of what was done was this time facilitated by a member coming from outside the movement, who shared his own experience of labor disputes in Paris and of the models that had been discussed in most of the sections of the International. Funds of solidarity originating elsewhere could only be accepted if they were accompanied by the adoption of practices and procedures aligned with the requirements of worker democracy, such as representative delegates, full disclosure of facts and figures, and absolute clarity about the goals being pursued. It was not uncommon to see the militants of the International visiting regions newly affected by strike action, to dampen the ardor of ill-prepared workers. The secretary of the Belgian general council, Eugène Hins, visited Liège and the Borinage in 1869 with this in mind, hoping to prevent strikers from going over the top too early. He then expected to consult with the authorities and convince the workers to organize thoroughly before they rose against their oppressors.[55]

Paradoxically, the ultimate aim of the resistance societies was not so much to multiply strikes ad infinitum as to make them so effective they would naturally become less frequent. Employers, it was hoped, would grow more aware of the dangers awaiting them if labor conflicts were allowed to go on too long. The rigorous "scientific" organization of the societies and their financial clout were both based on dissuasion. This was deemed an essential tool for consolidating the workers' power of negotiation, one that could make resorting to strike action exceptional, even superfluous.

Having a major fund at their disposal did not mean that strikes would occur more often: instead the plan was to impress employers and show them that, in the event of a major conflict, the workers could hold out for several weeks or even months. It was a question of power and credibility, intended to establish the authority of worker demands and demonstrate the strength obtained by "a compact organization of the working class."[56]

At a very early stage, the militants of the International were imagining a future in which the workers would be grouped in international professional federations — a movement that was to take off later, in the 1890s. They would be capable of assisting each other with strikes and lockouts, while preventing attempts by employers to hire foreign personnel. There was nothing to indicate that this was a vertical construction; its impetus did not flow from a central headquarters but from local associations. These were the basic cells of worker organization, tied into networks by modern communications and the physical mobility of the workers themselves. Some professions were already functioning like this in the 1860s and 1870s: the cigar makers, for example, had an international association of their own with a broad membership of English, Belgian, Dutch, and German workers.[57]

The project to make resistance societies include all professions was regularly discussed at the IWA's congresses, especially the one that took place in Basel in September 1869. There, the English trade unionist Robert Applegarth made common cause with Swiss workers from the Courtelary district, and their Belgian counterparts, who together were at the cutting edge of the issue.[58] At the critical Hague Conference in 1872, the "authoritarian" International of Marx and Engels broke forever with the Jurassian Federation of Bakunin, James Guillaume, and a group of Belgian, Italian, and Spanish militants. The reason was that the latter hoped for a federalization of the resistance societies, based on professional identities and in the absence of any central, coercive authority.

Their project to bring workers into horizontal alignment was to continue for decades afterward; in fact it lasted much longer than Marx's ideally centralized governing body with wide powers of coordination and decision. Meanwhile, the much debated plan for a European strike fund continued being postponed.

Beyond their functions of organization and professionalization, the resistance societies had a crucial role to play in the education of militants and their apprenticeship in the canons of collective life. The societies' financial strength was viewed as the means to a much more ambitious end, that of changing "non-solidarity" into "solidarity," thereby thoroughly training workers to defend their rights. As such, the societies were conceived as so many small "democracy schools,"[59] where the workers could learn to conduct themselves in obedience to common rules, to accept and share burdens and sacrifices, and above all, to define fair principles for the distribution and sharing of resources, which was their main recognized virtue and function. Society members received complete and continuous instruction in socialist and democratic values. Proposals from Swiss-German sections reflect the idea of a close parallel between economic solidarity and the democratic ethos: "Through the democratic principles of their constitutions, our production associations awaken and develop a need for — and love of — the Republic. They serve as preparatory schools for the Republic. They are pioneers of social reform."[60] In terms that were very different to the ones we use today, the societies were genuinely conceived as experiments in participative and deliberative democracy, of a kind that could make possible the political socialization of workers. This in turn could help them see beyond the isolation imposed on them by capitalism. In the eyes of their promoters, the societies were fully rounded institutions, equipped to take charge not only of the material destiny of the workers but also of their moral and political progress. In short, they favored the accumulation of a militant capital, which was at once material and immaterial, financial and relational, practical and intellectual.[61]

THE AGE OF SUBSCRIPTIONS

Economic and political emancipation belonged to distinct time frames. In the long-term, the goal was to create a credit-and-loan federation, independent of bourgeois institutions and run by the workers for their own benefit. In the medium-term, this meant the resistance societies collecting funds to support worker training in collective management, as well as in the development of services to help them in their economic exchanges and strike actions. But for the time being, solidarity would have to express itself through the payment of subscriptions. The militants of the International were regularly called upon to contribute money in addition to their regular membership fees, as a gesture of sympathy for struggling workers affected by industrial action or police repression.

A Polymorphous Nonpartisan Tool

Although it remains an important symbol of action for left-leaning political groups, subscription is actually a political and financial practice that is flexible and nonpartisan. It has the great advantage of bringing together several different repertoires in blends of militant mobilization, charitable inspiration, aggregation, distinctiveness, sound values, and fervent emotions. In no way is it the sole prerogative of the nineteenth-century workers' movement: in fact, it is the very opposite. The procedure is used in all kinds of different fields. It is strikingly ubiquitous. In its earliest sense in the nineteenth century, the word *subscription* was neither political nor charitable; indeed the subscriptions most often mentioned in the press of the time usually had to do with private or public bond issues. The term describes a financial maneuver backed by poster campaigns and publicity inserts in the economic and mainstream press between 1850 and 1860. The stock market bubble that took place in those years saw a proliferation of subscription offers, when railway companies issued bonds or governments sold public debt. In France, the Bonapartist regime boasted of having "democratized" the buying of debt securities by resorting to public subscriptions. The term laid great emphasis on the opening of this whole procedure, its purpose being to tap into the savings of various layers of the population by insisting that they were sharing in a collective enterprise.[62]

The origins of subscription are much older, dating back to classical Greece, when the wealthiest citizens of cities were asked to donate money for the building of such public assets as monuments or warships. Even then, the publicity afforded by the inscription in stone of the names of subscribers (along with the amount of their subscriptions) were essential features of the practice. Paul Veyne explained this to perfection in his study of magnate benefactors.[63] As the historian Léopold Migeotte has written, ancient Greek subscriptions mobilized the gift register as a source of finance for public expenditure, installing an economy that was symbolic of distinction and gratification.[64]

It is hardly surprising, given its fascination with classical Greece, that the French Revolution was all in favor of resurrecting such practices, especially within the context of its own *levées en masse* to defend itself against hostile neighbors. As in antiquity, but this time by appealing to the virtue and engagement of all citizens, the popular societies opened subscriptions to collect donations. But behind the apparent unanimity and patriotism symbolized by the act of subscribing money, there lurked a network of social and spatial hierarchies. The use of the technique to finance the building of ships had already proved itself under the ancien régime, when the duc de Choiseul launched several subscriptions after the Seven Years' War with a view to rebuilding the shattered French navy.[65]

Outside the patriotic context of *L'an II*, the subscription henceforth offered the possibility of collective finance for public infrastructure. Thus, in the eighteenth and nineteenth centuries, money was steadily raised to restore the village church bells of France.[66]

In the nineteenth century, subscription became a mainstream source of funds for philanthropic institutions. It was the main point of leverage of what was known as "philanthropic emulation," an idea embraced by elite figures looking for charitable projects that might bring them fame and public approval. The subscription lists, which publicized donations and the hierarchy of monetary symbolism they represented, lay at the heart of the philanthropic disposition from the 1820s onward.[67] At an early stage, this charitable repertoire assumed a transnational diversion: philanthropy without frontiers used subscriptions to create long-distance links between affected communities and their generous benefactors. It all began with the help given to the Greek people in the 1820s; international solidarity of this type took many forms, among them dispatches of money and aid in kind, following the publication and circulation of subscription lists. These included not only the names of leading liberals but also those of aristocratic grandees of the ancien régime.[68] As the century wore on, more and more philanthropic undertakings were thrown open to the punier donations of the general public, as the logic of aristocracy receded before a more egalitarian ideal — or at least a more socially open-minded one. In the United States, for example, calls for donations were aimed at the public-spiritedness of all classes during the Civil War. So the civic donation should not be viewed solely as a mark of aristocratic distinction but also as a vector of integration within the national community.[69]

At the same time, the practice of subscription became politicized, a change that the historian Emmanuel Fureix tartly qualified as the "political distortion of a philanthropical impulse."[70] Although it has come down to posterity as one of the central elements of the liberal and republican political repertoire in the nineteenth century, the subscription "crossed political currents." Between 1820 and 1830, the advent of funerary subscriptions designed to commemorate a political and/or literary personality by dedicating a cenotaph to his honor was used not only by ultra royalist militants following the death of the duc de Berry but also by their liberal opponents, who collected cash to build monuments to the glory of General Foy and other prominent figures in their own pantheon. The historian Emmanuel Fureix linked such subscriptions to a drive for publicity, to the expression of the "voice of the people," and to the logic of building a commonality of emotion and combat — all of which were significant prior to 1884 because they required no official authorization.[71] The sums collected had an importance that far outstripped their financial value, inasmuch as the lists of donors publicized certain militant groups, making them both visible and audible. Not surprisingly, the practice became widespread in republican circles from the 1840s onward.[72]

Under the Second Empire, subscriptions offered another way for republicans to make themselves known to each other, not so much physically as on paper. Perhaps the most celebrated subscription of the time was launched in November 1868 by a couple of republican newspapers, to finance the erection of a monument to a parliamentarian, Alphonse Baudin, killed on the Paris barricades on 3 December 1851. The memorial significance of this appeal for donations was inseparable from a will to somehow reassemble the republican family, at a juncture when the opposition was beginning to make its voice heard again.[73]

But in the last third of the nineteenth century, the subscription appeal was by no means the monopoly of progressive republicans. In addition to charitable Catholics, who were also invited to give regularly to the pope, other political forces more or less favorable to the Republic could be relied upon to respond. At the end of the century the Dreyfus Affair led to an all-out battle of petitions and subscriptions, initiated when twenty-five thousand people in the anti-Dreyfus camp came together to raise money for Colonel Henry's widow, many of them contributing anti-Jewish, anti-magistrate rants along with their cash. The defenders of Captain Dreyfus hit back by organizing subscriptions of their own that — like their petitions — served to unify his supporters and display their strength and determination in the press.[74]

Words and Money

With the proliferation of strikes and the creation of unions and resistance societies, the subscription became a permanent part of the repertoire of militant worker action during the 1860s. Of course it was already present, but at this time it became general practice, opening up to new social milieux. The International helped to make it a standard tactic, to be used in times of struggle or difficulty for the workers of Europe.

The militant subscription had several objectives. First of all it was the financial instrument that made possible the collection of funds under exceptional circumstances, with special emphasis on the usefulness and legitimacy of every donation, great or small. It also served as a support for mobilization and news coverage; by bringing causes squarely into the public domain, subscriptions made sure they received enough press coverage to influence opinion in their favor. Likewise, subscriptions made possible the creation of an informal community of militants whose names were constantly cropping up in the news. Before long, a significant development took place with the International. Subscriptions began to be more frequently registered in the names of militant collectives and worker associations, rather than bearing the identities of individuals. Last, the subscription built up an area of solidarity and reciprocity between the donor group and the beneficiary group: it served as a manifestation of just the kind of hardship-at-one-remove that the militants of the International sought to project across borders.

For social players with less abundant access to public discourse (or to what Michelle Perrot calls "voice" [*prise de parole*]), subscriptions were a popular way of expressing one's views — to powerfully liberating effect.[75] The sums of money were always accompanied by words of compassion and encouragement, which mobilized people on an emotional level. To give was to recognize the legitimacy of a cause or the injustice of a situation. It was hard evidence of one's personal solidarity. This dialectical relationship between words and money lies at the heart of the practice of subscription: written messages express a first form of solidarity, before completing the promise to donate, whereas the two should be indissociable. Mere writing offers a kind of relief, but it is not enough. The general council of the IWA was disturbed about this at the time of the Le Creusot strike: words but no money sent a very bad signal.

The proliferation of subscriptions can only be understood in terms of the militant press, which was the driving force behind it. The socialist workers' press had flourished since the 1830s. Often enough, the papers themselves had been started by subscription funds. In return, they made themselves mouthpieces for the industrial action that broke out all over Europe and, when necessary, opened subscriptions to which their readers could donate by sending contributions to the editors. In 1870, Henri Rochefort's *Marseillaise* launched a subscription on the behalf of the strikers of Le Creusot, recommending that its readers send fifty centimes a week to support the cause. Modest though they were, the contributions were so numerous that 10,000 francs were collected in barely three weeks and transferred to Le Creusot, in addition to 6,000 francs similarly assembled to help jailed militants and their families.[76] All the International's newssheets — the *Vorbote* in Switzerland, the *Volkstaat* in Germany, and the *Internationale* in Belgium — followed suit, with similar appeals on behalf of strikers and militant victims of repression.

The regular publication of subscription lists in the press made it possible to keep track of the sums of money pledged or paid. Their appearance was just as important in terms of making a public stand as it was in terms of money; moreover, the lists neatly took the place of account registers, when for one reason or another these failed to materialize. As in the case of membership dues, subscription funds could be seen by all in the columns of the press. Police informers tended to guess at the International's complement of members by reference to the subscribers mentioned in the militant press, hence their frequent exaggerations. In reality, the ordinary people who subscribed usually far outnumbered the IWA's adherents.

Fundraising Techniques and Locations

The opening of a subscription was never an automatic affair. It wasn't enough for a strike to break out for an appeal for solidarity to be instantly launched. Instead the decision to do so was always preceded by an exchange of correspondence, by a request for information, and by consideration of the local context, to avoid a possible clash with other subscription appeals already under way. It was clear and evident to the militants of the International that only workers' money could support the cause of the workers, a fact that obliged them to collect funds without waiting for help from other social groups. The liberal Spanish militants stated this with some force in 1873: "You should never forget that the emancipation of the working class must be the task of the workers themselves and that we cannot and must not expect any help whatever from the privileged classes."[77]

Nor did the assistance that a section of workers could supply immediately take the form of a subscription. The best-off societies, the ones that had funds of their own, began by advancing cash immediately (the slow delivery of aid money was a recurrent problem at a time when strikes never lasted longer than a few days or weeks) then went on to launch a special subscription to cover the loan. Veteran societies with long experience were thus able to use several different forms of finance, such as accumulated funds, loans, and subscriptions. In the case of the Paris bronze workers (1867), the strikers promptly received advances from several other groups, among them the tinsmiths, who passed on two-thirds of their capital, and the typographers and wood-carvers, who gave everything they had to spare.[78] During the strike called by the ribbon makers of Basel, the Geneva woodworkers and joiners' union held a general assembly and adopted a resolution combining two objectives: "Each member who is in work shall contribute a minimum of 30 centimes a week to help our brothers in Basel for as long as the crisis lasts; it is also decided that the entire sum shall be paid in advance every two weeks out of the section's own funds."[79]

The section's funds enabled money to be advanced, while an "extraordinary levy" — meaning the temporary increase in the sum owed weekly or monthly for regular dues — made it possible to hold enough cash in reserve to cover later industrial disputes. Thus, the funds advanced were considered repayable: this was not the case with other subscriptions, which were explicitly opened as vehicles for donations. A temporary increase in membership fees was required of the strikers themselves, as was shown by the interminable debates of the bronze workers in March–April 1867: the decision to raise the weekly membership from the usual 25 centimes to five francs per worker, whatever their wage or their family expenses, was strongly condemned by those who felt that contributions should be proportionate to each worker's salary. The mobilization of all workers was nevertheless deemed indispensable, especially since money was flowing in from all corners of Europe. On 3 March 1867 the president of the general assembly pointed out, quite angrily, "other corporations are subscribing to help us out. How is it that we are allowing them to make sacrifices greater than our own? Not one of the 4,000 people here should put up with that."[80]

These practices were also in use among the typographers of Germany, who were especially well organized in the 1860s. In March 1870, those of Berlin decided to place their funds at the disposal of the German Federation of Typographers so that it could immediately send 3,000 thalers (11,250 francs) to the striking workers of Vienna, in Austria. All available funds were requisitioned and extraordinary fees were imposed for four weeks to cover the advances already sent.[81] The vocabulary used for this was not "donation" but "extraordinary levy"; members who lacked the right to set the amount of their own subscriptions would have to resign themselves to regular payments for as long as the conflict lasted.

The collection of funds pledged as subscriptions took place in various locations. Participants could send their donations to the newspapers that had published the appeals. They might also open direct relations with the militants in charge of collecting the money, who officiated as treasurers; or the subscriptions might be deposited in the sections' premises on Paris, Geneva, or elsewhere, or at the treasurer's home. In Paris in 1868–1869 the job fell to Eugène Varlin, who ended up the focus of a judicial investigation. At his second trial in 1868, he acknowledged having collected 10,000 francs at the rue Chapon headquarters and at his own residence, on behalf of the construction workers of Geneva.[82] In the police search that followed, investigators searched in vain for a register containing the names of subscribers and the sums they had given. The documents they did find made it possible to reconstruct the successive stages leading up to the opening of the subscription: Varlin had first of all corresponded with a militant from Geneva, who supplied information about the conflict that was under way in Switzerland. After this he published an appeal for subscriptions in the press and placed several lists in circulation around the sections and workshops of Paris. These lists were then returned to him, with no indication as to the form in which the money had been passed to him.[83]

The circulation of subscription lists around factories and workshops was a noted feature of strike action. The *collecteur*'s task was to convince his worker comrades that the subscription had merit enough for them to trust him with their money. At Roubaix, in March 1867, the *commissaire de police* was actively searching for the identities of five "list peddlers" who made the rounds of local taverns and approached subscribers who might be favorable to the current weavers' strike.[84] At Le Creusot in January 1870, several workers were fired for passing the hat around on behalf of their strike committee. They were reproached with standing at the entrance to the factory cashier's office, soliciting contributions from workers as they came by to collect their pay.[85] Employers and authorities fought hard against such methods, which they qualified as moral and sometimes physical pressure applied to nonstrikers. The organization of a subscription was not just a matter of arms-length relationships, like that of a newspaper with its readers: it was a mission of real conviction, carried out face-to-face with the workers, on their own turf, in their homes, and in the factories where they labored. The *collecteurs* were well-known figures around the workshops, men who had to be above suspicion. Collections also took place during section meetings and at parties and concerts organized to top up resources by engaging the wider public. Although some militants hated this confusion of types, militant effectiveness depended on using any means that came to hand.

The decision to open a subscription had to obey certain precise strategic considerations. As was also the case in philanthropy, worker militants tried hard not to sour their public with too many requests. They had to be acutely aware of potential contributors' ability to give. A subscription appeal could be a double-edged sword: it could blossom into a broad movement of solidarity or it could be met with deafening silence. For this reason the general council of the IWA, the sections, and the professional *collecteurs* all advised prudence, especially when the number of strikes exploded between 1868 and 1870. Varlin emphasized that "subscription is a means we must use, but not abuse, because if we do we exhaust its potential; a strike must be sufficiently broad in proportion to allow of a general appeal for people to subscribe, with at least some hope that it will be heard."[86]

The fantasy of worker credit irrigated the discourse of many sections of the International. In London, the theoretical and strategic choices of Karl Marx might sometimes appear to have triumphed; but in local meetings, in the press, and in the letters between militants on either side of national frontiers, it was the dream of generalized credit, based on the circulation of workers' money and the ethic of reciprocity, that lay at the heart of most people's conversations and experiments. The 1860s were years of institutional and intellectual effervescence, with the creation of hundreds of aid societies, unions, and cooperatives in France, Germany, Belgium, Switzerland, and Italy, while in England the trade unions continued to spearhead a broad movement of organized, qualified workers. These experiments, some of which were very short-lived, familiarized workers with the rules and expectations of collective existence; above all they allowed them to develop the practice of collecting, managing, and circulating funds, which in turn prepared them for the social struggles that awaited them. The aspiration of worker autonomy had to undergo an apprenticeship in the sharing of social forms, and in the reappropriation of workers' money; the proliferation of strikes and lockouts in the late 1860s offered a chance to test these new militant resources in the service of transnational worker solidarity.

3 | STRUGGLE AND MUTUAL AID

During the 1860s, workers in several countries of western Europe won the right to organize in defense of their collective demands. At the time, political institutions were being liberalized in tsarist Russia, Bonapartist France, the Austro-Hungarian Empire, and the Kingdom of Italy; yet they were still heavily influenced by police surveillance, judicial repression, and military violence. The decade was also characterized by headlong economic growth coupled with a lowering of customs barriers, a mix that led to an explosion of strike action all over Europe as well as in England, the traditional stronghold of trade unions. An opening-up of politics in general and the granting of freedom of assembly allowed workers to band together in unions and to organize collective struggle in the form of strike action or resistance to lockouts imposed by their employers.

The IWA accompanied this movement at the same time as it contributed to its organization and growth. Its members may have taken part in strikes but they never planned or prepared them. Sometimes they even discouraged industrial action, but they did regard every strike action as an opportunity for its militants to gain experience of collective struggle and the benefits of international solidarity. Appeals for assistance were spread through the workers' press and the meetings of the IWA; the time had come to build universal solidarity. The construction of networks of solidarity and the learning of techniques of cooperation were bound to intensify contacts between European workers; these tasks also implied overcoming some of the misunderstandings that set those workers apart, most of which derived from different customs and interests.

THE EARLY STRIKES

Contrary to appearances, the surge of strike action around Europe between 1860 and 1870 was not always welcomed by the members of the IWA. Some questioned the usefulness of strikes, others their legitimacy and want of coordination. Nevertheless, strikes were the background against which workers' internationalism prospered in the course of these years. They provided prestige and an audience: for a while, all eyes were trained upon the IWA.[1]

Ideological Restraint, Strategic Calculation

During the first congresses of the IWA, speeches against industrial action were frequent and manifold. Supporters of Proudhon, who advocated free assembly and were critical of the right of coalition, spoke up vigorously, as did certain British militants influenced by the ideas of the utopian socialist Robert Owen.[2] Proudhon's position was affirmed at the 1865 London Conference, at the 1866 congress, and again in 1868 when the question of strikes and resistance societies was debated. The strike was seen as anti-economic and a threat to the principle of association and reciprocity that should regulate the rebuilding of economic relationships. Zéphirin Camélinat and others came out against the position taken by the English unionists, who saw strikes as instruments of social progress. In Geneva in 1866, Henri Tolain, Ernest Édouard Fribourg, and Johann Philipp Becker consented to admit that a strike, for the English, might be a temporary necessity, which should not, according to them, allow anyone to lose sight of the ultimate objective — namely, the demise of the wage-earning culture and its replacement by associations or cooperatives. The goal as far as they were concerned was not to obtain higher salaries but, rather, to destroy the relationship of subordination that bound the worker to his employer. In Lausanne in 1867, the Swiss militant Pierre Coullery suggested that "workers should be made to understand that striking is not in their best interest; and indeed that they are the first to suffer from their effects. The money used to support strikes would be much better used to create production associations." This automatic mistrust survives in the documents and official policy statements of the IWA, which are confined to seeing the raising of salaries by means of strike action as a kind of stopgap, a short-term goal ever subordinate to a grander strategy. At the Brussels Congress in 1868, the secretary of the association, Hermann Jung, who had championed the strikes in England two years earlier, announced that "the point of the Association is not to raise workers' wages through strikes or any other means: it is to break the bosses' stranglehold altogether."[3] The struggle against capitalism meant applying fundamental change to the human relations governing the production process. It did not mean making exploitation more bearable.

As strikes proliferated, this official position evolved apace. More and more sections expressed their belief in the usefulness of strike action, though they stopped short of acknowledging its full legitimacy. A convoluted stance, verbally typical of the time, was adopted by the Brussels and Geneva sections: "While we admit that strikes are contrary to certain principles of economy, we believe that as long as society continues to be organized as it is, capital will remain both judge and plaintiff, the worker will remain subject to the whims of the person exploiting him, and the working class will be taking a risk if it does not take energetic action to slow the steady decline of labor." The Brussels section suggested that strikes should be classified according to their objectives, declaring that the right to strike was "fundamental" when used to affirm the dignity of workers, defend freedom of assembly, or resist the more flagrant abuses of employers.

Proudhon-influenced French militants — notably among the striking bronze workers of 1867 — altered their position when they saw the extraordinary response to their mobilization from outside France.[4] Tolain, an engraver who extolled worker autonomy and the abolition of class divisions, acknowledged in 1868 that "the strike is an act of war. There may be unjust, bad wars, but there are also wars whose purpose is to defend people's rights, and these are sacred." This distinction between long-term goals and short-term demands, material claims, and simple dignity sums up the inherent ambiguity of the IWA, which ended up correlating strikes and even supporting them as opportunities to expand its influence. This was not quite so evident for those who had been part of it from the beginning, and for whom the degradation of the IWA into a network for managing industrial conflicts was deeply troubling. In 1870, Fribourg himself bewailed the IWA's contribution: "just strike after strike after strike; no serious reflection about anything, nothing of the sort," as if struggle and thought were totally incompatible.[5]

Strikes benefited from the almost mythical aura of the British trade unions at the time. Even the most revolutionary militants on the continent had to admit that the British made effective use of the strike as a negotiating tool. The reputation of their worker societies surpassed all others, especially following the success of the 1859–1860 strike by twenty-four thousand London masons, who, in standing up for their right to unionize, managed to raise £23,000, a record sum.[6] This unprecedented financial clout made it possible for the English workers to withstand several weeks of strikes and lockouts. Their concentration of manpower and method led to the formation of major "amalgamated" union centers within the various participating professions. In 1851 the union of mechanics showed the way by forming the Amalgamated Society of Engineers (ASE), and were followed by various other unions in the course of the succeeding decade. These included the Bricklayers' Operative Society and the Amalgamated Society of Carpenters and Joiners, whose president, Robert Applegarth, was a member of the IWA's general council.

The agreed aim of the amalgamated unions was to assemble thousands of adherents from the same professions on a national scale and, thereafter, to negotiate and raise funds on their behalf. In exchange for very high membership fees (the ASE charged a shilling a week, much more then any other union), members could expect generous sickness and accident compensation, provision for old age, and funeral expenses. Above all they had considerable backup funds, coordinated and managed in London by a financial secretary, that could be used in the event of industrial action. In the 1860s, the ASE had a membership of thirty thousand engineers and mechanics belonging to three hundred branches, with an annual turnover of £80,000 and reserves close to £140,000.[7] The Amalgamated Society of Carpenters and Joiners was smaller; still it had eight thousand members yielding an annual revenue of £10,000. Their plentiful funds allowed them to tackle strikes and lockouts with equanimity, unafraid that their struggling workers would end up destitute. The general secretary of the Carpenters and Joiners observed that nearly half the members of his association had been involved in work conflicts during 1865 alone. From now on, it seemed normal that strike action was a fundamental right and one of the conditions for improving the lot of the workingman. But its use required prudence and skill.[8]

The British unions were at the cutting edge of the European workers' movement, an inspiration to their counterparts on the continent. In the course of the general council's debates in

1865–1866, Karl Marx himself opposed John Weston, who had criticized the use of strikes on the grounds that higher wages obtained by the workers' struggle merely led to a rise in the cost of living and a fall in the value of money. Marx was against Weston, but also against the followers of Proudhon and Lassalle: he defended the British workers' resistance to "the encroachments of capital," even though he considered that they "fail generally for limiting themselves to a guerilla war against the effects of the existing system, instead of simultaneously trying to change it," for the "ultimate abolition of the wages system."[9]

The ideological reservations of the IWA members concerning strikes could be explained by their constant endeavors to silence the rumors that described it as a subversive organization capable of spreading a toxic effect throughout Europe and the United States. The International supported industrial action, but it stated categorically that it would neither plan nor sponsor them, despite the accusations brought against it by governments and employers. The French militants who were prosecuted in 1868 and 1870, despite their participation in the great conflicts of the time, were careful to minimize their own importance. Varlin sheltered behind the resolutions of the congress of Geneva as to the anti-economic effects of strikes, while acknowledging the need to support them out of solidarity, as the workers of Berlin had supported the London tailors' union.[10] The engraver Albert Theisz denied that the International was in any way responsible for starting strikes, which he attributed to poor relations between workers and capitalists: "The orders come from on high," he declared. "They come from your own industrial organization, from your economic regime which is in flagrant contradiction to your political theory and your universal suffrage." Léo Frankel used a medical metaphor: for him, strikes were no more than "symptoms of the disease affecting society."[11] He described them as phenomena produced by society itself, the militants having no role but to identify and orchestrate them.

Karl Marx, in a post-Commune interview with a journalist from New York's *The World* newspaper, said that, although the IWA supported strikes, it had always understood the political and financial risks involved: "The Society has no interest in strikes, though it supports them under certain conditions. It cannot possibly gain by them in a pecuniary point of view, but it may easily lose."[12]

The Need for Coordination

As usual, police authorities wildly exaggerated the International Association's ability to organize strikes on a continental scale. The general council's discussions largely focused on its members' dissatisfaction, as they witnessed a flood of calls for help without being able to coordinate or place them in any order of priority. The IWA was a victim of its own success, attempting to optimize the effectiveness of its appeals for solidarity by setting up rules and procedures to govern it.

The requirement of control and supervision was clearly behind the IWA's determination to collect information on shifts affecting jobs, prices, and wages, so that workers had the tools to understand their situation, the terms on which they had to compete, and what they were entitled to demand from their employers. At a very early stage, an intention was expressed in the general council and at the congresses of the IWA to assemble a statistical record, compiled from information about labor conditions in a number of different countries. This was already one of the resolutions contained in the report of the 1866 Geneva general council, which called for an inquiry to establish "statistics on the conditions of the working classes of all countries, gathered by the workers themselves."[13] The form sent out to all sections included questions on the size and organization of various industries, the sums of wages and guarantees, work and health conditions, and seasonal variations. This project came to nothing, despite a series of heated debates about it that continued until 1872. It failed not only because of the material difficulty of harvesting the information amid a chronic shortage of money: above all, its failure reflected the internal political and ideological contradictions within the association, with some members preferring purely descriptive statistical work, while others (such as Karl Marx) looked for something more comprehensively theoretical.[14]

Henceforth, militants were convinced of the fact that no coherent and coordinated action by the European unions was possible without hard statistical information. Their goal was to improve their knowledge of work and wage conditions throughout Europe, the better to adjust the claims of workers and make it easier for them to help each other. Worker solidarity could not flourish unless it had an area of publicity and commensurability, in which differences in wage levels and conditions among various worker groups could be appreciated along with possible convergences in their demands. Without such comparisons, appeals for international assistance were fruitless. The British unions, for example, were happy to help but only if they fully understood the reasons for any conflict they were asked to support. They were adamant: no funds for strike action could be lent or given without prior consideration of the economic and social conditions surrounding it. In the absence of thorough statistical data that could serve as a basis for an autonomous understanding of the labor market, any request for help had to come with a minimum of information.

The need to pair social conflict with a thorough knowledge of the working world was also understood by the Belgian militants of the International, who called for what they called *cahiers du travail* modeled on the lists of grievances compiled before the French Revolution in 1789. The positivist inspiration behind this project was clear, inasmuch as they sought to shed light on the true nature of the working world by objectifying it statistically, without reference to information supplied by official authorities, economists, or reforming elites. As with money, the internationalists intended that "the people" should repossess statistics and confront the state on its own terrain. Accurate knowledge was a prerequisite for action and protest, justifying the vital importance of statistical projects in the history of worker internationalism from the 1860s right through to the 1920s and 1930s. The only thing that changed over time was the confidence placed — or not placed — in the state and its authorities, to unriddle the social world for the benefit of the disenfranchised classes.[15]

In the absence of exhaustive and global statistical data, information from the various countries of Europe reached the IWA and its general council by way of national correspondents, who were told to archive copies of workers' newspapers published on the continent, so that the progress of strikes could be tracked as they took place and the groundwork laid for a history of the internationalist movement.[16] The correspondence that IWA members conducted with their local contacts — which today are among the most valued historical sources for the movement — played a vital role in the effort to coordinate collective action. At every general council meeting, the correspondents shared essential information such as the launching of strike actions, the progress of those strikes, and the funds requested or sent to help strikers. This chain of transmission might be damaged or broken by police surveillance or other material difficulties; at times it failed altogether because local correspondents were themselves ineffectual. When this happened, and local correspondents found themselves incapable of supplying reliable information to their colleagues in the council — or, more importantly, to the representatives of the British unions — they complained to their local contacts. In 1869 relations grew strained between the Belgian correspondent in London, Marie Bernard, and the militants of Brussels, whom Bernard accused of failing to provide the council with regular updates on the strikes in Seraing and the Borinage. Alphonse Vandenhouten angrily denied this, reminding delegates that his work as a correspondent — on top of his other obligations and his day job — took up all his time and more.[17]

Likewise, Hermann Jung, the Swiss correspondent, complained about the paucity of information supplied by Johann Philipp Becker (a German emigré who had taken part in the 1848 revolutions, now installed in Geneva); for example, an appeal for help from the workers of Basel in 1869. No request for money made in the absence of precise information would cut the ice with the English unions:

> What do you expect us to do with your letter? It asks us to help our brothers in Basel. Why do you want help? What's going on in Basel? We know nothing about this! You give us no news! ... [B]efore, people would at least tell us why they wanted money, but now they don't bother; they don't even say if it's for a strike, or for some other cause. We will always do our duty — but we can do nothing at all unless we are fully informed.[18]

This lack of information short-circuited any willingness to coordinate, though it was regularly pointed out that strikes and requests for help from outside could be subject to rigorous, predefined procedures, without slowing down the decision process. The increase in requests for help, which was very marked in 1869–1870, stalled the machine: the assistance of the general council was sought for strikes of whose motive and cause it sometimes had no inkling, any more than it knew the numbers of workers involved or their relative strength. So the general council was a victim of its own success and proved disappointing to many, for example the miners of Charleroi in Belgium, who were astonished not to receive the support they had been promised — rather prematurely — in 1872.[19]

Efficient strike coordination was indispensable, however, if appeals for solidarity were ever to be properly answered; above all, if the action was being launched haphazardly without previous overall planning. The task was all the more complicated in that local, independent, and heterogeneous movements had to be orchestrated all over the continent — a change of scale that proved a real challenge at a time when local organizational capacities were mostly nonexistent. The general council strove to find a balance between requests and offers of help, without recourse to any reserve fund that might have allowed it to make cash advances while it juggled its timing. This being the case, it risked having to cope with a sudden flood of international appeals for help, at a time when the English unions were heavily occupied with financing local and national strikes of their own.

This was a classic dilemma, which applied to philanthropic action in just the same way. Competing good causes, far from stimulating generosity, could have the opposite effect of discouraging it. The risk was that the costs of strikes would have to be borne by a minority of better-off workers: their goodwill was not in question, but in the end, the strength of their solidarity would evaporate if the pool of donor participants continued to shrink. In 1869, the Swiss newspaper *L'Égalité* pointed out the unexpected effects of the rising incidence of strikes, though in themselves they demonstrated the vitality of the workers' movement: "All that now remains is a small group of devoted men, strongly attached to the flag of solidarity, who view all the costs and loans contracted during the strike as a debt of honor that they are bound to repay."[20]

Ideally, internationalist militants dreamed of extending the procedures and practices used by the English movement to cover the entire continent of Europe. The success of the amalgamated unions derived from their capacity to centralize information and decision-making: no local strike could be launched without the prior approval of the central directorate, which alone decided whether it was useful or desirable to supply strike pay for the workers concerned.[21] Although this could be done locally, and sometimes nationally, at the time these consultation and authorization procedures could only be applied internationally with the greatest difficulty.

Help and Membership

The general council was aware that its reputation depended on its ability to support strike action. Nevertheless the dispatch of aid funds required a minimum of involvement on the part of the workers who asked for help. Solidarity worked in ever-widening concentric circles: local cooperation for the first weeks of a dispute when sacrifices had to be made, followed by an appeal for outside solidarity either within a given profession or on an interprofessional basis. Belonging to the IWA gave access to a network of solidarity, capable of mobilizing way beyond the usual limits. In April 1868, the Brussels membership congratulated the Geneva workers for coming under the wing of the association, rejoicing that now they could access all the resources of its "million-worker network of solidarity." Naturally this was a wildly exaggerated figure.[22]

The idea of making financial assistance conditional upon membership of the association was more theoretical than realistic. Often it was during the course of a strike, when workers were confronted by military repression or harsh measures imposed by employers, that workers looked to the IWA for help; and the IWA could not decently turn them down without trampling its own principles underfoot. It was a combination of the humanitarian logic of giving a helping hand to all workers, whether they were members or not, and the military logic of swelling the ranks of the association's adherents. In the latter case, aid would be solid proof of the International's usefulness, especially in the eyes of workers employed in industrial sectors that were barely unionized and structured hardly at all.

In the summer of 1869, two thousand *ouvrières ovalistes* in the Lyon silk industry — working women whose role in the factories was to prepare silk thread prior to the weaving process — went on strike to obtain better wages and a reduction of their shifts from twelve to ten hours a day. Their cause was strongly supported by the internationalist groups; the fact that these were striking women workers, a rarity at the time, was of great strategic importance, leading to the involvement of local militants (these included Albert Richard in Lyon, Émile Aubry in Rouen), as well as Swiss members and the general council itself.[23] Described as "martyrs of economic anarchy" and "unfortunate victims of monopoly," "crying in distress," in phraseology that was even more compassionate than usual, the *ovalistes* duly received more than 1,000 francs from Rouen, Marseille, Geneva, Locle, Brussels, and London.[24] The texts make it clear that the workers waited a while before launching their appeal for solidarity, making great sacrifices themselves before doing so. The promised funds were limited to members of the International, which explains why the *ovalistes'* strike committee decided on 10 July to join the association, one of the conditions insisted upon by militants before the women could expect their solidarity. They eventually announced their adhesion with a blend of gratitude and serious interest, each one pledging to subscribe 25 centimes per annum: "You may be sure that the help you have so generously sent to us, will bear fruit: the links of solidarity that you have established by your conduct toward us can never be dissolved, and in consequence all our efforts shall be focused upon this great idea: the emancipation of the proletariat. This we swear, and we will keep our word."[25]

A similar state of affairs arose a few months later, during the Le Creusot strikes of the first six months of 1870. The International section that was set up during this conflict added a new dimension to the movement, which members of the association learned about in the press and through the London general council's own informants. The subscriptions received were ever more abundant, because the Le Creusot strikers now belonged to a wider network with a serious long-term strategy. Despite the failure of their movement, the Le Creusot workers were not unhappy with its outcome:

"Sympathy for our cause was universal; we are proud of that, and when necessary we ourselves will know how to apply the principles of worker fraternity and solidarity. In the meantime, we declare our adhesion to the great international association of workers, the sublime freemasonry of the world's proletariat, and the hope of an egalitarian future. We thank all those democrats who fraternally came to our aid; and to proletarians everywhere, we cry out *solidarity!*"[26]

Making membership of the IWA a precondition for assistance, whether that membership preceded strike action or was the result of it, proved the determination of the members of the International to confront and eradicate opportunist behavior within the movement. This was explicitly stated in one of the association's slogans: "No Rights Without Duties, No Duties Without Rights." Worker solidarity was not an absolute universal right: it only made sense within the framework of a reciprocal relationship, in which the parties took turns to contribute and receive benefits. Appeals for help launched by little-known, not-very-organized worker groups lacking direct contact with the association were greeted with suspicion, so great was the fear of rampant stowaway behavior. If the "help in return for membership" logic was strategically useful, its opposite, "membership in return for help," might exemplify worker communities' ability to function autonomously. This was a source of worry to militants, as the Belgian Eugène Hins made clear in a letter to Albert Richard in Lyon:

Most of the time [strikes] are started by ill-organized workers who join the Association on condition that it helps them out. This is buying memberships at far too high a price and it is a dangerous path to follow....We have noticed that members won over by subsidies aren't worth a damn, they desert you shortly after the battle is won; whereas for a fraction of the cost we could have put out some active propaganda and gotten ourselves an army of serious comrades.[27]

Like any other form of solidarity, the one that the International meant to build could only work if everyone agreed to pay a price for it. This was why the general council, like the local sections, took umbrage at appeals for help from groups that begrudged their dues and forgot about the association when they no longer needed it. Universal solidarity did not escape this dilemma; certainly solidarity was a right and even a duty to workers suffering under the thumbs of their employers, but it could never be completely free from the existence of a financial, human, or organizational quid pro quo. The general council members were caught between their strategic desire to respond to the aspirations of thousands of workers who relied upon it and a more realistic approach to solidarity, viewed as a debt acquired by the association's members alone, like a mutual aid society or a trade union serving the interests of its own subscribers to the exclusion of everyone else.

In the absence of capital or funds held in reserve, the council was unable to function like the powerful local societies, which could advance cash by demanding higher dues. This financial insecurity and an acute awareness of the need not to make it any worse justified — in the opinion of treasurer Jung — the adoption of strict and rigorous procedures, even if these meant slowing the tempo of solidarity. Despite the nobility of their cause, the Basel ribbon makers' strike in the winter of 1868-1869 was (for Jung) symptomatic of the association's difficulties: "Again, if there was a fund to make immediate advances, that would work; but we don't even have the wherewithal to pay for postage stamps, because our members forget all about us when they need to make their contributions, offering nothing but promises as congress season approaches...but should a strike break out, or some other accident, all of a sudden they remember the General Council and start asking for money."[28]

This resentment was all the more palpable when the richer unions, British or German, prevaricated about paying their dues but called for instant support when they thought the association could be of use to them. In the summer of 1871, Karl Marx and Friedrich Engels were defiant when the ASE demanded help for their striking Newcastle engineers. There was no question in this case of a cash donation, given that the British had ample means of their own; instead they insisted that everything should be done to discourage Belgian workers from answering the appeals of any English employers who might come shopping for skilled people to replace the strikers. This request was greeted with reserve; Marx regretted that the "trades unions and labor organizations held aloof from the International until they were in trouble, and then only did they come for assitance....[I hope] in future societies [will] think of the International in a time of peace."[29]

In the same year Engels became enraged with the Tobacco Workers of Antwerp, who were beseeching the IWA for help even though they had always refused to take up membership. For him such failure to reciprocate was a rupture of solidarity that revealed a blatantly cynical attitude to the IWA:

> Do these gentlemen call it solidarity when they pocket English and other workers' money procured for them by the International, and then refuse to join our Association or prove that they are themselves ready to do the same for others? That's not the way we see it here. The International should not work for people like these. Anyone wanting to reap the benefits of our Association should be ready to share its burdens. The least they can do is join us.[30]

The general council was all the more vigilant because it knew how strongly the continental workers believed in the omnipotence of the IWA. Should the help expected from London or elsewhere be delayed or for some reason not materialize, all the council members' fine theories about universal solidarity would collapse in a heap. The inability of the association to help the German social democratic workers party (Sozialdemokratische Arbeiterpartei), founded in Eisenach in 1869 by August Bebel and Wilhelm

Liebknecht, was a case in point. These two German militants, who were close to Karl Marx, worked hard to obtain the adhesion of their party to the International; yet their requests for help went unanswered, for in London they were reproached with failing to impose the principal of individual contributions paid by each member. Despite their ideological closeness, Karl Marx and the German socialist activists were at odds on this subject. Bebel acknowledged later that German expectations of financial help for the strikers of Waldenburg in Silesia were overblown: all they got from London was a dressing-down and a lecture on how to manage their strike.[31]

Indeed the general council's attempts to supervise and coordinate European industrial action met with considerable obstacles, both material and ideological. Sounding board that it was, the council had no budget dedicated to helping strikers. Nevertheless, its existence made possible new ways of achieving solidarity between sections on a transnational scale, mostly through horizontal links forged by the sections' common membership of the association.

YEARS OF APPRENTICESHIP

Relationships of financial cooperation between workers of different countries proliferated in the 1860s. The sums involved were sometimes minimal, but they could become more significant during industrial conflicts led by better organized professions such as typographers, tobacco workers, tailors, and the like. Whatever their size, these financial transfers gave form to links of acquaintance, interdependence, and reciprocity that transcended frontiers, and most demands were focused on England, where the general council was based and whose unions were the richest and most powerful in the world.

London, Metropolis of Trade Unions?

In the 1860s, London was "the metropolis of capital," to use Marx's phrase. Only in London were there money and financial institutions large enough to invest in every corner of the world.[32] Access to the City and the London market in general was vital for every state and every corporation seeking to develop and modernize; yet London was also the capital of the union trade movement and its struggle against capitalism. The generosity with which the British had welcomed political exiles from all over Europe ever since the 1820s had created a major hotbed of political and social protest, in which the trade unions occupied a position of enviable strength. Just like the bourgeois states they fought against, socialist and anarchist militants placed all their hopes on the possibility of raising funds on the other side of the Channel, whether their intention was to build capitalism or to subvert it. In both cases, access to British money was subject to Draconian conditions. Worker solidarity did not escape the rule of exchange: it had to satisfy the interests of both parties and be reciprocal. This explains why relations between the English unions and the workers of the continent, despite signs of nascent cooperation and fraternity, were so rife with misunderstanding.

In fact, the general council of the IWA had no funds of its own to finance strikes, and this limited its power to centralize their control. The council had to content itself with relaying information and providing symbolic support for causes it judged worthy of interest. After that, it was up to the English unions to decide whether to lend or give money to help continental workers. Its members were not just go-betweens: they could intervene with the English unions to back up the requests of continental workers and convince them it was not only their duty but also their interest to release funds.

The London Trades Council (LTC), founded at the beginning of the 1860s, was the supreme authority over access to English help.

An outgrowth of the committee that coordinated the construction workers' movement in 1859, this council represented several dozen unions, among them all the larger amalgamated ones, and functioned as a veritable parliament for the London worker societies. The leading figures of local unionism were all members of its executive committee: they included Robert Applegarth of the Carpenters and Joiners, George Odger of the Ladies' Shoemakers, George Howell and Edwin Coulson of the Operative Bricklayers. These formed what their adversaries called a "junta," so great was their power over the English union world prior to the 1868 formation of the Trades Union Congress (TUC). Odger, for example, was secretary general of the LTC between 1862 and 1872; he was also a member and honorary president of the IWA's general council. By 1862 the LTC had 11,300 London members and represented over 50,000 workers through its various union leaders. Dozens of local societies belonged to it, but the amalgamated groups supplied most of its budget.[33]

The main function of the LTC was to field requests for help sent in by English strikers, assess the seriousness of their claims and their organization, and then provide its own moral guarantee by sending credentials that strikers could show to union chambers when they asked for financial assistance. In other words, the LTC was a fact-finding body that coordinated investigations and opened access to the funds of the trade unions that alone could decide whether they would lend the money at their disposal. The examination of applications imposed strict rules on workers appealing to union solidarity: every request had to be accompanied by a written report and followed by a hearing of its delegates by the assembled members of the LTC, who interrogated them about the origins of their movement, the sums they had set aside before downing tools, and their goals in general.[34] Only when they had been through this careful process were strikers authorized to contact the unions directly.

From the early 1860s onward, the members of the LTC maintained close relations with various workers on the continent, notably after the universal exhibition of 1862 and the dispatch of a delegation of French workers partly supported by the imperial authorities. In July 1862, the secretary of the LTC, Odger, and a number of other members signed an address advocating closer ties between the workers of England and those on the continent, to stamp out unfair competition.[35] The LTC was also behind the inaugural meeting of the IWA in September 1864, initially motivated by support for the Polish uprising. The top leaders of the LTC belonged to the general council and regularly attended its meetings. Karl Marx wanted the LTC to join the association en bloc as its English branch, but its leaders, who were strongly attached to the principal of complementarity, preferred to leave each union the choice of whether to do so. They merely expressed enthusiasm for communication between the workers of different countries, as an essential condition for the success of the British union movement, in a world of competing wages and work regulations.

Inquiries, Hearings, and Endorsements

The creation of the International made it possible for European workers to engage with the general council and then tackle the LTC to further their aims. Several delegations were auditioned during these years, some of which failed to obtain English help. The typographers of Leipzig, highly mobilized though they were, obtained no money in 1865, despite the official support of the IWA. The London typesetters merely informed them that they were in no position to donate. More successful was the sending of a delegation to London by the Paris bronze workers in April 1867. Three of their number — Arsène Kin, Zéphirin Camélinat, and Valdun — were appointed by the strike committee to go to London together with Tolain and Fribourg, who had excellent contacts there on account of their status as founding members of the IWA. This initiative met with a much warmer welcome. The representatives of the bronze workers, duly accompanied by the members of the International, were authorized to meet with a score of London societies and ask for loans. The LTC gave them its blessing:

> To all English working men's societies, our brothers! We write to certify that, after a full investigation of the facts and circumstances surrounding the strike of the Paris bronze workers, we have unanimously granted the necessary letter of guarantee to their delegates, whereby they may present their request for moral and material support to the workers' societies of England. We strongly recommend that this support be fully provided, all the more so because in similar circumstances French workers have declared their solidarity with the interests of their English counterparts. Your servant, G. Odger, secretary of the Trades Council.[36]

Having secured this validation, the members of the general council agreed to support and pass on the bronze workers' requests for donations and loans to the trade unions they controlled.[37] Twenty unions were contacted and voted to contribute sums varying between £5 and £20. In particular, the French delegation was received by the union of bookbinders in London, which offered £15 to the cause. Contributions flowed in from the boot makers, tobacco workers, and hat makers, as well as the French branch of the IWA in London; and on their return to Paris, the three delegates announced the good news to a general assembly of several thousand rapturous bronze workers. The militant wing of the IWA remembered the symbolic impact of this episode, which was viewed as illustrating the new relationship of solidarity existing between Paris workers and their London counterparts. The report submitted to the Brussels Congress in 1868 claimed a total contribution of 20,000 francs (£800), which seems exaggerated when compared to the usual sums provided by the English and the information we have about some of the loans.[38] Everyone, in Paris and elsewhere, was delighted with what Karl Marx presented as "a great victory," even though the funds arrived too late to be of much use to the bronze workers.[39] But more than money, it was mutual respect that lived on in internationalist lore.

Other delegations followed the Paris bronze workers to London, apparently with less success. The construction workers of Geneva, who went on strike in 1868, sent one of their members, François Graglia, to find money in Paris and then in London. Like the bronze workers, he had to depend on intermediaries at the IWA to reach the London workers' unions; disappointed in his efforts, he complained of the sluggishness of the English procedures, which at the best of times were ill-adapted to the urgent needs of strike action.[40] A delegate from the foundry workers of Paris was received by the general council of the IWA at the end of May 1870, accompanied by Jung. Despite his presence, the English workers refused to contribute any money at all, citing heavy expenses incurred in the preceding three years.[41] It was only after a second attempt that the union of mechanics finally voted a loan of £264. To save face, the London foundrymen followed this with a loan of £25.[42] More money was coming in, but access to it was a minefield for workers not familiar with the ways of the English.

Misunderstandings and Resentments

Profound asymmetries affected relations between the workers on the continent and those in Great Britain. The former clamored for help, and the latter studied their requests with extreme care before gratifying them with a positive response. The sums collected had a different significance, depending on whether they were viewed from a British or a continental angle. Loans of between five and £20 given by the trade unions were relatively insignificant compared to their overall budgets. Nevertheless they were riskier than loans given in England, inasmuch as the probability that they would one day be repaid was much lower. On the other hand, from a continental standpoint, money coming from London offered an unexpected boost to their strained strike resources. The sums lent to them were greater when such cooperation was offered at a national or international level, by highly coordinated professions like the typographers, tailors, or tobacco workers. Thus the English tobacco workers lent about £600 to their colleagues in Antwerp and Brussels in 1871, a much higher sum than any of the others yet mentioned.[43]

Apart from the case of the bronze workers, British aid was supposed to have played a significant role in the strike that broke out in the winter of 1868–1869 in the Bertel weaving workshops at Sotteville-lés-Rouen. The pretext for this industrial action was the withdrawal of a 20 percent bonus given to the workers by their employer a few years earlier. The Rouen Cercle d'études sociales published a detailed account of this conflict, with figures for the sums received and distributed to the two hundred workers involved in the strike. The contribution promised by the English represented one-fifth of the total funding made available to workers for the duration of the strike (500 francs out of a budget of 2500 francs). Again, the cash arrived too late to be effectively spent: the militant Émile Aubry blamed the Bertel mill workers, whose failure to prepare adequately had prevented the strikers from hanging on until the money from abroad could come to their relief. He estimated that 30,000 francs (£1200) could have reached them, given that the strike had been officially approved by the general council of the IWA after Applegarth and Marx vigorously intervened in its favor.[44] This shows that the reception of outside aid, which inevitably took several days or even weeks to arrive, could only be effective if the striking workers in the meantime could rely on resources of their own.

If the speeches and public addresses made by members of the IWA are anything to go by, the actual amounts of cash transferred mattered little. The simple fact that workers were connecting across frontiers, inquiring about shared difficulties, helping one another with contributions (however token) was hailed as significant evidence of solidarity. Any money they sent was a fruit of the liaison and mutualization work carried out by the networks of the International. Bakunin himself celebrated the coming of a new age of solidarity:

> There is but one law that is really obligatory upon all the members, individuals, sections, and federations of the International, for all of which this law is the true and the only basis. In its most complete form with all its consequences and applications, this law advocates the international solidarity of workers of all trades and all countries in their economic struggle against the exploiters of labor. The living unity of the International resides solely in the real organization of this solidarity by the spontaneous action of the workers' groups and by the absolutely free federation of the masses of workers of all languages and all nations, all the more powerful because it is free; the International cannot be unified by decrees and under the whip of any sort of government whatsoever.[45]

Bakunin's emphasis on the free and spontaneous nature of solidarity obscures the disillusion that could result. The continental workers complained loudly about the fussy rules imposed on them by the English unions. Proclamations of the solidarity and unity of the working class could be heard everywhere, but in reality, the interaction between workers of different nations was more than a little strained and not without an undercurrent of subordination. Hopes were all the more easily dashed when continental workers overestimated the wealth of the English unions and underestimated the thoroughness and precision of their inquiry procedures. The official representatives of the LTC were well aware of this. In 1865, William Randall Cremer was lucid about the possibility of rapidly mobilizing English funds: "People on the Continent may think [English trade unions] very rich and able to contribute to a cause which is their own," he said, "but they are tied down by petty rules which confine them to very narrow limits. They are difficult to move and, but for a few men that are among them, they are not worth anything for what they may do for their own emancipation or that of their fellow-men."[46] Graglia, a delegate sent to London by the Geneva section, had a bitter experience of this in the spring of 1868:

> The English societies are veritable fortresses, and I very much fear that we shall not raise a sum large enough to help our compatriots, this week. Without doubt, I am the first to acknowledge it, in some weeks these same societies will furnish us sums beyond our actual needs; but as I have made several of these gentlemen understand, it is immediate help that we must have. But what can you do? the laws forbid them in a positive manner. We must submit.[47]

The English workers' goodwill was not the only problem. A number of much more solid difficulties slowed the transfer of the sums collected. Two or three weeks could pass between the dispatch to London of information or delegates, the consideration of the request by the general council, the LTC, and the trade unions, the final release of funds, and their sending. Long-distance transfers by postal order or check were still quite rare, other than for transatlantic communications. Moreover, sending money by post when a strike was under way attracted the attention of the authorities, which were always looking for proof of foreign interference in domestic industrial actions. Consequently militants preferred to receive cash, delivered by hand. The question arose with a vengeance in July 1870, when the English engineers union decided to send the substantial sum of £264 to the Paris foundry workers. The political situation at the time was fraught; Franco-Prussian tensions and the ongoing trial of members of the International combined to make a postal transfer altogether too risky, so Applegarth opted to send a special delegation to France to hand the money over, in person, to the French strikers.[48]

For their part, the English unions were not short of reasons to be discontented with European workers. Although they were often accused of being "shams," they had good reasons for doubting the good faith of their supplicants.[49] People were always asking them for help, and the loans they made were seldom repaid without considerable fuss. Hence the ambiguity of cooperative, interest-free loans, with no fixed date for repayment, and no higher authority capable of intervening if there was a default. The texts show that the recipients felt these debts were real and that they were bound to reciprocate; what was missing was any sense that they were *limited in time*.

All this came to a head when the first loans remained unpaid. When the Paris bronze workers went to London in March 1867, the English engineers refused to help them, not so much out of principle but because they have never been reimbursed for any of the loans they had made to continental workers in the past.[50] In England prompt repayment had always been the norm (hence the distinction between sums of money *lent* and sums of money *given*). Not surprisingly then, English credit relationships with the continent were shrouded in uncertainty. Although the money lent to the bronze workers became part of the glorious legend of the association, afterward the English unions were obliged to make repeated requests for their money to be reimbursed. Until that money came back to London, it was awkward for anyone to request the help of British unions for other striking groups, such as the engravers of Geneva in early 1868.[51] Two long years went by before the Societé des bronziers parisiens officially voted (in principle) to reimburse the entire 1867 loan, minus the sums they had themselves lent to others on the continent out of the same funds. According to Fribourg, after a number of reminders and protests, this turned out to be the only loan ever properly paid back in the history of the IWA.[52] Nevertheless, the members of the general council sent to England to return the money were told before they left to "urge" the English to settle the backlog of their membership dues to the IWA. In other words, the two relationships of indebtedness became entangled, in a context where only the achievement of concrete results could actually motivate any sort of repayment.[53]

After 1869, the trade unions declined practically every request of help they received. Already in 1868 the help given to the workers of Sotteville-lès-Rouen had only been made possible by an arrangement suggested by Karl Marx himself: remembering that the English carpenters and joiners had lent £20 to the bronze workers in April 1867, he proposed that this sum — which had not been spent — should be transferred from Paris to Rouen. On this occasion, the general council asserted its power of supervision, managing at a distance the funds it had seen go through. Applegarth considered this money as "having been lent to the International; and hence he thought we were perfectly justified in transferring it from one body to another."[54] This order was duly transmitted to the bronze workers, who accepted the principle behind it. Thereafter, the militant Jules Johannard, dispatched from London to Paris, personally took charge of shipping the funds to Sotteville-lès-Rouen.

THE GEOGRAPHY OF SOLIDARITY

The English model had considerable influence during the 1860s. Requests for help flooded in, delegations were sent, sometimes funds were voted. These budding relationships of international solidarity were not confined to links between England and the continent. Similar actions were taking place all over northwestern Europe. In addition to the more high profile exchanges between London and the working centers of the continent — high profile, that is, because they were invariably discussed at the IWA's general council — relations were forged between the worker societies of France, Belgium, Switzerland, and Germany. This space of solidarity connected with that of the bastions of the first era of industrialization, which were concentrated on the North Sea coastline and along the Rhine.[55] As for financial transactions with the workers of America, these were still very limited at the time; they only became seriously important with the expansion of the Knights of Labor, created in 1869 (see chapter 5).

Actions of help and cooperation are always specific to the economic spaces in which they arise. Their intensity and the geography differ, however, profession by profession. Behind the unanimous appeals for disinterested solidarity there lurked a host of polarities and hierarchies, which revealed the limited and sometimes exclusive character of worker solidarity.

The Chains of Reciprocity

Although the funds contributed to strikers in the 1860s were frequently minimal, internationalist militants expected them to produce abundant effects, activating chain reactions through donations and counter donations, with loans received one minute and sums of money advanced to other workers the next. When English unions lent money to Paris bronze workers or strikers in Basel, the funds changing hands established much more than a bilateral relationship between lenders and borrowers. They encouraged people to pursue the cycle of reciprocity, especially vis-à-vis other workers' groups who might not have been included in the original relationship. The entire structure rested on the conviction that strikers benefiting from outside help would in turn help other workers, out of gratitude to their creditors and to all the other unions affiliated with the International. Through a practical demonstration of the positive effects of outside aid, a virtuous cycle of solidarity and generalized reciprocity would be created.

The priority for the workers who had been assisted was not so much to repay the money received from their creditors as to show themselves worthy of such solidarity when their turn came to do so, lending a hand to other workers struggling for better wages and conditions of work. They fully expected such transfers to broaden the capacity for action of communities beyond their national frontiers. Much more than the gift, which locked people into an asymmetrical relationship, the loan was — and is — perceived as an instrument conferring responsibility and autonomy. Financial aid is just as valuable for its monetary component as it is for the social capital it generates. Writing about the Geneva strike, one of Varlin's Swiss correspondents declared that the conflict "did us a power of good, in terms of solidarity among workers."[56] Even when the money arrived too late, the most important thing was that a relationship of mutual indebtedness and gratitude had been established.

These chain reactions of solidarity occurred frequently during the years between 1866 and 1871. Appeals for help always rested on the memory of earlier gestures of assistance, which either created rights for those who had already made loans or established duties for those who had already reaped the benefits of solidarity. The creation of the First International had the effect of setting up lasting cooperative relationships and making possible a succession of future gestures of gratitude and acknowledgment.[57] Thus the help sent by the English to the bronze workers of Paris in 1867 was not presented as something new or as a point of departure but, rather, as reciprocation for help given eight years earlier to the striking construction workers of London. This loan preceded and outlasted the Paris conflict by some distance; yet the five pounds sent from France in 1859–1860 was next to nothing, for a strike involving more than 24,000 workers and 235 companies.[58] Still it fed the memory of a real connection and justified the idea that the help given by English unions to Paris workers proceeded from a moral obligation, the logical result of a relationship of interdependence initiated several years earlier. After the 1867 conflict, the tailors of London called on the general council to relay their call for help to the workers of Europe and America, asking in their turn for solidarity from the workers of the International. The Paris bronze workers, who had expressed their eternal gratitude, reacted quickly: they decided to send a gift of £10 and a loan for the same amount, in effect adopting a standard practice of the English unions.[59] They provided a number of other loans to worker societies in France and abroad. Whether it came in the form of gifts or loans, the money received widened circles of solidarity, according to the economic philosophy whereby exchange was seen as the base of social relationships. And that is why the workers who were helped invariably expressed a desire to become benefactors in their turn.

The appeals for help received by the workers of Geneva show exactly how these links of reciprocation proliferated. Having been greatly helped during the construction workers' strike of 1868, the Genevois were later bombarded with requests from groups exhorting them to show themselves worthy of the support they had received. The German textile workers were the first to do this shortly after, reminding their Swiss brothers of their moral debt.[60] Next, in 1870, the miners of Waldenburg in Silesia asked for money, as a just reward for the help received from Germany two years earlier.[61] In the spring of 1869, the Geneva section also provided help to French workers in the form of an advance of 1,000 francs to the spinners of Elbeuf. As in the case of the Paris bronze workers, the great strike of 1868 created enduring bonds of trust and friendship, inasmuch as they inspired the Geneva sections to adopt similar patterns of behavior. The more closely strikers were connected to one another, the more relationships of solidarity were expected to accelerate and strengthen — on condition, naturally, that they did not exhaust all available resources.

As far as lenders were concerned, the very fact of having participated in worker solidarity generated a measure of trust and legitimacy. The example of the past conferred moral and financial rights in respect of the international worker community. What was important was not so much to establish an accounting equivalence between amounts lent and amounts borrowed as to appeal to the principle of reciprocity. The lender saw himself as morally entitled to ask for help later on, should he become involved in a social conflict. The lithograph printers justified their appeal for English union money in the summer of 1870 by reminding everyone that they had helped numerous other continental societies for months previously, to the tune of 18,000 francs. Their reserves were empty not because they were spendthrift but on account of their many acts of solidarity. Likewise, in 1871, the tobacco workers of Antwerp left no room for doubt when they called on their German counterparts for help: a simple reminder of the 3000 francs they had earlier paid to the workers of Leipzig was sufficient cause for their request.[62] Nevertheless, this chain of solidarities was a precarious one. If a single union stopped playing the game of reciprocation, the whole fragile edifice could collapse. Altruistic behavior patterns had to be demonstrated and repeated again and again, to prevent the kind of "non-solidarity" against which the entire project of the International was committed to fight.

Regional Cooperations

Such chain reactions of solidarity and reciprocation, ever proliferating and uninterrupted, created a geography of mutual aid that eluded the centralizing tendency of the English model. While at the time London appeared to be the center of the European workers' movement in terms of communications and institutions, pools of regionalized solidarity began to widen across the continent; and all this with the encouragement of the International, albeit without inheriting its polarities. Viewed from London, the continental workers' requests for assistance all reflected the same profound imbalance between the British unions' financial clout and the desperate need of their continental counterparts. This impression recedes when one observes the direct relationships that existed among the workers of the continent, whose networks were perfectly capable of circumventing London and its general council. If we look at the detailed subscription lists published in the contemporary press, we can see exactly how so-called universal reciprocity was geographically distributed.

Geographical proximity and linguistic familiarity were clearly factors that facilitated acts of solidarity. Over time, the French sections, especially those in Paris, made sizable contributions to French-speaking workers in Belgium and Switzerland. The 1869 subscription raised by the Belgian general council, on behalf of victims of the Seraing and Borinage massacres, revealed the predominance of funds sent from Paris, despite a situation that was difficult — to say the least — for internationalist militants under pressure from the authorities. Over half the sum of money entered in the subscription lists published by the Belgian Journal *L'Internationale* (1,317 francs out of a total of 2,242 francs, 53 percent of the total) came from Paris, as opposed to 36 percent (886 francs) from the Belgian sections, 8 percent from the general council of the IWA, and 1.5 percent from Germany. Among the Paris societies mentioned, the bronze makers furnished the largest sum (150 francs, almost as much as the 200 francs sent from London by the representatives of the IWA general council).[63]

Money from Paris also played an important part in the financing of strikes in Switzerland. In 1868, twenty-one hundred construction workers in Geneva on strike for wage increases and shorter working hours received funds from several French, German, English, and Austrian cities. On this occasion, Varlin collected nearly 10,000 francs, twice as much as the jewelers and engravers of Geneva itself. According to one Swiss historian, funds from Paris represented 10 percent of the total dispensed by the Geneva strikers, a figure that ought perhaps to be recalculated.[64] The rebuffing of Graglia, a representative sent to London, led him to conclude that, in the end, links of solidarity were liable to be stronger among French speakers.[65] The closeness of Paris and a greater ease in the exchange of information made interactions far more fluid. Furthermore, since 1867 Varlin and the Paris militants had acquired much solid practical experience in collecting funds.

The financing of the Swiss strikes in Geneva and Basel also show the minimal effect of the London money by comparison with the sums flowing from France, Germany, and Belgium. The social geography of solidarity was partly decentralized, given the institutional geography of the IWA. The same was true of the congresses of the association, most of which took place in Switzerland, one of the easiest places to reach for militants arriving from the north and south of Europe. Relying heavily on the platform provided by his newspaper *Der Vorbote*, the general council correspondent on the spot, Johann Philipp Becker, worked tirelessly to improve and increase contacts and mutual help between the German- and French-speaking sections of the association. The sums of money received by Becker from Germany increased steadily between 1866 and 1869, demonstrating his growing influence and his ability to integrate the German associations with the finances of the Geneva central committee. In 1869, the contributions the committee received from Germany, not counting subscriptions raised for strikes, represented one-third of its resources, as opposed to one-sixth in 1866. These financial links, which showed the strength of relations between the various German-speaking sections, were activated when strikes broke out in Switzerland and elsewhere.[66] Becker took care to publish brochures in German on the plight of the Geneva construction workers. He also maintained excellent relations with the Allgemeiner Deutscher Arbeiterverein party (ADAV), led by Johann Baptist von Schweitzer after the death of

Ferdinand Lassalle in 1863, along with the Verband Deutscher Arbeitervereine (VDAV), the party of the militants Bebel and Liebknecht. His influence on the complex web of the German-speaking sections began to decline after the creation of the Eisenach social democratic workers party in 1869, which "nationalized" the structure of the socialist and trade union forces of Germany and became the preferred interlocutor of the general council in London.

Becker's activism was reflected in the diversity of the sources supplying the Swiss strikers. Despite his limited number of members (six thousand at the most), he offered the International an effective financial weapon.[67] In 1868–1869 alone, the IWA paid over sixty-seven thousand francs to support strikes in Geneva, Basel, Lausanne, and Locle.[68] After 1868, funds were collected in Berlin through a mass concert for the benefit of the Geneva construction workers. The sum of 122 thalers (457,50 francs) raised at the time, surpassed all expectations.[69] A year later, the typographers' strike in the same city received more significant outside help: the funds received from six different foreign countries swelled the local militants' own war chest from 8,000 to 17,000 francs.[70]

The most compelling example of the ability of the Swiss to raise money in neighboring countries occurred during the Basel ribbon makers' strike in the winter of 1868–1869. In this case, France and the German territories were by some distance the most generous sources of finance. Just as in the Belgian subscription of the same year, half the sums received came from Paris, while London and Brussels sent much smaller contributions. The members of the general council had few illusions about the willingness to participate of the English trade unions.[71] Indeed Germany and German-speaking Switzerland sent the most money from the most societies. Becker contrived to mobilize a wide network of correspondence and a large number of German workers' associations (*Arbeitervereine*) based outside Germany who could identify with the struggle of the ribbon makers.[72] *Der Vorbote*, naturally, emphasized the close links between the workers of German, Austrian, and Swiss cities, independent of the IWA's general council.

In any event, we should take note of the fact that some zones remained on the sidelines of these exercises in cooperation, though they were IWA members and located close to Switzerland or France. Although they were closely associated with Switzerland, the hard-up militants of Italy, in particular, had great difficulty sending any money at all. In 1868, the members of the Naples section expressed all its sympathy with the striking Geneva workers, regretting bitterly that they were unable to help materially:

> We were moved to hear the news of your strike action, which is still under way. We wish we could be with you to share your struggle . . . we also wish we were rich enough to offer you effective help, but our association was only founded very recently, and alas we ourselves as individuals are as poor, and perhaps even poorer, than you are. Our will to act is in no way matched by our power to do so. Therefore we beg your pardon for the smallness of the sum attached, and ask you to accept it as proof of our fraternal and imperishable solidarity.[73]

Beyond solidarity, the International included societies that were more or less rich, and others that were considerably poorer. While the rhetoric of solidarity was shared equally between the Swiss and French workers and their Italian or Spanish neighbors to the south, the latter's margins for action were more limited, clearly showing the gap that can exist between a desire for solidarity and its achievement.

Migrations and Unfair Competition

Financial and material assistance were not the only forces driving international cooperation. If they were, it would be hard to understand why the English workers, who were comfortably self-sufficient, would agree to lend funds to others as they did, without any real expectation of getting them back. Nor why, in spite of the inequalities in wealth and status that characterized them, well-heeled workers should consent to come to the assistance of people in other countries whose fate held little interest for them. In the minds of contemporary militants, the priority was to develop modes of regulation and harmonization for a jobs market organized on a transnational basis; this would have more relevance to the coordination of worker action than a straightforward appeal to a supranational authority. Wherever employers used the pretexts of wholesale competition and differences in workers' wages to resist their demands, the militants of the IWA hoped to limit such competition through international cooperation during strike action. This was one of the obsessions of the English trade unions, which viewed the prudent and coordinated proliferation of strikes on the continent solely as an opportunity to improve the working conditions and wages of European workers, now that serious financial help was making it possible for them to carry on for longer and actually obtain satisfaction for their demands. It was also felt that there was a chance of closing the yawning gaps in living standards between Great Britain and her neighbors across the Channel, while slowing the importation of cheap labor from abroad by British employers determined to defeat collective strike action.

At a very early stage, the need to align workers' standards of living more fairly across frontiers was perceived as crucial to any successful mobilization of the working world against global capitalism. The framing of competition by the organization of professions and industrial action was part of a long tradition, which borrowed as much from the ancien régime ideal of the corporation as it did from such 1830–1840 socialist projects as those formulated by Louis Blanc in his *Organisation du travail*, published in 1841.[74] Blanc's idea was that it was up to the workers to organize themselves against the toxic effects of competition and prevent an unfettered market from producing a situation of every-man-for-himself. The self-regulation of the labor market through genuine transnational worker cooperation might be the forerunner of a "commune of the future," a world in which heavy competition for jobs, low wages, and widespread social neglect would no longer dictate the rules for working communities.[75] A general rapprochement of wage conditions would lead to an equivalence of functions and an attenuation of potential conflicts between the workers of different countries. For example, Marx thought it was a matter of vital importance for the workers of England to support the cause of the Sotteville-lès-Rouen textile workers in 1869 for, by trying to compete with the English industry by forcing wages downward, the Norman employers were threatening not only the condition of all other continental workers but also the higher standards enjoyed by British workers.[76] Weak or strong, workers on both sides of the English Channel had a common interest in helping each other prevent the evil of social dumping.

This kind of solidarity could function properly only if the tactic of temporarily importing foreign workers — an all-too-easy employer response to strike action during the 1860s — was short-circuited. In a publication on the merits of the International, the Belgian general council stressed the great benefits that might flow from closer relationships between European workers. Among other things, they would make it possible for workers to go on strike without fear that their employers would replace them with foreign "blacklegs":

> So there we are. What you need to do is build a union representing many, many workers, hailing not just from the same village, but from the same country, indeed from all over the world. Then it will be impossible to replace one set of workers with another from somewhere else; and you will be able to negotiate with your masters without fear of losing your jobs. In doing this, you will have founded an international association of working men.[77]

The recruitment of "blacklegs," as the English unions called them, was a well-honed tactic used by employers to replace striking or locked-out workers. The flow of manpower back and forth across the English Channel was so strong even in normal times that it was no more expensive to recruit a hundred or so workers in Belgium, Holland, Germany, or Denmark, pay their travel costs to England, and still be able to offer them wages well above those prevailing on the continent. This worked just as well at the local level as it did in the USA: the Geneva workers congratulated the "workers of the mountains" when the latter went on strike at Le Locle in August 1869, contributing to an alignment of the conditions and demands of workers from the same employment pool; meanwhile, far away on the other side of the Atlantic, the wallpaper workers of New York made clear their anxiety about the prospect of European workers usurping their jobs.[78]

Although they did not share the ideological views of the IWA, the English trade unions saw it as a useful instrument for limiting these temporary migrations by circulating information to discourage foreign workers from making the journey to England. For British workers, the important thing was to help continental workers to organize personally and financially in exchange for a better control of the flow of manpower, especially when strikes and lockouts were in progress. Beginning in 1866, the general council was committed to make this mode of cooperation one of the strongest elements in its overall plan.[79] The stopping of informal worker migration was presented as the principal short-term benefit the English workers could expect from their financial participation in the IWA.[80] A first serious example of the usefulness of the International emerged during the strikes launched by the tailors of Edinburgh, Manchester, and London, who were worried about the possible arrival of blacleg workers from the continent in 1865–1866. Thanks to the general council, the English unions were able not only to make their strike known to the workers' press on the continent, especially in Germany and Norway, but also to appeal to them to refuse any offers of employment by English bosses bent on breaking it.[81]

The well-documented case of the Newcastle engineers' strike in the summer of 1871 shows that information on strikes and migrations did not circulate as freely as all that. Alerted by rumors that the employers had sent a delegate to Belgium, the English strikers began to fear that workers were about to be recruited en masse to take over their jobs and break their collective action. The situation seemed to them so critical that it was thought not enough merely to send this information to the Belgian sections. Championed in the general council by the cigar maker James Cohn, the engineers demanded that a full delegation be sent abroad as soon as possible to convey their message face-to-face and discourage potential job candidates. Some of those present saw this as a costly overreaction, given the effective exchange mechanisms already in place between the general council and its Belgian counterpart, which were correctly structured and well established in the various industrial centers of the country. Cohn, however, took the view that "personal visits always carried more weight than letters could do however well they might be written."[82] He himself was eventually commissioned to go to Belgium on behalf of the engineers to meet the Belgian militants — who were duly outraged, given that the fears of the Newcastle engineers were completely groundless. All the same the general council relayed the English appeal to the Belgian engineers quite robustly:

> By demonstrations of justice in which the rights and duties of workers are balanced by reciprocity in the struggle for work, we shall convince them that their strength depends on their unity. They will easily understand that the competition they will have with English workers can only be disastrous for the proletariat, fatal for themselves, and entirely criminal, since it will inevitably bolster the iniquitous

activities of employers, whose strategy is to drive into hopeless poverty the very people to whom they owe their own excessive wealth.[83]

But since striking or locked-out workers were involved, their own mobility was seen as a way of alleviating the costs of the strike. They could find alternative sources of income while the conflict lasted. Help in the form of money was sometimes used to facilitate these short-term migrations and diminish the financial pressure on strike committees. This was the case of the weavers of Ghent, who went on strike in January 1869 and used the advances paid to them to go and work in Roubaix, just across the French frontier.[84] Instead of suffering the harsh effects of migrations that their employers wanted in order to break the strikes, the idea was to organize them in such a way as to fulfil the dual objectives of resistance and individual survival. Gradually those who were in principle hostile to the idea of workers moving around could adjust to the rhythm of strikes and conflicts. Their very mobility could become a factor of solidarity and resistance, instead of a means of competition to be exploited by employers.

A World of Priorities

The IWA's fresh commitment definitely marked a turning point in the history of international worker solidarity. Within the space of a few years, contacts proliferated, funds were exchanged, and debts both moral and material were contracted. But was this really the kind of universal solidarity for which earlier militants had yearned? The building of links in solidarity is always accompanied by a work of demarcation, between those who have a right to it and those who are excluded from it, as well as the identification of groups capable of cooperating on a grand scale and those whose means, financial or organizational, do not allow them to engage in the cycle of reciprocation.[85] It was not surprising that the universal language used by the International's militants glossed over a number of deeply entrenched professional and social hierarchies, in a Europe that contained so many different workers and unions.

Like many other international organizations of the time, the IWA contributed to structuring the world of work on a national basis, mainly through correspondents assigned to one or several countries within the general council or through delegations sent to its congresses and conferences. Its members used national categories to distinguish themselves from one another, identifying characteristic modes of organization and ways of behaving country by country. During his second trial in 1868, Varlin praised the solidarity expressed by "the English people" toward Parisian militants, subsuming beneath the English national tradition of etiquette certain gestures of mutual support built into social and professional milieux that were doubtless rather cooler than he let on.[86] Yet there was a definite national sympathy for the demands of oppressed minorities (such as the Poles or the Irish) and the appearance of new nation states (such as Italy or Germany). The historian Marcel van der Linden has shown very convincingly that, from the point of view of practices and exchanges, the internationalism of the IWA operated more on a "sub-national" than a national basis.[87] Relations of solidarity connected worker communities that mainly defined themselves by their local attachments. Obviously in countries like England, the unions were grouped into national structures, like the Trades Union Congress founded in 1868. But in most other cases, powerful national organizations that could pretend to some kind of monopoly of worker representation did not yet exist; there might even be several competing organizations, as was the case in Germany. For the moment, it was a matter of local sections joining in networks so as to implement exchanges. They were more decentralized than structured around national authorities.

The strongest principle of worker identification in these years was that of profession, which played a structural role in both local and transnational solidarity. Any action of human solidarity must involve a capacity to view somebody else as similar to oneself. This equivalence was led by the elite professions that formed the aristocracy of the contemporary working world. The intensity of contacts, exchanges, and solidarity was bound to be highest in organized professions with clearly identified skills and where the job markets were apt to be connected across frontiers and oceans. Thus between 1860 and 1870 capacities for cooperation were particularly developed among professional typographers, tailors, and tobacco workers. Because they were so close among themselves, these professions managed to coordinate their protest campaigns, control the movement of their workers across borders, and generally promote shared social and economic objectives.

The Leipzig typographers' strike of March–July 1865 was a high watermark for the internationalist movement. This long industrial conflict generated unprecedented gestures of solidarity between the typographers of several different European cities. Out of a total of 10,000 thalers (more than 37,000 francs), only one-tenth came from resources collected in Leipzig. The remaining 90 percent came from funds subscribed in 120 other places, two-thirds being from Germany (Berlin and elsewhere) and one-third from abroad (France, Switzerland, Austria, and Russia).[88] The typographers and typesetters of London, Paris, and Brussels also sent substantial contributions (the Bruxellois raised 200 thalers, a large sum by comparison with the usual amounts of subscriptions).[89] In the following year a German union of typographers was founded with around three thousand members, each of whom paid a membership fee of five pfennigs a month to the association's account.[90] The typographers were so successful that other professions were convinced they no longer needed to go on strike to win their disputes. The same was true of the tailors' profession, which in April 1867 was capable of orchestrating simultaneous strike action in London, Brussels, and Paris, backed by funds from both sides of the English Channel.[91]

Professions like these, which already had firm contacts with their counterparts in other countries, had less need of the IWA's input than other groups. They maintained a high level of information on current practices and above all they controlled the movements of their members. According to a study by the historian Ad Knotter, even before the IWA came into being the tobacco workers were noted for their high mobility and habit of coordinating action internationally.[92] The first contact between the English tobacco workers and those of the continent harked back to 1848, when English unionists were expelled from Belgium after trying to persuade their Belgian colleagues to restrict migrations and stop employers calling in manpower from abroad during English strikes.[93] In the 1860s, relations between the English, Belgian, German, Dutch, and American tobacco workers were closely maintained, showing up impressively in the spring of 1871 during the Antwerp strike. The five hundred workers at the Belgian port embarked on their action with a budget of £240 and promptly applied to their foreign counterparts for financial help in the hope that they could hold out for a few weeks.[94] Money poured in from the main centers of the tobacco industry in Amsterdam, Altona, Brussels, Ghent, and London. The English, represented by Cohn, sent more than £600. The Antwerp tobacco workers, who were jealous of their independence, made it very clear that they were not looking for charity: in its address, the general council indicated that they were not asking "for gifts, but for loans, and we know from experience that such loans have been faithfully repaid."[95] In 1871, the bonds established between the various tobacco workers' communities eventually led to the foundation, in London, of the Tobacco Workers' International Union: so strong was their transnational solidarity that the cigar makers were able to bypass the IWA, which explains their reluctance to join it.[96] In the 1860s, the craftsmen and industrial workers of elite professions like theirs formed the vanguard of international solidarity, and they were well aware of their superiority in every aspect of organization, deep pockets, and respect.

The weight of the métiers (professions) — whose proponents had a clear vision of an economy centered on credit, an ideal of self-sufficiency, and a concept of trade unionism founded on the levying of hefty union dues and the provision of services for the sole use of their members — was outside the IWA's sphere of action. The IWA was more concerned to project a brand of international "socialism of skilled workers" whose French manifestation was explored by the historian Bernard Moss.[97] Nevertheless, the International tried to support the industrial workers of Le Creusot, Belgium, or Silesia — with mixed results. The heavy demands of the amalgamated English unions and of the resistance funds of the continent provoked criticism because the solidarity they both envisioned was accompanied by practices of exclusion (toward heavy industry workers, agricultural laborers, etc). The heavyweights of the TUC, involved in the general council of the IWA, were denounced for their lordly manner and were depicted as a kind of "junta," seeking to impose their own model without ever opening up to other voices and professions (for example, the workers of the North and the Midlands were sparsely represented, despite the massive preponderance of those regions in British industrial production).[98] The English unions were also accused of pandering to Prime Minister William Gladstone's principles of liberal conservatism, with their respectability and insistence on financial integrity. All in all, the English trade unions were seen by their opponents as being an extension of the liberal capitalist world, whatever their strike-prone activism.[99]

Finally, the workers of the International may have come together in solidarity, but the vast majority of them were male. Only a few women played leading roles, all of them exceptional individuals. At the time, socialism and feminism were two distinct movements and, frankly, were even at odds. The question of women as workers, which was discussed in depth at Geneva in 1866 and at Lausanne in the following year, offered an opening for the French followers of Proudhon to reveal the full extent of their misogyny. For them, but also for many of the Belgian militants of the International, the idea of women as workers was quite simply against nature. There was nothing to prevent the average worker from being as "macho" as the next man: a woman's place was in the home, as much for moral reasons as for economic ones given that the work of women, just like the work of immigrants, was seen as depressing the wages of all.[100] Voices were raised against this blinkered attitude, most notably that of Varlin, but it is understandable that the IWA was hardly seen as a welcoming environment for women and feminists, who were better represented in other organizations at the time. Nevertheless a few militant women managed to negotiate this obstacle, such as Victoria Woodhull, the American campaigner for women's suffrage and free love who joined Section 12 of the International in New York, which itself was relatively self-sufficient and hence disapproved of by the general council. Virginie Barbet in Lyon, André Léo in Paris, and Elizabeth Demetrieff in Geneva did their best to to promote the cause of women in internationalist circles.[101]

Examples of strikes involving women were extremely rare, an exception being that of the *ovaliste* silk workers of Lyon in 1869.[102] When subscriptions were called for, women were above all presented as victims, wives, or mothers and were described in heavily compassionate terms. They were almost never acknowledged as full participants in worker solidarity or responsibility. The funds sent to the women silk workers in Lyon were presented as gestures of humanity, not of reciprocation or common interest.[103] In Geneva, the first people involved in collecting contributions for the silk workers were the "ladies" of the city, who organized themselves as a section and used the classic methods of feminine philanthropy (concerts, visits to people's homes, etc.). In London, Harriet Law — a member of the general council between 1867 and 1872 — attempted to collect funds from her own female friends.[104] She failed completely, noting afterward with some bitterness that "ladies did not like identifying themselves with strikes"; that kind of solidarity was still very much a matter for men, the role of women being chiefly confined to collecting money and displaying emotion. In spite of Marx's good intentions in allowing representatives of the silk workers (Philomène Rozan and Virginie Barbet) to attend the Basel Congress in September 1869, in the end it was Bakunin and Albert Richard who stepped in to represent the women workers of Lyon.[105]

■ ■ ■

In reference to France, the historian Michelle Perrot — a pioneer in the study of the workers' movement and the invention of the strike as a social practice, as well as a figure of reference in the history of women — noted that "solidarity flows from organization, much more than from sympathy, emotion or altruism."[106] Although these notions are more complementary than contrasting, Perrot's formula underlines the fact that the international solidarity of workers is never spontaneous. The facts are these: the First International opened a phase of apprenticeship in international worker solidarity, whose development it followed and attempted to institutionalize. The methods of loans and aid funds resonated especially with the ideals of economic emancipation and generalized reciprocation that inspired the militant workers of the era. The existence of a central headquarters in London facilitated exchanges of information and the forming of personal relationships, without creating any kind of centralized management of the mechanisms of mutual aid. Things were done at a local level, by individual professions, through their own locally maintained transnational connections, and as a rule it was these professions that decided on acts of solidarity.

Thus two rationales were blended into one, which went on to shape the hopes and methods of worker internationalism. The first was solidarity among workers who belonged to the same profession and who were brought together by their conditions of employment, their values, and their experiences outside their national frontiers. The second, which was harder to stimulate and organize, was the logic of interprofessional solidarity that grew progressively more distant from the local circumstances of its roots. This early phase of worker internationalism, strongly engrained in the globalization of the 1860s, was more relevant to the old professions of small industry and craftwork (such as typographers, bronze workers, building and textile workers) than to the growing masses employed in heavy industry (miners, steelworkers, dockers, and the like). The mobilization of the working masses and their insertion into networks of international solidarity presented new challenges at the same time as they heralded the possibility of actions unheard of in their breadth and geographical scope.

4 | THE PITFALLS OF COMPASSION

When workers were victims of injustice or repression, ordinary human compassion demanded that they be given immediate help, whether or not there was any real expectation that they would return the favor. As a result, the militant fraternity of the 1860s thrived on a diet of indignation and shared emotion. The gift of money — made manifest by subscriptions, concerts, and conferences — replaced the loan of money, which was more linked to the traditional structures of workingmen's associations. Meanwhile, charities distributed words of comfort, cash, and material help, in a concrete demonstration of the emotional links binding the members of the International, whatever their countries of origin.

The nature of the social relationship functioning through straightforward donations was considerably more ambivalent than the one involved in the contracting of a loan. Even if a gift between equals could exist in theory, there was always bound to be something about it that was out of kilter. Workers who value their independence have always loathed any suggestion of charity that might call in question their honor and dignity. The savagery of the French government repression after the Commune uprising in May 1871 forced some to compromise with their principles. For a period of two months (from 18 March to 28 May 1871), the working people of Paris put in place a municipal government of their own, refusing to acknowledge France's defeat at the hands of the Prussians in the war started by Napoleon III in July 1870. The emperor himself was forced into exile after the debacle of Sedan on 2 September 1870; a new French Republic was declared on 4 September. But the elections organized for 8 February 1871 at the height of the Prussian siege of Paris returned a conservative majority that advocated signing a peace treaty as soon as possible with Chancellor Bismarck and Kaiser William I. The population of Paris, fervently republican and patriotic, refused to surrender and rebelled against the government of Adolphe Thiers, based in Versailles. The Parisian and foreign militants of the International then joined the movement and took part in their unheard-of experiment in municipal federalism. After two months of violent and unequal combat, the "Versaillais" crushed the Paris Commune in the terrible Bloody Week (21–28 May) during which thousands of people — some well-known, others completely anonymous — were massacred in cold blood.

After this, thousands more penniless Parisian refugees went into hiding and exile to escape imprisonment or death, in a serious test of the IWA's power to activate real-life transnational worker solidarity for militants all over Europe. The experience quickly showed limitations, because neither the donors nor the fugitives they sought to help were comfortable with so one-sided a relationship. In this situation the clandestine former militants of the Commune — internationalist socialists, anarchists, or partisans of the extremist Auguste Blanqui — struggled to preserve links of solidarity between themselves and their comrades, now scattered to the ends of the earth. The way in which they contrived to resurrect the tried and true methods of philanthropy was not the least paradoxical aspect of this period of resourcefulness and exile, which ultimately led to the institutional breakup of the IWA.

FORMS OF DONATION

The workers' movement was thoroughly ambiguous about donations. On the one hand, it was omnipresent because it raised subscriptions for cooperation and mutual support, especially at times when there were violent repressions, arbitrary arrests, and collateral victims in need of help. Engagement came at a very high price, and any militant of the time might one day or another have to pay for it. Logically, any investment in union action, insurrection, or political debate had to be made in a spirit of mutual cooperation, especially within a political movement that was struggling against the power of capital and suspicious of anything smacking of charity.

Individual Assistance

The first form of mutual aid was the one given by individual militants to one another, when they were harassed by the authorities and were in personal difficulty or incapable of supporting themselves. Here the interpersonal dimension was fundamental, since the help came directly from a friend or another individual. Mutual aid was the compensation of association membership, and this was made up of providing a helping hand or some kind of service to fellow militants who might be in trouble, in hiding, or on the run. Mutual aid never surfaced in the press or at public meetings, but it was ever present in the daily interactions between comrades. Any militant on the move for political or any other reasons could be given some kind of cash assistance and a letter of recommendation and then be offered bed, board, or work by those receiving him.

Traces of such sporadic assistance can be found in the correspondence of the militants of the International, who backed each other up but also kept track of where the money went. Abundant documentation on the Belgian sections has survived, which shows how some militants used the funds they received as individuals.

This was the case of Paul Robin, who was given 100 francs by the Belgian council to get to Switzerland after being expelled by the Belgian authorities: the money was conditional on the fulfilment of a political mission, and in his letters Robin tried hard to justify the use he made of it. He also said he was prepared in turn to lend or even give the money he had received, in order to set in motion a form of reciprocation of the aid given to him, by participating in the expense of sending a Belgian delegate to the Basel Congress in 1869. Later, when forced to justify himself, he repaid the entire sum he had been given, to put an end to the rumors this story had engendered.[1]

Subscriptions opened for the benefit of veteran militants under pressure from the authorities were conceived as a veritable moral duty. In this case it was not a matter of coming to the rescue of anonymous workers, living in another town or in another country, but of helping personalities who were well-known locally and whose activities on behalf of the IWA were landing them in judicial or political hot water. The militant Pierre Vésinier, who was arrested in Belgium in 1866 after publishing a virulent pamphlet against Napoleon III entitled *Le Mariage d'une Espagnole*, had the privilege of seeing a "democratic subscription" opened to pay the fine imposed on him.[2] Despite his past stormy relations with the general council, on 30 June 1867 a sum of over 1,000 francs was raised for him, enough to settle his legal costs in full.[3] Having been set up as a martyr of the workers' cause, Vésinier quickly became a nightmare for the Belgian militants of the IWA. He was particularly fierce in his denunciations of the French militants of the International (Henri Tolain and Ernest Édouard Fribourg) whom he accused, without evidence, of taking money from the Bonapartist authorities. For this he was banned from the Brussels section of the IWC and then expelled from Belgium in 1868. Thereafter he was judged unworthy of the help that had been given to him when he was being persecuted by the authorities.

The lives of the exiled militants, buffeted as they were by successive political events and constant police surveillance, were often precarious — and this was also the case for the people at the head of the association. Without the support of his close friends, Karl Marx himself would probably never have been able to reconcile the writing of *Das Kapital* with his perpetual involvement with the general council during the 1860s.[4] Money and health problems are constantly mentioned in his correspondence with close friends and relatives.[5] He was constantly looking for cash to make ends meet. Ferdinand Lassalle lent him £75 in the early 1860s, but it was above all thanks to the fortune of Engels, who was always ready to support him, that he was able to relax somewhat in the late 1860s, when his health was beginning to deteriorate.[6] Better-off militants like Engels were often solicited for money by comrades in difficulty. These hard-to-track individual loans were a standard feature of militant life.

Rage and Censure

The setbacks and violence endured by worker collectives made people want to help them all the more. There was near unanimous denunciation of the violence wrought by governments and the forces of capital; at the same time, there was an unavoidable detachment from that violence, linked to the supposed ideology of the IWA and the determination of its leaders to steer clear of the politics of insurrection. One could — indeed one should — help fellow workers who were being victimized and repressed, but that need not stifle the expression of a moral judgment on their behavior or their involvement in workers' internationalism. This was the great paradox of the donation: while flaunting a surface solidarity, it reaffirmed the existence of a distinction — indeed a principle — of hierarchy between the victim and his benefactor. In this case, the donation was more a matter of honor. There was even something aristocratic about it. This type of relationship is also present in the working world, which is equally diversified, fragmented, and hierarchical. The donation takes on a very different function from those operating behind subscriptions to strikes and forms of credit. It can play a moralizing, guilt-awakening, educative role; it can stimulate people to join the ranks of internationalist workers. The rural recruitment base of the mining and steel industries, the bread of collective movements, and the difficulty of financing movements involving hundreds or even thousands of people in major pools of employment, all created a certain distance with respect to the more integrated workers of the International. This social distinction overlapped with national divisions that sometimes surfaced in the way militant practices were characterized. For example, Belgian workers occupied a paradoxical position: although it was a bastion of industrial Europe and the seat of a powerful section of the International, the country could not shake off an image of backwardness and inferiority, particularly in the great centers of Belgian employment around Liège, Charleroi, and Mons. Yet Belgium contained the largest number of factory workers affiliated with the IWA in all of Europe, at a time when the craftsmen and workers of city centers were dominant in other countries.[7]

An early episode in which International worker emotion was effectively mobilized took place in February 1867, during a conflict that took place at Marchienne, near Charleroi. To remain competitive, the ironmasters of the region decided to dock the wages of their workers and close down several major blast furnaces. The protest that followed became a full-blown riot, in which miners and steelworkers looted and burned property and soldiers shot and arrested them. The very composition of the strike revealed the international dimension of production, inasmuch as it involved French, German, and Belgian workers. Around fifty individual convictions were handed down for acts of rebellion, with prison sentences of between six weeks and six months. A year later, similar confrontations broke out at the coal mines of Couchant-de-Mons.

The Belgian internationalists immediately dispatched the printer Désiré Brismée to the scene, who assumed the defense of the workers being prosecuted and tried to calm everyone down. The administrative committee of the Belgian international even denounced the violent acts committed to the minister of justice and expressed disapproval of the methods used for the mobilization, which risked tarnishing the legitimacy of the strike and giving credence to false rumors about the brutal violence of the workers' International. The riot was driven by the legitimate and necessary energy of despair, but that energy would be dissipated once education and training had restored the workers to straight and narrow ways of association and cooperation:

> Yes, we are still prepared to tell our friends in the Charleroi basin: "When you went on strike, you were right to do so. You exercised and accomplished a duty." But we would add what you have correctly read into the words "the lot of the workingman is not seriously improved by strike action"; for we deplore the disturbances and shootings that resulted from the Charleroi strike, and if we still say that it was useful, urgent, and perfectly legitimate, it is because this was the only option for workers protesting the constraints of capital. Nevertheless we hope one day to emerge from the present state of struggle and enter an era of mutualism.[8]

In both Belgium and France, appeals were made on behalf of oppressed workers and their families.[9] The general council of the IWA seized on the mobilization of the Marchienne miners, which had been crushed in the violence, to amplify its international appeal for solidarity and denounce the ferocity of the bourgeois states. The reasoning here was ambivalent: indignation against the violence of the repression went hand in hand with condescending attitudes toward the immature behavior of the Belgian workers. Having occurred on the spur of the moment without the least preparation or organization, their uprising became a riot and gave the authorities a pretext for discrediting the whole enterprise. The appeal for contributions came as much from solidarity as from censure, and as much from empathy as from remonstrance. The miners were strongly advised to join the International, get some ideological training, and strengthen their capacities for action at a safe distance from any kind of violence. The language used in the address to the mine workers and steelworkers of the United Kingdom, written by Johann Eccarius on behalf of the general council, was not couched in any semblance of equality; indeed it sounded like an elder brother lecturing his novice junior:

> A great many of the work-people became exasperated, and not being organized and in the habit of deliberating upon their common affairs, thay had no plan of action for their guidance....This provoked an attack, the result is: killed, wounded, and prisoners. These poor-provoked and ill-used victims have left families outside the graves and the prison walls who are in dire want....Mistaken and misguided as these men were as to their course of action, they yet fell in labor's cause, and those they have left behind deserve sympathy and support. Some pecuniary help to the widows and orphans, and the moral influence it would produce, if coming from abroad, would raise the drooping spirits of the whole class, and might lead to communications and interchanges of opinion which would give our Continental brethren a better idea of how labor's battles must be fought, and what organization and education the fighting army require.[10]

At much the same time, in the spring of 1867, brutal riots broke out in Roubaix just across the border. This time they were centered on the more venerable weaving fraternity, with both French and Belgian workers involved. The demonstrators protested against the decision made by several employers to have each man working on two looms at once. There were violent clashes, with groups of workers smashing factories and machinery and even setting them aflame.[11] Just as it had been in Belgium, the repression was severe:

fifteen people were jailed on 6 April, among them a "ringleader" who was sentenced to sixteen months' incarceration. Official and worker observers alike quickly made the connection between these events and the ones that had broken out at Marchienne. The Internationalists saw this as proof that a spontaneous uprising, devoid of any ideological framework or procedure of collective deliberation, worked to the advantage of its repressors. The messages of support sent by the sections of the International used a rhetoric that was similar to the one addressed to the Belgian miners, albeit with a subtle blend of benevolent empathy and moral reprimand. The militants of Paris, whose bronze workers were currently at the cutting edge of the movement, did not hesitate to condemn a group that they referred to as "Brothers": "However justified your complaints, nothing can justify the destructive acts of which you are guilty. The machine, which is the tool you work with, should be sacred to you; acts of violence such as these endanger your own cause and that of all other workers. You have put weapons in the hands of the enemies of liberty and the slanderers of the people."[12] Thus the Luddite sabotage of machinery by workers was finally being denounced by the workers themselves, marking the end of a long process that the historian François Jarrige has so diligently traced.[13] The most enlightening aspect of this was that the workers of Roubaix actually took it on board, admitting their own position of inferiority and declaring their wish to follow the path suggested by the IWA. Three years later, a fraternal association of workers was founded in Roubaix to "educate them" and "free them from the state of moral inferiority" into which they had plunged.[14]

In 1869 this blend of appeals to solidarity and militant reprimands culminated in the "Belgian massacres," to use the expression coined by the IWA for the vicious crushing of the iron puddlers of Seraing and the Borinage, where the international struggle against capitalist violence was symbolized by factories founded at the beginning of the century by John Cockerill. The language of suffering and martyrdom was used copiously in this case, to shock and horrify the watching world.[15] Some directed rebukes at the workers of Seraing and the Borinage, but they were hardly unanimous. The Belgian Alfred Herman reminded Robin, a harsh critic of the strikers, that "it wasn't the workers who started this, it was the employers who for no good reason forced tyrannical conditions upon them." In his view, to shower the strikers with sanctimonious abuse at a time when they were already enduring a savage bout of repression was both morally wrong and an appalling tactical error. But Robin was only repeating the prevalent wisdom within the IWA, that no strike should ever be called without the prior accumulation of a substantial resistance fund. Without collective backing or financial means, the iron puddlers ought to have remembered that "every strike must be meticulously prepared, organized, discussed, and declared in cold blood." Yet these criticisms did not prevent the expression of solidarity, as contributions poured in from Belgium and abroad. German internationalists, for example, loudly denounced a crime against civilization and contributed the sum of 25 thalers (93.5 francs) via Bebel in Leipzig and Marx in London, to the victims of the riots in Seraing and the Borinage.[16] The route taken by the money across several frontiers was complicated in the extreme and in this case there was a necessary detour via London before it could return to the continent.

The Fate of Strikers' Families

When appeals for contributions were launched, the focus of attention was not so much on the suffering workers as on their suffering wives and children. It was felt that families needed help and relief far more than the fathers and husbands being arrested or killed. True enough, the men were pitied, but not enough to stem the moral condemnation of their actions. Here the logic was very different from the one applied to strikes in general; in effect the donations that came were acts of charity toward the collateral victims of the struggle between organized labor and capitalism. As ever, the humanitarian bent of the time required the sacrifice of defenseless innocents.[17] When he called on the general council for help after the events at Marchienne, Vésinier made explicit mention of widows and orphans, the prime targets for charity. A few weeks later, the Paris bronze workers — still locked in combat with their employers — consented to send a "small percentage" of the money made available to them to relieve the wives and children of jailed weavers, who were "the innocent victims of an impoverished, ignorant past."[18] In other words, their material help was tempered by a value judgment and a conviction that such acts belonged to a bygone age. This was still the case in 1869 with the massacres of Seraing and the Borinage, the donations being mostly intended to assist women and children; gifts of money were clearly less morally and ideologically awkward if given to people whose minority status made them magnets for compassion.

The attention paid to the collateral victims of strikes opened the way for new forms of symbolic action, particularly during the events at Le Creusot in 1870 — that occurred once again in a worker pool that was very different from those of the more active and better established centers of the International. The subscription appeals launched in the Paris press, and especially in Henri Rochefort's *La Marseillaise*, were couched in compassionate language toward the families of strikers. "Proletarian money alone remains, to dry the tears and relieve the pain of the proletariat," gushed the newspaper. Rochefort himself, languishing in prison, released a novel proposal to tighten the emotional and symbolic bond between the militants of the International and the workers of Le Creusot, on top of the material help collected by subscription. He suggested the temporary adoption by his newspaper, or by private individuals, of the families of militants sentenced to jail following the two Le Creusot strikes.

The process was aimed at making the aid relationship a personal one, by giving body to the often used metaphor of the universal family of workers, united in solidarity. Thus the adoptive family took the place of the biological one, for as long as the workers continued their struggle and resisted the strategies of impoverishment deployed by their employers. By taking in the children of men on strike, the militants of other cities and other countries would be contributing massive assistance in kind by relieving the strike committee of the responsibility to feed many mouths, while broadening the sphere of action of worker solidarity. This symbolic adoption was aimed at building a community of emotions and a solidarity of destiny: "You are no longer alone and bereft, *La Marseillaise* has adopted you and pledges to take care of you for as long as the imperial dungeons cling to their human prey," wrote the enthusiastic journalist.[19]

Parisian militants of the International demonstrated their willingness to help the wives and "orphans" of their jailed comrades. Private individuals wrote to the *Marseillaise* to offer their services. A Parisian couple volunteered to take in a child from Le Creusot until things improved. Another couple living on the Boulevard de la Villette did better, offering to look after a little girl of three or four, whom they would go fetch in person from Le Creusot — or welcome in Paris if her mother would prefer to bring her personally (they would naturally pay all travel expenses). A reader in Geneva made a similar proposal, saying that it was the workers' duty to help one another and match the employers' pseudo-charitable gestures: "We must rally round the families of the men given prison sentences in Autun" (Autun was the seat of the tribunal that tried the strikers) "and preserve them from the revolting charity of M. Schneider which threatens to engulf them sooner or later. I wish to persuade the wife of one of the prisoners to entrust me, my mother, and my sister with one of her children, to look after entirely during her husband's absence."[20]

Charity was a battlefield indeed. If the workers failed to stand together, their helpless families risked falling back into the employers' charitable clutches. This tactical concern, which converted the "solidarity donation" into one of the levers of protest, eventually won over a number of militants who would otherwise have viewed the procedure as repellently bourgeois. The Lyon federation outright approved the practice of temporary adoption and the principle behind it, despite some initial reservations:

> After the Autun verdicts fell, the federated workers' committee of Lyon decided unanimously somehow to help the families of the imprisoned workers, and its first idea was to ensure that the unfortunate and heroic victims of this injustice would continue to receive the same sums as they used to earn in wages, for the term of their detention. This seemed to the committee to represent an immediate application of the principle of solidarity that should unite all workers; moreover it might finesse that other principle, known as *charity*, which is so prevalent among the bourgeois and which in reality is just another confirmation of existing social inequalities. But confronted with the spontaneous act of the Paris sections of the International, whereby they adopted families stripped of their income by a contemptible legal judgment, the Lyonnais federation could only respond with applause, and with the immediate opening of a subscription for the striking workers of Le Creusot, and the families of those incarcerated.[21]

This was a clear change of course: to start with, the militants of Lyon thought of the assistance they might offer purely in terms of work and wages, within the customary framework of strike action and worker demands. But the wave of sympathy aroused by the cause of the Le Creusot captives obliged them to acknowledge the logic of charity, which was different in both form and principle. Workers' solidarity could not be confined to stumping up money to replace somebody's living wage or to amassing resistance funds; it had also to take account of the victims of military and judicial repression, fully endorsing the emotional register of charitable action.

The Right to Legal Defense

The subscriptions launched at the time of the trials of militants of the International in Belgium and in France were also intended to help arrested strikers organize their legal defenses. Subscription cash offered a means to mitigate suffering and prepare a decent resistance in court by settling fines and lawyers' fees; thus the human impulse to help was matched by a determination to assert every worker's right to a defense against police falsehoods. Money was needed to draw attention to the plight of the accused, with brochures aimed at making known versions of the facts that could rebut those put out by governments and their supporters in the press.

Although an official judicial inquiry was opened after the Borinage massacres, the Belgian general council engaged the militants to contribute, through their donations, to setting up a workers' commission to carry out a counter investigation of what happened. Worker emancipation meant challenging the state's pretension to a monopoly on truth, by reappropriating its tools of inquiry. Worker democracy had to cast the truth in the teeth of the bourgeois judiciary. The arrest of Eugène Hins, one of the most prominent militants of the International in Belgium, motivated the publication of an appeal, on 19 April 1869, that was intended not only to assist the victims of repression and their families but also to pay their legal costs and finance a workers' counter inquiry into the events of Seraing and the Borinage. This subscription, which remained open for several months, raised more than 2400 francs.[22]

Similar mobilizations of support took place during other court cases against members of the association. This was the case with the prosecution of the Paris sections in 1868 and 1870 and again in the wake of the events of 1870–1871. In Germany, the leaders of the brand-new social democratic workers' party were placed under tight surveillance after they refused to vote in favor of war credits in November 1870. Liebknecht, Bebel, and Adolf Hepner were finally sent to prison on 17 December 1870.[23] This was a heavy blow for the International, which had set much store on the development of its German branch; the latter was more unified thereafter and resolute in its support for the ideas of Karl Marx. Marx himself worked tirelessly in London to mobilize cash for his compatriots and their families. In this case the appeal for contributions was bereft of any negative connotations, since the German leaders were perceived as the victims of an unjust repression, which they had to endure simply because they had acted according to their internationalist and pacifist ideals. Their fate now threatened the entire project of the IWA. Only a few days after the arrest of the social democrat leaders, Engels sent money to Natalie Liebknecht, as did Marx several weeks later.[24] The three men were released from detention in March 1871 and then tried a year later in Leipzig, the process lasting from 11 to 26 March. Liebknecht and Bebel freely admitted their link to Karl Marx and the International but strenuously denied having committed violent acts. They claimed moreover that their use of the word *revolution*, which the prosecution tried to place at the center of its case against them, was "purely metaphorical."[25]

THE ORDEAL OF THE COMMUNE

The Franco-Prussian War of the summer of 1870, followed by the establishment of the Commune on 18 March 1871, changed the political history of Europe in the nineteenth century. The Paris insurrection was a tipping point for worker internationalism, which reached its zenith at this time before going into a period of decline because of government repression and its own internal divisions. The IWA in no way initiated this uprising, the causes of which were many, various, and mostly French in origin. Even so, the Commune and the solidarity it unleashed illustrated the vigor of internationalist engagement. Militants from all over Europe rushed to help the Paris revolutionaries, and international aid was organized outside the frontiers of France. The economic, social, and political concepts debated at the meetings of the IWA were brought to bear in a real-life experiment, even though the ideological influences feeding it were manifold and contradictory.[26]

The Commune episode was above all a chance to test the reliability of links built up within the IWA since the mid-1860s. The savage repression of the Bloody Week rovoked indignation throughout the movement; many from the ranks of the International were involved, having intervened physically to support the Commune. Links of solidarity might show best in adversity, but in this case the adversity was particularly excruciating for militants who suddenly lost the status of actors in their own revolutionary history and became hunted exiles, wretchedly dependent for survival on the generosity of their peers. More than any other event between 1860 and 1870, the Commune tested the basics of internationalism — reputation, trust, cooperation, and reciprocity — to their outer limits. Helping and providing for refugees was delicate in the extreme. Worst of all, all the work had to be done against the backdrop of an ideologically and politically polarized First International, in the period between the London Conference of September 1871 and the Hague Congress of September 1872, after which the general council moved its seat to New York. For over a year, the IWA's activities of solidarity were focused on the question of the refugees from the Commune, until its resources, both financial and emotional, were completely exhausted. The initial impulse of generosity faded rapidly as time went by and misunderstandings burgeoned.[27]

International Mobilization

The Commune was a brief event that generated contrasting positions, even if in general the members of the International were in favor of it. The stupefaction and panic that marked its brutal ending were every bit as strong as the hope and exhilaration of its beginning. Solidarity and mutual help were urgently needed by comrades trying by any means possible to elude death or arrest.

The IWA was one of the networks by which escape routes were organized. In fact, mobility had been at the heart of the association's project for several years past, its sections being fully prepared to take care of militants traveling throughout Europe for professional or political reasons. One of the first forms of mutual assistance was the furnishing of passports and false papers to circumvent ever-tightening police controls. Jean-Baptiste Dumay, the Le Creusot militant, mentioned in his memoirs the existence of a "passport bureau" whose mission was to facilitate the crossing of frontiers. All over the continent, IWA militants on the run had English, German, and Austrian passports at their disposal. When traveling to England, Belgium, Switzerland, or Spain they routinely operated in disguise, using identity documents supplied through the solidarity of professional, masonic, or municipal groups. Others might embark for England from Belgium, Spain, or the Netherlands.[28]

Clandestine escapes like these were rife with danger on account of the efforts made by the French government to secure the cooperation of its neighbors. In a celebrated circular dated 26 May 1871, the French foreign minister, Jules Favre, invited all European governments to extradite any former members of the Commune present on their soil, on the grounds that as common law "criminals" and "scoundrels" they had no right to political asylum or any other international legal protection. The IWA, like many far less radical political entities, mobilized strongly against this circular and the police motives behind it.[29] Some countries, such as Belgium and Switzerland, hesitated to comply. The arrest in Switzerland of Eugène Razoua on 17 July 1871 sparked a lively controversy as did certain declarations by Belgian politicians that belied their nation's record of hospitality since the creation of the kingdom during the revolutions of 1830.[30] Favre's request was ultimately turned down by both countries.

Great Britain, for one, maintained a wholehearted attachment to the right of political asylum. When France voted a stringent law against the International on 14 March 1872, intending to eradicate the organization and its militants altogether, it was not taken seriously by the British government. During a debate in the House of Commons on 12 April 1872, Home Secretary Henry Bruce declared that it would be perfectly pointless and counterproductive to ban the International. He preferred to rely on the virtues of free discussion, which in his view were far more likely to pacify and temper the revolutionary ardor of the IWA, which would then turn its attention to economic and social concerns.[31] On the other side of the Atlantic, meetings in support of the militants of the Commune were organized in New York on 2 July and 17 December 1871 by the local sections of the International, and several thousand people joined a march to show their solidarity.[32]

Thanks to the networks of mutual assistance and the passive complicity of foreign authorities, the exiles and fugitives of the Paris Commune found refuge in neighboring European countries and in America. Their exact number is impossible to compute, given their constant comings and goings within the area forbidden to them;[33] but we can safely say there were between 5,000 and 6,000 exiles, given that 3,313 were condemned in absentia by French courts of justice. Of these, about 1,500 were refugees in Belgium in the early 1870s, accompanied by several hundred dependent wives and children.[34] More than 2,000 communards settled in England; several hundred of these were based in London, where in 1872 a group of them founded the Refugee Society. Switzerland received about 800, half of whom were in Geneva, and a few more were sprinkled around other European countries (Spain, Italy, Germany, etc.). Likewise, several hundred militants emigrated to the United States with their wives and families. From the evidence available to us of their movements as refugees, we may calculate that about 83 percent of them came to rest in New York.[35]

These militants found sanctuary after periods of intense confusion, having left everything behind when they fled France. The lurid legend of the Commune, described in its aftermath by countless broadsheets and articles in the press, did them no favors. Conservatives accused the communards of looting, destroying property, and carrying out summary executions, making no reference to the savage repression they endured or to the pacifism that motivated so many of them. The Commune itself gave rise to a movement of international solidarity, which began even before the Paris insurrection was crushed. Contributions of all kinds arrived as soon as the Franco-Prussian War broke out in the summer of 1870, and later during the siege of Paris in the winter of 1870–1871; some of them were intended to help people in the countryside, others were meant for the revolutionaries in Paris. For example, funds arrived from Sweden that were explicitly reserved for French farmers; everything possible was done to stop these funds from falling into the hands of the communards.[36] Conversely, in Belgium, the militants of the International insisted that workers in Paris should not be forgotten, suffering acutely as they were during the winter siege of 1870. A subscription was launched in April 1871 on behalf of the Paris corporations, with the reminder that in the past they had generously contributed to the financing of the Belgian strikes and to the funds raised for the victims of Seraing and the Borinage. Giving to the Paris workers was presented as a fair return, and a way of compensating for the strong bias of philanthropic charity in favor of the Versailles camp. "Philanthropic appeals have been made; help has been rushed to people in the countryside; but for industrial workers nothing, absolutely nothing, has been done. So it is up to us, as industrial workers, to fill this void and prove that if farmers are worthy of sympathy, the workers of Paris, whose ordeal has been by far the worst of our time, are no less worthy."[37]

The cash raised in the United States was more substantial. Jung in London received and recorded payments into the fund that the general council had created in the month of July 1871 to assist the refugees flooding into England, and out of a total of about £200, more than half (£110) came from militants who had settled in the United States. This money came through so many different channels that the figures officially presented to the general council probably didn't tally all of it. But the amounts published in the newssheets of the International in the United States were in excess of $1,000 (£200), double those recorded for the United States in the accounts of the London refugee fund. Two-thirds of this ($687) were paid over by the five French sections in North America.[38]

Acceptable and Unacceptable Donations

In England, money was raised from the unions and from influential personalities. Karl and Jenny Marx alone contributed over £30 in the form of gifts and loans, some of which originated in Germany.[39] These gifts raised the question of principle, inasmuch as the IWA had always insisted that autonomy meant workers should be able to support themselves by building up reserve funds. But the humanitarian emergency demanded that compromises be made. Contributions demanded such compromises; but from whom should contributions be requested, and were all of them acceptable? There were deeply divisive arguments about this among the members of the Commune, who could not agree on the ideological concessions that would have to be made to keep them out of poverty.

Gifts of money were seldom mentioned during the sessions of the general council, and the gifts that were mentioned almost always came from anonymous donors. For example, Jung declared that he had received a gift of £40 (1,000 francs) in February 1871 from a member of the association who would rather not reveal his identity. Likewise, Karl Marx recorded a gift of £50 (1,250 francs) received in September 1871 from a friend whose name he also could not divulge. These substantial sums show that the IWA had a few generous benefactors that it was unwilling to expose. One detects a willingness to maintain a degree of secrecy concerning the inequalities of private wealth that existed within the association along with a concern not to allow this to damage its egalitarian objectives or otherwise bring it into conflict with the law. The arrival of so many refugees forced the association to launch a campaign to raise more money, however, including from influential personalities whose names would be made public this time, because they were openly speaking out in defense of the Commune. The general council even sent a delegation to the House of Commons to collect money from figures who were known to be favorable to the workers' movement.

A number of personalities contributed to the refugee fund, notably some of the English "Positivists" who had been watching the development of the International with approval since 1864; and whom Karl Marx (as usual) viewed with deep suspicion.[40] These were the only individuals who came directly to the assistance of the refugees. Among them was Edward Spencer Beesly, a professor at University College, London, and the founder in 1857 of the London Positivist Society, which had supported the English workers' movement ever since the building workers' strike in the early 1860s. Beesly himself had acted as honorary president of the inaugural meeting of the IWA in September 1864. There were also Frederic Harrison, a lawyer and man of letters who had supported the construction workers in 1860–1861 and participated in the 1867 royal commission investigating the finances of the trade unions, and other prominent figures such as Richardson, Charles

Dilke, and Hugh Williams, who contributed funds and publicly supported the cause of the Commune in the United Kingdom.[41] The contributions of these men were even more essential when the appeals launched among the English working and middle classes produced mixed results, throwing not only Engels but also a number of representatives of the British unions into a passion over the lack of empathy shown by their compatriots: "No more assistance could be got for the refugees from the middle class, and it was necessary to try what stuff the working class was composed of. He [Engels] thought the working class of England had behaved in a disgraceful manner; though the men of Paris had risked their lives, the working men of England had made no effort either to sympathise with them or assist them. There was no political life in them."[42]

Elsewhere in Europe, help for the communards also depended on the involvement of wealthy individuals. This was the case of Charles Beslay, a veteran republican militant born in 1795, who had been the Commune's delegate to the Bank of France before escaping as a refugee to Switzerland. James Guillaume described him as providential for the refugees, on account of the many donations he made to them. Although his bourgeois origins might have made him an object of suspicion, his actions in helping the exiles and refugees were deeply appreciated. Beslay paid due homage to the Commune while at the same time calling for a reconciliation between the people and the bourgeoisie through the association of work and capital.[43] Later, toward the end of the 1870s, a character like Louis Bologne, a bookseller and former member of the Commune, stood out for his generosity toward those who had been banished. His liberality was so great that he aroused the mistrust of several militants, who suspected him of being an undercover police agent trying to buy people's confidence the better to entrap them.[44]

The role of these wealthy personalities — who were few and far between — was a crucial question for the former communards.

Was it possible to accept donations indiscriminately, without selling out? For example, could they accept the compassionate help of those they had fought so bitterly, without abasing themselves or disavowing the cause? In general, the refugees felt they ought to expect help from within the working community alone, and money coming from figures outside the movement was frowned upon. There were political ways and means of turning down donations, when the more ideologically inclined militants were afraid of falling under the influence of benefactors. Some money was unacceptable: there were social and moral lines that could not be crossed without weakening the entire movement.

In the 1870s this problem several times became critical for the London contingent of exiles. Impoverished and desperate though they were, some of them flatly refused to take donations of doubtful origin. A meeting of support organized in London to coincide with a conference given by the freethinker and radical republican Charles Bradlaugh was hotly debated at the general council: the refugees refused to touch the money collected on this occasion, on the grounds that the orator had not only attacked Karl Marx but had also criticized the Commune.[45] According to them, no charitable gesture could be disassociated from ideological engagement. The interventions of Adolphe Smith and Victor le Lubez were required before the exiles could be convinced to put aside these reservations; they were reminded that the funding had come from English workers and to refuse it would be an affront to them. The Refugee Society was damaged by this episode, twenty-two of its members preferring to resign rather than benefit from funds raised by a meeting that was hostile to their own struggle.[46] The general council, which was running a number of initiatives to raise money, reacted with circumspection. In spite of all this, the refugees could rely on the understanding of John Hales, who considered that "they refused it as Bradlaugh's money and accepted it as being given by the working class."[47]

A second affair shook the London exiles in June 1872. One of their members was accused of accepting gifts from an English aristocrat, with a clergyman acting as intermediary. The religious function of this man and the charitable nature of his act were furiously denounced by those militants who were proud of the lay work done by the Commune in Paris and remembered the violent battles they themselves had fought with the church.[48] The purity of the communards' struggle obliged them to refuse these donations, which would signify a revival of the church's power over their rebel militants. Moral integrity was more important than material comfort: "Our principles are far above the puny details of our lives and they should take precedence over all else. The Commune fought against the priesthood, it had the heads of the clergy shot. No fusion and no transaction is possible...the well-being of the exiles was of only secondary importance," wrote Zéphirin Camélinat, another member who was present at the time.[49]

So it was better to persevere as an ascetic militant than to be in thrall to erstwhile enemies. Transfers of money were also vectors of a social relationship and of a quest for dignity; a few years later, when a raffle was organized on behalf of the deportees of New Caledonia (a Pacific archipelago annexed by France in 1853 and transformed into a penal colony), the origin of the lots donated for prizes was questioned and debated. Even the donations of moderate republicans were refused, because they came from personalities who favored the conservative French Republic and its institutions. In the eyes of the extremists, this was a matter of honor and self-respect; no bending of the rule could be tolerated and no exception to it allowed. This sensitivity to the moral implication of cash donations also cropped up in other countries that had taken in banished communards. When the Swiss refugees found out that one of their number had visited the Rothschild family to ask for money, their reaction was instant: "The refugees should ask nothing of their enemies and begging for M. De Rothschild's money is no different to proffering the hand of friendship to Maréchal Mac-Mahon" (president of the nascent Third Republic, and a conservative of monarchist leanings).[50]

Conditional Assistance

This intransigence was all the more astonishing in that each new account of the wretched poverty of communard refugees in London, Brussels, Geneva, or New York was more dismal than the last. Observers were horrified by the penury of the militants and their families: "These men are dying of hunger. Some of them have had to sleep in parks and we must remind ourselves that they sacrificed everything and have been reduced to their present condition after fighting bravely for their principles." Jenny Marx described the deplorable condition of many of the refugees on their arrival in London in the summer of 1871, as did Prosper-Oliver Lissagaray in his *Histoire de la commune de 1871*, which praised their still unsullied dignity. Help was urgently needed, and for many it was to be sought within the International, its sections, and its general council. To start with, it came in the form of personal assistance — some meals and a bed for a few nights. In Brussels, the refugees were looked after by Brismée, an influential figure in the Belgian general council; in New York, they received assistance from the French-speaking Republican Union and the IWA and were given lodging by a Swiss militant, Constant Christenert, until such time as they could support themselves adequately. In London, Karl Marx himself took in a steady stream of refugees and was tireless in organizing help for them.[51]

The distribution of aid in cash began in the month of July 1871, only a few weeks after the collapse of the Commune. At the end of June the general council opened a refugee fund administered by Jung, who had the task of handing out support money to militants who applied for it. The amounts distributed quickly dwindled as more people arrived. In the first weeks, the London refugees survived on 15 shillings a week. On 29 July, thirty-four of them received ten shillings each, a total outlay of £17. After that, the aid was reduced to seven shillings a week per person.

This influx not only forced the council to reduce its subsidies, it also made it necessary to inquire about the identities and honesty of the new supplicants, some of whom had come out of nowhere.[52] Solidarity could no longer be based on personal acquaintance; refugees were arriving in droves from all over Europe, and their identities, the part they had played in the Commune, and their relative wealth had to be checked. These precautions annoyed the refugees, who felt they had a right to expect unconditional help without hindrance by procedures that they found fussy and tiresome. The obligation to appear in person at sessions of the general council to receive their aid money was viewed as particularly tactless and insulting; they felt the immensity of their sacrifice deserved better. Moreover the members of the council took care to obtain information on the past behavior of individuals who presented themselves as refugees. Attempts were made to circulate information between Paris, London, and Geneva, with a view to understanding where these people came from, whether their stories were credible, and how exactly they had made their way to England.[53]

These difficulties, coupled with a rapid reduction in the amounts of the indemnities paid to them, fueled the refugees' discontent. They were already furious with the general council and disgusted by the lack of solidarity shown by English workers. The refugees, no doubt spurred by rumors of the IWA's fabulous wealth, expected far too much of the spontaneous solidarity of militants all over Europe. The reputation of the Commune was not good, in particular among British unionists who were still aghast at the violence they had read about in the press. The address written by Marx entitled *La Guerre Civile en France* precipitated a break with some of the more influential trade unionist leaders, who were irritated to see their names published, without their permission, beneath Marx's manifesto.[54] The refugees' disappointment gave way to anger in the summer of 1871, when they demanded an accounting from the general council, which they suspected of unfairly distributing the money it had raised.[55] The intense media coverage of the wave of solidarity for the refugees created a discrepancy between the funds that were supposed to have arrived (which had been announced with much fanfare) and the actual receipts (which were considerably less). Marx acknowledged, as did others, that inflated figures had sometimes been declared "to encourage others to subscribe." Thereafter, certain refugees who mistrusted the general council attempted to circumvent it; among them was Georges Melotte, who wrote directly to the Belgian council for help, going so far as to demand more money for himself than for his fellow exiles and claiming that he deserved higher payment for his service. Of this the Belgians took an extremely dim view.[56]

In the end, fatigue and mutual misunderstanding led to a parting of the ways. Marx became heartily fed up with the constant barrage of invective against the general council and the claims of the Commune "beggars" of a right to total financial support. Differences of opinion on the basis and breadth of solidarity burst into the open: though some saw solidarity as an unconditional right, others thought it could not be detached from criteria that guaranteed the solidity of relationships within the International, by way of careful procedures for identifying militants and weighting assistance according to the needs of each. The Belgian Alfred Herman shared Marx's skepticism, and moreover, with no residual compassion for the martyrs of the Commune: "To hear them talk, it would seem that the International is obliged to feed, lodge, clothe and supply them with the means to laugh and get drunk." The pressures were such that a decision was finally made to entrust a refugee committee with the task of distributing aid and to do what it could to sort out the contradictory claims being submitted. Jung ceased to pay money to individuals and instead transferred much larger sums to various leading exiles (Ernest Teulière, Albert Theisz, Zéphirin Camélinat, and Lucien Combatz), who were given the responsibility of sharing them out. In this way it was hoped that tensions would subside and the refugees could be left to settle their differences among themselves.[57]

Ultimately, these misunderstandings, combined, put off the last donors who might be tempted to give to the exiles. The funds voted ought to have provided temporary assistance to the refugees, who should then have gone on to look for work, learn English, and live off their own earnings. Instead the situation became bogged down, and peoples' attitudes changed radically toward the militants who had been helped. Engels criticized the refugees' want of commitment, although Jenny Marx understood why English employers were reluctant to give them jobs. Harrison complained that he had given advances to refugees that were never repaid; nor were the press articles they had promised him forthcoming. In 1872 he told the Refugee Society that he would provide no further advances and offer manual labor only. Thus the end of cash funding by the IWA made it possible to control the way help was deployed, while encouraging the French exiles to get back to work. According to one police informant, Harrison and other English defenders of the Commune were so depressed that one of them declared he "never suspected the party could contain such a throng of ne'er-do-wells, good-for-nothings and swindlers: if I had to repeat the exercise, I would do strictly nothing for them."[58]

These problems — and its own lack of funds — led the IWA to look for other, cheaper solutions. In December 1871, Jung suggested that the refugees could be helped to emigrate to the United States, while others spoke of colonizing New Caledonia with communard deportees. The prospect of seeing the backs of some of them was welcomed with relief, and in 1873, when a group of them announced their departure to join the communist revolutionaries in Spain, subscriptions were opened to pay for their voyage.

Departures for Cuba, New Zealand, and Latin America were also mentioned: these had the double merit of lightening the moral and financial burden of the help provided while exporting revolutionary ardor to other continents.

REFUGEES FENDING FOR THEMSELVES

The exile community continued to tear itself apart over money for the rest of the decade. The omnipresence of financial controversies derived from the ultra precarious circumstances of some of its members, and the central position occupied by the management of money in the political discussions and practical objectives of the international socialist movement. The 1860s idea was that the group was all the stronger and its solidarity more steadfast for pooling its resources, working out how to use them, and building mutual trust, but this was difficult to apply within the context of exile. The quarrels about money may have had personal, collective, and ideological undertones, but above all, they offered a chance to reassess the behavior of everyone under the Commune and to question choices and attitudes that might have betrayed the original ideal and weakened its supporters' resistance to the forces of Versailles.

The inequalities prevailing among the exiles were perpetual sources of conflict, duly relayed to the government by police informants against a background of generalized rumor and distrust. Money and its uses were bound to cause tension, especially when some of the refugees, who were themselves content with little enough, made it a point of honor to remain *solidaire*, even in adversity. Any member of the exile community whose style of life seemed unusually comfortable might be suspected of misappropriating funds or otherwise dishonestly enriching himself. A general suspicion paralyzed the practices of solidarity and collective management of resources. The members whose duty was to collect funds and supervise subscriptions were also viewed with distrust, and accusations of stealing subscription money were made not only against the general council itself but also against communard veterans. A case in point was that of the *blanquiste* Émile Dodot, who in June 1873 was summoned to explain how he had disposed of some money he received from Geneva. In 1874, the exiled Poles in London were powerless to prevent their treasurer from making off with money at a time when their society was heavily in debt.[59] Behavior like this weakened the worker societies and was a cause of great anxiety even for battle-hardened militants like Frankel or Vésinier, who deplored the decline of collective solidarity.

The politicization of financial subjects was all the sharper for bringing back memories of the Commune. For several years, erstwhile members attacked some of their former comrades, with the intention of assigning blame and explaining the failure of the movement. Even though solidarity was still strong among the exiles, acrimony was creeping in. The spectacle of inequality among the refugees — some managed a good deal better than others, either because they found work or because they had special support from outside — led people to chew over past events and question the integrity of fellow exiles. Investigations were launched against anyone who had handled public funds in 1871, notably François Jourde (delegate to the Ministry of Finance), Charles Beslay (delegate to the Banque de France), Gustave Durand (head cashier, public treasury), André Bastelica (director of indirect contributions), and Zéphirin Camélinat (director of the mint). In the spring of 1872, Vésinier took this initiative, one year after the collapse of the Commune, just as the refugees were settling into their life of exile. The subject was highly sensitive, especially in regard to the use of Banque de France funds, which Beslay and Jourde had preferred not to requisition: indeed they were furiously attacked for this throughout the next decade (1870–1880). Both men vigorously defended their policy of prudence, notably Jourde, who was brought before the Conseil de Guerre in August 1871. Their wish, which they fully assumed, to restore credit to France by depending on the Banque de France rather than confiscating its funds came in for savage condemnation. This renunciation — which showed, on the contrary, that some of the communards were attached to the respect of contracts and institutions — was never forgiven. Accusations against the two men were redoubled when Marx and Engels took them up a few years later, feeding a myth that persists to this day that the Commune could have hung on if only it had seized the money in the Banque de France.[60]

Indeed anyone who had had anything to do with the management of the Commune's finances was a target for denunciation, sometimes justified, sometimes not. Rumors that communard "looters" had made off with huge amounts of cash were all over the Paris newspapers. General Émile Eudes was accused of pawning items he had seized from the premises of the Légion d'Honneur, while Auguste Viard, former delegate to the Ministère des Commerces et aux Subsistances was believed to have arrived in London with 300,000 francs in cash. The atmosphere was such that the refugees spent their time comparing their living conditions and searching for suspicious departures from their standard ascetic norm. It was said that Jules Andrieu lived a high life that could not be explained by the income he earned from teaching. In 1872 the committee of inquiry into cases like his proposed to investigate any refugees who were "today in a financial position bearing no relation to the resources at their disposal prior to 18 March 1871."[61] Refugee groups in the United States were torn by the same dissensions: the brothers Gustave and Elie May were suspected of enriching themselves under the Commune and of having mishandled the funds of a subscription organized for the families of victims of the Commune. After an inquiry, they were expelled from the association.[62] Social and professional differences between the communards, with some having skills they could use and others not, sharpened jealousies and resentments that were a long way from the ideal of unity and militant detachment. The disenchantment of the 1870s once again made wealth a criterion for militant legitimacy, as though the idea that some should live in relative comfort and others in penury was unacceptable.

Peer Pressure

Social conflicts and inequalities led to the adoption of strict conditions of access to some of the societies funded by the refugees, whether their goal was political or social. The same kind of mistrust that existed between the general council and the refugees, also existed among the refugees themselves. The Social Studies Circle founded by them in London prescribed that all new members should submit to a process before they could be admitted: each candidate had to be of good standing, approved by more than two-thirds of the assembly, and backed by two sponsors.[63] This was very different from the unanimity of the early days, when anyone claiming to be a supporter of the Commune could claim assistance by appealing to international worker solidarity. By contrast, the better integrated members of the exile community did the opposite; they went ahead and reestablished clear distinctions between those accused of sponging off the community and those who were self-supporting as well as morally, politically, and professionally virtuous. Their dogged determination to keep control of all this shows how the refugees internalized the need to give their group credibility along with political and financial ballast. Their aim was much more in step with the first intent of the militant communards, who valued the emancipation and independence of all their members. Stronger engagements with the rest of the community would palliate their reputation as beggars and lessen their dependence on outside donors and the networks of the International, which after 1872–1873 had dried up anyway. Solidarity coming from the outside was no longer sufficient; funds had to be found within the exile community itself, and this meant working to a clear and effective set of rules.

The imposition of such rules, however, as a prior condition for defining a sphere of solidarity made up of rights and duties was bitterly resented by those who feared a resurgence of a police state like the Second Empire. Their purpose was to limit solidarity-based groups of individuals, excluding those whose means did not allow them to engage fully in mutual help societies by paying regular dues. The advocates of stricter rules used arguments similar to those deployed by the members of the International in 1871–1872: solidarity could never be a one-way street; the right to receive help came with a duty of responsibility, and former communards were not spared that duty. The motto of the Society of Refugees was an appeal to both assistance and work. Besides, workers who valued their independence would never dream of living at the expense of the community. In Geneva, a society entitled La Solidarité provided cash assistance, expecting to be repaid when its beneficiaries found jobs. This ideal of reciprocity was crucial, because the refugees were constantly on the move from city to city; they had a right to expect help, on condition that they belonged to a society to which they had themselves paid membership dues.

Basically, all these efforts were aimed at stopping benevolent people from handing money to refugees with no strings attached, which was tantamount to charity. Likewise, it was felt that regular attendance at sessions of the society promoting mutual aid and the appearance of actively looking for work were both necessary if refugees' independence and dignity were to remain intact. The same values were applied to mutual loans (*prêts mutuels*) by the Brussels society, which sought to resurrect the projects of collective emancipation that had flourished during the 1860s. Gradually, credit was coming back into favor. In London, in March 1872, the Social Studies Circle went so far as to ask its members to endorse a loan of £25 in lieu of directly distributed cash assistance. The development of financial practices like this was taken as evidence of an economic, moral, and symbolic renewal among the refugees, after the misery they had endured in 1871–1872.[64]

This new philosophy, more cautious and more focused on individual responsibility, led to a change in the way collected funds were managed at a time when every penny counted. The funds of La Solidarité (the society established to help exiles in Geneva) were deposited in the workers' credit bank (the Banque du crédit ouvrier). In London, the money raised for the New Caledonia deportees was also placed in an interest-paying account. These new practices may have allowed treasurers to duck criticism, but they were still viewed as inexcusable concessions to capitalism by hard-core militants, for whom banks and interest-bearing loans were anathema. The *blanquiste* Bernard Landeck, an exile in London, made this money a matter of principle, excoriating the subscription committee on behalf of the banished communards for using a bank account to manage it. This raised material and ideological issues; Landeck, for one, thought it a vile betrayal of the autonomous dream of the Commune and the International, to profit from the services of a capitalist institution.[65]

Proletarian Philanthropists

The most surprising thing about this was how former militants of the Commune were brought around to embracing some of the most emblematic methods of bourgeois philanthropy, within a context of great social urgency. Confronted by a serious lack of money, the refugees clamored ever more loudly for generosity and mutual help. Door-to-door and individual collections were organized on behalf of penniless families, following political meetings and festive reunions. Concerts were arranged in support of militants in real difficulty, as in Brussels where funds were raised for the children of a militant who had fled to America in October 1877. Before a concert or a dinner, tickets were distributed among the exiles to make sure enough money would be raised. Conferences were given by famous figures from the Commune, and these worked well. Gatherings of exiles plunged into militant socializing, political discussion, and mutual help activities. Objects and souvenirs were sold, such as portraits of Théophile Ferré or Eugène Varlin, for the benefit of the Commune's deportees.[66]

Crucially, the aid supplied to the communards and the New Caledonia deportees made it possible to try out methods borrowed from philanthropy. Suffering, even at one remove, strengthened links with fellow militants banished to the far side of the world.[67] Over four thousand communards had been deported or transported, some condemned to forced labor, others to incarceration in fortified prison colonies, others simply to exile in a foreign land. The successful escape of several exiles (among them Henri Rochefort, Paschal Grousset, and François Jourde) brought attention to the plight of the deportees and shocked international public opinion. When they disembarked in San Francisco, Rochefort and his companions were helped by French militants in California and were given money raised by subscription. They then crossed the United States, holding conferences and giving interviews as they went. This ploy caught the world's attention: the organization of "remote" solidarity was galvanized as soon as the American and British newspapers seized on the wretched conditions in which the deportees in New Caledonia were living.[68] The arrival of Rochefort's fugitives in London a few months later set up the cause of the deportees as a fresh solidarity imperative for the exiled community; militants embraced it in the hope of sinking their differences while preserving the memory of the Commune. After all, there were comrades on the other side of the world who were a lot worse off than they were and outright philanthropy was clearly the remedy best suited to the urgent, immediate distress of the deportees.

The communards in London then took the initiative of launching a permanent subscription for their brothers languishing in

New Caledonia, with the idea that it might achieve among communards the same success that the Catholic Church had achieved with its "pennies for the Chinese" campaign. Moreover, a financial connection like this would maintain existing moral and political links until combat could resume on the political battleground. This was the emotional and humanitarian register that underpinned the quest for funds to help the deportees: "Everyone should set aside one sou per week, starting now. But instant momentum won't suffice; we need to supply steady assistance, not a flash in the pan. So let there be individuals and committees in every city working to gather contributions and send them to us, let there be auctions, lotteries and conferences for the cause."[69]

The promoters of the permanent subscription did not conceal the philanthropic inspiration of their gesture. For them it was a way of defusing the suspicion of the police authorities: by placing themselves in the register of fraternal assistance, they hoped their action could be rendered banal, void of any sign of protest or political intent. The investigators, ever anxious that mutual aid activity might be a cover for subversion or conspiracy, did not let down their guard. The reestablishment of a long-range connection with the Caledonians gave credence to the idea of an international network with multiple ramifications, capable of linking militants across frontiers and oceans. Once again, subscription lists were sent to the main clusters of exiles in Belgium, Switzerland, and Paris, where *collecteurs de quartiers* could be relied on to bring in funds. The operation was placed under close surveillance by the refugees themselves, given the highly sensitive nature of anything to do with money or accounting at the time.

The result of the first round of the appeal, though not exactly spectacular, was encouraging. In London, the equivalent of 3,000 francs was collected in 1874, and a further 1,000 francs the following year.[70] After that, the permanent subscription dwindled and other methods had to be found to stoke people's generosity. In

July 1877, to the disgust of militants known for their loathing of the bourgeoisie and their charity, it was suggested that a raffle should be organized to help the deportees. Various well-known personalities donated lots as prizes for those with winning tickets. Once again a controversy arose as to whether a genuine communist could accept gifts from any quarter without selling his soul; and more precisely, whether such gifts could come from people who had been all too forthright in their attacks on the subscription committee. Militant generosity was also a serious bone of contention, around which personal quarrels and ideological differences continued to fester. Donations came in, all the same, from Switzerland (via the Jurassian Federation), and from Germany (via Liebknecht), while prominent figures such as Gustave Courbet contributed paintings and other works of art. The lots were put on show in London, as much to encourage subscriptions as to disarm members who were complaining loudly about the time all this was taking. Finally, the long-awaited raffle was held; it yielded about 20,000 francs, a sum surpassing all previous subscriptions (but only because of a huge donation of 5,000 francs by one single individual, Louis Bologne).[71] Tickets were bought in countries as far away as the United States, Brazil, Switzerland, and Canada. Nevertheless, the operation ended in failure: its organizers had rashly announced the sale of sixty thousand tickets, which was unrealistic. To make matters worse, on 18 October 1877 the Paris *Figaro* led with an article criticizing the raffle and raising doubts not only about the informers who had supplied its information but also about the use made of the funds and even the integrity of the committee that had collected them. Above all, the organizers failed to present winning ticket holders with the lots contributed by private donors, which were valued at about 25,000 francs. All in all, by the end of the 1870s, the exile communities looked to have lost their edge; fatigued as they were by the many demands made on them, they were quite incapable of contributing significantly to any more solidarity initiatives.

Nor did material obstacles make the success of the deportee subscription any easier. Long-distance help required that militants transfer the funds they received with reasonable efficiency, in the certainty that they would reach their destination. They also had to allay the concerns of the authorities, who might suspect there was another escape attempt in the offing. At the meetings of the subscription committee, those in charge were regularly questioned about the networks they would use to transfer the funds; since they had to be discreet for fear of losing their contacts, they revealed next to nothing to reassure potential donors. Disasters accumulated: in 1875, the transfer of a sum of £100 to the Caledonians failed completely to arrive. It reached Sydney, Australia, without difficulty, but the correspondent who was supposed to carry it from there to New Caledonia suddenly died. His widow sent the money back to London where Jourde, who had run the finances of the Commune and was himself an escaped deportee, decided that it should be "lodged in a bank till things take a turn for the better."[72] The most prudent course was to fall back on financial services the militants had once rejected.

Occasional suggestions that the civil and military authorities might be used to expedite funds were roundly dismissed. To avoid arousing suspicion, it was decided that donations in kind should be sent instead of cash — shoes, tobacco, and clothing, for example. This obviously limited the use the convicts could make of the aid, but its humanitarian value was reinforced. In consequence, a case filled with merchandise finally reached the Ile des Pins in the fall of 1877. It had been expedited through the good offices of the Ministère de la Marine, which appalled the more intransigent communards. Landeck said he would have preferred to give cash to the widows and orphans of the Commune rather than accept so craven a compromise with the Republic; but his position was rejected by the members of the subscription committee, who were concerned not to change the destination originally intended for the donations it had called for.[73]

This raffle experience illustrates the contradictions with which the refugees had to wrestle, and the philanthropic expedients forced upon them by their poverty. The requirement of solidarity remained sharp, because it was one of the conditions for the survival of the militant group. Nevertheless it was contradictory and a source of division. A world-weary informer concluded that it was all up with the entire project, which was now too hollow to be realistic: "They'll send forty or fifty francs to Paris... in return they'll receive a grateful letter dripping with praise for the stouthearted-ness, spirit of 'solidarity' and devotion shown by the citizen refugees of the Commune. And so on. They'll just go on performing the usual cartwheels."[74]

Returns from Exile and Competitive Solidarity

He was right. In the late 1870s the mood of the communard exiles was one of lassitude, even exhaustion. The prospect of a partial or total amnesty was all they could think about.[75] After 1877, moderate republicans were in the majority in France and were busily marginalizing conservative forces. Many among them had been hostile to the Commune and to the radical socialism it embodied, but now the time had come for a reconciliation; it was clear that the socialist workers' movement had been rudderless ever since 1871 and had ceased to be much of a threat. It was not until 3 March 1879, however, that a first partial amnesty was voted by the Third Republic, to be followed by a full amnesty on 11 July 1880. At this point the way was opened for the communards to return to France, from wherever they happened to be: London, Geneva, New Caledonia, and elsewhere. Nevertheless, they were far from done with conflicts linked to the exercise of solidarity. Their arrival in France instantly started a squabble between the fiercely independent veterans of the Commune and the moderate bourgeois republicans who had campaigned for their amnesty.

Two committees were responsible for helping the refugees coming back, and they were at loggerheads from the start.[76] It was a confrontation between two models, one predicated on republican bourgeois charity, the other on socialist worker solidarity, equality, and mutual respect. These tensions had been present throughout the 1870s, but the actions of the aid committee looking after the convicts' families — coordinated by Jean Greppo, a deputy for Paris and a municipal counselor — particularly enraged the exiles.[77] They strongly objected to the priority given to the families by the committee, while exiles and deportees were left in grinding poverty. They were concerned that this charitable action masked a republican attempt to cover up the outrages committed by their forces during the 1871 repression. Moreover, they viewed the decision of the Paris municipal council to fund this committee as contentious in the extreme.[78]

Next, on 6 February 1879, there was an outcry in London following the creation of a centralized aid committee, sponsored by Victor Hugo and Louis Blanc, to help the amnestied communards. With the backing of prominent individuals and the Paris municipal council, this committee set about raising funds that were substantial beyond any comparison with the Communard group's own meager contribution. Between February 1879 and July 1881, the committee gathered more than 300,000 francs to assist 3,352 amnestied militants. Food and clothing were distributed, and efforts were made to find work for them.

The more politically active refugees went on to define their own socialist aid committee on behalf of their comrades, amnestied or not, emphasizing class solidarity over the charitable paternalistic tilt of the republicans. The emotions mobilized by these rival committees were thus markedly different: the former appealed for empathy, class reconciliation, and benevolence, while the latter attempted to reactivate militant solidarities. Their aim was to thwart the discourse of fusion and appeasement, on the grounds that it threatened to dilute the memory of the Commune and euphemize the vicious killings that had taken place.[79] Their rivalry burst into the open on the arrival of the trains bringing the exiles home to Paris, when members of the two committees assembled on the platform and fought each other to shake hands with the returning martyrs.[80] The aid they eventually distributed was split between republican integration and reconciliation, on one hand, and socialist determination to perpetuate the memory of the workers' Commune through solidarity, on the other.

The circles within which the two subscriptions were launched were very different in scale and produced very different results. The socialist committee struggled to collect 30,000 francs, in other words one-tenth of the amount assembled by the so-called bourgeois committee (which included an extra 100,000 francs contributed by the Paris municipality). Militant intransigence came hand in hand with financial difficulties; militant solidarity affirmed its principles loud and clear but could not match the unifying logic behind the republican subscription, which was supported by the ordinary people of the Paris arrondissements. This was a major issue at a time when the socialists in France were trying to regroup under the aegis of Jules Guesde, and afterward around the leaders who had returned from exile, such as Jean Allemane, Benoît Malon, or Paul Brousse.

The socialist committee launched its appeal "to all socialists, given that solidarity is not an empty word: every one of them must bring his contribution, and participate by every means possible in the work of reparation and justice now under way, which will only be confirmed on the day that a full and complete amnesty shall have become an accomplished fact."[81] But as far as the police were concerned, the true motive behind this initiative was something rather different: "It seems that the organizers of the committee were above all concerned, beneath the veneer of a humanitarian endeavor, to regroup, and meet frequently to discuss all political and social questions to which the events of the day might lend a topical interest."[82] Humanitarian aid continued to be seen as a cover for political action; the two registers were merged, in a demonstration that politics did not end where solidarity began, because solidarity made possible the building of a collective, the strengthening of links, and the affirmation of real autonomy.

The fact was that the paroxysm of violence that annihilated the Commune had tested the reality and effectiveness of militant solidarity to its limits. Compassion, however sincere, confirms the irreducible distance between benefactors and the people they help. Donations reflect and magnify an existing hierarchy, at the same time creating resentment. The IWA had proclaimed the advent of universal worker solidarity; the year 1872 revealed an internationalist world that was ever more divided. The English trade unions and the wealthy donors who had agreed to support the cause of the communard refugees were now at a loss for words to describe the refugees' abuses, laziness, and dishonesty. The refugees countered by denouncing the hypocrisy of the International, which they accused of abandoning them. These tensions all flowed from a disagreement about the nature of the aid that should be given. For some, it was a one-off, temporary thing, justified by the exceptional circumstance of a wave of repression flooding across Europe after 1871. But for the communards, solidarity was something to which they had a right; and that right stemmed from the sacrifices they had made on behalf of the entire workers' movement. At the same time, they could not bear to be locked into the role of assisted persons, incapable of looking after themselves. Such contradictions explain why, after a few months, aid to the refugees became for everyone involved a subject of tension, not communion.

All this came into the open when the IWA, crippled by ideological bickering, suspicion, and power rivalries, self-destructed at the

Hague Congress of 1872. Marx and Engels proposed that the general council be transferred to New York, rather than see it fall into the hands of their enemies or emptied of its substance by people advocating an international worker federation with no center and no command. The rival organizations of the general council and the Jurassian Federation of Bakunin and James Guillaume staggered on until 1875–1876. At that point, almost nothing remained of the links of solidarity that the workers of France, Germany, Switzerland, Austria, and the United Kingdom had forged with such difficulty in the years since 1864.

And yet the disappearance of the International as an institution did not erase the practices it had tested and developed. They survived.

PART TWO

The Years of Consolidation

5 | THE REVIVAL OF INTERNATIONALISM

The experience of the First International ended in blood and dissension, and its failure was of a piece with the hopes it had aroused. Even so, the links of solidarity established between 1860 and 1870, the contacts made, and the networks patiently woven continued to exist in ways that were semi-clandestine and all but invisible. The Italian historian Maria Grazia Meriggi has called this the period of "International relations without an International."[1] Some of the initiatives rehearsed at the time of the IWA, such as financing foreign strikes or helping oppressed comrades, survived to show that its networks of solidarity would last the course; the militant and relational capital built up by the IWA had not evaporated overnight. Despite the fierce determination of the authorities to eradicate all memory of the International, there remained an array of habits, achievements, bonds of trust, and friendship, all of which were ready to be reactivated the moment the pressure of the authorities began to relax.

The 1880s were a decade of transition, with an ideological, economic, and sociological context that profoundly transformed the world of European workers and their attitudes to international collective action. At this time, the construction of socialist and syndicalist movements was mostly carried out on a national basis, while a general economic crisis fueled protectionist tensions over trade and migration.[2] Despite this, worker militants did not abandon the project of international entente, which in 1889 was reborn in institutional form with the creation of the Second International at the Paris Universal Exhibition. The rapid progress of a second wave of industrialization, the globalization of financial flows, and the growth of transatlantic migration were modifying the shapes and contours of worker solidarity. Little by little, the balance of forces on which the IWA had been built was called in question by the growing implication of the masses in politics and social struggle. All over Europe a new form of union activism was emerging, based on the participation of heavy industry's unqualified workers and on new counterbalances to the ideological and financial domination of the British trade unions during the 1860s. The Europe of mutual support and solidarity no longer amounted to an asymmetrical relationship between qualified workers in London and their counterparts in Europe. The world's advance into an age of mass unionism was catching up with its British exception: America, Germany, and the Scandinavian countries were emerging as new bastions of worker struggle and as models of organization that could be exported in their turn.

THE STRENGTH OF WEAK TIES

Despite its failure, the IWA had a lasting influence on the careers of the militants who had been involved with it. The International continued, even in adversity, to sustain their dreams and projects of coordination for the socialist workers' struggle. In this sense, the tenuous links it had helped to forge survived its dismemberment.

Militants under Surveillance

In the 1870s, the annihilation of the Commune led to a dramatic tightening of police surveillance over the militants of worker internationalism. Whenever militants made contact with people in a foreign country, the fact was interpreted as a resurgence of the International, which terrified the governments of the time. Even after its official disappearance in 1876, police authorities remained obsessed with the International: the merest hint that it might be stirring again was a matter of deep concern.[3] The activities of the refugees were closely watched, as were those of the militants and the leaders of the Jurassian Federation. Police analysts perpetuated the use of the notion of "the International" to cover a wide variety of political tendencies.[4] Gradually, as the term *Internationale* began to be used in reference to existing contacts between European anarchists more than to trade union or socialist movements, the existence of those links became more doubtful. On several occasions, police informers erroneously reported a refounding of the International, most notably in July 1881 when anarchist militants converged on London to form a (completely ephemeral) International Worker Alliance.

For a while, the repressive 1872 legislation adopted against the International managed to hold in check the reactivation of cross-frontier links. The crippled French socialist movement did not begin to recover before the end of the 1870s, by which time the Republic was secure enough to vote a Commune amnesty into law. The French militant Jules Guesde returned home from exile in Switzerland in 1876, having maintained relations with the German socialists Bebel and Liebknecht, who themselves had been under heavy police surveillance ever since their trial in 1872. It was Guesde's ambition to turn his newspaper *L'Égalité* into an organ for the entire proletarian International.[5] Following its congress in Lyon in February 1878, the Workers' Party reconvened a Socialist workers international congress in Paris the following September. The anxiety of the French authorities about this was extreme — so much so that the meeting was banned by the Interior Ministry and thirty-nine of the congress organizers were arrested, prosecuted, and tried for taking part in an illegal association of more than twenty people. The trial caused a sensation, and Guesde himself was fined 200 francs and imprisoned for six months. Despite the ban, the list of foreign personalities invited to the congress was proof that the network of relationships set up by the IWA was still intact: among them were several Belgian militants (Désiré Brismée, César De Paepe, Eugène Steens) and a number of prominent figures from the English trade union movement (Eccarius, Hales, and others).[6]

The repression of the time, which isolated networks and closed the narrow window of toleration that had been opened in the late 1860s, grew even tougher in Germany in 1878 with the adoption of Bismarck's first anti-socialist law after his abandonment of *Kulturkampf*. The chancellor hoped this move would marginalize the social democrats who, in 1875, had joined forces with the followers of Lassalle and condoned their party platform, the Gotha Programme. But far from weakening German social democracy, the legislation helped it take root and increased its electoral weight. The movement's newspaper, *Der Sozialdemokrat*, was published in exile outside Germany, first in Switzerland and then in London. Historians of German social democracy claim that Bismarck's laws actually strengthened the party's capacity for action by galvanizing what they called an authentic "organizational patriotism."[7]

Thus the trap Bismarck had set for German social democrats backfired spectacularly, unleashing waves of solidarity in Europe and on the other side of the Atlantic. International cooperation was forced on the defensive, within a generally repressive context. Italian internationalists, like the German ones, were arrested or forced into exile after their attempted insurrections of 1874 and 1877. But demonstrations of support for the German socialists were held from 1878 onward in Belgium, France, Italy, and Austria-Hungary, raising funds to help the social democrats with election campaigns in which they still had a right to take part.[8] German emigrants, embedded in many countries and still true to the cause, rallied to the call. In 1878, donations came from the USA (4,000 deutsche marks), Switzerland (1,100 marks), Belgium (1,200 marks), England (600 marks), and France (400 marks). Support came from the same pools that had contributed in the late 1860s, when Johann Philipp Becker in Geneva mobilized the German-speaking worker communities of several European countries. There was also an overwhelming new response from the USA, which showed the growing importance of European immigration; links were particularly strong with North America, where emissaries were sent in 1881, followed by Liebknecht himself in 1886. Funds to help with elections flowed steadily into Germany throughout the 1880s; these reached a high point with the elections of 1890, in the last year of serious repression. Thirteen thousand marks were received from abroad at that time, including funds from Brazil and Argentina. The results obtained by the Sozialistiche Arbeiterpartei (over 1.4 million votes, one-fifth of the total votes cast) showed the extent of Bismarck's legislative debacle.

Diminished and repressed though they were, in the 1880s German social democrats made it a duty to help other striking European workers — whether they were in France, Russia, Poland, Italy, or Denmark. The repressive context of the time did not stifle solidarity. On the contrary, it sustained a proven model of militant fraternity and encouraged acts of reciprocation, whatever the political and legal situation in which worker militants might find themselves.[9]

Ineradicable Traces

When the members of the International helped one another in the late 1860s, they were convinced that the links of solidarity they were creating would have long-term effects. The high-minded declarations they made when they sent out donations and loans were partly illusory, and the implosion of the IWA soon confirmed this. These experiments, fragile and one-off though they may have been, did not disappear overnight; the connections built up at that time only depended on a small part of the institutional framework created by the association. Individually and collectively, the practice of solidarity forged reciprocal links that were both durable and reusable. The people involved acquired skills, knowledge, and mutual trust in one another that could eventually be redeployed in other circumstances. In this sense, the experienced crew of the IWA did not sink with it. The contacts they had fashioned were anything but ephemeral. Indeed, they were the first steps in a process that would later become a planetary movement.

Certain prominent figures later made themselves into "professionals" in the field of worker community relations. One of these was the militant Zéphirin Camélinat, who for a long time served as a regular intermediary between the French and English trade union movements. He began as a member of the delegation sent to London in March 1867 to raise funds on behalf of the Paris bronze workers. Later he was exiled to London and then to Birmingham, having been the director of the Paris mint under the Commune. In Birmingham he joined a trade union as a member of the local section of the Amalgamated Society of Engineers, where he formed friendly working relationships. These he maintained after his return to France in 1882.[10] Camélinat's qualities as a manager and accountant and the fact that he was one of the few leaders whose reputation emerged untarnished from the collapse of the Commune made him the ideal choice to organize the affairs of the bronze workers' union in Paris in the 1880s. Furthermore, his international support networks and his mastery of several languages fitted him for the role of French delegate to workers' congresses in other countries. He was present at international exhibitions in Amsterdam (in August 1883) and Boston (in 1883–1884); in Boston he used the occasion to hand over funds raised by Paris workers to help the tobacco workers of New York, reviving links of solidarity among skilled workers from the IWA years. The goal of his delegation was to leave behind it "ineradicable traces, through the establishment of international relationships between workers of all nations."[11] Camélinat was a hugely appreciated figure on account of his past as a militant bronze worker, internationalist, and trade unionist. His engagement in favor of international cooperation made him a strong proponent of understanding among workers of all nations. He also supported the establishment of international labor laws, which he proposed in December 1885 shortly after his election to the French Parliament.[12]

Individual links like Camélinat's were backed up by solid contacts between worker communities. The minutes of meetings of the London Trades Council show that the disappearance of the IWA did not interrupt either the sending of written requests for help or the dispatch of delegations from the continent. Some professions, which were by now thoroughly accustomed to dealing with their English counterparts, continued to apply for help as if nothing had happened. The makers of Limoges porcelain, who had already staged a strike in 1864, returned to the charge in 1883 and received £50 in aid funds. Likewise, workers in Vienna (1879) and in Roanne and Lille (1882) also successfully appealed to English solidarity.[13] Meanwhile, English trade unionists continued to visit the continent in hopes of discouraging worker migration to Britain. After his first visit to Belgium in 1871, James Cohn returned there in 1877 to defend the cause of the stonecutters and marble workers then on strike in London. Memories of the Newcastle strike six years earlier, on behalf of which the tobacco workers' leader had made the same trip, were still fresh when he arrived.[14] Later, in 1886, the Decazeville strike in France received generous international and British support.

So, beyond the International and right up to the turn of the century, links of mutual assistance survived among skilled professions. They rested more on local solidarities than on relationships between organizations on a national scale. The bond between the lace workers of Calais and Nottingham was very much a case in point. The establishment of the mechanized lace industry in France stemmed from a transnational connection, after the first tulle machines were brought there from England — and from Nottingham in particular — during the first decade of the nineteenth century.[15] The two lace manufacturing centers, French and English, continued thereafter to maintain professional and family links on either side of the Channel. Work conditions, wages, and price variations were constantly scrutinized and compared between them, and any time a dispute arose with employers, English or French, efforts were made to coordinate claims in both Nottingham and Calais. Thus a Calais lace worker, Georges Hazeldine, who was related to a union leader in Nottingham, was sent to England to seek financial aid for a strike in 1890.[16] On this occasion, two delegations were heard by the LTC, which then agreed to issue a letter of credit.[17] The local press in Nottingham provided day-by-day coverage of events in Calais, and the French workers received serious assistance in the form of £257 (6,425 francs). This supplied only a small percentage of their needs — a week's half pay for four hundred strikers — but it certainly helped.[18]

Ten years later, in 1900, a fresh strike broke out in the Calais area, in protest against long working shifts that exceeded twelve hours a day. Jean Jaurès considered this dispute to be highly symbolic in the struggle for an eight-hour day. Twenty-two hundred workers downed tools and were locked out by the employers in a reaction that directly affected a population of fourteen thousand people, including the workers' families. The activation of cross-Channel solidarity was immediate: Camélinat was called in, as usual, to plead the cause of the lace makers before the Trades Union Congress, the LTC, and the London Chambers of Trade. The secretary of the Amalgamated Society of Lace Makers provided decisive support by accompanying the French delegation and afterward collecting the funds contributed by the trade unions.

In December 1900, the committee of the TUC published an official circular in support of the Calais lace makers.[19] The attitude of the French industrialists was denounced, and the workers' stand against it applauded; for the French lace makers had taken care to organize themselves officially as a trade union and, as such, had framed their request for mutual aid. In the eyes of the TUC, the adoption of the English model was a guarantee of their seriousness and credibility.

Shortly afterward, a representative of the TUC arrived in Calais with an initial check of 10,000 francs to reassure the strikers that their English counterparts were behind them. The language of reciprocity and moral debt was, as usual, a central feature of all this: the long-standing relations between the communities of Calais and Nottingham were celebrated, as was the help the French lace makers had given to the English engineers in 1897, with a collection made for them every seven days over a period of several weeks. Concerned as they were to show themselves equal to this generous gesture, the English workers responded three years later by using the same practices that had prevailed in the 1860s: in addition to an immediate donation of 1,500 francs, the lace makers of Nottingham agreed on a loan to their Calais colleagues of 25,000 francs, financed by an exceptional weekly subscription of £50 (1,250 francs). This aid was augmented by a contribution of 22,500 francs sent by the Amalgamated Society of Engineers.

All this money made the secretary of the French union of lace makers overconfident. In the belief that his reserves were inexhaustible, he engaged his troops in a long, attritional strike. But the funds at his disposal — about 296,000 francs, with 107,500 coming from England and barely 10,000 from French unions sources — were still not sufficient for a strike on such a scale, and this quickly became apparent as payouts shrank from 15 francs per striker, per week at the start of the dispute, to three francs in the third month of the strike. According to Léon de Seilhac (a researcher from the Musée Social, a conservative think tank created to study social and industrial issues), the money from England actually fueled a conflict that the workers had no real hope of winning. Solidarity from abroad could only supplement local or national mutual assistance, which was indispensable to the success of any such major industrial action. The lace makers, whose wage levels were much higher than those paid in other industries, were seen as privileged by other French workers. De Seilhac, suspicious of the solidarity shown by the English unions, went so far as to suggest that their help was not as selfless is it seemed, given that the prolonged French strike allowed the English to sell their own products more readily and compete more effectively with the Calais lace manufacturers. According to this conservative and pseudo-impartial reading of the case, British solidarity was no more than a ploy aimed at securing a greater share of the lace market.[20]

However, the lace makers' strike does show beyond doubt that the practice of mutual assistance among skilled workers persisted well beyond the era of the first International. Help was even channeled from England to new recipients: in 1891, British funds were sent to striking print workers in Berlin, adding to the list of special relationships already in place with certain communities in France. The same solidarity was shown to textile workers in St. Petersburg and Belgian carpenters in 1896, Hamburg dockers in 1897, and Danish workers in 1899.[21] The sums in question during the 1890s were also substantially larger: the German printers received £3,440 from the English unions, and the Danes over £3,000, so it is clear that the methods first used in the 1860s were broadening considerably during the second wave of the industrial revolution.[22]

Finding a Common Language: The Congresses of the 1880s

The way mutual help and exchange steadily continued to function showed that their methodology would last. Even so, there was no certainty that the movement could go further than acts of solidarity, pick up the stray threads of internationalism, and develop an altogether more ambitious project based on shared ideology and objectives. The gradual relaxation of police surveillance in the 1880s enabled contacts to be reestablished; and though the old links of solidarity had not completely disappeared, ideological divisions and national confrontations were the cause of deep concern, notably among British workers alarmed by the rising tide of collectivist socialism. Whether they involved trade unions, socialists, or anarchists, the international worker congresses of the time tended to replicate the tensions that had led to the IWA's demise, by relentlessly exposing the practical and ideological drawbacks common to all internationalist projects.

The first outlines of an organized international union appeared in the late 1870s. Following a congress held in Ghent in September 1877, a group of former members of the IWA general council who were still at odds with the authorities (Eccarius, Hales, Jung, Mottershead, and others) founded a short-lived International Labour Union.[23] On the other side of the Atlantic, an organization of the same name but differently spelt — the International Labor Union — rallied American syndicalists and former internationalists (notably Friedrich Sorge and Eugène Dupont) with the aim of defending the interests of unskilled immigrant workers. However this project's scope of action remained confined to the east coast of America.[24] Another congress was planned for Paris in 1878 but was prevented from convening by the authorities. After this, the LTC — which had fully expected to send a strong delegation to the French capital — reconsidered the feasibility of an international meeting to bring together the various syndicalist movements of Europe.[25] In the end it was not until the early 1880s that militants were again able to work together like before, and even then it was much easier for some than for others.

In July 1881, a group of anarchist militants gathered in London, hoping to rebuild some kind of new International. To do so they had to overcome many obstacles, in particular the grip of governments on postal services throughout Europe.[26] Ostensibly the intention of its forty-three delegates (among them Pierre Kropotkine, Louise Michel, and Errico Malatesta) was to re-create an international body of sorts; but not surprisingly the IWA experiment was viewed with horror by the heirs of Bakunin and the Jurassian Federation, who preferred "propaganda by the deed."[27] In 1883, at the next anarchist congress at La-Chaux-de-Fonds in Switzerland, a proposition to create an international assistance fund was firmly rejected, but not before it had opened some old wounds. The Swiss militant Georges Herzig opposed the idea of an international fund that, he said, would "paralyze propaganda by the deed." As far as the anarchists were concerned, accumulating funds from workers' savings was a waste of energy and resources, a useless distraction with little relevance to the revolutionary ideal. Indeed a number of speakers were more inclined to rob and hang the bosses instead of "asking workers to hoard reserves of cash, like a bunch of accountants."[28]

Debates about European solidarity and genuine forms of social and political action were more likely to take place within the various networks of syndicalist and reformist socialism.[29] Reformist and syndicalist worker congresses were held in Coire, Switzerland, in 1881, in Paris in 1883 and 1886, in London in 1888, and then once again in Paris in 1889, where two meetings took place, one syndicalist and reformist, the other collectivist.[30] During these years, former members of the IWA acted as facilitators. For example, a star turn at the Paris Congress of 1883 was Jules Joffrin, a member of the IWA and a key figure of the communard exile community in London who had also appeared at Coire with Benoît Malon. On several occasions in his speeches, Joffrin recalled the solidarity shown by British workers toward French refugees in the early 1870s. The delegations sent to Paris in 1883 were mainly French and English, with a smattering of representatives from Italy and

Spain; three years later these were joined by militants from Germany, Austria, Belgium, Sweden, and even Australia.

In addition to the ideological differences among their participants, these congresses had to cope with ways of debating and acting that were sometimes widely different. Reporting back to their respective organizations, the English delegates sent to Paris in 1883 and 1886 were critical of the conditions under which the meetings were held. It amazed them that no fees were paid at the entrances of the meeting rooms, and that delegates were not expected to produce printed credentials.[31] Furthermore, the Paris voting rules were bitterly contested between a minority who favored one-man-one-vote, in conformity with the internationalist ideal, and a majority who preferred one-nationality-one-vote, thus prioritizing national over individual disagreements about basic issues and methods.[32] These organizational quarrels, which were inherent in the practice of internationalism because of the many disparate worker and syndicalist cultures involved, were made worse by linguistic difficulties. Worse, the need for interpreters tended to make the debates drag on interminably — which was no help to mutual understanding.

During the 1880s, the English trade unionists were basically alarmed by the growing clamor of socialist demands. The three English delegates sent by the TUC to Paris in 1883 (Alfred Bailey, John Burnett, and Henry Broadhurst) were all moderates; predictably enough, they were outraged by the revolutionary tenor of the speeches they heard.[33] They also deplored the conciliatory approach of continental militants to state intervention, which went against their deepest convictions about the majesty of self-help and worker autonomy in organizational matters. But it was the sheer amateurism of their continental partners that worried them most. Their fire was mostly concentrated on the inability of French syndicalists to collect funds, which was apparently total, as stated in a report of 1887:

So far as we have been able to observe, this characteristic self-abnegation and pecuniary privation has no permanent existence in the Continental conception of Trade Unionism. Let us hasten to make clear that we do not insinuate that Frenchmen or Germans are less brave or self-sacrificing than ourselves in a national cause, but we have not noticed that they have yet exhibited these qualities in the cause of Trade Unionism. It has been seen from the report presented to the trades by the deputation which attended the International Congress in Paris in 1883 that there existed great difficulty in getting French workmen to regularly make effective contributions to any permanent trade society, and, so far as we are aware, this difficulty still prevails.[34]

Some of the French militants were irritated by the patronizing tone of all this and duly lost their tempers. The anarchist Joseph Tortelier, a carpenter by trade, replied to the English that they were making a serious mistake if they thought French workers were not as good as they at finding solutions to social questions. People would always operate as their national temperaments and habits dictated. The Englishman, with his cold character, might reach his goal by moving slowly and methodically; "but we French get more done, more rapidly than you do."[35] The speeches of the English seemed lukewarm to the French militants, whose anti-capitalist positions were much more pronounced. They turned against the English their own claim to organizational superiority, scoffing that the Anglo-Saxon obsession with scrupulous money management was the direct consequence of an intellectual and political compromise with liberalism. The cult of organization was conservatism under a different name — to such an extent that the trade unionists sounded as prim and priggish as their liberal Victorian countrymen. Moreover, the two camps extravagantly overplayed their antagonisms: one side represented the pragmatic English trade unionist approach, obsessed by cost-effectiveness and coddled by social conservatism, while the other stood for French revolutionary lyricism, incapable of organizing effectively but always ready to harangue crowds and perorate from podiums.[36]

Many militants attempted to mitigate these divergences so as to keep afloat the ideal of international cooperation. This was noteworthy in the case of Adolphe Smith (aka Smith Headingley), who worked as the official translator during this series of congresses. Smith did everything he could to iron out differences and convince his English comrades that their feeling of superiority was ill-conceived and wrong.[37] Yet the minutes he supplied for international meetings tended to stray from the neutrality officially required by his role as a translator as he strove to reassure the British and keep them inside the circle of worker Internationalism. Smith acknowledged that the French unions were "weak in funds and in discipline."[38] That said, he urged British trade unionists not to oppose the reestablishment of international contacts out of simple ignorance of the progress made by other workers on the European continent. According to him, France's innovative Fédération des Bourses de Travail offered an example worthy of interest. In his desire to reassure everyone, Smith also validated a tendency to categorize social behavior according to workers' nationality, which would differ according to the "race" of the various groups concerned: "Though it is true that the Latin races do not pay their subscriptions regularly, this is not the case with respect to the Flemish, Dutch, Scandinavian and German workmen," he wrote.[39]

The 1888 London Congress was a missed opportunity, largely because the German, Austrian, and Russian socialists were not represented. The English organizers, who were heavily criticized for this lapse, explained that the rules of trade unionism forbade them to admit delegates from the ranks of the bourgeoisie. Only French, Belgian, Italian, and Danish delegates were present, notwithstanding the loud protests that this provoked among the participants themselves. This absence was explained by the strong internal tensions then affecting British trade unionism. The boy-cott of socialism had become steadily more contested within the English movement, notably since 1881 and Henry Hyndman's creation of the Democratic Federation (which changed its name to "Social Democratic Federation" three years later).[40] The elites of the TUC were attacked by militants who denounced their limpness and egoism. Thus the international congresses were not only opposed to national sensibilities: they also provided an opportunity for internal dissidents to make their voices heard before crowds of foreign militants, a tactic that shook the power then held by the "aristocrats" of the TUC.[41] The German social democrats, even though they were absent from this meeting, were delighted by the decline of the moderate elites within British trade unionism, which was bound to strengthen their own position in the galaxy of European socialism and trade unionism.[42]

The two congresses held in Paris in July 1889 confirmed these divisions. On one side were the *possibilistes*, who included French reformists, moderate socialists of the Social Democratic Federation, syndicalists, and trade unionists. On the other side were militants of the German and Belgian socialist parties, as well as the Marxist-leaning followers of Jules Guesde (known as the *Guesdistes*). Close links between the French and the German delegations made possible the creation of a Second International and a glimmer of hope for a new phase of institutionalization. Yet there were basic disagreements galore over theory and methods; the debates at the two meetings were also markedly different in tone. The *possibiliste* congress was mainly concerned with international work regulations and the need to set up international information offices to promote interaction with foreign countries — all without re-creating an International central committee, which was deemed "too dangerous."[43] By contrast, the *collectiviste* congress, which ultimately generated the Second International, depended on socialist parties that were built on a national base — nineteen nations were represented — with a clear political and electoral strategy at their core.[44]

THE NEW WORKING WORLDS

During the 1880s, the revival of long-distance international contacts and solidarities could no longer rely on methods developed twenty years earlier. The working worlds of Europe and America were undergoing profound changes in their composition, their modes of organization, and their social demands. Geography and the balance of power in Europe were modified for the duration, as new layers of labor and industry emerged, transatlantic exchanges intensified, and new and more powerful poles of unionism emerged in Germany and the countries of Scandinavia. The world of worker solidarity, formerly dominated by British trade unionism, was broadening its spheres of action to embrace the new technical possibilities and new models for syndicalist action opening up on the continent.

Internationalism and Protectionism

After 1873, the growth of nation states and colonial empires, along with mass migration from the European interior to the United States, offered new challenges to the European labor movement. The post-1880 phase of intense globalization of economic and financial relations exposed a number of paradoxes. Mass migration facilitated long-distance relationships and the circulation of ideologies, but it also aroused xenophobic reactions and national antagonisms. At the same time, financial liberalization was accompanied by a raising of customs tariffs everywhere — except in the United Kingdom — that in turn accelerated economic nationalizations. In the final decades of the nineteenth century, the parallel phenomena of a world opening up and societies distilling into nations effectively reconfigured worker internationalism and shifted its centers of gravity. In a word, globalization was a piece of luck for the cause; again paradoxically, the huge challenge of nationalism and the advent within each national space of policies of social and commercial protectionism, offered rich opportunities for *internationalism*.[45] This dual dynamic explains why, right up to the outbreak of the First World War, questions of migration featured so strongly in socialist and syndicalist debates on the definition of solidarity.

Although it did not exactly choke off worker activism, the intermittent economic crisis rendered the unions vulnerable. The use of strike action was obviously less prevalent in a period of slump.[46] But while economic conditions were unfavorable to the expression of worker demands from the mid 1870s to the mid 1880s, at least they forced the invention of new forms of action. The great British trade unions — whose power and reputation depended primarily on their ability to raise huge financial resources — floundered in this economic climate. Obliged as they were to pay benefits to large numbers of workers stricken by the crisis, they no longer had the means to pay for a policy of generous assistance to every striker who applied for it. The economic model — and the credibility — of the Amalgamated Societies were thus seriously compromised; henceforward, a relative decline in the weight of British unions in actions of international aid can be explained by the obstacles met by traditional organizations in adapting to a straitened economic context. This in turn fed an ambition to build a new mass model of syndicalism, designed to force major social reforms on such issues as work hours or the provision of basic collective benefits.[47]

The toxic mix of migration and rising nationalism stirred sharp debate in Europe and the United States. Labor unions, just like states, viewed migrant workers as straight-up unfair competition, especially when they steered resolutely clear of mainstream worker organizations. Statistics from the period reflect a spectacular increase in migrant worker numbers: at the turn of the twentieth century, more than a million men and women a year were arriving in the United States, a country from which Chinese immigrants had been officially barred ever since 1882. Within Europe, the largest numbers of foreign workers headed for France, flocking there from Belgium, Italy, and eastern Europe. The immigrant question had changed both shape and scale: no longer was it a matter of managing trickle migrations from neighboring countries, as had been the rule in previous decades. The issue now involved massive and durable movements that sorely tested the capacity of unions to represent all workers, regardless of their nationality.[48]

Not surprisingly, the legitimacy of international worker migrations was a key topic for discussion at worker congresses from the 1880s right through to the outbreak of the First World War. The principal of worker mobility was not questioned, except in the event of strikes or lockouts.[49] Nevertheless, it worked more to the advantage of incoming migrants than to the detriment of workers already present. The 1883 Paris Congress acknowledged this unequivocally: "With respect to the use of foreign workforces in any country, the International Conference…above all invites workers looking for jobs in foreign countries to accept the working conditions established by the local and national trade unions of those countries and by no means to accept work for wages that would devalue indigenous work to the exclusive advantage of employers."[50] At the next congress, which was held in Paris in 1886, the Belgian militant César De Paepe — formerly a leading figure of the IWA — stressed that the migration question had changed in scale since the 1860s: the international circulation of manpower was now part of the international organization of capital, and capital would feed competition with low wage levels should wage levels not be structured to reflect strong social demands. This went way beyond controlling migrations to and fro across the English Channel, an objective that the First International had sought to promote via exchanges of information and dispatches of English money. From now on, the challenge was to operate on a global scale, taking account of the gigantic movements across the Atlantic and Pacific Oceans — and especially from China to the United States. According to De Paepe, union coordination was not sufficient to regulate economic migration; in the new "world republic" he envisioned, only the adoption of international legislation would make it possible to mitigate the worst effects of migration.

Yet the racially biased "Chinese question," which was a growing concern for workers from 1880 onward, by no means obscured the danger inherent in short-distance migration.[51] The Belgian militant Édouard Anseele declared at the same debate that, depending on the scale at which one studied the problem, Belgian workers could be called the "Chinese of Europe" if one compared their wages with those of English workers. The globalization of capital, work, and migration raised issues that were at once inside and outside Europe (every worker was somebody else's Chinese migrant), but the objective of improving wages and work conditions lent further justification to conflicts that were both local and international.[52] In 1891, the question of anti-Semitism, then rampant in eastern Europe, was raised at the socialist congress in Brussels where the majority of delegates felt it was pointless to adopt an official condemnation of something so omnipresent in the world of work. The British trade unions were concerned that there was an obvious link between shrinking salaries and the arrival of "multitudes of Jewish workers expelled from Russia." Yet their general disapproval of anti-Semitism did not prevent them from acknowledging its role in local issues affecting wage levels and social change in London's East End.[53]

Calls for the adoption of an international regulation of migrations were not unanimously welcomed by workers' parties and unions, many of whom were reluctant to entrust the state with the business of establishing standards for wages and social protection.[54] At the 1880s congresses and at the meetings of the Second International, pride of place went to workers' unions, whose task it was to integrate foreign workers and help them take an active part in the struggle for social justice, instead of staying marooned on the margins of industrial wage-earning communities. The program of the Marxist workers' party, drawn up by Guesde and Paul Lafargue in the early 1880s under the direct influence of Karl Marx himself, recommended "a law against employers hiring foreign workers at wages lower than those paid to comparable French workers." Thirteen years later, the resolutions of the 1896 socialist congress in London invited unions to open their ranks to foreign workers, specifically to stop them accepting salaries lower than those of locals; for only the unions would be capable of imposing such collective discipline as would function on behalf of all, no matter what their nationality or their place of origin.[55]

In practice, this was far from simple. The British trade unions were regularly accused of slowing the integration of foreign workers, by reason of their vise-like financial strictures — which also excluded a major segment of their own unskilled, impoverished industrial proletariat.[56] In France in the 1880s, it was more or less customary for workers' unions (unlike the socialists Guesde and Jaurès) to support proposals for a tax on foreigners.[57] Prior to 1914, lines of battle were drawn between militants trying to protect the national workforce against competition from foreign workers, on one hand, and on the other, militants who believed in the primacy of an internationalist project that would bring everyone together as allies in the collective struggle, irrespective of their national or racial origin. In the United States, the immigration question and the integration of African Americans profoundly divided unions and socialists, some of whose organizations became outright protectionist despite their seemingly internationalist discourse.

Atlantic Crossings

The difficulty encountered by European syndicalists in weathering the crisis of the 1870s, and afterward in picking up the threads of internationalism, coincided with the affirmation, in the United States, of new worker organizations for whom international action on migration had become an absolute priority. During the 1860s, western Europe had been the focal point on which internationalist worker aspirations had been concentrated, but the IWA's transfer of its headquarters to New York in 1872 and, above all, the rapid growth and organization of the American workers' movement between 1870 and 1880 combined to reshuffle the cards. London was no longer the epicenter of internationalism, because international solidarity had also become a necessity for huge numbers of American workers. The waves of migrants from England, Ireland, Germany, and Scandinavia, and then from southern and eastern Europe, were not always favorably received in the USA at a time when Americans themselves were mobilizing to defend their wages and fight for an eight-hour day.[58] Just like the support given to European workers by the English trade unionists in the 1860s, the support American organized labor gave to the immigrant newcomers was far from disinterested. Organized labor was ready to help workers in other countries strengthen their capacity for organization so as — if possible — to discourage them from emigrating to the New World. Thus, on a grander scale, the intensification of solidarity exchanges on both sides of the Atlantic reignited the same difficulties the IWA had formerly experienced between England and the countries bordering the North Sea.

One of the most influential union movements in the United States at the time was the Noble and Holy Order of the Knights of Labor, a secret society founded in Philadelphia in 1869 by nine garment workers. Within a few years this organization had become a major driving force for international worker action, more especially after the great railway strike of 1877, which caused panic from Baltimore to Chicago and San Francisco by convincing employers in the industry that they were witnessing the birth of a new Paris Commune.[59] Instead the railway strike marked the beginning of a period of intense social agitation in the USA, which lasted until the late 1880s. By 1885–1886 the Order of the Knights of Labor, which had begun as a small group, counted nearly a million members — including numerous women and Black workers — in the midst of a period that was known as "the great upheaval."[60] Its epic battle with the business magnate Jay Gould, the owner of several American railway companies, was a high-water mark for the Knights, who were well entrenched among the qualified workers of the city centers and the mining industry.[61] Their activism finally led to a wave of strikes and boycotts on a scale never seen before in the USA, whose core demand was the blanket legal adoption of the eight-hour working day.[62]

At the same time, former members of the IWA like Johann Most and Victor Drury, who had emigrated to the United States and were now anarchist fellow travelers, were militating within the International Working People's Association, created after the London Congress of 1881. This was to be the Knights' undoing, when their campaign reached a climax with the famous Haymarket drama in Chicago on 4 May 1886. On that day, a bomb exploded during a peaceful rally for the eight-hour day, killing several policeman and demonstrators. Eight anarchist militants were arrested and brought to trial; four of them were executed in November 1887, despite the weakness of the evidence against them.[63] While this episode certainly influenced the Second International's choice of the First of May for its International Labor Day, it also led to the rapid decline of the Knights of Labor, who were accused — wrongly — of fomenting violence and were brutally repressed by the authorities.

The core mission of the Knights was to defend the condition of established workers in America. For this reason, immigration and the denunciation of contract labor were always central to their demands. The Knights sanctioned the prohibition of Chinese immigrants in 1882 and were far from happy about the disembarkation of masses of immigrants from south and east Europe. On the other hand, they were more open to integrating African American workers and enabling them to play their part in the social struggle. The Knights' biggest problem was how to restrict immigration within the context of a slowing economy that was bound to create bitter competition between wage earners.[64]

Above all they wanted to correct the rosy stories swirling around Europe about the state of the jobs market in America; and for this they had to engage with European labor organizations and make clear the stark reality that awaited immigrants. The policy of "fraternity at a distance" that the Knights implemented was at least partly designed for this purpose, inasmuch as showing transatlantic solidarity would allow them to economize on more immediate, face-to-face encounters with the risk of resurrecting old antagonisms. Thus the international attitude of the Knights of Labor was paradoxical to a degree, given the organization's close association of nationalism with internationalism and its defense of national labor with support for European workers — provided they stayed put, in Europe.

Like the British in the 1860s, the American Knights considered that the best way to discourage immigration was to help European workers to organize themselves, struggle effectively, and in consequence win better working conditions. For this reason the Order tried to establish itself in England, Ireland, Australia, New Zealand, and throughout the vast British Empire as well as in other countries such as France and Belgium. The historian Steven Parfitt thought that this swarming effect justified describing the Order of the Knights of Labor as a kind of "First International and a Half," which could stand in for the vanished IWA until such time as an official international workers' organization could be set up. During the 1880s, the Order was undoubtedly the "most successful international workers' organization in the world."[65] Its ability to project itself was undeniable, as was shown by the emissaries it sent to the

Old World to promote the formation of international professional unions. The Universal Federation of Window Glass Workers was one of these, founded in England in 1884 with the direct support of the Knights, to the tune of 15,000 pounds sterling. The Knights were not content merely to make contact with European unions: they actually sent serious funds to help develop new sections. The roles were now reversed: like the English trade unions, the Knights applied a policy of centralization of human and financial resources that allowed them to release money for international aid projects.[66] Several strikes organized in England on their initiative, in 1888 and 1889, were accompanied by copious subscriptions and promises of help that powerfully impressed employers. The Knights were also sympathetic to nonqualified workers (unlike the Federation of Organized Trades and Labor Unions, then led by the cigar maker Samuel Gompers) whom they exempted from paying the kind of heavy dues demanded by the British trade unions; in consequence the Knights became an alternative model for militants looking for union renewal in the 1880s.[67]

The Knights saw no contradiction between their promotion of universal solidarity and their determination to restrict immigration. For them this was the only way to reconcile worker internationalism and a rejection of the negative consequences of globalization. The export of their organizing methods would contribute to improving the social and economic position of the workers of the Old World, while turning the struggle for an eight-hour day into an authentically transatlantic cause. Although immigrant workers were never directly targeted, immigration as a global phenomenon was severely condemned, especially when it was used by employers as an excuse to cut salaries in periods of crisis. A member of the Knights of Labor, Paul T. Bowen, presented this case without hesitation at the *possibiliste* congress of July 1889 in Paris, when he proposed a resolution condemning all recourse to immigration at times of industrial difficulty.[68] The resolution was unanimously approved; but it remained an object lesson in the sheer ambiguity of international action as envisaged by the Knights of Labor, who believed that being internationalist in a protectionist world was ample justification for compromise with the values of mutual aid and solidarity. Convinced of the superiority of their structures and demands in the industrial society of the 1880s, the Knights viewed solidarity as a possible vector for Americanizing European syndical organizations. However, this ambition was thwarted for lack of money: without funds, proclamations of solidarity stood no chance of winning over the workers of Europe and Great Britain.

The Knights' loss of influence after the Haymarket events dealt a heavy blow to the internationalist cause among American workers. Founded in the early 1880s, the American Federation of Labor (the AFL, as it called itself after 1886) turned its attention to the domestic scene within the United States, in spite of the international links that its leader, Samuel Gompers, continued to maintain with the International Tobacco Workers' union. Always wary of socialism, the AFL was attached to a form of "pure and simple politics" that was deliberately kept void of excessive ideological substance.[69] Its rejection of the radical approach favored by the Knights of Labor was balanced by a much stronger continuity in its attitude to immigration; the AFL supported measures to limit the latter, without perpetuating the "brotherhood from a distance" that had colored the experiments of its predecessors.[70] Samuel Gompers waited until 1909 before attending an international syndicalist congress organized in Paris (see chapter 7). Once again, the leader of the AFL reminded delegates that in the opinion of his union the control of worker migration should be a priority of international worker cooperation, just as the American socialist party had announced two years earlier before the socialist International in Stuttgart.[71]

The New Unionism: A Turning Point

In the 1880s the fading dominance of British trade unionism was challenged not only by internal debates but also by the emergence of a new form of mobilization that further embedded unskilled workers in the world of heavy industry. This was the start of what the British called the *new unionism*, in a time of collective action characterized by a change in the social recruitment of unionized workers. This was made possible by the adoption of a new strategy of mobilization and by the gradual, inevitable acceptance of closer links with socialism.

During the 1880s the conservative stance of the British trade unions was regularly challenged by continental workers at the international congresses. It was also confronted by a new crop of militants who felt closer to socialist ideas and criticized the "aristocratic" character of the trade unions.[72] In 1881 the Marxist Henry Hyndman founded the Democratic Federation.[73] Disputes arose in the ASE, under the leadership of two rising Federation members, John Burns and Tom Mann, who were inspired by the Knights of Labor, their crusade for the eight-hour day, and the agitation they coordinated in the mid-1880s. Rejecting the high-and-mighty attitudes that had prevailed in the trade unions since the 1860s, the new generation openly embraced socialist doctrines, concluding (for example) that clear legislation on work hours had to be a prime objective of the workers' movement. They also criticized the hermetic nature of the British organizational model, which for the last twenty years had been predicated on sky-high membership fees in exchange for promises of generous aid when needed. Burns, Mann, and Ben Tillett, the founder of the Dockers' Union, defended the necessity to integrate new workers into collective action, which meant slashing the dues they were expected to pay.

The leaders of the TUC put up a strong resistance to these propositions, particularly during the national congress of 1887, which revealed deep fissures in the movement.[74] A generational conflict pitted the heirs of the 1860s "junta" — men like George Howell and Henry Broadhurst, whose priorities were the financial power and credibility of the trade unions — against the faction of Keir Hardie and Tom Mann, who favored the better integration of unskilled workers and a rapprochement between union action and socialist struggle. At the TUC congress of 1890, a resolution for the adoption of a law on the eight-hour day caused panic among older syndicalists, who were against state intervention in an area that they believed should be dealt with by union action via intricate adaptations of the rules, profession by profession. Howell, leading the forces of the old unionism against the new, denounced these statist leanings, which he deemed contrary to the spirit of independence characteristic of the English people.[75]

These ideological disputes grew sharper in the years 1886–1890, which saw the development of a whole new set of social issues in the United Kingdom. The rise of the "new unionism" was driven by popular and unprecedented strike movements, which reached layers of society that had hitherto taken no notice at all of mass worker unrest. The original amalgamated chambers of working men were no longer alone on the front line after strikes organized by the Women's Union of Matchmakers (1888), bus conductors, and gas company employees in the East End of London.[76] Each of these was bitter, long-lasting, and amply covered by the newspapers. More importantly, these strikes completely demolished the tradition of cautious strike action, based on careful long-term preparation and limited to qualified, professional male workers. The support of public opinion was growing ever more important, in an era of cheap newspapers offering prompt international coverage of political and social events. New issues such as healthy work conditions or the eight-hour day were now firmly at the forefront of workers' demands.[77]

The great London dockers' strike in the summer of 1889 was a decisive event. Led by Burns, Mann, and Tillett, one hundred thousand workers engaged in a bitter struggle for better wages that entirely blocked the port of London for four weeks between August and September.[78] Strike action was entering its own industrial age; no longer was it enough to provide aid to a few hundred or even a few thousand workers, according to the principle of solidarity founded on the identity of professions. From now on, strikers would fight on a much grander scale, involving tens of thousands of people, with dockers and dockers' families all carrying out different tasks for the cause. Social struggle had ceased to be the privilege of the best organized professions: the newspapers covering the conflict focused on the women and children who had to go hungry for as long as the strike lasted. This new, much more widespread version of struggle duly changed the practices of solidarity: union finance was no longer sufficient, because unskilled workers with limited savings now had to be accommodated along with the rest. The support of public opinion was indispensable, in particular when it came to supplying the strikers and their families with food during their strike.[79] Moreover, the credibility of the movement was closely linked to its capacity to distribute assistance effectively and fairly around the many quarters of the port. And finally, the dockers' success sealed the triumph of a new generation of syndicalists who wanted international action and the mobilization of workers in the sectors of heavy industry (mining, transportation, steel, etc.). Other famous conflicts followed this, particularly in the London district of Silvertown, where three thousand workers at a rubber factory downed tools for three months. This strike further deepened the rift separating the new unionism from the ASE, which was unwilling to support the strikes of unskilled workers.[80] The wave of protest carrying it was due to a significant increase in the numbers of unionized workers, which rose from 750,000 in

1888 to 1,500,000 in 1892. Spectacular though it was, this growth again left many female and unskilled workers by the wayside.[81]

Another consequence of the dockers' strike of 1889 was to show workers the point to which outside help could be useful to the British, who were more accustomed to handing out aid than receiving it. It is important to note that most of the foreign contributions to the British dockers came not from Europe but from Australia; funds from France, Germany, and even the United States were minimal by comparison. Australian dockworkers sent no less than £30,000 from the other side of the world, two-thirds of the total sum raised during the conflict (£48,000) and a record for the time. These funds were raised at meetings, soccer matches, and solidarity drives, supported by national newspapers that alerted public opinion in Australia to what was going on in London. Communication by telegraph also made it possible for the strikers themselves to receive prompt news of solidarity and mutual aid from other countries — and this in turn motivated them to hang on and prolong their strike; moreover, cash support also arrived with dispatch, thanks to improved bank transfer techniques of a kind unavailable in earlier years. The Australian aid effort was roundly applauded by the English press, which showcased mutual aid and the different directions it could take. All in all, the dockers' strike proved the effectiveness of the new syndicalism, which was more advanced in Australia where unions were already well on the way to embracing socialism.[82] This made it possible to maintain regular supplies of aid money and distribute food coupons to strikers, as a complement to the distributions carried out by the Salvation Army.

As usual the solidarity expressed in this way needed to be reciprocal to be fully effective. An opportunity to reciprocate came the following year, when the Australian dockers initiated a social conflict of their own. In a gesture of gratitude, the British trade unions decided to send a loan of £20,000.[83] The London societies rushed to contribute, but the Australian strike was too short-lived for their élan of solidarity to be of use. Besides, the Australians, determined to affirm their independence, politely refused the money and gifts promised by the English. The sums of money transferred through the London Honesty Bank were returned and were subsequently distributed among the various professional chambers. After this, integrated professional solidarity became a potent force throughout the British Empire, which in 1890 made British workers less inclined to strengthen their links with workers on the European continent.[84]

Thereafter, white, imperial solidarity became the pride of British workers. Professional identities played a part in this, along with the conviction that solidarity was all the stronger when it concerned workers who spoke the same language, shared the same skin color, and belonged to the same empire. This form of mutual aid — highly effective in 1889 — represented nothing more than a vector of distinction and the affirmation of a reciprocal and exclusive affinity: "Men of the United Kingdom, Canada and America — bound by ties of blood and of language — arise with giant strength to determine that the cause of our compatriots in Australia shall not be lost. Show to the world by the splendor of example that indomitable courage — which never acknowledged defeat — is still as ever the type of all our race."[85] The great dockworkers' strike marked not only the end of the old unionism but also the first example of solidarity among the white peoples of the British Empire, which was to spread even further in the early twentieth century in parallel with the exclusion of African or Asian workers.[86]

Emerging Poles of Union Activism

While the British were experimenting with the new unionism and the tight links binding them to their Australian counterparts, their hegemony was beginning to falter on the continent with the advent of new poles of industrial action in Germany and the Scandinavian countries. The old British domination, overdependent on affinities between skilled professions and ill at ease with the great ideological debates of the moment, now had to grapple with organizational models that were at once more open and more effective than their own — the forerunners, in a word, of the mass syndicalism of the future. This rebalancing of forces on a European scale had repercussions on the concepts of international worker solidarity of which the Germans were gradually assuming the leadership.

Ever since its first adoption in 1878, the law against socialism had failed to produce the result Bismarck expected of it. Nor had the creation in the 1880s of an innovative system of compulsory social insurance proved any more successful in enticing German workers away from socialism. The social democrats, despite all the obstacles placed in their path, continued to prosper within German society. Although its way of functioning was authoritarian, the German Reich held elections with universal male suffrage and permitted the development of strong oppositions, both socialist and Catholic. The departure of Bismarck after a fundamental disagreement with the new Emperor Wilhelm II, along with the abandonment of the anti-socialist law in 1890, accelerated the process of growing union organizations, in particular the social-democrat-inspired "free unions" (*freie Gewerkschaften*).[87] Already firmly established locally but still widely dispersed, in 1890 the free unions set up a general committee (the Generalkommission) whose headquarters was first in Hamburg, then in Berlin.[88] Its president after 1891, the former woodturner Carl Legien, established himself within a few years as a dominant union figure in Germany. By the turn of the century Legien was a leader of international syndicalism; he was finally elected to the Reichstag as a Social Democratic Party deputy in 1893. Like everywhere else in Europe, free unions in Germany were rife with controversy between members who advocated setting up professional federations and those who envisioned dividing industries into groups; also between those who favored immediate collective action and those who preferred to complete the organizational donkey work before committing to strikes. Legien took the latter view and quickly concluded that the effectiveness of workers' unions depended on their ability to build up structures and resources comparable to those of their German employers.

Looking back at the international congresses of the 1880s, at which the principle of local autonomy was nearly always reaffirmed, Legien saw the centralization of resources and decision-making as the key to success for the union movement. According to him it was not enough for the general committee merely to federate local initiatives: it had to give real structure to the union movement, coordinate its actions, and generate the kind of knowledge that would be useful and positive in defending the interests of workers. One of his major initiatives was the introduction of a union-created statistical resource, with a view to rivaling the state's own knowledge of working conditions, the frequency and duration of strikes and lockouts, and wage fluctuations. This "statistical obsession" was one of the levers for standardizing union action that Legien subsequently attempted to apply on an international scale.

Just as important, for him, was the ability of the general committee to provide itself with a serious budget to support strikes, and thus to send a clear message to employers and public authorities that unions had the means to get what they wanted. Nevertheless, this rational, centralizing vision had difficulty gaining traction. The general committee wasted a lot of money on the Hamburg typographers' strike in 1891, because on this occasion the imbalance between the substantial funds advanced and the paltry income from membership dues generated a debt that it could not repay. Legien solved this problem by adopting the principle of a one-off contribution to discharge all liabilities, alongside higher membership dues that were rewarded by access to various services.[89]

Legien had a dual objective: to create a stringent financial model for trade unions as an essential condition for effective social struggle, which could at the same time be opened to a wider public. This was the dilemma that the English trade unions were having such trouble resolving and that the free German unions would eventually surmount, thanks to their hugely increased numbers of industrial workers at the end of the nineteenth century. A steady growth in memberships and resources combined to leverage their strike power between 1890 and 1900, even though they had to compete with confessional and liberal workers' unions that operated more along English mutualist lines.[90] The example of the typographers' union, which to begin with was seen as a privileged worker "aristocracy" of small importance, was extended to cover entire segments of the new industrial proletariat. Legien's general committee reaped the benefit: now it could count on the annual dues of every union member and also raise exceptional subscriptions for strikes and lockouts. In consequence, its spending soared, from 73,000 marks in 1892–1893 to 1,500,000 marks on the eve of the First World War.[91]

The financial health of the German free unions allowed them to offer their members a broad range of aid and services, just as the old corporations and mutual help societies had once done, from the financing of strikes to the payment of travel costs (*viaticum*), sickness and unemployment benefits, and funeral expenses.[92] The diversity and breadth of the assistance given, which flowed from the substantial dues paid by members, established the unions firmly in the daily lives of ordinary people in such a way that even the extreme centralization of the general committee did no harm to local roots. The experience of the anti-socialist law had a lot to do with this emphasis on help provided by the unions, at a time when the workers needed to protect themselves.[93] This produced the outline of a kind of "total syndicalism," which would take care of every aspect of working life alongside the system of compulsory insurance put in place by Chancellor Bismarck in the 1880s. The unions invested massively in this idea during the 1890s, by having their representatives elected to the boards of local savings banks. Likewise the union presence functioned in neat symbiosis with the "counter culture" maintained for workers' benefit by local sections, libraries, and social clubs of the Social Democratic Party.[94]

Meanwhile, the aspect of conflict and protest was not neglected. Thorough preparation for industrial action was one of the priorities of the general committee, which was kept informed on a weekly basis about the development of strike projects. In this way it was able to piece together basic statistics, unique in the German Empire, on the number and intensity of ongoing social conflicts. The purpose of centralizing information in this way was to give the best possible assistance to movements that lacked money. There could be no solidarity without a regular exchange of information; this idea was crucial to free unions like the German Federation of Metallurgists, which allowed no strike to be launched in the industry without the consent of its federal committee, based in Stuttgart.[95] For Legien too, organization was a prior condition for any gesture of solidarity.[96] Revolutionary enthusiasm and raw emotion could achieve next to nothing unless they were backed by a quasi-scientific understanding of the strengths and weaknesses of the workers' movement.[97]

This new model for mass union action, which retained aspects of the English system while adapting them to the second wave of industrialization, did not entirely sideline the French movement, although it was still far from being able to — or even wanting to — compete. In France the *syndicats* were not officially legalized by the Third Republic until 1884, and it was not until 1895 that the Confédération générale du travail (CGT) was created — nearly thirty years after the foundation of the Trades Union Congress in the United Kingdom and ten years after the foundation of the American Federation of Labor. France's originality in this field lay in its Bourses du Travail (labor exchanges), which coalesced into a national federation in 1892, five years after the foundation of the Paris Bourse du Travail. Although the number of its members was limited, this movement represented an extension of the reach of unions, which in France were kept very much at arm's length by the political parties, unlike in Germany. The Bourses du Travail provided services, found professional positions for job seekers, managed financial aid for temporary workers, opened libraries, and ran evening training courses. The Fédération des Bourses, created in February 1892, even fulfilled some of the functions (notably, the compilation of statistics) exercised by the General Committee in Germany. For Fernand Pelloutier, president of the federation from 1895 onward, the Bourses played a crucial role in "the organization and education of the workers," with the ultimate goal of "reorganizing the jobs market."[98] Their sociological grip was much weaker than that of the British, German, and Scandinavian unions, and above all the Bourses, partly out of principle and partly for lack of means, seldom involved themselves in assistance to strikers, at least in the 1890s.[99]

■ ■ ■

After a phase of lows and uncertainties in the aftermath of the repression of the Commune, the collapse of the IWA, and the economic crisis, international worker solidarity grew to unprecedented levels in the 1890s. By this time, the funds collected and distributed during strikes no longer bore the slightest resemblance to those seen in the 1860s. The symbol of this development was the great London dockworkers' strike of 1889, whose colossal budget was unequaled at the time. The help for the dockers that came from Australia, to the tune of £30,000, caught the contemporary imagination and for good reason. A rapid increase in union memberships, the consolidation of national organizations, and new means of communication via the telegraph, the press, and the bank transfer, all made it possible to raise and exchange funds to support massive strikes with the potential to mobilize tens of thousands of people for several months at a time. In twenty years, the world of worker solidarity had changed completely. The British trade unions were no longer the only institutions that could extend their aid across frontiers. A diversification was emerging at a time when institutional internationalism was entering a slack period, despite the corporative congresses held in the 1880s and the foundation, in 1889, of the Second International, which openly acknowledged the tenets of Marxism. Thereafter a powerful organizational movement dominated the socialist and syndicalist worlds all through the 1890s, alongside a growing participation of the masses in political life and a spate of social unrest. The strike weapon had finally reached a maturity of sorts; now it desperately needed new structures and new procedures for comparison and exchange.

6 | SOLIDARITY AND THE MASSES

A storm was gathering over Europe at the turn of the twentieth century. Everywhere the working masses were organizing and mobilizing into unions, parties, and cooperatives. The workers' movement was no longer marooned on the margins of politics, while anarchist militants sowed terror all over Europe with their "propaganda by the deed." Socialist members of parliament were elected in Germany, Sweden, France, and Belgium; strikes proliferated, reaching a paroxysm in the years 1905 to 1912. In the United States, social agitation continued unabated despite the decline of the Knights of Labor. The Pullman strike of 1894 in Chicago brought down a bastion of industrial paternalism. Even though no great political victories were won, American socialist leaders like Daniel De Leon or Eugene V. Debs (who ran several times for president at the head of the Socialist Party of America, founded in 1901) were careful to build up links between socialists and syndicalists, in stark contrast to the "pure and simple politics" of the AFL, which remained stuck in the logic of professional unionism. Finally, in 1905 a revolutionary internationalist organization emerged in the United States, with the creation of the Industrial Workers of the World (IWW).

The end of the economic depression restored confidence and hope to workers both male and female, who coordinated campaigns across frontiers for such causes as the eight-hour day and the six-day week (with Sundays off). Meanwhile the numbers of union organizers and strikers increased beyond measure; the option of repression, which the authorities continued to use in France — notably at Fourmies in 1891 and at Villeneuve Saint-Georges in 1908 — provoked general outrage. Important social reforms began to be secured from the 1890s onward, and from these evolved the first forms of social protection, the right to work, and a formal recognition of the political rights of workers. In the United States the progressive movement, allied with independent social reformers, called for a regulation of capitalism and a general improvement of the condition of the working classes. All this was directly inspired by what was going on in Europe at the time, particularly in Germany.[1]

The massing of worker action depended on a parallel movement: the organizing and structuring of syndicalism internationally. It was no longer limited to skilled artisans united across frontiers, it also affected workers in heavy industry such as miners, dockers, transport workers, and textile employees. Now more numerous and better organized than ever before, workers were more likely to emphasize their class identities, even though their corporative allegiance remained fundamentally important too. Because of this, the strikes affecting every country in Europe took on a fresh dimension: henceforth they were to involve tens of thousands of strikers for several months at a time, under the persistent scrutiny of international public opinion. Local and transnational solidarities became essential tools of social struggle: the metaphor of *war*, so often used at the time to describe this new type of conflict, implied that thousands of workers and their families would need to be protected from extreme poverty and hunger. The organized power of employers had to be matched by an equally powerful force, able to systematize international solidarity within the workers' movement.

AN INTERNATIONAL OF TRADES

The resumption of economic activity in the 1890s coincided with a relaunch of institutional internationalism. Possibilities for a much broader fabric of connections were opening up to workers all over Europe. The Second International, although it widened the rift between political parties and unions, accompanied the creation of new professional federations that extended the scope of older associations of skilled workers.

A Law of Evolution?

After 1889, every congress of the Second International spawned a series of corporative, parallel congresses. International professional federations multiplied between 1890 and 1914: there were twenty-eight of them on the eve of the First World War, of which twenty-four were headquartered in Germany, reflecting the worldwide predominance of German syndicalism.[2] As structures they were light and flexible, taking the form of offices or secretariats whose main purpose was to facilitate exchanges of information and coordinated actions. Their composition and their geographical location varied in function of the profession or industry they represented. The spread of such federations, with differing statuses, geometrical compositions, and headquarters, reflected the diversity of economic and social realities on the ground; no monolithic institution, imposing a common framework on every sector of activity, could ever do that. Their multifaceted model answered specific industrial considerations that necessarily took precedence over national and interprofessional ones.

For many contemporaries, whatever their political views, the formation of international professional federations was more the result of a spontaneous process than of social conflict or a growing awareness on the part of the workers. Union members saw this process as a natural expression of the solidarity between workers of the same profession, transcending national frontiers and cultural differences. In this sense, trades and professions symbolized belonging and solidarity in their most basic forms. International professional federations attracted fellow workers to one another who had probably shared the same experience of employment; hence their individual struggles meshed together. Liberal internationalists used a rhetoric that identified similarity as the crucible of solidarity.[3] Seen in this way, solidarity was the logical, inevitable consequence of a similarity of conditions. In his widely translated book *L'Entr'aide* (1902), the anarchist Pierre Kropotkine, whose political background could hardly have been more extreme, wrote that solidarity stemmed from a natural evolution leading all living things to cooperate with each other. He welcomed a world in which altruism would become the rule, popularizing the idea that the groups of workers most likely to succeed would be those who united to help one another.[4]

In trade union terms, many saw this development as a counterpart to the internationalization of economic life, migration, and labor reform; indeed, as a kind of symmetrization of the international coordinating capacities of capital and work. The champions of liberal internationalism were thrilled by the spectacle of professions organizing themselves on a European scale. They hoped that globalization would harbor its own forms of regulation and saw no trace in it of class conflict or of an emerging internationalization of strike action; rather, they treated it as a spontaneous and logical evolution toward international understanding, indeed as a rationale for the whole process of economic globalization.[5] As far as they were concerned, an international organization of workers untainted by ideology or partisanship would be no more than a stage in the unstoppable march toward universal understanding.[6]

This rush of optimism seems poignant in the light of what happened after; nevertheless, it reflected a deep belief in liberal circles that human history was firmly on course for international union. Liberals and socialists, despite their antagonistic ideologies, were convinced that the regulation and outstripping of capitalism would be achieved by a simple change of scale. Responding to liberal internationalists, the French socialist Paul Louis — who wrote a number of studies on the progress of European and international syndicalism — described international entente in the following terms, as the precursor of the coming collapse of capitalism: "The great proletarian advance has universal sides to it that are much more striking to the observer than the individual natures of countries. It correlates to the universal diffusion of the capitalist system.... Day by day, the capitalist world is being worn down by forces that are spreading within its structure and preparing its collapse."[7]

Conclusions like this masked the slowness and complexity of the process, which mobilized the efforts and energies of hundreds of militants over a period of decades. It is quite true that the rapidity with which the federations came into being and structured themselves between 1890 and 1900 was very impressive; yet they could not hide the innumerable national or professional disputes and rivalries that were such a drag on the wider movement. We should therefore make a distinction between the older skilled professions, which already had relationships of exchange and mutual help as early as 1860–1870, and the new industrial sectors, whose international organization began much later.

The first international unions or federations had emerged at the time of the First International: by 1871 the tobacco workers had formed their own international federation that was largely independent of the IWA, having no need of the IWA to establish the federation's relationships. The other professions that had already developed the habit of cross-border links (especially during strikes) were among the first to arrange international structures after 1889. This was the case of the typographers, who held their first congress during the 1889 Universal Exhibition in Paris.[8] At the same time International congresses were held in numerous other sectors positioned between the craft unions and the industrial ones, such as the hatmakers (1889), the glove makers (1892), the textile industry workers (1894), and the diamond workers. All these federations or secretariats assembled professions whose members were limited in numbers — accounting for only a few thousand or tens of thousands — of workers all over Europe. All these shared preoccupations about training, apprenticeship, and the movement and organization of their work.

More important, in terms of existing forces, was the movement among workers in the heavy industries, whose priority was mass unionism. The three largest international professional federations were, on the eve of the Great War, those of the miners, the metallurgists, and the transport workers, all of which appeared during the 1890s in the wake of the "new unionism" and the expansion of German and Scandinavian syndicalism. The first International congress of miners took place in 1890 at Jolimont in Belgium, against a background of multiple strikes at European mining centers in the Nord-Pas-de-Calais, the Ruhr Valley, Hainaut, and the Sarre — and also in Wales, across the Channel in the United Kingdom. The total number of mine workers belonging to the Miners' International Federation (MIF) was impressive (1.3 million members in 1911–1912); overall, the unionization of the sector was very high indeed (between 40 and 50 percent of the workforce were MIF members, country by country).[9] The great industrial powers of western Europe — British, German, French, Belgian, and Austro-Hungarian — were all strongly represented in the federation.[10] By comparison with the miners, European metallurgists and steel-workers were aggressively activist; at their first meeting, held in Zurich in 1893, they voted to create their own international information bureau.[11] The German unions were naturally in the vanguard in Zurich, just as they were almost everywhere else.

Before long, the 335,000 member Association of German Metallurgists (Deutscher Metallarbeiter-Verband), had gained total ascendancy over the venerable ASE, whose membership was stuck at around 92,000. Moreover the headquarters of the International Metalworkers' Federation was symbolically transferred from England to Stuttgart in Germany after 1904.[12] Finally, the world's third-largest union federation (882,000 members) was the one founded in London at the instigation of Tom Mann in June 1896, to unite first the maritime transport workers and then all transport workers (Mann's International Federation of Ship, Dock, and River Workers quickly evolved into the International Transport Federation in 1898).[13]

Trades without Frontiers

Whatever form they took, these international professional federations attempted to implement some of the projects already formulated in the 1860s, so as to develop relationships of solidarity with, and control of, workforces in other countries. The smallest of these were linked to older professions that were still close to the culture of the artisan; these were also the best fitted to carry the ideal of mutual understanding, in terms of training, apprenticeship, mobility, and industrial action. Their goal was to organize professional practices of solidarity, designed to limit competition for jobs at the base, and to counter the undercutting strategies used by employers. The federations sought more to internationalize a corporative organization unfettered by professional identities than to promote cross-border solidarity. This dimension was just as present among the old professions as it was in the giant new miners' federation.[14]

The question of worker mobility was one of the subjects most frequently discussed at the international corporative congresses of the time. Indeed it was the condition for the very existence of a profession on a transnational scale, which made possible contacts, solidarities, and dependences. The issue consisted, for the professional federations of the most cohesive professionals, in promoting the mobility of their members while protecting them against the negative effects of competition over wages and working conditions.[15] This model could only function properly in areas where the majority of workers were unionized and prepared to share the same sets of rules. Federations attempted to systematize and enlarge aids to labor mobility, but the passage of a bilateral logic (for example, assistance for travel from one country to another, presupposing an agreement on compensation between the two) to a fully international approach could hardly be taken for granted. For this reason, glove makers and typographers — again for example — explored the possibility of entrusting their international bodies with the responsibility of managing a federal aid fund for jobless workers presented with the choice of moving to another area, or staying put, to work for rock-bottom wages. This circulation of workers had the added advantage of offering a transnational adjustment mechanism between supply and demand, without worsening employment conditions. The fact remained that not everyone liked the idea of a perennial source of help: the glove makers of Grenoble declared they would prefer to raise a one-off subscription when one of their members wished to travel, rather than setting up a permanent aid fund financed by the payment of regular fees. Similar debates took place at the international typographers' secretariat, with countries traditionally attached to paying travel expenses like Germany, Austria, and the Scandinavian countries, pitted against those like Belgium, Spain, or Italy that were unwilling to indulge jobless or temporarily employed foreign workers.[16]

The positive aspect of worker mobility came into its own in the event of strike action. At such times there was a veritable duty of solidarity — not to mention a practical strategic benefit — in treating comrades well. In the course of a long conflict carried out by the glove makers of Denmark in 1893, ten of them were temporarily lodged by fellow workers in Brussels: this hospitality was indispensable in helping the Danish strikers to reject the degrading work conditions their employers were attempting to impose upon them. The issue was the defense of all glove workers, wherever they were. Had the Danes agreed to work for less, this would have opened the door to competition through lower salaries, which the workers of other countries would have had trouble opposing. This autonomous management of a workforce across frontiers was only possible within the context of a small industry whose workers had very specific skills.

The federations now added another obligation to their duty of hospitality, that of showing material and financial solidarity with foreign strikers. Profession by profession they made a reality of something the general council of the IWA had struggled to impose — namely, the centralization and exchange of information about ongoing strikes and lockouts, dispatches of official requests for the granting of subsidies, publications of financial records, and the results obtained by various social movements.

The capacity of the federations to coordinate strike action was most effective in heavily unionized professions, where worker numbers were limited and concentrated in a few pools of employment. In cases like this, measures could be used that were out of the question in the heavier sectors of industry, where personal acquaintance within working communities was outweighed by anonymity. For example, the Europe-wide network of the glove makers was so restricted (their international federation had only seven thousand unionized members in 1914) that it was possible to pinpoint nonstriking workers individually and exclude them from unions or prevent them being employed in other production locations. It was also possible to impose boycotts of products from nonstriking factories, a principle enshrined by the congress of Scandinavian unions in 1901, which declared its intent to do everything to block distribution of merchandise from plants affected by lockouts. The diamond cutters went even further in their logic of solidarity: when local strike funds ran out of money, their international bureau stepped in to help — as stipulated in their statutes — by raising subscriptions from all members of the federation.[17] Mutual help was also dependent on the creation of a cooperative workshop at Foncine in the Jura, one of whose missions was to shelter workers deprived of means by a strike or lockout.[18]

Some federations took a different path, preferring reformist legislative action to the internationalization of social struggle. One of the most famous cases was that of the miners, which involved the largest number of workers just prior to the First World War. Contrary to the legend of great nineteenth-century coal miners' strikes, the Miners' International Federation was resistant to the proliferation of industrial conflict between 1890 and 1900. British and French miners generally preferred parliamentary action and regulatory state intervention to the idea of concerted pan-European struggle.[19] In 1891, at the second International Miners' Congress, Belgian delegates proposed resorting to a general strike to force recognition of the eight-hour day. The British opposed this, insisting that parliamentary reform was the wiser course for a sector that needed proper oversight by the authorities to limit the worst abuses and — as far as possible — avert professional risks.[20]

Strikes in the Industrial Era

The creation of international professional federations did not necessarily result in the setting up of powerful, centralized financing tools for strike action. Nor did it facilitate the circulation of cross-frontier information exchanges. Thus the 1890s saw a wave of strikes breaking out across Europe, during which international solidarity crossed a new threshold. Loans and funding assistance provided by national movements, with or without the blessing of international federations, reached an unprecedented level. International aid was no longer an occasional, one-off business prompted by emotional reactions to such and such a strike or repressive act by the authorities; from now on it was part of the routine of collective international struggle, at a time when the resources of German trade unionism were so great that their effect was perceptible all over Europe. Nevertheless, such conflicts were still confined to specific industrial sectors; in this sense, the movements of the 1890s were still about the logic of professional identification rather than the dream of an all-out strike of the entire working class.

The old professions with histories of trade union internationalism continued to depend on routines established in earlier decades. This was the case for the tobacco workers and printers, when successive strikes breaking out in several areas of the continent opened a cycle of reciprocal gestures of solidarity. The tobacco workers of Bremen helped their counterparts in Holland, while in 1891 the German printers and typographers received the then-colossal sum of £7,000 (144,000 marks) in aid from nineteen different countries, including £3,500 from England alone. After 1892 it was the turn of the German typographers to send 75,000 marks to their striking Austrian colleagues in Vienna.[21] In a similar chain reaction, strikes hit the construction industry between 1888 (Paris), 1890 (Hamburg), and 1891 (London, with the great carpenters' strike for the eight-hour day).[22]

At this point the strike weapon entered an industrial age of its own. In keeping with the great dockworkers' strike of 1889, conflicts began to last longer and the numbers of strikers and their families hit by serious want became immeasurably greater. The issue of financing became a crucial factor in the battle to win over public opinion.[23] Not surprisingly, help from workers in other countries increased in volume, though this did not necessarily give strikes a better chance of success: the sums contributed simply grew larger as their places of origin became more manifold and diverse.

The example of workers in the transport and maritime sectors, whose activities connected the great ports of northwestern Europe, was significant. At the time, few sectors were as comprehensively internationalized as that of maritime commerce. The impact of a strike or a lockout in one of the Channel or North Sea ports immediately affected the entire maritime sector. Right up to the 1890s there remained a significant asymmetry between the capacities for international action of private shipping companies and those of their workers. The private companies worked through the North Atlantic Steamship Association, which coordinated the defense of their economic interests and devised collective strategies to counter the demands of — for example — dockworkers. Social protest as a weapon might have gained ground among the dockers since the great London strike of 1889, but in the 1890s international solidarity was still stuck in its infancy. It was to do something about this that the English trade unionists now set about aligning themselves more closely with workers on the continent: Tillett traveled to Antwerp, while Mann, a tireless propagator of internationalist ideas and a member of the Independent Labor Party, visited the dockers in Rotterdam and Hamburg-Altona in November 1896.[24] His subsequent arrest and expulsion by the German authorities unleashed a wave of protest, especially when Mann was expelled again when he attempted to enter Germany a second time. A few weeks later, a major strike broke out when thirteen thousand workers at the port of Hamburg stopped work for eleven weeks. Nearly forty thousand people were affected by this conflict between the dockworkers and the city's Employers' Association.

The Hamburg strike had a steadily broadening international dimension from the very start. The context was a favorable one:

Mann was president of the International Federation of Ship, Dock, and River Workers, which he had helped to found in June 1896.[25] As he saw it, the Hamburg dockworkers' strike offered an ideal opportunity to demonstrate the effectiveness of coordinated struggle. In Stockholm, Sweden, in Bristol and Hull in England, and in various French ports, local dockers agreed — at least on paper — not to unload ships out of Hamburg whose cargoes might have been handled there by nonstriking workers. The dockers of Amsterdam and Rotterdam then walked out in sympathy, while the Swedish trade unions actively prevented strikebreaking workers from traveling from Sweden to Germany.[26] Meanwhile, in Hamburg itself, employers were reduced to recruiting men from local athletics associations to replace the city's striking dockers.[27]

Foreign financial help proved most useful of all. Just as in London in 1889, daily union payments to workers and their families were key to keeping the movement going. The number of people involved meant that colossal sums had to be raised; the strike committee spent a total of 1.75 million marks in three months, between indemnities to workers, the cost of paying would-be strikebreakers to go home, and propaganda expenses. An appeal launched by university professors in support of the strike called on wealthy and middle-class people to contribute money for the support of strikers' families. Aid from outside Germany remained relatively sparse: only 69,000 marks, 4 percent of the strike's total outlay, which came from thirteen different foreign countries. But this financial effort could not be sustained in the long term, especially after the government made it illegal to collect contributions door-to-door; also the Hamburg dockworkers had trouble rallying public opinion behind their strike, unlike their London counterparts of 1889. Inter-professional solidarity, even when multiplied tenfold over previous benchmarks, was not enough to overcome the obstacles facing so massive a strike. The combination of total intransigence on the part of the employers of Hamburg-Altona and brutal repression by the authorities — over five hundred strikers were indicted for violent attacks on "blacklegs" — ultimately forced the strike committee to call off the conflict, a move voted by the strikers in early February 1897.[28] Given the extent of the battle, Legien — who had followed its developments closely — concluded that trade unions should not only be far more involved in the leading of strikes but also develop far better organizations to keep them afloat.[29]

The British funds sent to help the Hamburg dockers produced a reciprocal effort several months later, this time on behalf of the metallurgists of the ASE. Here again, unions militating for the eight-hour day found themselves confronted by well-organized employers who rejected any hint of conciliation. In the summer of 1897, the employers forced a lockout of nearly one-quarter of their workers. At this point the metallurgists' union decided, after consulting with its base, to raise funds for a prolonged strike. Ninety thousand workers took part in the ensuing stoppage.[30] The ASE was not short of reserve funds: in all, it spent £180,000. Of this sum, £30,000 (16 percent of the total) arrived from abroad, notably by way of the information bureau of the International Metalworkers' Federation. Half the foreign funds came from Germany and one-quarter from colonies of the British Empire (South Africa, Australia, and New Zealand). Solidarity was heavily polarized, with, on the one hand, a British-German connection that reflected a struggle for influence within the International Metalworkers's Federation and, on the other, the same kind of mutual aid within the British Empire that had surfaced earlier during the dockworkers' strike of 1889.[31]

The metallurgists' strike committee used any means available: funds were raised from factories and cooperatives but also from the general public through concerts, religious services, and even soccer matches.[32] To keep going, the strikers fought to place their movement in the public eye and to touch every level of society. Of

the strike aid available, 44 percent was paid to non-union workers, evidence that there was a real will to unite, in tandem with
an appeal for subscriptions to the general public. Despite this
unprecedented mobilization, the ASE was forced to call off the
strike after thirty weeks of struggle, amid bitter recriminations
against the other professional unions for their failure to step up.
In England, just as in Germany, solidarity had proved itself unable
to prevail unless it spread beyond the frontiers of the professional
community.

Yet this failure was not without consolation. It was to be hoped
that the episode would make employers think twice in the future
before committing themselves to an industrial conflict that had
already caused them heavy loss. The Metallurgists' International Bureau of Information saw the episode as a defeat — but an
encouraging one that might help pave the way to "a reign of peace
and goodwill" among the workers of the world.[33]

So the German dockworkers' strike of 1896, like the English
engineers' strike of 1897, worsened an already considerable paradox. The fact was that the financial capacities of the unions were
still too weak, notwithstanding their appeal for foreign contributions. A broader alliance, extending way beyond professional affinities, was clearly required.

A BLUEPRINT FOR PAN-EUROPEAN SYNDICALISM

In terms of action, the professional federations occupied the first
level of international solidarity. At the turn of the twentieth century there emerged an ambition to merge these federations into a
single inclusive structure, which would improve their coordination and facilitate the use of good practices. The implementation
of this plan was assigned in 1901 to the International Secretariat
of National Centers of Trade Unions, which, in spite of the mod-
esty of its means, proved an effective forum for exchanges and

discussion. The decision to create it was taken in 1901, during a Scandinavian trade union congress held at Christiania (Copenhagen), which was attended by several foreign representatives. The example supplied by the Swedes and the Danes was a spur to action, especially after the broad mobilization provoked by the locked-out Danish workers in 1899, who had launched appeals for help and received substantial foreign funds in response, most notably from England.[34] The resultant project grew from an alliance between the Scandinavian and German trade unions, which were closely aligned both ideologically and in their systems of organization. A year after a second conference at Stuttgart in 1932, the headquarters of a new international institution was set up in Berlin, with Carl Legien, the leader of the German Generalkommission, installed as director of the secretariat, a post he held until 1913.

The International Secretariat represented for some the "confederative" stage of trade union internationalism: it was no longer a matter of grouping trades and industries or of trying to unite the various syndicalist forces into the same single organization. Although it was far from well-funded, the secretariat succeeded in establishing a model of what a rational Europe-wide organization of workers ought to look like. The secretariat would deal with no more than one organization per country, which obliged often fractious national trade unions to look for common ground. Countries like France, where trade unionism was in pieces, were underrepresented; to the considerable advantage of countries where the working classes were already assembled under the banner of a single dominant organization, as in Scandinavia (where there tended to be single national federations) and Germany (where free trade union members heavily outnumbered confessional and liberal ones). This architecture explains why, on the eve of the First World War, the international confederation had no fewer than 6 million adherents, of whom 2 million were German and 1.7 million were American (following the AFL's official adhesion in 1910).

Comparisons

The existence of professional federations, the creation of the International Secretariat, and the many trade union conferences held between 1901 and 1913 had the combined effect of multiplying practices of observation, comparison, and exchange among union militants all over Europe. In fact this was probably their most important accomplishment: coordination and solidarity made progress, but it was above all in the domains of knowledge, technique, and syndical expertise that the European landscape was radically altered in the early 1900s. The constitution of these transnational networks of knowledge and expertise affected every area of public action leading up to the Great War, from social reformers to magistrates implementing laws for the protection of children and from international jurists to specialists grappling with educational dilemmas.[35] In this sense, trade unionists did not escape a larger movement, by which national experiences and the building of networks of expertise were scrutinized and compared. Even though nationalism and national pride were on the rise, it was obvious that there were still valuable lessons to be learned from other countries. Thus the German Social Democrat Eduard Bernstein, who was known for his revisionist positions on Marxism, made clear his interest in exchanging and sharing experience at a conference in Brussels in 1908:

> Nobody will acknowledge more willingly than I that Germany has still much to learn from other countries; nor in my opinion should any German social democrat ever forget the debt owed by the German workers' movement to its English and French precursors, or lose sight of the fact that in many instances we have been shown the way by smaller countries. But I would not be the internationalist that I am, simply because I belong to the workers' movement, if when invited to speak about German matters to a non-German audience, I

were to hesitate for a moment to say how much these things are worthy of study and imitation.[36]

The practices of observation and comparison derived from the circulation of printed brochures and statistical compilations. This was one of the principal functions of the International Secretariat, which set about extending the effort of statistical codification carried out by Legien's Generalkommission in Germany, through the latter's publication, the *Correspondenzblatt*.[37] It was also an application of the general directives adopted by the world congress of international associations in 1901. Relations between the International Secretariat and its member confederations mostly revolved around this statistical imperative: far from being a simple information issue, it forced an objectivization of the ways in which people and resources differing widely from one country to another were actually managed. Collecting statistics about membership levels, resources, expenses, strikes, and lockouts of trade unions, and the results obtained, exposed deep disagreements about the very concept of industrial action, its priorities, and its effectiveness. As long as the International Secretariat lasted, Legien deplored the reluctance of the English, French, and Italians to fill out the forms he sent to them. In effect, the secretariat was at the heart of a symbolic statistical battle: the Germans and Scandinavians were proud of sending complete and accurate figures relating to their activities, while others were secretive and opaque about their members, what they were doing, and why.[38]

This "statistical" superiority justified the pretension of the Germans and Scandinavians to leadership of the European movement. They aligned their practices with international standards for the good management of trade union human resources and their ways of preparing for strikes. For Legien and many others, the capacity of the workers' movement to produce its own statistics was key not only to its credibility but also to its capacity to fight its corner against state power; moreover, reliable statistics were essential to any collective strategy for struggle at the European level. Without them there was no way of knowing the strengths and weaknesses of the workers' movement, or what it could reasonably expect to gain by plunging into a given conflict. Comparative statistics could be used with confidence by the authors of books and articles on European and international syndicalism, which was now a force in its own right.

Still, in spite of its potential to expose fault lines between models and practices, the dry work of statistical quantification would never replace the sheer quality of observation and contact that militants could draw from itinerant research and participation in international congresses.[39] Tours, inquiries, and travels to and fro were part in the process of self-discovery, by its own agents, of the European trade union world. The English socialist Tom Mann, a towering figure of European syndicalism at the turn of the century, offers an excellent example. In the late 1890s Mann was highly active between England, Germany, and the Scandinavian countries, but also in France and Spain.[40] His unwavering goal was to strengthen workers' collective capacity for action and to facilitate their use of observation and exchange. After going twice to Hamburg at the end of 1896 to mobilize German dockers and defend the projects of the International Federation of Ship, Dock, and River Workers, he traveled to Denmark, there to observe how his own counterparts operated. Unlike the English syndicalists of earlier generations who were consciously ignorant of continental realities, Mann always sought to learn from others and thus accelerate the transformation of both English and international syndicalism. He became aware of the power of Danish trade unionism — at the time a closed book to his compatriots — by seeing it for himself and meeting its leaders. On his return, he saluted the many successes of the Danish workers: apart from the fact that they seemed to collect huge sums of money (which won the hearty approval of the English), the Danes maintained close links with the socialist movement and constructed highly symbolic buildings such as their Trades Hall, used as a kind of "parliament of the people." Mann was impressed. On his return from Denmark Mann called on his compatriots to abandon their superiority complex: "Britishers," he wrote, "seem to think that the Continental men either can't or won't pay for their Trade Unionism. I venture to declare that the Trade Unionists of Denmark and Sweden are subscribing to Trade Unionism and the Labor Movement, for the purpose of fighting their industrial battles, a larger proportion of their income than does the corresponding section of British Trade Unionists."[41] Later on, Mann continued to be inspired by his experiences abroad while continuing his own syndical and political career. At the beginning of the second decade of the twentieth century, after a long stay in Australia and New Zealand, he turned to the revolutionary unionism of the French as a more competitive and libertarian model for action, applying its principles during the Liverpool general strike in the summer of 1911.[42]

The continuing attractiveness of the Scandinavian and German brand of syndicalism did not fade at the turn of the century. On the contrary: the Parti ouvrier belge, the Belgian workers' party (POB), also decided to send an observer to the 1901 Scandinavian congress at Christiania (Copenhagen). Cofinanced by the party and by the unions, this mission of observation was entrusted to Alphonse Octors, a former teacher who had become secretary of the party's syndical committee.[43] Octors traveled to Denmark by way of Germany. Just like his British counterpart, he returned from his trip full of enthusiasm, having understood that statistics could only offer cold, imperfect conclusions: "It was vital to go in person, in order to see, hear and experience what was going on.... We are glad to say that nothing of what we read about it previously was in any way exaggerated."[44] Denmark's high level of trade union membership (77 percent of the workforce) was based on the willingness of the unions themselves to offer services to members, to entrench the fact of syndical action in the lived experience of the population, and to coordinate the actions of Scandinavian workers beyond their national frontiers. During his trip, the Belgian delegate met Legien himself, also present at Christiania, and was party to his decision to found the International Secretariat.[45]

All these exchanges of information painted a picture that was anything but flat and homogeneous: instead, the circulation of knowledge and statistics, the travels, and international congresses led to the emergence of national classifications of organizational styles. Better and closer acquaintance led to growing hierarchization, much more than to uniformity. Again, this was the paradox of international congresses: they favored the emergence of transnational communities of expertise, while at the same time identifying so-called national models. With its statistical publications, the International Secretariat clearly demonstrated the difference between unions that were capable of collecting enormous amounts of money and offering their members a wide range of services like financial help for striking workers and sick leave payments, and more ideological unions that were content to operate on small budgets without tackling the primary risks of human existence. Financial power was an explicit criterion for hierarchization: in this sphere the German unions may have raised record contributions per worker, year after year, but others remained a long way behind. Thus the Socialist International, which had its own ideas about how best to organize unions, officially sanctioned the German model during the Stuttgart Congress of 1907.[46]

Syndical Savoir Faire

Exchanges of information were not an end in themselves, their underlying objective being to promote solidarity between European workers. Professional, unionized federations, like the International

Secretariat, were primarily interested in the mechanisms of mutual aid and solidarity that lay at the heart of the internationalist ideal. Here again, their deliberations in international arenas were just as focused — if not more so — on questions of procedure as they were on the substance of the aid given to other workers.

Strike action was more and more often compared to warfare, necessitating a plan of attack, a strategy, and a high degree of coordination, as explained by Bernstein in the early 1900s: "A strike is a conflict, a kind of war. War requires an overall strategy, meaning an understanding of how to move and position forces, and of tactics, meaning the arts of attack and defense." The workers of Germany seemed to have all the necessary qualities for this kind of contest. "The dominant qualities of the German worker are discipline, a talent for organization, a spirit of solidarity, and tenacity: and I believe that these qualities make up for the lack of a revolutionary temperament, of which German workers are sometimes accused."[47] Like his predecessors, Bernstein was nevertheless convinced that thorough preparation for a strike could have no other goal than that of rendering resort to a strike entirely pointless. And it was up to the unions to master this art of preparation at a time when strikes were unionizing, as Michelle Perrot has demonstrated.[48]

International organizations held frequent debates on how recourse to strike action could be codified. Those who were most concerned with the procedure sought to place the launching of strikes, and the dispatching of aid to support them, within the routines of collective action: this would make it possible to engage international solidarity for strikes in real need of it and to save time in the transmission of information and money, the golden keys to success. From this emerged a growing determination to promote a technical, quasi-scientific approach to strikes and solidarity. To maximize their chances, unions needed to stop counting on their own resources and the ever-fluctuating generosity of the general public: it was more by the establishment of regular, stable, and automatic mechanisms that solidarity would become an essential cog in the machine of industrial action, detached from the vagaries of mobilization or public attention. This was a change that coincided with the transformation of the state and its financing methods; the invention of standard procedures of collection and redistribution was aimed at creating durable financial systems discounting individual cases and voluntary choices. The codification of international assistance for strikes made it possible to activate practices of solidarity without having to repeat, every time, the work of winning over public opinion and engaging workers to collect gifts and subscriptions. The aim was nothing less than the passage, at an international level, from a mechanical solidarity to an organic one (to borrow the terminology of Durkheim).[49]

Those who believed in rationalizing strike action insisted on the need to manage resources properly. The unions had become powerful financial institutions; the wise investment of their ample funds and the ability to mobilize those funds promptly when needed were strategic imperatives. Mann in particular was delighted with the advent of professional federations that could shatter the inertia of union capital and make it work profitably. He had seen how the Danish metallurgists resisted a lockout in the summer of 1897, and how their victory was made possible by the circulating and loaning of mutual aid funds, just what the supporters of "resistance" funds had yearned for back in the 1860s. "None of these [Danish] unions keep, or attempt even to obtain, any large sums in hand. Being federated, they have the requisite machinery at their disposal to raise what money is required."[50]

The financial position of the free German unions was unique in Europe at the beginning of the century. By then the entire cost of strikes in Germany was covered by union money, a sea change since the early 1880s, when they could afford only 58 percent of their expenses.[51] No other European syndical entity spent so much money on the financing of strikes in the early 1900s. Because of their high dues and substantial numbers of members, the free German unions had amassed huge reserves that they invested in German state bonds, as did some of the international professional federations headquartered in Germany.[52] The idea that unions could protect their funds by investing in state equities had been unimaginable two decades earlier, when Bismarck was on the warpath. At the beginning of the new century it was no longer a matter of establishing a network of solidarity on the fringes of the bourgeois state and the stock markets but, rather, of actually relying on them to strengthen and support industrial action.[53] The unrivaled wealth of the German unions produced a fundamental dichotomy: they became net exporters of capital to countries in Europe, where syndical organizations lacked anything approaching their resources. The funds that fed the great European strikes of the early twentieth century no longer came from London. They came from Berlin.

However, the obsession with financial preparation and economic independence was loudly denounced by the supporters of revolutionary syndicalism, who somehow viewed poverty as a militant virtue. The effectiveness of a given strike was not measurable in their eyes by the quantity of financial help supplied to it, which would tend on the contrary to blunt workers' enthusiasm for the fight: "In France, our struggle has produced concrete results, despite the scarcity of union funds. This is because money alone is not enough for success! The spirit of struggle that has developed here, and which is lacking in practically every other country, is also necessary," wrote Victor Griffuelhes.[54] The confrontations between ardor and rigor, spontaneity and professionalism, continued steadily, even though by the early 1900s some of the leaders of the CGT were admitting — off the record — that there was a need to build massive reserves if employers were ever to be confronted effectively.

Subsidiarity

The increasing quantities of money being transferred across frontiers prompted the professional federations to reflect on the adoption of an international procedure for financing strikes. There were undeniable conclusions to be drawn from the industrial actions of the 1890s, which had received plenty of international aid but had never quite prevailed: particularly that solidarity was worthless if not implemented within a well-defined framework, with national and international aid working in harmony rather than as substitutes for each other. The strikes and lockouts of the industrial age could no longer depend completely on local initiatives and improvized mutual aid; hence the workers' movement had to raise its capacity to assist, to the same level as that already reached by the employers' organizations. If the workers did not, the result would be a resounding failure to improve their conditions. According to the more fervent internationalists, rationalization and a change of scale in its procedures for assistance would enable European syndicalism to win symbolic victories.

There was a significant precedent for this in the experience of the Swedish and Danish unions, which had agreed on the principle of obligatory bilateral aid, whenever a strike mobilized at least 20 percent of members of a neighboring country's central trade union directorate. This model, hammered out during their 1907 congress, established that international assistance was neither a favor nor an impulse of generosity. Instead it was a *right* belonging to those who asked for help and a *duty* acknowledged by those who dispensed it; and it was inscribed as such in the trade union statutes of all nations. The purpose of international assistance was to give strikers every possible chance to stay the course for as long as it took to overcome the resistance of employers. The codification of bilateral mutual aid was meant to strengthen the resistance of workers and their power to negotiate.[55]

These innovations were discussed post-1900 both within the International Secretariat and during its conferences, especially after the Swedish general strike of 1909. That episode marked the beginning of a major cycle of worker protest (known in Great Britain as "The Great Labour Unrest"). In 1909 the Swiss delegates filed a proposal to systematize requests for help from foreign countries, with the aim of entrusting the secretariat with an active role in the channeling and orientation of funds donated. As in the 1860s, the idea of giving some international body a mandate to judge the opportuneness of strikes and to devise a plan to raise funds raised plenty of hackles. Such was the resistance that the rules set down in writing after this discussion clearly formalized a principle of subsidiarity that dictated exactly how strikes ought to be financed. During a trade union conference held in Budapest in 1911, solidarity was presented as a mechanism functioning in wider and wider concentric circles. It was seen as beginning within a given professional community, then widening to achieve international status using different forms of bilateral aid. After this, international worker solidarity would surely ensue, overarching the differences between trades and industrial sectors.[56]

The extension of networks of international mutual aid was viewed as part of a more general trend toward collective struggle. The longer a conflict lasted and the more workers it mobilized, the more it acquired a form of universality, which in turn justified appeals for international help. When it came to action, this entirely theoretical architecture placed national and international professional federations in the role of prime movers; the International Secretariat was merely seen as a focus for the collection of information and, thereafter, as an agency for the "trans-professionalization" of aid. Plenty of union militants believed that the effectiveness of social movements had initially to be built up nationally; international aid was no substitute for the preparation any self-respecting union had to make if it meant to be ready for industrial conflict. Centralization was mostly of use at the national level: as things stood, the contemporary leaders of international trade unionism were more in favor of the decentralized model, *à l'anglaise*.[57]

THE DEPLOYMENT OF SOLIDARITY

A gulf had always existed between procedural discussions and the real life practices of mutual help. The former did not dictate the latter; at best they could provide a framework and show the way forward. Yet contacts established through international federations and the secretariat broadened the scope of international aid and coordination. The years between 1900 and 1914 carried worker solidarity to new heights; its influence, though mitigated, at least made international mobilization a central issue in the duration and success of strikes.

Confronting Employers

The coordination of mutual action to such a point that it became routine was also of vital importance, for workers now faced employers whose organizations were constantly improving and who no longer allowed themselves to be caught napping by sudden strike action. Workers' alliances were mirrored by those of their bosses. The international dynamic of coordination took care of itself, with each party justifying its cooperative efforts by a need to be on equal terms with the opposition, and never the underdog.

Militant workers habitually presented their internationalism in a reactive light: confronted by employer solidarity and the globalization of capital, the forces of labor needed to coalesce and make their struggle symmetrical. Tom Mann repeated a conclusion already reached by the founders of the First International in the 1860s: "The owner of capital is already cosmopolitan as regards the use of that capital for the purposes of exploitations.... What we do now stand in urgent need of, is, an international working alliance among the workers of the whole world."[58] The fact was that labor was way behind capital in the race for globalization and international coordination. This did not mean that the circulation of capital should be resisted, or that protectionist barriers should be erected: only that the objective of many syndicalists was to counterbalance the power of capital by pooling labor resources internationally, across frontiers. Mann called this process "international fraternization." The goal of confronting employer organizations and winning decent work conditions was better served by an internationalist approach than by nationalist retrenchment. The cosmopolitan nature of work had to counterbalance the cosmopolitan nature of capital, despite differing linguistic, cultural, and national notions of political rights. In Germany, for example, unions had languished under restrictive anti-socialist laws for over a decade, while employers were left at leisure to organize themselves into efficient professional groups.[59] The same was true of Sweden and Denmark, where full syndicalist unity (trade union confederations were created in these two countries in 1898) was the workers' response to a robust coalition of employers.

Employer associations strove mightily for a better coordination of their forces, in the awareness that workers were steadily developing their own practices of international solidarity. They were concerned by the new mass character of strikes, in particular the increased capacity of unions and professional federations to exchange information, synchronize industrial action, and help one another promptly when required. The threat of "falling behind" was used by employers just as it was by union organizers: clearly both sides were mobilizing and appraising, constantly reminding their own members of the danger represented by the other side. In consequence, the years between 1890 and 1900 saw major employer organizations uniting in the various countries of Europe in response to the coalescing of worker forces.[60] In France, this period led to the founding of the Union des industries métallurgiques et minières (UIMM) and the Union des syndicats patronaux des industries textiles de France. In Germany, two more umbrella associations were formed in 1904, which merged in 1913 into a single German employers' federation, the Vereinigung der deutschen Arbeitgeber. In Sweden, the Confederation of Swedish Employers (SAF) appeared in 1902, while in Switzerland a new Union centrale des associations patronales suisses set about coordinating employer resistance to the workers' movement in 1908.[61]

Thus Europe's employers responded to worker solidarity with a solidarity of their own, not only organizing themselves into pressure groups but also helping one another when worker protests were under way. In 1890 a German employers' defense union for the first time established a loan fund for use during the strikes in Hamburg-Altona; in the following year, the Federation of German Metallurgists was founded. This impulse on the part of both unions and employers to strengthen their defense mechanisms continued through the early 1900s and was epitomized by a very long textile workers' strike at Crimmitschau, in Saxony, in 1903–1904. On this occasion, German trade unions sent gigantic sums of money (5,000 marks per day) for a total of 1.25 million marks distributed; this was answered by funds contributed by the central union of German industrialists (Centralverband deutscher Industrieller, founded in 1876), which voted to raise periodical subscriptions.[62] This strike degenerated into an all-out economic battle between industrialists who wanted to limit losses without giving in to worker demands and strikers attempting to continue their struggle without endangering either their own well-being or that of their families.

One of the the novelties of the turn of the century was the introduction by employers of insurance policies against strike action. Obviously, strikes did not occur with the regularity and predictability of other objective risks, but from this time onward they were perceived as being inherent threats to productive activity, costing more and more the longer they dragged on. The strengthening of workers' capacity to resist led bosses to invent new ways of protecting themselves from the potentially disastrous effect of social conflict on the survival of their businesses. Just as trade union organizations looked for ways to systematize the practices of mutual help, employer associations turned to insurance companies to anticipate — and attenuate — the cost of strikes. The first policies of employer insurance against strikes were devised in Germany, Austria, and Sweden, the three European countries where trade unions were most powerful and best organized. After this, employer unions functioned like "mutual insurance societies against the damage wrought by strikes."[63]

These new forms of protection did not supplant the more traditional practices of employers' resistance, most of which relied on appeals for local and foreign workers to take the places of striking employees, shattering their united front. The system of importing foreign workers was a crucial issue for the conflicts at the beginning of the century: the employer associations depended on firms offering interim work and on recruiters who, in a few days, could provide a cheap and docile workforce to take the place of strikers.[64] This addition to the equation worked much like a kind of insurance against strikes, because it lightened the financial burden on employers. The struggle against the importation of strikebreaking workers thus became a major concern for international syndicalists, who officially condemned the practice at their 1907 and 1909 congresses, along with the importation of workers during periods of economic slump.

This theoretical question lay squarely at the heart of the methodology of strike action. Imported workers were sometimes stopped and ordered to leave, albeit compensated by money withdrawn by the resident workers from their strike fund. Physical confrontations sometimes occurred; strikebreakers were violently attacked in Sweden in 1908, at which time a man was killed and a score of others injured by a bomb explosion.[65] Seamen were accused of agreeing to load their ships when the dockers were on strike, behavior that in 1911 saw them officially reprimanded by the international trade union conference in Budapest.[66] However, in a wider context, it was the emergence of "yellow syndicalism" that blurred the lines, when a third force attempted to position itself between employer organizations and the strike-supporting trade unions. Here the intention was to unite nonstriking workers, especially in sectors where there was plenty of manpower to spare and qualifications were less essential than they were in other trades. Employers were sometimes directly involved in the creation of "yellow" unions, as they were at Le Creusot, Montceau-les-Mines, and Longwy between 1899 and 1905.[67] After this the movement broadened with the creation, by Pierre Biétry, of the Fédération nationale des jaunes de France (1902), which from 1908 onward became a serious nationalist political force, whose chief aim was to reconcile employers and workers.[68]

International Mobilization: Sweden, 1909

The social conflicts of the 1900s clearly showed the new breadth of international worker solidarity and the variety of its outlets, as well as the concentration of its original flow. At the same time the wave of strikes in the 1908–1914 period marked the apogee of the pre–First World War worker protest movement; in those five years, industrial disputes attained record levels everywhere in Europe. In 1905 a major strike in the Ruhr valley started a cycle of protest in Germany that peaked in the following year, when 3,300 conflicts — nine per day, on average — took place. More than 270,000 workers were involved, numbers that required colossal expenditure by the unions, in the order of 13.2 million marks. In 1909, about 11 million workdays were lost overall in Germany. In

1908, France saw the famous strikes of Draveil and Villeneuve Saint-Georges, which were violently repressed.[69] These were only the tragically visible aspects of a much larger movement that was playing out in all the major industrial areas of Europe. The same things were happening in Austria, Belgium, Holland, and Sweden. The United Kingdom experienced "The Great Labour Unrest" between 1911 and 1914, with a general transport workers' strike in Liverpool in 1911, followed by a coal miners' general strike in 1912.[70] These disputes mobilized workers of more and more different professions and were supported by national and international organizations that were able to launch actions of solidarity on a scale never seen before.

The most celebrated case of the time (although it is virtually forgotten today) was the Swedish general strike of 1909. This event crystallized all the main developments that had been at work within international syndicalism since the beginning of the 1900s. Scandinavian workers had played a decisive role in the formation of the International Secretariat and had worked tirelessly to extend the range of cross-border mutual aid. They had also moved closer to the social democratic Workers' Party, the better to coordinate social conflict with political action. For this reason the general strike that broke out in 1909 was a shining example, being one of the most prolonged and expensive conflicts of the period, indeed of the entire history of the workers' movement.[71] The Swedish trade union confederation, in the face of intransigent employers, hoped to force the Swedish government to intervene in their strike and open negotiations. It responded to an initial employer lockout, which involved nearly eighty thousand workers, by proclaiming a general strike, which resembled none other that had come before: no fewer than three hundred thousand workers were concerned, of whom ninety thousand were not unionized.[72]

This spectacular mobilization won an overwhelming international response. The equivalent of three million French francs poured in from abroad, half of it contributed by German unions. The Danes, who had worked in close harmony with the Swedes since the late 1890s, advanced eight times more money to their neighbors than they usually spent on themselves in a single year.[73] International trade unions were also solicited for contributions, since the strike was such a major one: the International Federation of Metallurgists sent 50,000 francs, plus a loan of 540,000 francs. Money also arrived from Norway and the USA, but the British remained on the sidelines, sending only about 2 percent of the total aid. This penny-pinching was roundly criticized by the Germans, who pointed out that certain individual cities in the British Empire had given more than all the workers of Britain combined.[74]

The massiveness of foreign help showed that the practices and procedures so long discussed by the international federations were producing substantial results. Even so, they were not sufficient to ensure the movement's triumph. Contrary to the hopes of the syndicalists, the Swedish government refused to intervene and chose a stalling strategy instead. So extravagant was the workers' outlay of energy, means, and sheer sacrifice that when the strike committee — realizing it was unable to continue raising enough money to pay its members' indemnities — proposed to bring an end to the conflict, the workers twice refused to do so. This was only one of the paradoxes of national (and international) mobilization: the help received would encourage people to prolong the struggle, even when resources were running critically low. The employers had their war strategy: either solidarity would make it possible for the workers to hold on and win, or poverty and hunger would force them back to their jobs, powerless to find alternative means of survival. Naturally, the provision of aid, financial or in kind, was not the only factor that explained the capacity of a strike to succeed or fail. In the Swedish case, there was also the defection of certain segments of the working class to consider: a recent study has shown, for example, that the general strike of 1909 was bound to falter without the support of the dockers and sailors, whose standing aloof made it impossible to shut down the maritime traffic in the Port of Stockholm. Had they engaged, the resultant commercial damage might have forced the employers to be more flexible. Above all, the strategy of the Swedish unions hinged on what turned out to be a serious analytical error: despite the unprecedented breadth of the strike, the government never made the smallest effort to help find a solution, as the unions had hoped and expected it would.[75]

At the same time, the international mobilization behind the Swedish strikers showed how there had been an expansion — out of all proportion — of a practice that in the 1860s had seldom concerned more than a few hundred workers or gone on for longer than two or three weeks. Moreover, the lists of countries that gave and countries that received had altered substantially in forty years. The most outward-looking bodies of workers were now the Scandinavians and the Germans. The Scandinavian unions had the backing of an international solidarity of neighborhood, as shared by the bulk of workers within Scandinavia where worker cultures and organizational form were relatively homogeneous. The German unions, on the other hand, had become the biggest source of funds for strikes all over the continent of Europe. Their huge workforces and the rigorous organization of their syndical structures had the double effect of sparing them any need to look abroad for funds to pay for their own strikes since, for all intents and purposes, they were self-sufficient. Moreover, these funds empowered them to send help to a growing number and variety of other countries. German money was mainly steered to east and south Europe, affecting workers who had previously been remote from international aid and its benefits. Between 1911 and 1913, German metallurgists provided refundable loans to their Italian, Croatian, Serbian, and Bulgarian counterparts.[76]

Geopolitics, spurred by intermittent conflicts in the Balkans, became a feature of mutual aid between workers. The German donors were intensely proud of their role as leading contributors to industrial action: in 1913, half the funds received by the Italian metallurgists came from Germany, the rest flowing from Austria, Sweden, and Denmark. Successive annual reports published by the International Secretariat confirmed the preeminence of German workers in actions of international solidarity.[77] By contrast, French and British unions were almost completely absent from these practices of international mutual assistance: the former had no money to spare, while the latter were distracted by an unprecedented wave of domestic strikes in 1911 and 1912, which involved up to a million workers.

Help and Assistance

The growing numbers of strikers and the lengthening of the conflicts themselves created situations of extreme vulnerability for workers' families. The costs and privations were only bearable if some kind of aid was given by communities, in the form of cash, services, or help in kind. The starvation faced by strikers, their wives, and their children was a core feature in the portrayal of strike action as a social experience, like the business of gathering for rallies and protests. The fact that conflicts were lasting longer than before made it easier for reporters to cover them more extensively: from 1889 onward, the London newspapers assiduously documented the living conditions of dockers and their families with written reports, drawings, and performances in theaters. Strikes attracted media attention; they also supplied subject matter for literature and the mobilization of sympathy.

Feeding strikers was a giant strategic issue. Starving workers left to fend for themselves were totally incapable of maintaining any kind of lengthy struggle, and from the start this meant building up resistance funds. These had to provide strike indemnities ample enough to keep morale high and hold off the blandishments of employers, who were always ready to recruit blackleg labor among the more impoverished workers. In England, charitable associations were much moved by the plight of people smitten by strike action, but still they made a distinction between "innocent victims" — meaning wives, children, and nonstriking workers — and the actual strikers, both leaders and led, who were thought to be honor bound to assume full responsibility for what they were doing.[78] By the same token, it was felt that active strikers should be refused access to soup kitchens, which apparently "rewarded laziness" and so offered indirect support for the workers' struggle. Certain philanthropists went further in this cold reasoning: it was better to let strikers languish in poverty than help them persevere in their struggle.

The distribution of aid and food was one of the essential tasks of strike committees, along with the fixing of strategic objectives for the movement. During the Swedish strike, aid received from outside Sweden made it possible to distribute coupons to strikers that could be exchanged in cooperatives for food.[79] Thus a roughly parallel workers' economy was in place to serve those involved in the struggle. Between 1904 and 1905, the first "communist soup kitchens" appeared — most notably during the Fougères shoe industry strikes of 1906–1907. Later, in the course of the Graulhet tanneries strike (1909–1910), "communist" meals were distributed to the tune of thirty-five hundred a day. Indispensable as it was to keep the struggle alive, food was placed at the disposal of workers in strike canteens, which lessened people's suffering and offered refuges where strikers could meet, talk, and mobilize. The food they distributed came either from donations in kind or from purchases made using money collected from worker cooperatives. As their historian François Jarrige has written, the *soupes communistes* became one of the symbols of worker solidarity during strikes and lockouts.[80] They gave locations — and a human face — to mutual help by providing it to individuals and groups and demonstrating its collective power. Strike committees could also count on the support of socialist municipalities, which, if required, could vote subsidies to finance the people's soup kitchens (as they did at Limoges).[81]

In consequence, financial, material, and alimentary preparation for strikes soon reached unheard-of levels of organization and sophistication within the context of mass strike action. An important example was the Belgian general strike of 1913, which was called for entirely political purposes. In the spring of 1913, the Belgian workers' party and the Belgian trade unions, whose clear strategy was to establish universal suffrage in the country, gave warning comfortably in advance of their decision to launch a general strike. The weeks that preceded it were used to set up a committee for food and census-taking, whose responsibility was to organize in advance the forms and locations for collective meals and to distribute food access coupons to some 350,000 workers and their families. Working in parallel, a finance committee pieced together a reserve fund and created a cooperative. To hold the union resistance funds in reserve for as long as possible, workers were asked to save money personally, ahead of the coming conflict.[82]

One major issue confronting the *soupes communistes* and other syndical food distribution networks was how to place the resources of the agricultural sector at the full disposal of striking workers. An alliance between urban and rural areas had been one of the priorities already identified in the 1830s by William Benbow, an early English theoretician of general strike action.[83] To lighten the load on strike funds, any strikers or their families able to do so were asked to head for the countryside, where food was more easily and cheaply available. Thus large numbers of Swedish strikers evacuated Stockholm during the general strike of 1909.[84] Even more astonishing was the practice of "children's exodus," as it was called at the time, which seems to have started around 1905–1906, most notably during the Breton strike at Fougères. Léon de Seilhac, the researcher for the Musée Social commented on the originality of this tactic in his study of the 1906 lockout at Verviers in Belgium. At this time, thirty-five hundred strikers' children were packed off to the Brussels, Antwerp, and Liège areas, where they were sheltered by sympathizers.[85] Shortly before the outbreak of the 1913 Belgian general strike, contact was made with both rural and city-based families in France and the Low Countries, with a view to asking them to look after children. Twenty-five hundred offers of shelter came immediately from the Netherlands and five thousand from the north of France. Precise questionnaires were sent to all candidates by the strike committee, inquiring about their resources, their diet, and the state of their health. Support committees were formed with the aim of temporarily rehousing up to five thousand strikers' children.[86] Finally, candidatures from abroad awakened the hospitality of the Belgians themselves, so most of the children ultimately remained in Belgium, even though a few hundred were sent abroad, particularly to Lille, Roubaix, and Tourcoing in France.[87]

■ ■ ■

Food coupons for use at cooperative stores, free meals in soup kitchens, moving children away from strike locations in times of industrial action, all were innovations that completed and extended the repertoire of solidarity inaugurated by the workers' movement in the 1860s. Implementation of these procedures on a grander scale offered a means of strengthening the workers' struggle overall and of tightening the bonds among working communities so they could resist employer lockouts for longer periods.[88] For the Belgian socialist leader Louis de Brouckère, the author of a report on this question in 1907, the workers' movement now had the tools to launch much more massive protests than ever before. The strike had become a "composite weapon" that could assemble political demands, financial organization, and the provision of services and food under a single banner. It now had a permanent "socialist apparatus" at its disposal: "acts of proletarian solidarity that used to be mere accessories to strikes were growing more essential every day."[89] For this reason the Second International, while remaining at the time outwardly detached from union matters, was quietly — but very seriously — pondering the revolutionary use it could make of this already well entrenched form of mobilization.

7 | A REVOLUTIONARY WEAPON?

The generalizing of union action, recurrent economic conflicts, and the fact that acts of solidarity had become routine, all triggered a new range of aids and actions that caused a degree of controversy but ultimately forged closer links among European workers. The major strikes in the first decade of the century led to exchanges of funds and ways of helping that crossed frontiers. Might these practices of solidarity prove useful across an even wider spectrum? This was a central question at the dawn of the twentieth century, as the European socialist movement steadily gathered way. The means mobilized in conflicts enabled solidarity and interdependence to advance. Was this a sign that a generally broader political solidarity was emerging, which would one day transcend professional and national frontiers? It was no longer just a matter of reflecting on the opposition between work and capital but, rather, of seeing exactly how solidarity could contribute to political gains for the working world. These debates lay at the core of the Second International, which relied on new techniques of solidarity to create a broad movement promoting socialist ideas. Ever since its foundation in Paris in 1889, the "new" International, as it was called at the time to distinguish it from the old one, had wrestled with the idea that political parties and union organizations had to be separate entities. The wall dividing them, which was porous to begin with, grew much more solid during the 1890s, in particular during the London Congress of 1896 that officially excluded anarchists and enshrined the principle of a separation between political and corporative congresses.[1] This separation, which resulted in the creation of the International Secretariat in 1901, existed internationally (but not necessarily nationally) between parties and unions in different countries. It ranged from the highly conflictual situation in France right through to the strongly interpenetrative relationships prevailing in Germany and the Scandinavian countries. Even in countries where an overlap between the two structures was well under way, the unions clung to their control of operations of solidarity, being much better at it than the political parties. Meanwhile in the United States, the internationalist ideal was perpetuated within a revolutionary, syndicalist structure known as "Industrial Workers of the World."

THE PRIMACY OF NATIONAL ORGANIZATIONS

Although it claimed to be the natural heir of the IWA, the Second International was determined not to repeat the mistakes of its predecessor. For this reason, for over a decade it "refused to see itself as any kind of institution," as the historian Georges Haupt has noted.[2] Prior to 1900, it only existed through its congresses, which were held every two or three years and brought together a number of completely autonomous national groups. There was a strict rule that the International would recognize only one political party in each country, and little by little this nudged the various brands of socialism into a single united front at national level. This period of relative uncertainty came to an end in 1900, with the creation of the International Socialist Bureau (ISB), which was based in Brussels at the Maison du Peuple. The ISB, which enjoyed strong human and financial resources, was designed to play a liaison role, rather than replicate the model of the IWA's general council. Its principal mission was to assemble the archives of the First International, with a view to compiling a written history of the socialist workers' movement.[3] Its first secretary was the Belgian Victor Serwy, succeeded in 1905 by Camille Huysmans, who was the driving force behind it until the outbreak of the First World War. Bitter memories of the general council of the First International, and the divisions it created, explain why the means allocated to the ISB remained strictly limited. Its budget came from the membership dues of the member parties: some of these were well-off and good payers, but many others had difficulty keeping their pledges, either for lack of the will to do so or for lack of money. Huysmans was extremely prudent as well as a skilled diplomat; he did his best to bring in membership fees on time and impose a minimal budget — much less than the resources available to national parties — on the structure he directed.

This financial weakness was just what most of the socialists of the period wanted, given that they were firmly opposed to working from a powerful policy-oriented center. Ever since 1889, priority had been given to Engels's wish to build powerful national parties in preference to international structures.[4] This is why there were so many who, like Édouard Vaillant, saw the ISB as a simple instrument of "correlation," which did not require substantial funding. Nevertheless, the moment had come for socialists and social democrats to grow into mass organizations and electoral juggernauts; a takeover of political power by means of universal male suffrage looked to be within their grasp. In Germany, Austria, Belgium, Sweden, and Denmark, socialist parties were securing between one-quarter and one-third of the vote just before the outbreak of the First World War.[5] In other words, socialists were major participants in parliamentary life — and by the same token, in the nationalization of private companies. The national echelon was much stronger and offered a sounder structure for the internationalism of the turn of the twentieth century than it had done in the 1860s, when "translocal" relationships still predominated and there was no centralized institution to mediate.[6] This trend was further reinforced by the first stages of social legislation that all over Europe and ever since the 1880s, had helped workers integrate into national life by giving them rights and protections guaranteed by the state. Even if the origins of these measures, which involved labor legislation, social insurance, and social assistance, were more international than previously thought, they created rights and duties that were relevant to the concepts of nation and citizenship.[7]

The establishment of socialist parties and unions brought the practices of solidarity directly to bear on the daily lives of militants. Encouraged by their electoral successes, they built a wide network of groups, associations, and cooperatives, creating a form of "counter society" in which solidarity was a feature at every stage of workers' lives. The best exemplars of this were the German and Austrian social democratic parties, whose activists in the larger cities ran kindergartens, cooperatives, libraries, choirs, and sporting associations of their own. Solidarity-generated facilities like these helped to strengthen worker culture by integrating women and young people, in preparation for future battles.[8] They also opened the way to new forms of internationalism, such as the creation in 1907 of the Socialist Women's International, with Clara Zetkin as its president; among other things, this marked a decisive rapprochement between feminism and socialism. Such institutions benefited from the extra support given to them by socialist municipalities, which had been constantly growing in numbers since the 1880s. The winning of local power made it possible for elected socialists to apply their programs in earnest, without waiting for the universal triumph of socialism. In Belgium, Germany, and France (first in Lille, then in Roubaix and other major urban centers), socialist towns supported education for the people and assistance for the poor, while giving control of utilities to municipalities and subsidizing cooperatives, labor exchanges, and cultural associations.[9] Nor did these local bases exclude the transfer of know-how and skills across frontiers, by way of international networks for social reform.[10]

THE SPREAD OF SOCIALISM WORLDWIDE

Despite the preponderance of national organizations, some militants considered entrusting the ISB with special responsibility in the coordination and organization of solidarity campaigns on a European scale, operating like the International Secretariat. This question was placed on the discussion agenda for the Copenhagen Congress in 1910, article 7 of which outlined the possibility of improving the organization and structuring of international solidarity, thereby making it easier for European socialists to take collective action. Just as it had over union matters, the German delegation objected. The members of the Sozialdemokratische Partei Deutschlands (SPD), who invariably preferred national to international action, dismissed the idea of organizing international solidarity as hopelessly utopian. They warned against the use of public subscription campaigns on behalf of international causes whose effectiveness was limited at best. Such campaigns should be reserved for "cases of major importance, that would impress the masses"; if overused, they would result in failure. Any broad appeal to public emotion should be viewed as an addition to, not a substitute for, the regular collection of funds by national organizations. The Swedish and Belgian representatives did not share this view, to put it mildly; especially the Swedes, who were still sore that foreign help had taken too long to reach them during their general strike in 1909.[11] They wanted the ISB to be given extraordinary powers for the coordination of international solidarity, without waiting for the representatives of every country to decide what they thought about it. The Belgians proposed, in vain, that the ISB should be authorized to raise exceptional levies of up to one-tenth of the annual subscription totals of member parties (though no more than once a year). What was feasible for certain international professional federations was unthinkable for the political parties, which jealously protected their procedures and prerogatives. The congresses had to settle for statements expressing the International's moral support for certain causes, and for arranging collections when workers in different industries were striking simultaneously (as was the case for the miners of Fourmies in 1891 or the Stuttgart strikers in 1907).[12]

Although its means were limited, the ISB set out boldly to promote the planetary spread of socialism. This objective went hand in hand with the conviction, affirmed by Émile Vandervelde at Stuttgart in 1907, that "our ideal encompasses the entire universe, which is why we will conquer the world."[13] One of the first vectors of this spread was the worker and socialist press. This explains why the German social democrats regularly helped socialist newspapers in other countries when they ran into financial difficulties, as did the Dutch newspaper *Het Volk* in the fall of 1906, which received 25,000 francs from the SPD only a couple of years after it began publishing.[14] August Bebel himself attended a solidarity meeting in Geneva to help Jean Jaurès's newspaper, which had "deserved well of international socialism," in particular with the funds it had raised in 1905 on behalf of the Russian revolutionaries.[15]

The propaganda activities of the ISB were deployed through the many manifestos and appeals it published over the years in support of socialists implicated in the constitutional revolutions in Russia in 1905, in Persia in 1906, and in China in 1911.[16] It also announced the violence against Jews in the Russian Empire, against Armenians and Greeks in the Ottoman Empire, and the lynching of Negroes in the United States.[17] This use of the written word could result in the organization of major demonstrations, whose effect was to place worker solidarity at center stage. Lacking the power to dispense financial and material aid of any significance, the IBS concentrated on symbols, in the hope that solidarity would flow from the great gatherings it sponsored. The historian Kevin Callahan refers to this as "a mass-based political culture of demonstration that effectively displayed a united image of socialist solidarity in the public sphere while promoting a sense of common purpose and fraternity amid great ideological, national and cultural diversity within its sections."[18] This culture of symbols reached its apogee between 1900 and 1910, when international collective action was ritualized at the funerals of prominent European socialists. For example, when Wilhelm Liebknecht died in 1900 a subscription was raised for a lavish monument to his memory.

This universal solidarity, proclaimed everywhere at demonstrations and in speeches, was expected to apply well beyond the European working class. Up to a point it was subject to restrictions, because racial frontiers were still present even in internationalist circles.[19] These limitations to the concept of universalism came into the open whenever the question of immigration was under discussion. The congresses of the Second International did their best to reconcile the opposing positions, and in a perilous balancing act they reiterated their commitment to the legal protection of foreign workers — against whom there should be no discrimination based on their origins. This general principle also had to exclude blacklegs and foreign workers imported by employers during strikes; free circulation of labor was perfectly legitimate on condition that it did not impinge on the rights of workers. But the representatives of the countries targeted by immigrants — like Argentina and the United States — wished to go further. In 1904, at the congress of Amsterdam, the Argentinians, Americans, Australians, and South Africans militated for the control and restriction of migrants. The Argentinian socialists considered that it was imperative not only to restrict the "artificial immigration policy" maintained by their governments but also to make European workers fully aware of the true working and living conditions on the other side of the Atlantic.[20]

This debate over immigration also brought to light a racially biased view of workers and their rights. The first attacks were on what was known as the "yellow peril" of the Chinese and Japanese, as opposed to white European immigration. The American delegate Morris Hillquit, of the Socialist Party of America, declared his determination to fight against the "Chinese coolies" whom he accused of "negating the proper organization of unions." His remarks were contradicted by several other speakers, among them another member of the American delegation, Nicholas Klein.[21] The debate resumed in 1907, and the Americans and Australians repeated their positions, which were based on the supposed inability of Asiatic workers to organize themselves, and solidarity could therefore not be applied to them. An Australian representative, Victor Kroemer, put this in the crudest terms: "White emigrant workers easily organize, whereas colored ones object to the very idea. This is what led the Australian Labor party to impose the principles of white Australia on yellow immigrants. We make this exception only for Asiatics, who are incapable of being an integral part of the organized working-class." In case there was any further doubt, Hillquit, the American delegate, made it even clearer: "the Chinese...are still too far behind us, to be organized." Only one Japanese representative, Kato Tokijiro, dared to protest: "The Japanese are victims of capitalism just like any other people, and if they emigrate abroad, it is because they cannot find the sustenance they need in their own country."[22]

The prohibitionists were in a minority: the Amsterdam Congress ruled against any legislative measure intended to hinder emigration. The socialist ideal promoted equality in civil and political rights and favored the integration of foreign travelers into trade unions. All racial discrimination was condemned at Stuttgart, with the exception of certain contract laborers, about whom manipulative transportation companies and capitalist enterprises were accused of spreading disinformation.[23] Nevertheless, the French delegates Jules Uhry and Adéodat Compère-Morel were appalled by the protectionist attitudes of the Americans and Australians. Solidarity had certainly become international, but it was still far from being universal.[24]

SUPPORT FOR THE RUSSIAN REVOLUTION

The 1905 Russian Revolution revealed an area in which the ISB and the Second International could experiment and mobilize on an international scale, with solidarity ceasing to be mere lip service. On 18 February 1905, a few days after the Bloody Sunday massacre of scores of demonstrators in St.Petersburg, the ISB began publishing a circular recommending the opening of subscriptions all over Europe to help the Russian and Polish socialist parties. Newspapers were asked to publicize the appeal and open subscription registers.[25] Later, on 30 June 1905, a more formal manifesto was adopted, calling for international help for the liberal and socialist opposition in its emblematic conflict with the Russian tsarist government. The ISB also played its part in attempting to mobilize public opinion and tighten the links between socialists of all nations: "The International proletariat cannot remain indifferent to this titanic struggle against blind reactionary forces. Our voice of protest must be heard everywhere; above all we must help our brothers in Russia with every means at our disposal! Our solidarity must be translated into action!"[26] Words were no longer enough. Strikes and demonstrations of support were organized, notably on 22 January 1906, one year after the revolution began. The workers of Europe were asked to give up half a day's work, or the wages of one hour, to help the Russian cause.[27]

The ISB went on to focus its operations by opening a Russia Appeal, a rare example of the central committee of the Second International directly putting together a subscription fund. Money poured in: November 1906 saw 82,000 francs collected, considerably more than the ISB's own entire budget for that month.[28] In July 1907, just before the opening of the Stuttgart Congress, the Russia Appeal was assessed at a total of 141,996 francs.[29] The Russian diaspora in the United States had contributed handsomely.[30] *L'Humanité* opened a subscription that raised 20,000 francs.[31] The French socialists, like the ISB itself, did their best to persuade French workers and holders of savings not to subscribe to any Russian government loan. As Jean Jaurès put it, "any French citizen who subscribes to the Russian Loan is an accomplice to the organized murder of an entire people."[32] All the same, in spite of his efforts, Russian government bonds were indeed massively subscribed.[33]

Figures published by the ISB were partial in nature, because they did not include money sent directly by German social democrats to the Russian revolutionaries. Just as they did in union matters, the Germans gave priority to bilateral relations. The funds they collected in this instance far exceeded those sent by the ISB: at the margins of the many strikes and demonstrations organized in Germany in sympathy with the Russian cause, the various sections of the SDP managed to raise 340,000 marks (400,000 francs) for the Russian revolutionaries prior to 1907, to which was added a payment of 22,000 marks made by the party's directorate toward the election campaign of December 1906 for the first Russian Duma (parliament). Thus a total of 435,000 francs was contributed to the Russian Revolution by the SDP, three times more money than all the other socialist parties combined.[34]

As usual, the contributions that came from Germany outweighed all the other forms of mobilization. The financial power of German social democracy was unparalleled: the SPD amassed no less than 1.6 million francs in 1906, while the Section Française de l'Internationale Ouvrière (SFIO) managed a mere 180,000 francs to pay for its own budget in 1913, which logically flowed from worker solidarity.[35] But German aid took other forms as well: exiled revolutionaries were taken in, supported, and helped to find work or continue their journey westward. The SPD also supplied legal aid to immigrants and protested against their expulsion from Russia. The ISB complemented this action by helping individual activists, who were given money to tide them over.[36]

Aid to the Russian Revolution also came from the United States, by way of the networks of solidarity woven by the Jewish diaspora, above all after the mass emigration that followed the pogroms of 1880–1890. The General Jewish Labour Bund, founded in 1890 in Poland and Lithuania, was instrumental in transferring the most significant sums of money in this regard. In 1905, the Bund union had about thirty-five thousand members, scattered across the territories of the "Zone of Residence" to which the Russian Empire's Jewish population was confined. Members were also present in western Europe (the foreign committee of the Bund was based in Geneva) and on the East Coast of the United States.

As an anti-Zionist organization, the Bund favored the formation of self-defense committees against Russian pogroms and against violence in general.[37] Its ability to raise funds on both sides of the Atlantic was remarkable for its time: the American committees were transferring an average of $40,000 per year to Europe in the years immediately prior to the First World War. These funds were not the fruit of charitable gestures by wealthy people but were from much more modest contributions — typically between fifty cents and two dollars — made by thousands of Jewish workers, particularly during solidarity strikes organized in the United States.[38] Numerous collections were launched when news of the events in Russia reached America: the Bund was proud of having initiated a flow of American gold to help the revolution, largely thanks to a fundraising that achieved the impressive total of 1.3 million francs between 1904 and 1906, of which 610,000 francs were allocated to its foreign committee.[39] As the historian Frank Wolff has shown, the Bund's network of mutual aid was instrumental in weaving the many strands of global solidarity into a local context.[40]

The brutality of the tsarist repression brought about a diversification of aid and assistance. It was no longer a matter of helping to keep strikes going with food and money but also of arming revolutionaries in what looked like it was becoming an authentic civil war. The ISB received numerous appeals confirming this. For example, the Russian exiles in San Francisco wrote, "the Russian nation needs support from outside to overthrow this dynasty of massacre and pillage, of tyranny and barbarity incarnate. The Russian proletariat should not have to wait a single day longer for the books and weapons the world's socialists can provide."[41] Arms and munitions were needed in addition to cash. The Armenians opened a subscription clearly indicating that the money collected would help them "arm themselves," in the most literal sense.[42] Huysmans, without openly saying so, participated in arming the Bolsheviks: it was through him that the money used to buy weapons was transferred, after he agreed to receive and invest the money expropriated in controversial fashion by the Bolsheviks.[43] In Germany too, the police suspected the SPD of having covered up paramilitary trafficking operations carried out with the Russian revolutionaries.[44]

The buildup of funds for Russia raised awkward questions about how it should be shared out. The ISB was obliged to justify its choices as to how this would work, within a particularly difficult context where theological and national divisions were constantly gnawing at the socialist world.[45] The various Russian parties, the Poles, the Bund, and the Armenians all wanted their share of the cash and demanded that the ISB explain its policy; hence the collection launched in the name of revolutionary solidarity was still far from eliminating innate conflicts and suspicions. The bureau, having decided to hide nothing, revealed in its bulletin exactly how funds had been divided among the various parties.[46] Many of them were disappointed: for instance, the Armenian socialists were particularly outraged by what they took to be an imbalance strongly favoring the Russian socialists.[47]

All these questions of attribution reflected a more fundamental issue: that of the unity of worker representation and the multiple conflicts that were tearing apart the socialist world in eastern Europe. This eventually led to a famous controversy between Lenin and Rosa Luxemburg in 1911–1912, when Luxemburg refused to give the Russians the right to speak in the name of the Polish socialists whom she purported to represent. Conversely, the Russian Social-Democratic Workers' Party tried, through an intervention by Lev Kamenev, to monopolize international aid and minimize the shares of it allocated to other national political parties.[48] He suggested that the ISB centralize all funds and redistribute them more efficiently.[49] No single nation was unaffected by squabbles of this kind. In 1914, when it wished to help Bulgarian socialists, the SPD opted to use the ISB as its intermediary — specifically to avoid having to choose between two organizations that were bitterly at odds over the right to represent their country.[50]

THE GENERAL STRIKE: A BURNING ISSUE

The ultimate aim of all these campaigns was to promote socialist solidarity and the expansion of the International within a number of different countries. But subscription appeals, as the German delegates hastened to point out, were only possible on a one-off basis, when provoked by events of extreme violence. On the other hand, the unions possessed a weapon of great power that had proved its value in the 1880s. Would it be possible to use the strike and its accompanying practices of solidarity in struggles other than those linked to wages and work conditions? This was the issue at stake in the debate over the usefulness and legitimacy of general strikes, which opened deep fault lines within the Second International. The difficulty lay in working out exactly how union action and political action might complement each other (an ideal state of affairs devoutly wished for by Jaurès in 1896).[51] If this could be resolved, there was no reason that an effective general strike should not advance the objective of worker emancipation to the point of winning overall political power.

Discussion of the potential of the general strike began in France in the 1880s and 1890s, within the Bourses de Travail and the CGT. Unlike the parliamentary system, which their militants opposed, the strike was viewed as a revolutionary mode of action, more in line with the anarchist-syndicalist approach. When it was debated by corporative worker groups and unions at the 1892 Marseille Congress, the general strike at first found supporters in the labor exchange milieu like Fernand Pelloutier and the young Aristide Briand, while Jules Guesde and his Workers' Party were bitterly opposed to its use.[52] But those who favored the general strike as an option were at odds about how and when it could be used. To begin with, Pelloutier acknowledged that a general strike should be actively prepared for. Later, he changed his mind: "The idea of organizing a general strike is frankly absurd," he concluded, adding that the whole principle of resistance funds for strikes and unemployed workers was also misguided.[53]

Later, between 1900 and 1914, the general strike was strongly supported within the CGT, with Georges Sorel, Émile Pouget, and Hubert Lagardelle its leading theorists. Indeed it swiftly attained mythical status among ordinary workers as the harbinger of general revolution. When asked about its realistic chances of success, advocates like Georges Yvetot replied that it was better to fail than do nothing, the classic line of defense for French partisans of the general strike; in other words, although there was no guarantee that it would work, without it the workers' party would be doomed to inertia. Where the French Socialist Party sought to achieve power through parliament, the CGT opted for the more radical road of the revolutionary general strike, which resulted in a string of failures in 1902, 1909 (postal services), and 1910 (railways). The idea won most traction in France, where workers were proportionately among the least unionized: but as far as its opponents were concerned, revolutionary syndicalism was demonstrably deadlier in word than in deed. Supporters of general strikes were convinced that they perpetuated the original ideal of the First International. The conclusion of the CGT was that "in countering the theory that socialism should be expressed through political parties, we stand for the syndicalist theory that logically derives from the ideas of our predecessors in the International Workers' Association."[54]

Elsewhere in Europe, a different concept of the general strike was developing, which would have it subordinate to political objectives. Several such strikes took place in Belgium, Holland, and Sweden during the first decade of the century, for the extension of voting rights. The socialist parties of these countries considered that the parliamentary route, however legitimate it might be, would always be a sham unless every worker had the right to vote. From this realization sprang a project for making political use of the general strike to obtain new rights and new constitutional guarantees. The first strikes of this type took place in Belgium in 1893 and 1902; these were followed by action in the Low Countries in 1903 (transport workers) and Sweden. The 1893 Belgian strike, which was supported by the Belgian Workers Party, demanded a full reform of the country's electoral system. It resulted in the adoption of universal voting rights, though this was balanced by a curious mechanism known as the *vote plural*, whereby richer individuals were awarded several votes. However, the next strike, in 1902, ended in failure despite the mobilization of nearly three hundred thousand workers, as did another in 1903 when thirty thousand Dutch workers downed tools.

Prior to its Amsterdam Congress in 1904, the International commissioned a report from the Dutch workers' party on their political action of the previous year. The report was critical of the anarchist fantasy of the general strike. At the same time its text recommended the idea of temporary, limited recourse to general strikes as the only means available to workers for bringing serious pressure to bear in countries where they still lacked the right to vote. It concluded that the success of politically driven strikes was conditional on the unity, sound organization, and collective awareness of the workers.[55] The Amsterdam Congress concurred with the Dutch resolution, rejecting a French one that it deemed tainted by anarchism: thus recourse to a general strike was not excluded, even though the delegates refused to see in it any promise of a dawning revolution.

For the Belgians, this concept signified a growth in the more general nature of trade union demands, since the formerly piecemeal approach to strike action was giving way to the pursuit of more general objectives. It was now acceptable for union savoir faire to be used for the advancement of reformist political projects. This meant clamping down on "neutralists" intent on preserving union strike action from any association with political action. Émile Vandervelde was delighted by the development of politicized reformist strikes that promised to go far beyond the pinched framework of the old corporative ones.[56] The theory was put into practice again in 1913, when the Belgian socialists voted for the principle of the general strike and then patiently organized one as if it were an economic endeavor, building reserves of money, encouraging workers to save up individually, and anticipating all forms of aid that might attenuate the cost to workers of the coming conflict and help them to keep going for as long as necessary. This peaceful strike, which involved 350,000 workers across the board (except the transport workers, whose absence proved decisive) at least obtained the nomination of a state commission and a number of other engagements from the government.

At first, the French theories about general strikes left German socialists cold and even hostile, but the debate nevertheless caught up with them in the mid 1900s. The events in Russia in 1905–1906 illustrated the revolutionary potential of the general strike, at least in the opinion of Rosa Luxemburg, who became one of its most fervent advocates. For her the idea was the demonstration of a brand-new concept, the "mass strike," at the heart of a broad doctrinal conflict within Germany in 1905–1906. Luxemburg deliberately used the expression *Massenstreik* to emphasize her difference with the anarchist propagators of the general strike. As in Belgium and Sweden, the German socialists reflected on the possibility of making limited use of the strike for political ends, with the aim of forcing a change in a Prussian electoral system that hinged on the existence of three distinct classes (the richest being politically overrepresented). The discussion was opened at the SPD Congress at Jena in 1905, against a backdrop of uprisings in Belgium, Sweden, Austria, and Finland. Several high officials of the SPD, among them Eduard Bernstein, were reluctant to extend the use of the strike to cover any purposes other than electoral ones. But, here again, Luxemburg was enthusiastic about the revolutionary possibilities of the mass strike: rather than establishing a definite line where the industrial strike ended and the political struggle began, she saw in it an opportunity to start a process by which the economic strike would gradually become a force for revolutionary change, in the wake of repressive intervention by government authorities. If the general strike had so much promise, it was because of a potential for participants' energy and emotion to overflow and become full-on violent and revolutionary. For this reason it was pointless to organize and prepare any particular action: according to Luxemburg, an effective organization would spring naturally from the energy and massive scale of the event itself. Thus she was able to justify both the spontaneity of the masses and the need to channel it, on condition that this did not relapse into bureaucratic rigidity.[57] In short, her vision was diametrically opposed to that of the Belgian socialists, who so carefully prepared their political general strike in 1913.[58]

In 1906 at the SPD Congress at Mannheim, Luxemburg proposed the adoption of the principle of the mass strike as an offensive revolutionary weapon that could be used without the formal approval of unions. This would also make it possible to broaden the sociological perimeter of German unionism. Any overdependence on the mechanisms of union organization would get in the way of a direct appeal to the masses: "The rigid, mechanical-bureaucratic conception cannot conceive of the struggle save as the product of organization at a certain stage of its strength. On the contrary, the living, dialectical explanation makes the organization arise as a product of the struggle."[59]

These ideas provoked an outcry among the free German unions, which were determined to keep control of an instrument of mobilization they had been patiently perfecting since the early 1890s. Legien and the leaders of the Generalkommission feared a possible hijacking of the strike weapon, which they believed would lose its effectiveness if in any way harnessed to political demands or revolutionary projects.[60] The internal debate within the German social democratic milieu culminated in 1906, in which year the syndicalists finally prevailed. Without categorically rejecting the general strike (though it might be considered in exceptional circumstances), the party roundly condemned its use for revolutionary purposes.[61] The main objective of any strike was to raise wage levels and improve working conditions, and all other issues should be decided by elections and parliaments. This point of view, which was obviously contrary to Luxemburg's, reflected the free unions' contemporary domination of the German socialist galaxy. Although less familiar to the public than the SPD, the unions had more adherents and hence a wider sphere of influence. The historian Stefan Berger describes their determination to syndicalize the SPD, whose 384,000 members were dwarfed in 1906 by the 1.7 million free unionists. In the event, the membership of the SPD increased threefold, up to the outbreak of the Great War, by which time it had surpassed one million.[62]

REVOLUTIONARY SYNDICALISM IN THE USA

In 1905, the debates over general strikes found an echo on the other side of the Atlantic, with the creation in Chicago of a new union, the Industrial Workers of the World (IWW). The craft unionism promoted by the American Federation of Labor was heavily criticized in American socialist and anarchist circles, which had lacked a powerful organization ever since the sudden collapse of the Knights of Labor in the late 1880s. The AFL was viewed as altogether too conservative, timid, and closed to the various minority groups within the working class — for example, women, Black workers, and recently arrived immigrants were scarcely represented at all.[63] In the spirit of unity and revolutionary radicalism, two hundred delegates came together in June 1905 to found "One Big Union" and bring the internationalist ideal to America. The members who were present for the occasion illustrate the social and political openness of this new umbrella union, which at its start brought together socialists (Eugene V. Debs, Daniel De Leon), anarchists, and unionists. Lucy Parsons — a militant anarchist and the widow of Albert Parsons, one of the martyrs of the Haymarket executed in 1887 — took part in this first meeting and gave enthusiastic backing to the idea of an industrial union resolutely in favor of radical strikes and radical action in general.

The working linchpin of this organization until the end of the First World War was the syndicalist and socialist William D. "Big Bill" Haywood, who was involved in many strikes during these years.

The "Wobblies," as the roughly one hundred thousand activists controlled by the IWW were known when it was at its peak, were fairly close to the "anarcho-syndicalist" ideas of the French CGT, whose Amiens Charter of 1906 had laid out a set of guiding principles (union independence from political parties, primacy of class struggle, and recourse to the general strike).[64] In the European syndicalist world, by comparison with the German juggernaut, the French theorists of the general strike had aroused considerable interest outside France, particularly in the United States. For example, the American anarchist Emma Goldman closely followed the debates launched by Gustave Hervé and Georges Sorel.[65] The themes of sabotage and direct action remained popular, even as the attempts of the CGT to provoke a general strike in France were failing one after another.

Like the First International fifty years earlier, the IWW gained its reputation by the strikes it organized all over America and by its conviction that solidarity had to be expressed in action and had to go beyond any conceivable limits of type, race, nationality, craft, or trade. It was the return of a phase of intense worker mobilization, thirty years after the great upheaval of the 1880s, that depended on workers from the European diaspora (Italians, Finns, eastern European Jews, etc). As in Europe and the United Kingdom, the American struggle reached its height in the years 1912–1913. The strikes of textile workers in Lawrence, Massachusetts (1912), hop field laborers in Wheatland, California (1913), and the famous "free speech strikes" for the defense of union liberties were among the best-known episodes in this wave of mobilization. Interestingly, the practices of solidarity applied on these occasions sometimes quite closely resembled the ones in Europe. For example, during the

Lawrence strike, Margaret Sanger and other activists organized the transfer of strikers' children to sympathetic families in New York and Vermont, just as was happening in Belgium and France at the same time. Money was also sent from various unions and from the Socialist Party of America, to help the strikers. Most of these had come to the USA in the latest surge of immigrants and were consequently ill-defended by the AFL, if they were defended at all.

The Wobblies appropriated the messianic tone of the internationalist discourse forged in the 1860s, whereby unions should overarch all frontiers and work toward the ultimate goal of universal emancipation of all workers, both male and female. Their leading newspaper was — significantly enough — entitled *Solidarity*: the imperative of solidarity, so ubiquitously present in the words of the founders of the first International, was the banner behind which every activist of worker internationalism stood. Obviously, the IWW had to cope with obstacles that were much the same as those faced by the associations that had gone before. Whereas the Second International had made a choice in favor of political action and socialism at the risk of cutting itself off from a large section of the syndicalist world, the anarchist-influenced American organization was reluctant to engage directly in the political struggle. At the same time, the old internal battles continued to rage between activists who wanted to decentralize the movement and those who wanted to see it even more centralized than it was already. Finally, the internationalism of the IWW, which was a real force in the USA given the extreme national and ethnic diversity of its members, came overwhelmingly into play at a continental level. Whereas the First International had been a fundamentally European association, despite a few more distant connections, the IWW was a quintessentially American union, of great importance in the social history of the nation, which managed to maintain vital links with Mexico, Latin America, and the surrounding English language countries.[66] What the two had in common was ferocious repression by government authorities that had enfeebled both — in the wake of the Commune, in the case of the IWA, and during the First World War, in the case of the IWW, whose members were hunted, arrested, and deported first in 1917 for their opposition to the war and then, in 1919, at the time of the first "Red Scare" and the Bolshevik revolution.[67]

THE ROUT OF ANTI-MILITARISM

In Europe, the general strike took on fresh importance as military and diplomatic tensions grew around the Moroccan crises (1905 and 1911), involving France and Germany, and persisted through to the Balkan Wars (1912–1913). These tensions threatened to force the implosion of the vast zone disputed by the Ottoman, Austro-Hungarian, and Russian Empires, and thence — by diplomatic association and networks of alliances — the entire European continent. The Second International was alert to the threat of war at a very early stage and did what it could to further the anti-militarist cause, just as the First International had done in its time. But socialists disagreed about the means to be used. The suggestion of a general strike to head off a war was not a new one, having been raised during the 1890s by the Dutch anarchist Domela Nieuwenhuis. It reemerged in the 1900s, championed by the French militant Gustave Hervé, and after that was regularly discussed at professional federation congresses. At one international meeting of the metallurgists' federation, English trade unionists took strong issue with the French, deeming them both weak and unreasonably bellicose.[68] The supposed "spontaneity" of their response was also heavily criticized. The debate grew sharper following the congress of the International at Stuttgart in 1907 and led to a confrontation between German and French concepts of the general strike. Legien, as always seeking to draw a line between syndicalist action and political struggle, declared that the general strike should never be part of the union repertoire:

> The employer class cannot be overcome by mere force of temperament. Only when the French have a serious union organization, will they stop going on and on about general strikes, direct action, and sabotage. Of course, I understand that the general strike may under certain circumstances be a political weapon, but I certainly don't see it as any kind of weapon for unions. The day the French have a serious union organization, they will stop acting like they did last spring. They will cease to imagine that the eight-hour day can be achieved at a single stroke. If you want reforms like that, you must first build large and solid organizations — and that means hard work and sacrifice.... You don't fight the bourgeoisie with rhetoric; you fight them by bringing workers into organizations that all pursue the same goal and are willing to struggle side by side to achieve it.[69]

The discussion was started by a resolution introduced by Gustave Hervé and opposed by Jules Guesde.[70] For Guesde, the "military-style" strike was a derivative that would distance the workers from the real battle. "By concentrating all the workers' efforts on the suppression of militarism in today's society, whether we like it or not, we will be operating to preserve the status quo by diverting the working class from that which should be its sole preoccupation — the seizure of political power for capitalist expropriation, and a socialist appropriation of the means of production."[71] Jaurès and Vaillant were less direct in their response, acknowledging that recourse to the general strike "was possible" in the event of armed conflict breaking out, which naturally provoked the vigorous opposition of right-wing SPD German delegates such as Georg von Vollmar. In his view, "The idea of stopping war with militant industrial action is just about as absurd as the idea of stopping capitalism with a general strike."[72] Luxemburg distanced herself from her German comrades over this, on the grounds that the Russian

Revolution had hastened the end of the Russo-Japanese War in 1905. As far as she was concerned, mass strikes were entirely legitimate. Eventually these widely differing positions led to an impasse: no strategy against war was resolved, and no single coordinated course of action was agreed upon.[73]

The debate was a bitter one, and it left scars. Hervé blamed the Germans, who were under the influence of their free unions and so were nothing but "an admirable machine for voting and paying dues." He went on to tell them: "You have no idea of revolution. You can float as far as you like in clouds of thought, but faced with a government, you prevaricate, you run away. You're scared of going to jail."[74] This onslaught infuriated the German socialists, many of whose older delegates had endured arrests and trials during the anti-socialist period (1878–1890). Bebel, himself an icon of the international socialist movement at that time, responded with gusto. He pointed out that a general strike, quite apart from being extremely difficult to implement, would only worsen the state of workers, who might lose their jobs and sink into poverty should economic life and international exchanges be curtailed in any way. Above all, he accused Hervé of ignoring the aid and assistance the Germans had given to their European neighbors, from the ample funds they had themselves amassed:

BEBEL Hervé calls the German Social Democratic Party a voting-and-dues "collecting machine." I say nothing about our votes, because you vote just as we do. As for our bulging coffers, I don't see what's wrong with them. . . . I even think they exemplify a virtue worthy of imitation (*laughter*). Our comrades from other countries know very well that we don't always contribute according to our own selfish interest. Often enough we have had the pleasure of placing our "machine" at the disposal of parties much less fortunate than ourselves. (*Quite right!*)

JAURÈS We know this, and we are grateful to you.

BEBEL It is our hope that in future our "machine" will contribute even more.

ADLER We will accept, with pleasure (*loud laughter*).[75]

Rejection of war was a shared sentiment within the International. The universal horror felt by European freethinkers, anarchists, and socialists at the execution of Francisco Ferrer in October 1909 gave way to a conviction that henceforth the masses would be ready to rise up in support of anti-militarism and anti-clericalism.[76] How that would work was a matter for discussion; obviously, demonstrations alone were not sufficient. For some, the general strike was the most effective and threatening weapon of worker solidarity; but was it possible to make use of it for a project as vast as this, or even to apply it outside the sphere of trade unionism? The debate over means and objectives was closely involved here: the participation of trade unions appeared vital in guaranteeing the effectiveness of a form of mobilization requiring so high a degree of coordination. Consequently, in 1910 the Miners' International Federation announced that it would call for a general suspension of work if any state, whether monarchical or bourgeois republican, should threaten the peace of Europe.[77] Resolutions in favor of a general strike in the event of war were tabled again in 1910 by Jaurès and Keir Hardie, and in 1912 Vaillant declared his belief that the militarist danger could be met by this means.[78] In short, the proletariat saw itself as fulfilling a messianic role in preventing the outbreak of war.

■ ■ ■

These convictions were to collide with the harsh reality of geopolitical conflict in the years 1912–1914. In spite of its pacifist assurances, the Second International failed to mobilize European workers against the war. A few acts of solidarity were arranged on behalf of socialists in the Balkans in 1912–1913, but no agreement was ever reached for a general uprising.[79] Socialists were far from alone in this failure; many, many others were blinded and misled by the macabre chain of events that led to disaster.[80] But socialist disillusionment was all the more bitter, insofar as activists had for years been aware of the danger and had tried in vain to raise the alarm. The Second International was supposed to dissolve all national frameworks by making class solidarity universal; yet it too found itself seduced by nationalism, which in the end led most of the world's socialist parties to join one or another holy alliance.[81] In a few countries this was not the case — in the United States, for example, where the IWW was firmly against the country's joining the war and was immediately repressed. Politically unable as it was to transpose the trade union movement's experience of strike action, worker solidarity foundered on its own fundamental contradictions and ultimately on its refusal, inherited from the First International, to entrust a genuinely international body with the responsibility of engaging and coordinating actions of protest and mutual assistance.

8 | FOOTPRINTS AND LEGACIES

Worker internationalism failed dismally to raise the masses against the war of 1914. The issue looked to be settled once and for all: national war mobilizations trumped class solidarities, and socialist pacifism was an illusion. The story might have ended there, with an acknowledgment of defeat, an abject surrender to violence and the abandonment of all ideals. Yet when the Great War was over, the appeal to international worker solidarity was brought back to life by the communist revolution, by socialists, and by trade unionists convinced of the need to carry the international struggle for social justice to a new level.[1] Far from being forgotten, the accumulated experience of the years between 1860 and 1914 — when the worker solidarities that concern us here were hatched and brought to maturity — was to overshadow the twentieth century right through to the 1970s.

The goal in this concluding chapter is not to analyze in detail the way that practices of mutual aid proliferated after 1918 (a trunkload of books would scarcely begin to do that) but to highlight the legacies and derivations by which they were connected to the nineteenth-century infancy of worker internationalism. Indeed, it was in the twentieth century that international worker solidarity became truly global and universalist, despite its context of rival ideologies and mobilizing masses.

COMPETING BENEFITS

Although they were mostly suspended during the Great War, socialist and worker solidarities were quickly reactivated with the coming of peace. The institutional and political failure of the Second International did not obliterate the repertoire of ideas and practices it had helped to forge. The great novelty of the post 1917–1918 world was the emergence of a new fault line between socialists and communists, when the myth of a united working class was shattered by the establishment of a Bolshevik regime and the revolutionary years between 1918 and 1920. During this period, the organization of solidarity became more than ever a political battlefield, as the frontiers between trade union action, humanitarian engagement, and revolutionary agitation were far less clear than they had been in the early 1900s. Strikes, fundraising, the relief of famine, and political mutual assistance had become so many complementary facets of a global battle between communists, socialists, and liberal philanthropists. In this fight, ferocious competition among the different brands of solidarity was bound to put an end to any lingering dreams of unity.[2]

The reduction in actions of solidarity in the immediate postwar era came about through the creation of new international organizations that were both antagonistic and complementary to one other. A new International Federation of Trade Unions (IFTU), inspired by social democratic ideals, was refounded in 1919 in Amsterdam (whence the "Amsterdam International" sobriquet). Under its new leader, Edo Fimmen, this federation was soon competing directly with the red syndicalist international (Profintern), created in Moscow in 1921, which was largely made up of Soviet trade unions and minority groups within professional federations already attached to the IFTU.[3] In the United States, the Wobblies were sharply divided over whether to take part in this new adventure. The IFTU and the Profintern had strategies and convictions that were polar opposites, right up to their final rapprochement in 1937 with the Popular Front movement. Their repertoire of actions during strikes and movements of solidarity was freely adapted from the past, but their attitude to reform and to other international institutions created in the wake of the Treaty of Versailles was markedly different. The IFTU, in addition to its many other projects of solidarity, aligned itself with the International Labor Organization (ILO), where it strove to represent the syndicalist working world. Albert Thomas, the first general director of the ILO, attended the 1924 IFTU Congress to explain the links between reformist syndicalists and the institution that he headed.[4] At this time, the international professional federations that had originated in the 1890s were reconstituting themselves, most of them choosing to have their headquarters outside Germany.

Meanwhile, a much more pronounced imbalance was emerging on the political front: the Communist Third International, highly centralized and based in Moscow, was disrupting the scheme of things to which international worker organizations had been accustomed for decades. For a start, the quarrels that had so divided activists of the First and Second Internationals were rendered irrelevant by the Comintern's view of itself as a straightforwardly bureaucratic, centralized organization serving the interests of Soviet Russia. The intrinsic fragilities of previous international associations that had once expressed the vitality of a culture of worker autonomy abruptly ceased to be an issue after the Comintern's Moscow base assumed its position as central controller of world revolution. Never before had an international workers' organization developed such a degree of "discipline, centralisation and bureaucratisation," or such a formidable network of agents abroad.[5]

As in the 1860s, but far more systematically, the circulation of men and money hinged on the distribution of false passports, sophisticated new means of transferring funds and information, and the promotion of exemplary "militant individualities" by way of autobiographical memoirs.[6] For Lenin, the lesson of the Second International's failure was crystal clear: revolution was an undertaking not for amateurs but for highly organized professionals. In an article written in September 1917, he appropriated for his own use some of the favorite dictums of the International Workers' Association: "For internationalism consists of *deeds* and not phrases, not expressions of solidarity, not resolutions."[7] As a result, the Comintern had lavish means at its disposal, with which the Labor and Socialist International (LSI), reconstituted in 1923, could not compete. The LSI, of course, counted on the League of Nations to resolve trade union issues, preserve the peace, and bring about social reform. The Comintern counted on nothing but all-out revolution.[8]

Apart from maintaining close connections with communist parties in various countries, between the wars the Comintern put in place a series of new mutual help organizations that increased its capacity to take action and spread propaganda. The organization of its solidarity devolved from the creation of Workers' International Relief (WIR, also known as the Internationale Arbeiterhilfe) in 1921, which was followed in 1922 by International Red Aid (Internationale Rotehilfe).[9] The WIR was based in Berlin and directed by the activist Willi Münzenberg, in conjunction with the German Communist Party (KPD); its goal was to orchestrate worldwide worker solidarity on behalf of civilians, persecuted militants, and strikers of all nations. Red Aid's more limited raison d'être was to help victims of revolution and communists on the run from the authorities, wherever they might be. Tightly controlled by Moscow, which wanted to provide the communist world with an institution comparable to the International Red Cross, its first presidents were the Pole Julian Marchewski and after him, in the mid 1920s, Clara Zetkin, who had earlier been a leading figure in the prewar German Social Democratic party. Red Aid was present in no fewer than forty-four countries, a significant aftereffect of the First World War.[10] Its speciality was helping victims of repression in postrevolutionary circumstances. Between them, these two complementary but differing organizations shared the mission of enlarging the meaning and practices of international worker solidarity, at the meeting point of trade union action, humanitarian aid, and mutual political assistance.

During the 1920s the promotion, improvement, and celebration of international worker solidarity became a central issue for Soviet propaganda and its struggle against American imperialism. These institutions were certainly not exclusively at the beck and call of Moscow (this view of them has anyway been largely rejected in recent years by historians of communism), but they did play a crucial part in political communication and the overall battle for influence. In this area, the organizing and propagandizing gifts of Willi Münzenberg stood out. A major figure and militant socialist at the crossroads between communist activism, propaganda, and artistic action, Münzenberg had spent the war as a refugee in Switzerland; he was a supporter of the Spartacist revolt in January 1919, as well as various other revolutionary movements. The WIR gave him a key role in the world of international solidarity, and in the 1920s he arranged a series of aid and fundraising initiatives through a network of cultural mediums (theater, cinema, literature, and newspapers) to publicize his actions and promote the universal merit of communist solidarity. Never before his time had solidarity been so important a vector for political mobilization and celebration.

From the beginning of the 1920s, the communists were determined to show they were capable of helping and serving the people in a broader and more effective way than their reformist adversaries. Lenin and Münzenberg were both intent on competing with American philanthropy in the name of anti-imperialism.[11] The first experimental attempts at international assistance were made in Vienna and in Poland in 1919, and later in Russia, where the population was ravaged by poverty and famine. These contexts offered an opportunity to the United States — operating through the American Relief Administration founded in 1919 by President Wilson and directed by Herbert Hoover — to use food supplies, expertise, and economic aid as barriers against the spread of revolution.[12] Depending on which camp one belonged to, solidarity was a weapon either to attack or to defend the revolution; but for both sides it was a vital element to convince people of the benefits of their own model and showcase the generosity of the various organizations competing for attention. The WIR tried to blindside American Relief and the socialist ISF with aid shipments to destitute people in Vienna and Russia: they managed to do better than the ISF, but were significantly outspent by American Relief, whose financial clout came from a subtle combination of public money, philanthropic donations, and capital funding.[13]

The Russian famine inaugurated ten years of relentless solidarity action for the WIR, culminating in Berlin in 1931 when Münzenberg organized a world congress of international solidarity to celebrate the tenth birthday of the institution. A work of several hundred pages, soberly entitled *Solidarität*, synthesized all the areas of action where the WIR had intervened, including photographic illustrations, drawings, and reproductions of posters. Münzenberg was at pains to present international relief as a "total" institution, which had raised funds, financed strikes, and distributed food and clothing on every continent, while relieving the suffering caused by natural, social, and political disasters. Solidarity had become an ideological and political battlefield: doing good had now to demonstrate the moral and economic superiority of one system over the other.

BLURRED BOUNDARIES

Perhaps the most intriguing phenomenon of these years was the despecialization of worker solidarity. Prior to 1914, for example, the German trade unions had attempted to draw a clear line between the strike weapon, which was used for labor conflicts, and political mobilization. The model of a strong trade union membership slowly but surely imposed itself as the most effective form of defense for the interests of the working world and for the organization of solidarity in the event of strikes. After 1920, the WIR and the IFTU conjugated their activities and methods of intervention: support for strikes remained a central element of worker solidarity, but it was balanced henceforward by closer attention to humanitarian issues and political conflicts.

In this sense, both motivationally and practically, worker solidarities were enlarged and hybridized with forms of action that had previously been kept at arm's length. At the time of the First International, when trade unions had little power, all this was indeterminate; specialization and the division of tasks were uppermost at the turn of the twentieth century, despite the appeals of advocates of the revolutionary strike such as Rosa Luxemburg. After the war, organizational weaknesses were addressed, and there was a return to combined action on the trade union, political, and philanthropic register, based on a newfound immense ability to raise funds and expedite them to Europe and elsewhere. Solidarity was now a total and global phenomenon, embracing humanitarian, trade union, and political causes at a single stroke. Solidarity coincided with projects for social change, some communist, others socialist or reformist in nature, "whose organisms had in common the idea of inserting concrete aid activities (reception, lodging, economic support, and legal help for workers) into a wider strategy of social and political change, struggle against injustice, and the elimination of social and political inequalities," wrote the historians Gotovitch and Morelli.[14]

Support for strikes and the aid given to the mobilization of workers obviously remained at the core of mutual aid practices throughout this period, but they could not be independent of contemporary social and political conditions. In 1921–1922, both the IFTU and the WIR brought massive aid to the workers and trade unions of Germany, hard hit by inflation. Among the reformists, the Swedes and the Americans were also major contributors; indeed, the help given by the Swedes showed that the relationship they had formed with the Germans before the war remained intact, since one-third of the money raised by the IFTU for German workers came directly from Sweden (less than 1 percent came from France).[15] International mutual help during periods of strike action still depended on practices and procedures put in place prior to 1914. The general miners' strike in Great Britain in 1926 left nobody indifferent. The IFTU sent money to the British miners on this occasion and loaned additional funds to the British Trades Union Congress.[16] Not to be outdone, the WIR made its own substantial effort to help the British workers, sending money, food, and clothing. Just as it had been before 1914, solidarity was expressed by actions aimed at countering employer strategies: for example, the workers of Hamburg struck in sympathy with the British and prevented the passage through their port of eventual strikebreakers.[17]

Interestingly enough, at this time both communist and socialist solidarity organizations began to adopt the terminology and practices of philanthropy. This had started with the help initiatives organized for the inhabitants of Vienna in Austria struck by famine in the immediate aftermath of the war, which were followed by aid to Russians similarly affected.[18] Obviously, the primary motivation here was one of humanity and compassion for those suffering from hunger. Hoover's American Relief Administration combined with the two socialist organizations to send food, with mixed results on the ground. The IFTU, which was not the most active agent on these two fronts, managed to raise one million florins for the Viennese workers, and two million for "starving Russians." Their methods of collecting money and involving donors used classic procedures of philanthropic action; for example, sales of stamps encouraged members of the CGT in France to send small sums on a regular basis to help the Viennese workers.[19] This philanthropic playbook, after the experience of total mobilization during the war, easily laid the foundations for a mass form of philanthropy, which counted just as much on generous donations by the very rich as on the offerings of workers and ordinary people.[20] The funds also yielded aid in kind, which was transported by rail. Basic provisions like margarine, cheese, and potatoes were sent in this way, at a time when galloping inflation made cash assistance problematic. The Danes even managed to send ten railway cars packed with salted herring through to Vienna.

The compassionate tone of these first actions was further reinforced by the care taken to prioritize the most vulnerable people — meaning children. In May 1919, the English philanthropist Eglantyne Jebb founded the Save the Children Fund, a new humanitarian charity that quickly won the support of American Quakers, among others. Save the Children immediately began sending food aid to those children worst hit by the hunger crisis in Vienna, Germany, and Russia, while implementing a program to evacuate them into the care of families abroad.[21] The child exodus strategy, which strikers had tested before the war and that was common practice during it, became one of the most recurrent forms of long-distance solidarity in the 1920s. The IFTU orchestrated one exodus of Viennese children in 1919, and another of German ones in the early 1920s, in the course of which Sweden took six hundred Austrian and four hundred German children; Denmark took one hundred and Holland more than two thousand Austrians.[22] Later, Münzenberg's WIR organized a "children's week" over Christmas 1924, after mobilizing the youngest during a fundraising for the Russian people in 1921. Nevertheless, the reception of refugee children met with obstacles: when more than one thousand French families volunteered to take care of German children in 1923, the Poincaré government refused to provide the necessary authorizations.[23] Red Relief also made considerable efforts on behalf of suffering children during the 1920s.

Political action and cooperation formed a third essential dimension of practices of solidarity between the wars. They were already present at the time of the First and Second Internationals, when imprisoned, hunted, or exiled activists were at issue; but the revolutionary context of the late 1910s and the early 1920s, followed by ever sharper conflict between democracies and authoritarian and fascist regimes, made the exercise of political solidarity imperative. For communists, this meant working to spread the message of revolution; for socialists, it meant stemming the tide of authoritarianism. Anti-militarism and protests against attacks on democracy were part and parcel of the 1920s and 1930s. The IFTU instigated boycott operations in Hungary and Poland at the beginning of the 1920s, protesting against the "White Terror" and blocking the flow of munitions to authoritarian regimes. It also denounced atrocities committed by the Hungarian government against worker activists and their families, appealed to the League of Nations on their behalf, and then decided — when it became clear that no international action would be forthcoming — to promote a blockade of the country by immobilizing railways, shipping, and postal services.[24] In 1922 the federation went on to start an antiwar fund, fed by the proceeds from sales of stamps and posters designed by Steinlein and Käthe Kollwitz.

In the meantime, a fascist government came to power in Italy in 1922, while the Weimar Republic's position in Germany continued to weaken. The IFTU, with the support of the Labor and Socialist International, responded by placing anti-fascism at the heart of its political and social action. A "Matteotti Fund" was created in 1926 to help Italian activists repressed by Mussolini's regime, but the political dangers to it eventually became so dire that in 1933 this fund, which was jointly administered by the two organizations, had to be renamed the "International Solidarity Fund." Cofinanced by socialist parties and trade unions, its mission in the 1930s was to bring material and legal help to exiles and proscribed victims of fascist and Nazi repression, whether they were Italian, Jewish, or Austrian.[25]

The Bund, the trade union of eastern European and American Jewish workers, was another mutual aid network, combining class struggle, actions of solidarity, and support for people resisting fascism. Money was raised for it as far away as Argentina to finance strikes, build schools, and draw attention to the fascist threat. Like its fellow organizations, the Bund blended trade union techniques and philanthropic savoir faire, constantly enlarging its networks of solidarity, despite the forced exile of many Bund members after the arrival in power of the Bolsheviks.[26]

GLOBAL STRUGGLE

Ever since the 1860s, the rhetoric of the First and Second Internationals had been universalist, and its effects had seldom spread beyond the frontiers of western Europe and the USA. Prior to 1914, worker internationalism had remained a movement focused on Europe, with progressively more significant extensions into eastern Europe after the first Russian Revolution in 1905. On the other side of the Atlantic, the IWW integrated migrants from Europe and deepened connections with the workers of Mexico and Latin America, but Black workers remained largely outside their action. The language of international solidarity covered methods and practices that, to begin with, concerned relatively small numbers of qualified white workers in western Europe and America, but which later broadened and became more democratic at the end of the nineteenth century. The endless debates over immigration and how to control or even prevent it showed how far racial frontiers could explicitly limit the internationalist horizon of workers. After the First World War, with reaction to the Wilsonian project and the onset of anti-colonialist protest, international workers' solidarity took on a new and much greater significance, spilling far beyond the European context.[27] Beginning in the 1920s, the language of class solidarity broadened its field of application to include workers in countries outside Europe, many of which were under colonial domination.

The Comintern was highly active in all this, even though other solidarity organizations like the IFTU also ventured well beyond European frontiers. Communist solidarity was now thought of as existing throughout the world, with the Comintern as its center of coordination and impulse for revolutionary and anti-colonialist movements. This "global communism," which balanced centralized resources with local dynamics, was henceforth to be at the heart of the historiography of communism, consistently favoring a closer integration of the transnational movements and exchanges that communism involved.[28] The Soviet view was that socialist internationalism flowed directly from the idealistic melting pot of the First International, which it claimed to be overtaking and extending. Thus, centralization and universalization would be the two driving elements of "progress" added by the Bolshevik revolution to earlier forms of internationalism, whose means and ambitions were now viewed as pitiable at best. Lifetime socialists who turned to communism in the early 1920s contributed eagerly to this version of history: among them were Zéphirin Camélinat, who was praised to the skies by the French section of the Communist International; and Charles Rappoport, who declared that the "authentic communist spirit" was already present in the IWA, a claim easily refuted by anyone who has read the debates of the general council.[29]

The global and political dimension of these campaigns of solidarity was perfectly illustrated by mobilizations all over the world on behalf of two anarchist militants of Italian origin, Nicola Sacco and Bartolomeo Vanzetti, who were accused by American authorities of having committed a murder near Boston in 1920. All the ingredients of international workers' solidarity immediately came together to make these two men martyrs of the global cause, which was very popular with the masses and intellectuals — even more popular, in fact, than the cause of the Haymarket martyrs in 1886. Their belonging to the Italian diaspora, so numerous in the United States and South America, and their devotion to the anarchist movement earned Sacco and Vanzetti the support of workers and militants alike for at least three decades and on several continents. But the anarchist revolt was not what it had been prior to 1914.[30] Communists quickly grasped the advantage to be gained from supporting the two Italian American anarchists, despite their ideological differences with them: indeed, the gulf between Comintern-style centralization and anarchist federalism had never been so profound as it was in the early 1920s. The case of Sacco and Vanzetti, however, neatly encapsulated the violence, injustice, and sham of American capitalism. The charge brought against them symbolized the inhumanity of the American system, especially after that system's brutal repression of anarchists and socialists in the years 1918 and 1919. Best of all, the Sacco/Vanzetti affair not only dented the image of the United States as a land of freedom and equality; it also allowed communists to distract international public attention from the even uglier events taking place at the same time in the USSR. Just as the anarchist Francisco Ferrer had lent his image to the furious opposition to the Roman Catholic Church in 1909, Sacco and Vanzetti became the heroes of a mobilization directed against the USA and its judicial system. The unions (the Confederazione Generale del Lavoro in Italy, the CGT, the Confederation générale du travail unitaire [CGTU] in France), plus communist organizations and socialist parties, called on workers everywhere to strike and demonstrate in support of the anarchists Sacco and Vanzetti, who were finally executed in August 1927 after they ran out of legal options to appeal their sentences. In Argentina, China, Germany, and many other countries, activist workers loudly protested this injustice around American consulates.[31] There can be no doubt that without the participation of worker organizations of all stripes, this mass mobilization would never have spread as widely as it did.

The Comintern's embrace of anti-colonialism gave its action an unheard-of global heft, which became a powerful feature of the operations carried out by socialist and social democratic organizations. Strike relief assistance was no longer confined to European and American workers: in 1925, the IFTU and the WIR turned to India and China, where worker movements and revolutionary protests were gathering strength. The IFTU sent money to striking Indian workers in 1926, though very little by comparison with what was sent to the Russians in the early years of the decade. The more openly revolutionary WIR gave financial support to strikes that broke out in Shanghai, Beijing, and Canton in 1925. This support was designed to help the preparations of communist forces for the coming revolution.

This dynamic comforted and invigorated the anti-imperialist project of communist internationalists, who were no longer content merely to rant about the evil financial power of America. From the 1920s onward, they worked to establish interlocking solidarities between communist workers and anti-colonialist militants, to create a junction that the earlier workers' Internationals had never quite managed. The Comintern forged links with Indian revolutionaries through figures like Manabendra Nath Roy, who connected southern Asia with Central America by taking part in the foundation of the Mexican Communist Party in 1919 and developing a radical critique of colonialism. They also made contact with such militants of the Black, Pan-African cause in the USA as the

Communist Party member George Padmore, a Trinidadian immigrant.[32] Münzenberg himself contributed in 1927 to the creation in Brussels of the league against imperialism and colonial oppression, while the Pan-African Congress held in the same year in New York debated possible points of convergence between Pan-Africanism and communism. The Comintern, in concert with the Profintern, in July 1930 created an International Trade Union Committee of Negro Workers, based in Hamburg, whose mission was to deploy militant activism among the workers of the Atlantic world and to denounce imperialism in Africa.[33] These clandestine solidarities mostly affected maritime transport, as when Italian ships were boycotted after the outbreak of Mussolini's war against Ethiopia in 1935. In the seaports of Britain, South Africa, and the USA, militant solidarity united Black and white workers in a common cause.[34] The publication of the *Negro Worker* newspaper (sponsored by the International Trade Union Committee and published by Padmore) under the aegis of the League Against Imperialism, brought about a convergence of struggles at a time when the Nazi and fascist threats were making international worker solidarity ever more necessary and urgent. For the first time, the workers' movement had made a clear commitment against racial discrimination and colonialism.[35]

The despecialization, politicization, and extension of international worker solidarities and their effects all came together during the Spanish Civil War (1936–1939). All the practices that had been drafted before that time were suddenly systematized, in a new context of rapprochement between socialist forces and communist parties. The aid provided to the Spanish Republicans, who were engaged in combat from July 1936 onward against the troops of General Franco supported by Nazi Germany and fascist Italy, launched an unprecedented international campaign of support. The International Solidarity Fund, managed by socialists, received contributions from nineteen countries, international union organizations, the Bund, and young socialist associations, with the largest donations coming from France, the United Kingdom, Belgium, and the United States. As it had been ever since the early 1920s, aid to the Spanish Republicans and the foreigners fighting alongside them took many different forms, from food and cigarettes to spare parts. The war in Spain above all marked a high point in communist-internationalist action, not only through the creation of the International Brigades, which attracted thirty-five thousand volunteers from more than fifty different countries, but also by way of the help supplied by Red Relief, which was then at the top of its game.[36] The International Brigades were a kind of babel of solidarity, with scores of different languages, trajectories, and cultures represented in their ranks.[37] In August 1936 Münzenberg, who remained perpetually active within the communist movement until forced to distance himself during Stalin's purges, set up an international committee of coordination and information to assist the Spanish Republic, which raised more than 100 million French francs.[38] Eight committees sprang up on several continents, making it possible to send quantities of food and medicine to Spain, along with medical doctors, weaponry, and munitions. Money came from fundraising efforts in which Soviet citizens were strongly urged to participate. Just like before, during the pre-1914 working men's strikes, and during the operations of humanitarian assistance to Viennese and Russian workers in the early 1920s, a massive evacuation of Spanish children was arranged by trade unions and associations whereby fifty-one thousand Spanish children found refuge abroad, fifteen thousand of them in France alone.[39] In general, the war in Spain made it clear that international workers' solidarity was no longer confined to factories and major economic protests. Henceforth it was at the very heart of armed conflicts, wherever the great confrontation between democracy, fascism, and communism was being played out. Far from being spectators of history, committed workers played a major part in it, even though the great powers sometimes took advantage of their internationalism and they found themselves crushed by imperialist-militarist nation states.

BIPOLAR SOLIDARITIES

For nearly a century, from the 1860s right through to the 1970s, worker internationalism had witnessed phases of great hope followed by cruel disillusion, especially during the two world wars. But the accumulated store of experience remained solid. The first age of worker solidarity, in the years between 1860 and 1900, was one of project, experimentation, and apprenticeship. The initial reluctance of militants to found permanent organizations was overtaken between the two wars, under the effect of bitter competition for the fruits of solidarity between communist and socialist Internationals, Christian trade unions, and American philanthropic foundations. During the same period, the sociological and geographical frontiers of worker internationalism were pushed back in spectacular fashion. The integration of the masses into political parties and unions diversified the actors and beneficiaries of solidarity, which henceforth included not only masculine workers in heavy industry but also their wives and children, immigrant and colonized workers, and what remained of the old professions that had played founding roles prior to 1914. Universal solidarity was no longer an empty promise: in embracing anti-imperialist, anti-colonialist, and anti-fascist causes, the workers' movements of the 1920–1930 period, whatever their affiliation, spoke to everyone. The awareness of functioning in a globalized world, where major ideological conflicts could easily leapfrog frontiers, was comforted by the real and solid capacity of organizations to raise funds, provide assistance in the form of food and weaponry, and transfer activist savoir faire from one country to another or even from one continent to another. The repertoire of actions of solidarity, composed of words, gestures, rituals, and methods of mutual aid developed ever since the 1860s, bestowed a political and symbolic centrality on the working world that in the mid twentieth century could no longer be denied.

The three decades that separated the end of the Second World War from the beginning of the age of deindustrialization and the end of the Cold War, at the close of the 1980s, were at once the zenith and the tipping point of this phase of history. The great crosscurrents of change between the two wars were exposed all too clearly by the global confrontation between the Soviet and capitalist blocs. The idea of internationalist engagement was omnipresent in the communist world and had taken root among the working classes of the Western world's liberal democracies, at a time when the mobility of capital and labor was far more limited than it had been prior to the Great Depression of the 1930s.[40] Hence the great paradox: internationalism was inherent to both of the dominant political ideologies of the era, even though the world's economies had grown less globalized and more regulated than before. The workers had won new rights; they had mobilized for wars for their countries and defended their national organizations, while continuing to see themselves as members of a universal working class that transcended frontiers. The refounding of the great structures of worker internationalism immediately following the Second World War showed this very clearly: despite the savagery of the conflict that had just ended and the immense power amassed in the course of it by nation states, the trade union movement went ahead and reconstituted the great organizations responsible for the management of international solidarity. A new World Federation of Trade Unions — founded in 1945 on the ruins of the prewar International Federation of Trade Unions — embodied the aspiration for worker unity, in a context where trade unions were expected to control the regulation of work, the adoption of social policies, and the establishment of "built-in" liberalism.[41] That unity was far from perfect because, ever since the years between the wars, an autonomous Christian-leaning syndicalist federation (the World Confederation of Labor) had continued to thrive. Above all, as it had done in the early 1920s, international syndicalism was split by the advent of the Cold War, whereupon the main American and British centers of influence (the AFL and the TUC) decided to create their own regime to amalgamate the unions of the "free world" and prevent a communist takeover of the World Federation of Trade Unions. From this decision sprang the International Confederation of Free Trade Unions (ICFTU), founded in 1949, which perpetuated the institutional infighting of the 1920s and 1930s.[42]

The logic of confrontation between two blocs, with parallel structures of exchange and solidarity, did not stifle other forms of internationalism, which prospered in vacant crevices between the two rival behemoths in the 1950s. Third Worldism was already active and established by the beginning of the 1960s; the critique of colonialism and the attainment of independence by numerous African and Asian countries placed the problem of development at center stage for international organizations, trade union movements, and Great Power governments alike.[43] The rivalry between free unions and communist ones found in this a new area of expression: solidarity with workers recently freed from imperial domination was decisive in embedding the seductive potential of imperial domination's direct opposite. The British and American unions worked hard to reconcile solidarity with geopolitical considerations, and communist militants did much the same. For example, in 1956 the ICFTU opened a fund to support the victims of repression in Hungary, at a time when the Stalinist edifice was under heavy fire from all quarters. A year later, it launched another international appeal for solidarity toward the countries of the Third World; and just as they had done in 1860–1870 vis-à-vis the European continent, British trade unionists called for active political support for African workers, on condition that they adopt British modes of organization and set aside all socialist aspirations.[44]

The AFL-CIO (so called since the AFL's 1955 amalgamation with the Congress of Industrial Organizations, an autonomous movement founded before the war) was the sole major American union at the time, and as such, it had no difficulty endorsing the objectives of American foreign policy during the 1950s. The money it dispensed, particularly in South America, offered a way to combat the communist unions and propagate "pure and simple politics," a model completely innocent of revolutionary ambition against which, in their time, the Knights of Labor and the Wobblies had fought both tooth and nail.[45] Communists found it easy, in return, to denounce the imperialism of Western trade union leaders. In East Germany, "international solidarity" took on a decidedly Third World–ish tinge between 1960 and 1970; the population was called upon to mobilize relentlessly to help solidify socialist unity abroad. The authorities sent more and more cash, experts, and volunteers to "build" socialism in newly independent countries.[46]

In the end, the two blocs fell a long way short of channeling international methods of solidarity. Moscow's star continued to fade in the face of the new power of attraction displayed by the Chinese and Cuban revolutions; while the reputation of the Americans foundered in Vietnam as leftists, trade unionists, and Third-Worldists borrowed the language and methods of international solidarity, more to subvert the two-pole logic than to make it work. This explained the emergence of composite coalitions that, in the 1970s, orchestrated massive campaigns of protest against attacks on the freedom and rights of workers. From the end of the 1960s, the AFL-CIO was worried about the rising frequency of contacts between trade union figures on either side of the Iron Curtain. Because of this it decided to leave the ICFTU, which it had itself helped to create, rather than see it adopt slogans for worker action against official American foreign policy.

Nor were these fears unfounded. On 11 September 1973, a CIA-backed coup d'état in Chile led by General Pinochet against the socialist president, Salvador Allende, led to a wave of protest and solidarity that transcended political differences and frontiers, even though it was a bit rich for communists to be denouncing American fascism and imperialism at that time. The warm welcome extended to Chilean exiles abroad, the bitter condemnation of the Chilean military and its exactions, and the overwhelming support in other countries for the building of a foreign-based Chilean opposition galvanized scores of unions, associations, humanitarian NGOs, artists, and intellectuals in Europe and South America.[47] It was hardly an accident that the trade unionists of Chile's central workers' union (Central Unicá de Trabajadores de Chile) were the first victims of Pinochet's repression, for they embodied a set of values cordially loathed by his putschist government. In response, the socialists rebuilt their organization and networks from Europe, long range, with the support of the two main international trade union federations (communist and free social-democratic). These federations mounted aid projects in cooperation with the ILO, as well as with national organizations such as the TUC in Great Britain.[48] The traditional base of worker internationalism, reminiscent of the glory days of anti-fascist mobilization to help the Spanish Republicans in the 1930s, was reinforced by Third-Worldist, religious, and humanitarian organizations (among them CIMADE, a French NGO, and Amnesty International) that operated on a transnational scale and were wholly independent of Moscow or any other government. The campaign for Chile produced the first signs of a rift between class struggle and principled humanitarianism. The language of the rights of man, focused on violations of fundamental rights, secured widespread support for Chile in all manner of different quarters; but at the same time, it led worker militants to distance themselves from the revolutionary political ambitions of international solidarity.[49]

Indeed, a combination of trade union mobilization and humanitarian engagement was to characterize all the last international movements within which workers proper were able to play a decisive part. This was especially the case in the struggle against apartheid in South Africa and, more generally, in the critique of communist regimes. The solidarity movement of the Polish workers in Gdansk in the early 1980s mirrored the campaign for Chile of a few years earlier, and this time American imperialism was not at issue: the target was the authoritarianism of the so-called people's democracies, against a background of growing anti-totalitarian sentiment within the intellectual and political elites of western Europe. The Solidarnosc union, founded by Anna Walentynowicz and Lech Walesa after the great Polish dockworkers' strike in the summer of 1980, became the symbol of protest against the power of the communist state, supported by the Catholic Church and by noncommunist international labor institutions like the ILO. The first to join this campaign of solidarity abroad were syndicalist organizations (the AFL-CIO in the United States, the CFDT in France, and the DGB [Deutscher Gewerkschaftsbund] in West Germany), all of which sent huge quantities of money — $4 million from America alone — along with food and vital supplies of ink, paper, and presses to print newspapers and tracts. Nevertheless, the language of the rights of man supplied ample cover for the mobilized Polish workers, especially after the imposition of martial law by General Jaruzelski in December 1981.[50]

■ ■ ■

The widespread solidarity campaigns of the 1970s were also, in a way, the swan song of worker internationalism, on the brink of a decade that was to be marked by crisis in industrial societies, neoliberal assaults on the legitimacy of unions (particularly in the United Kingdom and the United States), and the steady erosion of militant union membership. Between the early 1970s and the late 1980s, industrial society cracked and crumbled. Worker collectives, though still active, were at the same time permanently tested by mass unemployment, polarization of the labor market, and in some countries, relentless government attacks on trade unions (which were blamed for social unrest), inflation of salaries and prices, and prevailing states of rigidity and economic inertia. Although trade unions had led the "first globalization" in the late nineteenth century, this new phase of it — later to result in the growth of finance-driven, deregulated capitalism at the turn of the twenty-first century — could not emerge until worker organizations had been brought into line and their goal of international solidarity replaced by one of consumerist individualism.

Not that the world of the workers suddenly disappeared with the crisis that began in the 1970s. Far from it. But the organization and international impetus that had held trade unions together since the end of the nineteenth century fell apart so emphatically that they started to look old-fashioned and incapable of collective action. In more recently industrialized places such as China or Southeast Asia, the existence of unions would be instrumental in improving working conditions and wages; but in areas hit hard by deindustrialization, such as the USA and western Europe, the decline of syndicalism and the near disappearance of political parties representing workers' interests left a keen sense of abandonment. This sense was all too frequently expressed in demands for protection, or in racial and nationalist conflicts; the effects of this weakening rippled outward beyond national frontiers, even though trade unions still claimed to represent a certain idea of international solidarity and worker combativeness. Thus the way was opened for a version of globalization at once less regulated and more unequal than before, whereby capital prospered and wages languished. Worst of all, this played out against a background of implacable competition for jobs, among workers unprotected by any trade union and hence in deadly peril.[51]

Conclusion

The globalization of the nineteenth century produced many new types and conditions of international solidarity. Workers were not alone in wanting to extend mutual assistance across national borders: philanthropists, missionaries, and political exiles also sought to establish long-distance relations with one another for exactly the same purpose. Nevertheless, the internationalist workers' project that took hold in the 1860s had strong characteristics of its own. Its aim was to unite the workers — regardless of their nationality, language, or culture — against the globalization of capital and the oppression of bourgeois governments. The initial objective was not so much to seize power and place limits on people as to construct an alternative form of international solidarity. This project was inspired by a horizontal approach to economic and social relationships, whereby the sharing and circulation of worker-generated wealth might benefit everyone instead of stirring up rivalry and contention. The conclusions of Marx and the founders of the First International were irrefutable: for as long as no universal solidarity existed among them, the workers would always be be losers in the race for globalization, perpetually contributing to their own enslavement and bickering over narrow particularist demands.

The original internationalist workers' project was clear enough in theory, though in practice it was chaotic and contentious. It was, however, a notable achievement. Within a few years of the project's beginning, sound guidelines for establishing loans and mutual aid had been developed among workers based in different countries. The tactic of strike action offered golden opportunities to test these new links of solidarity at a time when the collapse of a dispute in one place could have a tangible effect on conditions in another. Thus the "solidarity of struggle" was shown to be no vain concept. After the 1860s, those who argued in favor of international solidarity could do so in the serious expectation that resources invested in social conflicts would lead to an all-round, collective improvement in workers' wages and conditions — as opposed to leaving the market to reward the lowest bidder, as usual. In the years between 1860 and 1870, the desire for a collective regulation of the jobs market by strengthening workers' capacity for struggle and negotiation ceased to depend on an appeal to the state or to international law. Instead, the International Workers' Association envisaged a broader "socialism of skilled workers," of a kind typified by the more qualified professions during the first phase of industrialization. Social harmony was not something that could be decreed: it had to be won, through a process of struggle and mutual aid.

The centralizing ambition of the London general council evaporated with the collapse of the First International in the 1870s. By that time, more important things were happening elsewhere, as worker communities fell into the habit of exchanging views, dispatching aid across frontiers, and comparing different ways of emancipating and organizing themselves. Their approach to internationalism rested for a while on the identities and solidarities of the surviving skilled professions, but before long, tensions and divisions appeared between the better organized sets of workers, who were proud of their autonomy and power, and those who came from the heavy industrial sectors, who were still largely non-syndicalist and ill-prepared for major social conflict. By the close of the century this sociological constraint on worker internationalism, which derived from inequalities based on types of profession, was mostly a thing of the past. At a time when skilled workers' practices of mutual aid were becoming the norm among international professional federations, workers in heavy industry were launching strikes of a completely different kind, on a scale never seen before in terms of sheer size, duration, and social and international impact. The strike weapon was entering its own industrial age, fully dependent on the mass character of trade union organizations. Although the advocates of spontaneous revolution continued to improvise, the reality was that trade unions now sat at the fulcrum of international solidarity. The American Knights of Labor offered a first transatlantic demonstration of this in the 1880s; within ten years, German and Scandinavian unions had progressed to a model based on mass worker membership, huge fundraising, and the provision of a range of services from assistance to strikers to sickness and travel allowances. All of these features made it possible for them to introduce their members to a broad network of established rights and dependable emergency aid.

This expansion of union involvement coincided with a new centralization of decision-making. National and international solidarity had to be professionalized if they were ever to compete with the new forms of organization invented by employers. At the beginning of the century, the biggest strikes in Germany, the United Kingdom, and Sweden attracted substantial aid from abroad, yet foreign help never seemed to be enough to guarantee their success. It became clear that strikes were far more expensive when they were generalized to a point where male and female workers and their families had to endure weeks, even months of privation, confronted by employers determined not to give an inch. The payment of a strike salary was emphatically not sufficient. New initiatives appeared, such as feeding strikers at soup kitchens, encouraging them to take jobs elsewhere for as long as a conflict lasted, or sending their children to the countryside (or abroad) to ease the load on family budgets. The model of the "good" strike, well-prepared and highly effective, gradually became settled and even routine: before anything else happened, reserves had to be built up, local solidarity had to be deployed, and appeals had to be made to public opinion and international worker solidarity for support in a prolonged dispute. As in the 1860s, foreign mutual aid might take the form of gifts, but loans were much preferred. Loans were seen as the heritage of an era when internationalist worker militants were especially touchy about their financial autonomy.

International aid never ensured the success of any strike. On the contrary, it might signal despair or surrender, if bereft workers were seen to beg others for help. Money transfers could meet with all kinds of obstacles, even though the technical and banking conditions open to workers had changed rapidly for the better between 1860 and the beginning of the new century. Such improvements did not signify that solidarity had become simpler or more automatic. For one thing, the frontiers of its effectiveness were constantly changing, so much so that by 1900 the ongoing inclusion of workers in heavy industry sectors had led to people making distinctions between European workers and those of the rest of the world. At every stage, again and again, worker internationalism was forced to confront its own limits and contradictions. The First World War shattered many expectations; in its aftermath, it seemed that the hopes placed in the general strike would come to nothing, in the absence of any clear will to promote the internationalist cause against national resistance.

Despite all this, the long debates, growing knowledge, and repeated setbacks of worker internationalism — from the founding of the First International in September 1864 to the death of Jean Jaurès fifty years on — bequeathed a deep reservoir of experience, argument, and technique that ultimately favored the expansion of international solidarity between the wars. Communist internationalism appropriated to itself the tools and reflexes put in place at the end of the nineteenth century, by incorporating them into a project that, for the first time in human history, fully embraced the centralization of its organization and its ambition to orchestrate solidarity on a global scale. Any objective assessment would reveal everything that the Workers' International Relief (to take only one example) owed to the experiences of the past, even though the exercise might mean mixing up the practices and registers that earlier activists had strived to keep separate. The age of the masses, of propaganda, and of intense struggle between the systems of fascism, communism, and democracy projected international solidarity into another dimension altogether. This dimension was not only global but also far more political than ever before, as was shown by the answered appeals of the Spanish Civil War. The issue was not only to unite the workers and help them win their battles but also to place solidarity in the service of a cause and a struggle for influence.

What is left of that brand of working-class internationalism today? Communist activism lingered stubbornly until its hypocrisies became untenable. Its disappearance in the 1970s coincided with the collapse of the trade union movement that had powered the actions of international solidarity for a century past. Indeed, the support given to the Polish unions in the 1980s represented the last great Cold War manifestation of syndicalist mutual assistance for political objectives, after which unions and workers ceased to symbolize internationalism in any meaningful way. Today, NGOs and humanitarian associations have taken their place, appropriating a repertoire of actions based not on similarity and struggle but on "otherness" and compassion. Thus, the promotion of human rights triumphed at the very moment when the ideal of reducing economic and social inequalities was in terminal decline.[1] The "solidarity of humanity" remains far from compensating — in terms of rights and redistribution — for the "solidarity of citizenship" upon which the socialist states of the twentieth century were founded.[2]

The decline of the internationalist worker ideal has had profound consequences. The hope that capitalism might be regulated through social struggle and international cooperation has been largely dashed, though in the last two decades anti-globalization militants have achieved a measure of internationalist engagement by way of taxing financial transactions and mitigating climate change. On the whole, this internationalist critical approach to liberal globalization did not attract so many people from the lower working classes,[3] while the impossibility of reconciling globalization of capital with the fragmentation of the world of work looms just as large — and just as worrying — as it did in the 1860s. Within the European Union, employers exercise huge influence and lobbying power (without having the coherence that some claim is theirs) to compete with the mobilizing capacities of a European syndicalist confederation struggling to preserve the solidarity of social harmonization from above.[4] The differences in trade union cultures that arose at the end of the nineteenth century continue today to divide the representative organizations of European workers, according to whether they prioritize negotiation between equals, provision of services, or social conflict. Despite repeated calls to do so, the unions and social democratic parties have failed to create a European society driven by the dynamic of extending rights and protections for all. The free circulation of workers may still be functioning, but it does so in a climate of deteriorating social protections and ever more tenuous conditions of work.

All over the world, the rise of authoritarian populisms has been sustained, at some point, by a basic hostility among the working classes to immigrant workers, whom they are encouraged to see as competitors and threats to their future. National solidarities, which rest on the foundations established between 1945 and the

1980s, continue as best they can to resist the swirl of capital, rising unemployment, and declining work conditions. For all this, the analysis of the founders of the IWA remains as compelling as ever: without cooperation and organization, the working people of the world stand little or no chance of freeing themselves from unbridled competition. The integration of solidarity into the mechanism of globalization remains more than ever the greatest task and duty of humankind.

Acknowledgments

Throughout my research, I have been assisted by numerous colleagues and archivists, for whose generous encouragement, advice, and ideas I will always be grateful. In particular I wish to thank Nicolas Barreyre, Fabrice Bensimon, Axelle Brodiez-Dolino, Gilles Candar, Alain Chatriot, Marie-Emmanuelle Chessel, Michel Cordillot, Quentin Deluermoz, Patrizia Dogliani, Jean-Numa Ducange, Sabine Dullin, Juan Flores, Marion Fontaine, Étienne Forestier-Peyrat, Eric Geerkens, Rebeca Gomez Betancourt, Nicolas Hatzfeld, Gerd-Rainer Horn, François Jarrige, Paul Lagneau-Ymonet, Marc Lazar, Jeanne Lazarus, Claire Lemercier, Jeanne Moisand, Mary O'Sullivan, Michel Prat, Christophe Prochasson, Pierre Rosanvallon, Paul-André Rosental, Stephen Sawyer, Claire Silvant, Andrew W. M. Smith, Iain Stewart, Julien Vincent, Jakob Vogel, Charles Walton, and Odd Arne Westad, for commenting on earlier versions of this project during seminars and conferences, between 2015 and 2019.

At Seuil, I wish to express my heartfelt gratitude to Séverine Nikel and Patrick Boucheron for their steady belief in my project, and for their constancy in seeing it through to its original publication. This American translation has been made possible by Judith Gurewich's enthusiastic support and intellectual friendship. Since

2019, our numerous conversations on the relevance of transnational labor solidarities for understanding our contemporary political challenges, both in Europe and in the United States, have greatly improved the quality and scope of the manuscript. Anthony Roberts and all the team at Other Press, especially Alexandra Poreda and Yvonne Cárdenas, have done an incredible job in crafting this revised American version.

List of Acronyms

AD	Archives départementales
ADAV	Allgemeiner Deutscher Arbeiterverein
AFB	Académie François Bourdon (Le Creusot)
AFL	American Federation of Labor
AMAE	Archives of the Ministère des Affaires étrangères (La Courneuve)
APP	Archives of the Paris préfecture de police (Le Pré-Saint-Gervais)
ASE	Amalgamated Society of Engineers
CFDT	Confédération française démocratique du travail (French Democratic Confederation of Labor)
CGT	Confédération générale du travail (General Confederation of Labor)
CGTU	Confédération générale du travail unitaire (United General Confederation of Labor)
DGB	Deutscher Gewerkschaftsbund
FMSH	Fondation Maison des Sciences de l'Homme (Paris)
ICFTU	International Confederation of Free Trade Unions
IISH	International Institute of Social History (Amsterdam)

ILO	International Labor Organization
ISB	International Socialist Bureau
IWA	International Workingmen's Association
KPD	Kommunistische Partei Deutschlands (German Communist Party)
LSI	Labor and Socialist International
LTC	London Trades Council
MIF	Miners' International Federation
POB	Parti ouvrier belge (Belgian workers' party)
SAF	Confederation of Swedish Employers
SFIO	Section française de l'Internationale ouvrière (French Section of the Workers' International)
SPD	Sozialdemokratische Partei Deutschlands (Social Democratic Party of Germany)
TUC	Trades Union Congress
UIMM	Union des industries métallurgiques et minières
VDAV	Verband Deutscher Arbeitervereine
WIR	Workers' International Relief (Internationale Arbeiterhilfe)

Notes

INTRODUCTION

1. Suzanne Berger, *Notre première mondialisation. Leçons d'un échec oublié* (Paris: Seuil/République des idées, 2003); Christopher A. Bayly, *The Birth of the Modern World (1780–1914)* (Malden, MA: Blackwell Publishing, 2004); Jürgen Osterhammel, *The Transformation of the World: A Global History of the Nineteenth Century* (Princeton, NJ: Princeton University Press, 2014 [2009]); Pierre Singaravélou and Sylvain Venayre, eds., *Histoire du monde au XIXᵉ siècle* (Paris: Fayard, 2017).

2. Kevin H. O'Rourke and Jeffrey G. Williamson, *Globalization and History: The Evolution of a Nineteenth-Century Atlantic Economy* (Cambridge, MA: MIT Press, 1999).

3. Samuel Bernstein, *The First International in America* (New York: Augustus M. Kelley, 1962); Michel Cordillot, "Socialism v. Democracy? The IWMA in the USA, 1869–1876," in *"Arise Ye Wretched of the Earth": The First International in a Global Perspective*, ed. Fabrice Bensimon, Quentin Deluermoz, and Jeanne Moisand (Leiden: Brill, 2018), 270–81.

4. Bensimon, Deluermoz, and Moisand, *Arise Ye Wretched of the Earth*, 387.

5. *Instructions for the Delegates of the Provisional General Council*, written by Karl Marx, August 1866: https://www.marxists.org/archive/marx/works/1866/08/instructions.htm (consulted on July 13, 2022).

6. Mikhail Bakunin, *Trois conférences faites aux ouvriers du Val de Saint-Imier, mai 1871*, in *Oeuvres complètes de Bakounine* (Paris: Champ Libre, 1979), 7:244–45 (translated into English from the French).

7. E. P. Thompson, *The Making of the English Working Class* (London: 1963).

8. E. P. Thompson, *Customs in Common: Studies in Traditional Popular Culture* (New York: New Press, 1993).

9. David Featherstone, *Solidarity: Hidden Histories and Geographies of Internationalism* (London: Zed Books, 2012).

10. Steinar Stjernø, *Solidarity in Europe: The History of an Idea* (Cambridge: Cambridge University Press, 2004); Marie-Claude Blais, *La Solidarité. Histoire d'une idée* (Paris: Gallimard, 2007); Serge Audier and Léon Bourgeois, *Fonder la solidarité* (Paris: Michalon, 2007); Serge Paugam, ed., *Repenser la solidarité. L'apport des sciences sociales* (Paris: PUF, 2007).

11. Mariuccia Salvati, "Solidarietà: una scheda storica," *Parolechiave* 2 (1993); Alain Supiot, ed., *La Solidarité. Enquête sur un principe juridique* (Paris: Odile Jacob/Collège de France, 2015).

12. William Sewell, *Work and Revolution in France: The Language of Labor from the Old Regime to 1848* (Cambridge: Cambridge University Press, 1980); Bernard H. Moss, *The Origins of the French Labor Movement: The Socialism of Skilled Workers, 1830–1914* (Berkeley and Los Angeles: University of California, 1984); Gérard Noiriel, *Workers in French Society in the 19th and 20th Centuries* (New York: Berg, 1990 [1986]).

13. Seymour Drescher, *Abolition: A History of Slavery and Antislavery* (Cambridge: Cambridge University Press, 2009); Denys Barau, *La Cause des Grecs. Une histoire du mouvement philhellène, 1821–1829* (Paris: Honoré Champion, 2009); Hervé Mazurel, *Vertiges de la guerre. Byron, les philhellènes et le mirage grec* (Paris: Les Belles Lettres, 2013); Lisa Moses

Leff, *Sacred Bonds of Solidarity: The Rise of Jewish Internationalism in Nineteenth-Century France* (Palo Alto: Stanford University Press, 2006); Davide Rodogno, *Against Massacre: Humanitarian Interventions in the Ottoman Empire, 1815–1914* (Princeton, NJ: Princeton University Press, 2011).

14. Luc Boltanski, *Distant Suffering: Morality, Media, and Politics* (Cambridge: Cambridge University Press, 1999 [1993]); Pierre Rosanvallon, *The Society of Equals* (Cambridge, MA: Harvard University Press, 2013 [2011]).

15. Gauthier Chapelle and Pablo Servigne *L'Entraide. L'autre loi de la jungle* (Paris: Les Liens qui libèrent, 2017); Dean Spade, *Mutual Aid: Building Solidarity during This Crisis (and the Next)* (London: Verso, 2020).

16. Michelle Perrot, *Workers on Strike: France, 1871–1890* (New Haven, CT: Yale University Press, 1987); Jacques Rancière, *Proletarian Nights: The Workers' Dream in Nineteenth-Century France* (London: Verso, 1992 [1981]); Xavier Vigna, *L'Insubordination ouvrière dans les années 68. Essai d'histoire politique des usines* (Rennes: Presses universitaires de Rennes, 2007); Nicolas Hatzfeld, Michel Pigenet, and Xavier Vigna, eds., *Travail, travailleurs et ouvriers d'Europe au XXᵉ siècle* (Dijon: Éditions universitaires de Dijon, 2016); Michelle Zancarini-Fournel, *Les Luttes et les rêves. Une histoire populaire de la France de 1685 à nos jours* (Paris: La Découverte/Zones, 2016).

17. P. Rosanvallon, *La Question syndicale* (Paris: Calmann-Lévy, 1988); Jean-Louis Robert, Friedhelm Boll, and Antoine Prost, eds., *L'Invention des syndicalismes. Le syndicalisme en Europe occidentale à la fin du XIXᵉ siècle* (Paris: Publications de la Sorbonne, 1997); Dominique Andolfatto and Dominique Labbé, *Histoire des syndicats (1906–2006)* (Paris: Seuil, 2006).

18. Perrot, *Workers on Strike*; Leopold H. Haimson and Charles Tilly, eds., *Strikes, Wars, and Revolutions in an International Perspective: Strike Waves in the Late Nineteenth and Early Twentieth Centuries* (Cambridge: Cambridge University Press, 1989); Friedhelm Boll, *Arbeitskämpfe und Gewerkschaften in Deutschland, England und Frankreich. Ihre Entwicklung vom 19. Zum 20. Jahrhundert* (Bonn: Dietz, 1992); Stéphane Sirot, *La Grève en France. Une histoire sociale, XIXᵉ–XXᵉ siècle* (Paris: Odile Jacob, 2002); Beverly J. Silver, *Forces of Labor: Workers' Movements and Globalization since 1870* (Cambridge: Cambridge University Press, 2003); Kim Kelly,

Fight like Hell: The Untold History of American Labor (New York: Simon and Schuster, 2022).

19. Jean-Christian Vinel, "Introduction," in *La Grève en exil? Syndicalisme et démocratie aux États-Unis et en Europe de l'Ouest (XIXᵉ-XXIᵉ siècle)* (Nancy: Éditions L'Arbre bleu, 2014), 15.

20. Christophe Prochasson, "La gauche et l'argent," in *La Gauche est-elle morale?* (Paris: Flammarion, 2010), 115–58.

21. E. P. Thompson, "The Moral Economy of the English Crowd in the Eighteenth Century," *Past and Present* 50 (February 1971): 76–136; James C. Scott, *The Moral Economy of the Peasant: Rebellion and Subistence in Southeast Asia* (New Haven, CT: Yale University Press, 1976); Laurence Fontaine, *Moral Economy: Poverty, Credit, and Trust in Early Modern Europe* (Cambridge: Cambridge University Press, 2014 [2008]); Dominique Margairaz and Philippe Minard, "Marché des subsistances et économie morale: ce que 'taxer' veut dire," *Annales historiques de la Révolution française* 352 (2008): 53–99; Didier Fassin, "Les économies morales revisitées," *Annales. Histoire, sciences sociales* 64, no. 6 (2009): 1237–66.

22. Viviana A. Zelizer, *The Social Meaning of Money* (Princeton, NJ: Princeton University Press, 1995). See also Karl Polanyi, *The Great Transformation: The Political and Economic Origins of Our Time* (New York: Farrar and Rinehart, 1944).

23. V. A. Zelizer, "Payments and Social Ties," in Viviana A. Zelizer, *Economic Lives: How Culture Shapes the Economy* (Princeton, NJ: Princeton University Press, 2011), 136–49.

24. Jacques Julliard, *L'Autonomie ouvrière. Études sur le syndicalisme d'action directe* (Paris: Gallimard/Seuil, coll. Hautes Études, 1988).

25. Zelizer, *Social Meaning of Money.*

26. Mark Mazower, *Governing the World: The History of an Idea* (London: Penguin, 2012); Glenda Sluga, *Internationalism in the Age of Nationalism* (Philadelphia: University of Pennsylvania Press, 2013); Patricia Clavin and G. Sluga, eds., *Internationalisms: A Twentieth-Century History* (Cambridge: Cambridge University Press, 2017); Éric Anceau, Jacques-Olivier

Boudon, and Olivier Dard, eds., *Histoire des internationales. Europe, XIXe– XXe siècle* (Paris: Nouveau Monde Éditions, 2017).

27. Patrizia Dogliani, "Socialisme et internationalisme," *Cahiers Jaurès* 191 (2009): 11–30.

28. G. D. H. Cole, *A History of Socialist Thought*, vol. 3, part II, *The Second International* (London: MacMillan, 1956); Annie Kriegel, *Les Internationales ouvrières, 1864–1943* (Paris: PUF, 1964); Jacques Droz, *L'Internationale ouvrière de 1864 à 1920* (Paris: Center de documentation universitaire, 1965); *La Première Internationale. L'institution, l'implantation, le rayonnement* (Paris: Éditions du CNRS, 1968); Georges Haupt, *La Deuxième Internationale, 1889–1914. Étude critique des sources, essai bibliographique* (Paris/La Haye: Mouton, 1964); Frits van Holthoon and Marcel van der Linden, eds., *Internationalism in the Labour Movement, 1830–1940*, 2 vols. (Leiden: Brill, 1988); Michel Cordillot, *Aux origines du socialisme moderne. La Première Internationale, la Commune de Paris, l'exil* (Paris: Éditions de l'Atelier, 2010); Mathieu Léonard, *L'Émancipation des travailleurs. Une histoire de la Première Internationale* (Paris: La Fabrique, 2011); Maria Grazia Meriggi, *L'Internazionale degli operai. Le relazioni internazionali dei lavoratori in Europa fra la caduta della Comune e gli anni 30* (Milan: FrancoAngeli, 2014).

29. Emmanuel Jousse, "Une histoire de l'Internationale," *Cahiers Jaurès* 212–13 (2014): 11–25.

30. Martin H. Geyer and Johannes Paulmann, eds., *The Mechanics of Internationalism: Culture, Society, and Politics from the 1840s to the First World War* (Oxford: Oxford University Press, 2001); Marcel van der Linden, *Workers of the World: Essays toward a Global Labor History* (Leiden: Brill, 2008); "Travail et mondialisations," *Le Mouvement social* 241 (2012).

31. Madeleine Herren, *Internationale Organisationen seit 1865. Eine Globalgeschichte der internationalen Ordnung* (Darmstadt: Wissenschaftliche Buchgesellschaft, 2009); Paul-André Rosental, "Géopolitique et État-providence. Le BIT et la politique mondiale des migrations dans l'entre-deux-guerres," *Annales. Histoire, sciences sociales* 61, no. 1 (2006): 99–134; Sandrine Kott, "Les organisations internationales, terrains d'étude de la

globalisation. Jalons pour une approche socio-historique," *Critique interna-tionale* 52 (2011): 11–16.

32. Benedict Anderson, *Under Three Flags: Anarchism and the Anticolo-nial Imagination* (London: Verso, 2006); Ilham Khuri-Makdisi, *The Eastern Mediterranean and the Making of Global Radicalism, 1860–1914* (Berkeley: University of California Press, 2010).

I | A WORKERS' STATE?

1. Geoff Eley, *Forging Democracy: The History of the Left in Europe, 1850–2000* (Oxford: Oxford University Press, 2002), 30–32.

2. Oscar Testut, *L'Internationale. Son origine, son but, son caractère...* (Paris: Lachaud, 1871 [3rd ed.]), 61–62 (translated from the French).

3. Maurizio Isabella, *Risorgimento in Exile: Italian Émigrés and the Lib-eral International in the Post-Napoleonic Era* (Oxford: Oxford University Press, 2009); Jean-Noël Tardy, *L'Âge des ombres. Complots, conspirations et sociétés secrètes au XIXᵉ siècle* (Paris: Les Belles Lettres, 2015).

4. Jonathan Sperber, *The European Revolutions, 1848–1851* (Cambridge: Cambridge University Press, 1994).

5. *L'Égalité*, no. 32, 3 September 1870.

6. Article in *La Liberté*, May 1872 (translated from the French), BA 434, Archives of the Paris préfecture de police (APP).

7. Letter to the police prefect, 16 January 1874, BA 434, APP.

8. London, report of 14 February 1883, BA 435, APP.

9. Frédéric Monier, *Le Complot dans la République. Stratégies du secret, de Boulanger à la Cagoule* (Paris: La Découverte, 1998); Vivien Bouhey, *Les Anarchistes contre la République 1880–1914. Contribution à l'histoire des réseaux sous la troisième République* (Rennes: Presses universitaires de Rennes, 2009); Richard Bach Jensen, *The Battle against Anarchist Terror-ism: An International History, 1878–1934* (Cambridge: Cambridge Univer-sity Press, 2013).

10. During the decisive Hague Congress of 1872, James Guillaume for-malized this idea just before he was expelled from the IWA: "In the move-ment, two main ideas exist side by side: that of the centralization of power in

the hands of a few, and that of the free federation of those whom the equality of economic conditions in each country has united around the concept of interests shared by all countries.... Should we be asked, does the IWA need a head, we will answer: 'No!'" (translated from the French) Hague Congress, 5 September 1872, in *La Première Internationale. Recueil de documents publié sous la direction de Jacques Freymond* (Geneva: Droz, 1962), 2:351.

11. M. Bakunin, *La Politique de l'Internationale* (Paris: Éditions de la Vie ouvrière, 1913), 18.

12. M. Bakunin, article published in *L'Égalité*, 28 August 1869. English translation available at: https://www.marxists.org/reference/archive/bakunin/works/1869/policy-iwma.htm (consulted on 13 July 2022).

13. M. Bakunin, "Two speeches to the Congress of the IWA at Basle (1869)," intially published in French in *L'Égalité*, September 18, October 1, 1869, English translation available at: https://www.libertarian-labyrinth .org/bakunin-library/bakunin-two-speeches-to-the-congress-of-the-iwa-at -basle-1869/ (consulted on 13 July 2022).

14. On paper, the provisional rules of the association adopted in 1864 make it clear that "While united in a perpetual bond of fraternal cooperation, the workingmen's societies joining the International Association will preserve their existent organizations intact," https://www.marxists.org/history/international/iwma/documents/1864/rules.htm.

15. Henry Collins and Chimen Abramsky, *Karl Marx and the British Labour Movement: Years of the First International* (London: MacMillan, 1965), 86; K. Marx, letter to F. Engels, 19 October 1867, in K. Marx and F. Engels, *Correspondance* (Paris: Éditions sociales, 1971–2020, 13 vols.) July 1867–December 1868, 9:66.

16. "Report of the General Council to the Fourth Annual Congress," in *Minutes of the General Council*, August 1869, 3:328–29. All the English quotes of the minutes of the IWA General Council come from: Institute of Marxism-Leninism, *The General Council of the First International: Minutes*, 1864–1872, 5 vols. (Moscow: Progress Publishers, 1964).

17. Hague Congress, 5 September 1872, in *La Première Internationale. Recueil de documents*, 2:355.

18. *Minutes of the General Council*, 6 November 1866, 2:58.

19. *Minutes of the General Council*, 26 July 1870, 4:34.

20. Ibid., 35.

21. Ibid., 20 December 1870, 4:96. The figures advanced by the authorities were mostly fantasy, with no relation to the real strength of the association. A police report in February 1872 at the APP mentions "official accounts held at the general secretariat of the Association," the existence of which is highly improbable. Apparently these official accounts stated that the association had around 700,000 members in the United Kingdom, the same number in France, 290,000 in Germany, 86,000 in Switzerland, and more than 1 million in America. All this was baseless speculation; it fed the police machine, without reflecting the reality of the human extent of the association. London, report of 4 February 1872, BA 428, APP.

22. The internationalist militant Charles Rappoport remembered this at a conference he gave in May 1920, on the history of the IWA: "At that time the millions of the First International were uppermost in people's minds. When a strike broke out anywhere in Europe, the gold of the Internationale was instantly blamed. When I was in London in 1891, I remember that Engels, one of the founders of the Internationale and a close friend of Marx, laughed a lot about this legend: he said, 'In the First International, we never had anything but debts!'" (conférence de Charles Rappoport à l'école du propagandiste, fédération de la Seine du Parti socialiste, 10 May 1920, art. 54, 8D3, Georges Haupt Papers, FMSH Archives).

23. E. É. Fribourg, quoted by Camille Pelletan, "Questions d'histoire, II. L'Internationale," *Le Rappel*, 2 May 1876, BA 34, APP.

24. Rapport sur la Fédération des sociétés ouvrières, s.d. [fin des années 1870], BA 439, APP.

25. Alastair J. Reid, *United We Stand: A History of Britain's Trade Unions* (London: Allen Lane, 2004), 93, 130–55; Sarah Roddy, Julie-Marie Strange, and Bertrand Taithe, "The Charity-Mongers of Modern Babylon: Bureaucracy, Scandal, and the Transformation of the Philanthropic Marketplace, c. 1870–1912," *Journal of British Studies* 54, no. 1 (2015): 118–37.

26. Royal Trades Union Commission, *Reports of the Commissioners Appointed to Inquire into the Organisation and Rules of Trades Unions and Other Associations, with minutes of evidence* (London: Eyre, 1867–1868); George Howell, "The Financial Condition of Trades Union," *The Nineteenth Century* 12, no. 68 (1882): 481–501.

27. Margot C. Finn, *The Character of Credit: Personal Debt in English Culture, 1740–1914* (Cambridge: Cambridge University Press, 2003).

28. Collins and Abramsky, *Karl Marx and the British Labour Movement*; Gareth Stedman-Jones, *Karl Marx: Greatness and Illusion* (Cambridge, MA: Belknap Press of Harvard University Press, 2016), 470–75.

29. *Minutes of the General Council*, 26 July 1870, 4:35.

30. Ibid., 18 October 1870, 4:76.

31. London report, 8 March 1872, BA 428, APP.

32. *Minutes of the General Council*, 26 April 1870, 3:230; 9 August 1870, 4:45; 11 October 1870, 4:69.

33. Marx defended the bad management of the general council's accounts in the following terms: "The general council wished to leave bookkeeping in the hands of workers and above all, English ones, because of their general suspicion of financial matters. We also needed to find someone completely trustworthy" (9th session of the London Conference, 22 September 1871, in *La Première Internationale. Recueil de documents*, 2:212, translated in English from the French transcript).

34. *Minutes of the General Council*, 25 October 1870, 4:80.

35. *Minutes of the General Council*, 2:283–84 (Balance sheet of the International Working Men's Association, 1 September 1866 to 23 April 1867). Between 1865 and 1867, expenditure amount to over £100 (£103, to be exact), of which the expenses of the congress (for the London Conference of 1865 and the Geneva Conference of 1866) represent more than £60 (i.e., three-fifths of outlay). As for current expenses, these were divided between printing costs, correspondence, rental payments, the secretary's salary, and travel for delegates to attend conferences outside London. Had salaries been fully covered, the shortfall would have been far greater.

36. *Minutes of the General Council*, 10 May 1870, 3:233.

37. *Minutes of the General Council* 18 October 1870, 4:76. On the ambiguities of voluntary work in contemporary militant associations, see also Maud Simonet, *Le Travail bénévole. Engagement citoyen ou travail gratuit?* (Paris: La Dispute, 2010).

38. *Minutes of the General Council*, 18 October 1870, 4:75; 16 May 1871, 4:193–99; 10 October 1871, 4:201.

39. See also 9th session London Conference, 22 September 1871, in *La Première Internationale. Recueil de documents*, 2:211.

40. 9th session London Conference, 22 September 1871, see above.

41. Congress of the Hague, session of 7 September, in *La Première Internationale. Recueil de documents*, 2:363.

42. *Procès de l'Association internationale des travailleurs. Première et deuxième commissions du bureau de Paris* (Paris: Éditions d'histoire sociale internationale [EDHIS] Reprint, 1968 [1870]), 199.

43. H. Collins, "The International and the British Labour Movement: Origin of the International in England," in *La Première Internationale. L'institution, l'implantation, le rayonnement*, 37.

44. *La Première Internationale. Recueil de documents*, 1:29.

45. *Minutes of the General Council*, vol. 3, 273–78 (translated from the French).

46. *La Première Internationale. Recueil de documents*, 1:175.

47. Meeting of the Geneva tailors' section, *L'Égalité*, no. 3, 6 February 1869.

48. *La Première Internationale. Recueil de documents*, 2:177 (translated from the French).

49. William Otto Henderson, *Marx and Engels and the English Workers, and Other Essays* (London: Frank Cass, 1989).

50. *Minutes of the General Council*, 19 December 1865, 1:147.

51. Collins and Abramsky, *Karl Marx and the British Labour Movement*.

52. *La Première Internationale. Recueil de documents*, 1:163–73.

53. Geneva Congress, 8 September 1866, in *La Première Internationale. Recueil de documents*, 1:55.

54. Hague Congress, 1872, in *La Première Internationale. Recueil de documents*, 2:338.

55. *La Première Internationale. Recueil de documents*, 2:189ff.

56. Édouard Glaser de Willebrord to Karl Marx, 26, 30 April 1872, in *Documents relatifs aux militants belges de l'AIT. Correspondance, 1865–1872*, texts assembled and annotated by Daisy Eveline Devreese (Louvain-Brussels: Éditions Nauwelaerts, 1986), 374–82.

57. Report on the Verviers (Belgium) section of the International (only card-carrying members admitted), BA 436, APP.

58. London Conference permanent committee, 25 September 1865, in *Minutes of the General Council*, 1:235.

59. Arthur Hérisson, "Une Mobilisation internationale de masse à l'époque du *Risorgimento*. L'aide financière des catholiques français à la papauté (1860–1870)," *Revue d'histoire du XIXe siècle* 52 (2016): 175–92.

60. Jean-Philippe Schreiber, "L'Alliance israélite universelle, une forme pionnière de solidarité internationale?" in *Les Solidarités internationales. Histoire et perspectives*, ed. José Gotovitch and Anne Morelli (Tournay: Éditions Labor, 2003), 112–27; André Kaspi, ed., *Histoire de l'Alliance israélite universelle de 1860 à nos jours* (Paris: Armand Colin, 2010).

61. Henrietta Harrison, "'A Penny for the Little Chinese': The French Holy Childhood Association in China, 1843–1951," *American Historical Review* 113, no. 1 (2008): 72–92.

62. "To Trade, Friendly, or Any Working Men's Societies," June 1865, in *Minutes of the General Council*, 1:297.

63. Gérard Noiriel, ed., *L'Identification des personnes. Genèse d'un travail d'État* (Paris: Belin, 2007); Ilsen About and Vincent Denis, *Histoire de l'identification des personnes* (Paris: La Découverte, coll. "Repères," 2010); Keith Breckenridge and Simon Szreter, eds., *Registration and Recognition: Documenting the Person in World History* (Oxford: Oxford University Press, 2012).

64. Kenneth Arrow, *The Limits of Organization* (New York: Norton, 1974); Diego Gambetta, ed., *Trust: Making and Breaking of Cooperative Relations* (New York: Basil Blackwell, 1988); Pierre Rosanvallon, *Counter-Democracy:*

Politics in the Age of Distrust (Cambridge: Cambridge University Press, 2008 [2006]).

65. *Minutes of the General Council*, 18 July 1871, 4:236.

66. Copy of the statutes of the "Paris Section" of the International, founded in London in 1872, BA 439, APP. On the practice of "novitiates" in workers' unions and its decline at the end of the nineteenth century, see also Maxime Leroy, *La Coutume ouvrière. Syndicats, bourses du travail, fédérations professionnelles, coopératives. Doctrines et institutions* (Paris: Éditions CNT, 2007 [1913]), 1:132–33.

67. Statutes of the "Cercle révolutionnaire de 1871," in London, BA 437, APP.

68. Octave Van Suetendael, letter to "X," Brussels, 20 July 1872, in H. Wouters, *Documenten betreffende de geschiedenis der arbeidersbeweging ten tijde van de Ie Internationale (1866–1880)*, Centre interuniversitaire d'histoire contemporaine, Cahiers 60 (Leuven: Éditions Nauwelaerts, 1971, 3 vol.) 1:419 (translated from the French).

69. *Minutes of the General Council*, 26 September 1871, 4:281 (Boon's quote), and 4:530, note 274, on the context; London Conference, 22 September 1871, in *La Première Internationale. Recueil de documents*, 2:230–32.

70. Ernest Édouard Fribourg, *L'Association internationale des travailleurs* (Paris: Armand Le Chevalier Éditeur, 1871), 49. On Hermann Jung, see Marc Vuilleumier, "À propos d'un centenaire. La Première Internationale en Suisse," extract from *La Revue syndicale suisse* 9 (September 1964): 3–13.

71. César De Paepe to Alfred Herman, 23 August, 1871, in *Documents relatifs aux militants belges de l'AIT*, 321.

72. Ladislas Mysyrowicz, "Karl Marx, la Première Internationale et la statistique," *Le Mouvement social* 69 (October–December 1969): 51–84 (in particular 52–53); E. Jousse, "Les traducteurs de l'Internationale," *Cahiers Jaurès* 212–13 (2014): 181–94.

73. Congress of Lausanne, 6 September 1867, *La Première Internationale. Recueil de documents*, 1:142.

74. Antony Taylor, "'Sectarian Secret Wisdom' and Nineteenth-Century Radicalism," in Bensimon, Deluermoz, and Moisand, *Arise Ye Wretched of the Earth*, 282–96.

75. *Minutes of the General Council*, 21 June 1870, 3:253; 1 November 1870, 4:81; Address of the General Council *"Al consejo federal de la region española de la asociacion internacional de trabajadores,"* 13 February 1871, 4:346–349; 14 and 21 February 1871, 4:133 (on the Birkbeck bank); copies of two letters from Paul Brousse, Charles Alerini, and Camille Camet to the militants of Saint-Étienne, 3 and 29 June 1873, BA 437, APP; doc. no. 201, in H. Wouters, *Documenten betreffende de geschiedenis . . .* , op. cit., 1:143–44.

76. E. Varlin, letter to É. Aubry, 18 August 1869, reproduced in *Troisième procès de l'Association internationale des travailleurs à Paris* (Paris: Armand Le Chevalier, 1870 [Reprint EDHIS, 1968]) 22; Alphonse Vandenhouten to Marie Bernard, Bruxelles, 26 February 1869, and Marie Bernard to César De Paepe, 8 June 1869, in *Documents relatifs aux militants belges de l'AIT*, 131, 162; *Minutes of the General Council*, 16 November 1869, 3:178.

77. *La Première Internationale. Recueil de documents*, 1:57; *The International Courier*, 12 January 1867; letter from James Guillaume to Eugène Hins, 17 July 1871, in *Documents relatifs aux militants belges de l'AIT*, 284–85; Léonard Laborie, *L'Europe mise en réseaux. La France et la coopération internationale dans les postes et les télécommunications (années 1850 – années 1950)* (Brussels: P.I.E. Peter Lang, 2010).

78. *Almanach de l'Internationale pour 1870* (Liège: Alliance typographique, 1870).

79. Fifth Congress, Belgium, 5–6 June 1870, in C. Oukhow, *Documents relatifs à l'histoire de la Première Internationale en Wallonie*, Centre interuniversitaire d'histoire contemporaine, Cahiers 47 (Leuven: Éditions Nauwelaerts, 1967), 260; article from *La Nouvelle Tribune du peuple*, 4 April 1869, doc. no. 259, in H. Wouters, *Documenten betreffende de geschiedenis*, op. cit., 1:180–82.

80. Report of the administrative committee of the local Barcelona Federation, signed by José Pons, 1 October 1872, BA 437, APP; *Minutes of the General Council*, 15 August 1871, 4:258–59 (on Caporusso).

81. Marx, letter to Dr. Kugelmann, 23 February 1865, in K. Marx, *Letters to Dr. Kugelmann* (New York: International Publishers, 1934), 27–32. As to

the differing views of Marx and Lassalle on the nature and role of the state, see also Stedman-Jones, *Karl Marx: Greatness and Illusion*, 446–48.

82. Hague Congress, session of 6 September 1872, in *La Première Internationale. Recueil de documents*, 2:354.

83. *The Civil War in France*, 1871, report in the name of the General Council of the IWA, 30 May 1871, in *Minutes of the General Council*, 4:411.

2 | WORKERS' MONEY

1. The notion of *insolidarité* (non-solidarity) was used by the Rouen militant Émile Aubry in his critical report on the workers' strike at Sotteville-lès-Rouen, *Publication du cercle d'études économiques de l'arrondissement de Rouen. AG du 7 février 1869. Suivi du compte rendu moral et matériel de la grève de Sotteville-lès-Rouen*, in *Les Révolutions du XIXᵉ siècle, 1852–1872*, vol. 5, *L'AIT en France* (Paris: EDHIS, 1988), 15.

2. On the resurrection of these ideas following the 2008 financial crisis, see Michel Feher, *Rated Agency: Investee Politics in a Speculative Age* (New York: Zone Books, 2018 [2017]).

3. Olivier Chaïbi, "Entre crédit public et crédit mutuel. Un aperçu des théories du crédit au XIXe siècle," *Romantisme. Revue du XIXᵉ siècle* 151 (2011): 53–66; Clément Coste, "Imposer ou créditer. Réformes et révolutions fiscales dans les économies politiques socialistes du XIXᵉ siècle français" (economic science thesis directed by Ludovic Frobert, University of Lyon III, 2016).

4. Louis Hyman, *Debtor Nation: The History of America in Red Ink* (Princeton: Princeton University Press, 2011); Monica Prasad, *The Land of Too Much: American Abundance and the Paradox of Poverty* (Cambridge, MA: Harvard University Press, 2012); Sarah L. Quinn, *American Bonds: How Credit Markets Shaped a Nation* (Princeton, NJ: Princeton University Press, 2019).

5. Pierre-Joseph Proudhon, *Solution du problème social, Banque d'échange. Banque du peuple (1848)*, introduction and notes by Hervé Trinquier (Antony: Éditions Tops/H. Trinquier, 2003); Société Pierre-Joseph Proudhon, *Le Crédit, quel intérêt? Actes du colloque de la Société P.-J.*

Proudhon, Paris, 1er décembre 2001 (Paris: Publications de la Société P.-J. Proudhon, 2002).

6. P.-J. Proudhon, *De la capacité politique des classes ouvrières*, in *Œuvres complètes*, new edition, vol. 3 (Geneva-Paris: Slatkine, 1982 [reprint of the Paris edition, 1923–1959]), "Du crédit mutuel," part 2, ch. 12, 175–84.

7. P.-J. Proudhon, *De la justice dans la Révolution et dans l'Église* (Paris: Fayard, 1988),vol. 1, étude III, 470–75; K. Marx, *Les Luttes de classes en France, 1848–1850* (Paris: Messidor/Éditions sociales, 1984 [1850]); Frédéric Bastiat, *Gratuité du crédit. Correspondance avec Pierre-Joseph Proudhon* (Paris: Arctic, 2006 [1849]).

8. *Le Manifeste des soixante*, reproduced in P.-J. Proudhon, *Œuvres complètes*, new edition, op. cit., 6:411.

9. Marx couldn't find words bitter enough to describe "the emptiest Proudhonist phrases," as repeated by French militants at the Geneva Congress in 1866. "Ignorant, vain, prolix, presumptuous, chattering" were some of them. Marx to Dr. Kugelmann, 9 October 1866, in Marx, *Letters to Dr. Kugelmann*, 39–41.

10. *La Première Internationale. Recueil de documents*, 1:190.

11. Charles Gide, *La Coopération. Conférences de propagande* (Paris: L. Larose, 1900); Michel Dreyfus, *Liberté, égalité, mutualité. Mutualisme et syndicalisme, 1852–1967* (Paris: Éditions de l'Atelier, 2001); M. Dreyfus and Patricia Toucas-Truyen, eds., *Les Coopérateurs. Deux siècles de pratiques coopératives* (Paris: Éditions de l'Atelier, 2005); Julien Carenton, *Les Fabriques de la "paix sociale." Acteurs et enjeux de la régulation sociale (Grenoble, 1842–1938)* (thèse d'histoire sous la direction d'Anne Dalmasso, université Grenoble-Alpes, 2017).

12. One of the points of order at the congress that would have been held in Paris in September 1870 (had the Franco-Prussian war not broken out) referred to the "need to abolish public debt." Agenda drawn up by Karl Marx, 12 July 1870, Fifth Congress of the IWA, in *Minutes of the General Council*, 3:268.

13. Report of the Belgian section, Lausanne Congress, September 1867, in *La Première Internationale. Recueil de documents*, 1:194–95.

14. During the 1860s an English newspaper, *Bee Hive*, noted a significant growth in deposits in the Post Office Savings Bank created by the government in 1861: "Savings of the Working Classes," *Bee Hive*, 4 May 1868. On the international development of savings banks in the nineteenth and twentieth centuries, see also Sheldon Garon, *Beyond Our Means: Why America Spends while the World Saves* (Princeton, NJ: Princeton University Press, 2011).

15. Lausanne Congress, 9th session of 6 September 1867, in *La Première Internationale. Recueil de documents*, 1:137.

16. "Correspondance d'Italie," *L'Égalité*, no. 8, 13 March 1869.

17. Report of the Belgian section, Lausanne Congress, 1867, in *La Première Internationale. Recueil de documents*, 1:193–201.

18. Brussels Congress, 12th session, 11 September 1868, ibid., 1:360.

19. Lausanne Congress, 9th session, 6 September 1867, ibid., 1:135.

20. Brussels Congress, 12th sesion, 11 September 1868, ibid., 1:359–60.

21. Julian P. W. Archer, *The First International in France, 1864–1872: Its Origins, Theories and Impact* (New York: University Press of America, 1997).

22. Claire Lemercier and Claire Zalc, "Pour une nouvelle approche de la relation de crédit en histoire contemporaine," *Annales. Histoire, sciences sociales* 67, no. 4 (2012): 979–1009; Anaïs Albert, *Consommation de masse et consommation de classe. Une histoire sociale et culturelle du cycle de vie des objets dans les classes populaires parisiennes (des années 1880 aux années 1920)* (history thesis directed by Christophe Charle and Anne-Marie Sohn, University of Paris I Panthéon-Sorbonne, 2014).

23. *Minutes of the General Council* 17 October 1871, 4:543n335.

24. General Assembly of the Geneva sections: debate on resistance and cooperation funds, *L'Égalité*, no. 46, 4 December 1869.

25. *Minutes of the General Council*, 6 July 1869, 3:117; 25 January 1870, 3:205.

26. *The International Courier* 14 (11 September 1865); Brussels Congress, session 12, 11 September 1868, in *La Première Internationale. Recueil de documents*, 1:358; Stefan Berger, *Social Democracy and the Working Class in Nineteenth- and Twentieth-Century Germany* (Harlow: Longman, 2000), ch. 2, 19–53; Thomas Welskopp, *Das Banner der Brüderlichkeit. Die deusche*

Sozialdemokratie vom Vormärz bis zum Sozialistengesetz (Bonn: Dietz, 2000).

27. See also the statutes of the IWA voted at the session of 5 September 1866 in Geneva and reproduced in *Les Révolutions du XIXᵉ siècle, 1852-1872*, 5:10-11. A provision entitled "International Credit" laid down that all sums loaned between sections should be duly recorded.

28. See also, for example, the statutes of the Paris section that decreed that any group had a right to a travel credit provided it was up-to-date with its subscriptions and prepared to pay back the loan within three months. E.-É. Fribourg, *L'Association internationale des travailleurs*, op. cit., 92.

29. Agricol Perdiguier, *Mémoires d'un compagnon*, introduction by Maurice Agulhon (Paris: Imprimerie nationale, 1992 [1854-1855]).

30. *La Première Internationale. Recueil de documents*, 2:247.

31. Jean Peeters to X., December 23, 1868, in *Documents relatifs aux militants belges de l'AIT*, 105.

32. Assemblée générale des sections genevoises, in *L'Égalité*, no. 46, 4 décembre 1869.

33. B. Moss, *The Origins of the French Labor Movement*, op. cit.

34. P.-J. Proudhon, *Œuvres complètes*, new edition by C. Bouglé and H. Moysset, introduction and notes by Maxime Leroy, vol. 3 (Slatkine, Geneva-Paris: 1982 [reprinted Paris edition, 1923-1959]), 413.

35. Julien Grimaud, *L'Âge du bronze de l'Internationale. L'Association internationale des travailleurs à Paris et la grève du bronze de 1867*, master's thesis, supervised by Christophe Prochasson, École des Hautes Études en Sciences Sociales, 2008, 71 (for the quote); see also *Historique de la grève du bronze en 1867* (Paris: typographie de Gaittet, 1867); Fernand L'Huillier, *La Lutte ouvrière à la fin du Second Empire* (Paris: Armand Colin, 1958); Albert Thomas, *Le Second Empire (1852-1870)*, volume of *L'Histoire socialiste*, ed. Jean Jaurès (Paris: J. Rouff, 1901); Cordillot, *Aux origines du socialisme moderne*, "La Commission ouvrière de 1867," 57-70.

36. Richard White, *The Republic for Which it Stands: The United States during Reconstruction and the Gilded Era, 1865-1896* (Oxford: Oxford University Press, 2017), ch. 21.

37. Gérard Noiriel, "Du 'patronage' au 'paternalisme.' La restructuration des formes de domination de la main-d'œuvre ouvrière dans l'industrie métallurgique française," in *État, nation et immigration. Vers une histoire du pouvoir* (Paris: Belin, 2001), 167–87; Robert Castel, *Les Métamorphoses de la question sociale. Une chronique du salariat* (Paris: Fayard, 1995); Alain Dewerpe, "Conventions patronales. L'impératif de justification dans les politiques sociales des patronats français (1800–1936)," in *Logiques d'entreprises et politiques sociales des XIXᵉ et XXᵉ siècles*, ed. Sylvie Schweitzer (Villeurbanne: Center de coopération interuniversitaire franco-québécoise, 1993), 19–62.

38. Third Belgian Congress, May 1869, in Oukhow, *Documents relatifs à l'histoire de la Première Internationale en Wallonie*, 248.

39. *L'Égalité*, no. 1, 23 January 1869.

40. *Société Cockerill à Seraing. Ses institutions de bienfaisance envers son personnel, 1842–1880* (Liège: Imprimerie Léon de Thier, 1880); Louise Henneaux-Depooter, *Misères et luttes sociales dans le Hainaut, 1860–1869* (Brussels: Institut de sociologie Solvay, 1959); Jean Puissant, *L'Évolution du mouvement ouvrier socialiste dans le Borinage* (Brussels: Palais des académies, 1982), ch. 2, "Le socialisme importé," 119–47.

41. *L'Égalité*, no. 23, 26 June 1869; *L'Égalité*, no. 49, 25 December 1869, 3; "Aufruf an die Mitglieder der internationalen Arbeiterassoziation, *Der Vorbote* 1 (January 1870): 1–2; *Minutes of the General Council*, 4 January 1870), 3: 197–98 (on the Waldenburg's strike); Ulrich Engelhardt, "Zur Verhaltensanalyse eines sozialen Konflikts, dargestellt am Waldenburger Streik 1869," in *Soziale Innovation und sozialer Konflikt*, ed. Otto Neuloh (Göttingen: Vandenhoeck & Ruprecht, 1977), 69–94.

42. Règlement de la caisse de prévoyance des usines du Creusot, 1861, article 1, dossier DH0011-19, Académie François Bourdon (AFB).

43. Céline Bellan, *Grèves et conflits sociaux au Creusot, 1848–1871. Une résistance face au patronage?* (Master 1 memoir, directed by Maurice Carrez, université de Bourgogne, 2009).

44. Outline of workers' demands, 1870, file 01I0019-07, AFB.

45. Pierre Ponsot, *Les Grèves de 1870 et la Commune de 1871 au Creusot* (Paris: Éditions sociales, 1957).

46. Henri Chabrillat, "Grève du Creusot," *Le Figaro*, 22 January 1870.

47. M. Cordillot, *Eugène Varlin, internationaliste et communard* (Paris: Spartacus, 2016 [1991]); Claude Latta, "Benoît Malon et la grève du Creusot (avril 1870)," in *Benoît Malon. Le mouvement ouvrier, le mouvement républicain à la fin du Second Empire*, ed. M. Cordillot and C. Latta (Lyon: Jacques André Éditeur, 2010), 115–32.

48. *Le Public*, 9 April 1870, file SS0311-04, AFB; "Travailleurs et capitaliste," *La Marseillaise*, 24 January 1870; "Les grèves et la légalité," *La Marseillaise*, 10 April 1870.

49. "Adresse du conseil général belge aux travailleurs du Creusot," *L'Internationale*, 24 April 1870; *L'Égalité*, no. 5, 29 January 1870; "Manifeste de la section rouennaise en soutien des ouvriers du Creusot," reproduced in Jean-Baptiste Dumay, *Souvenirs d'un militant ouvrier (Le Creusot, 1841–Paris, 1926)*, introduction and notes by Pierre Ponsot (Le Mans: Éditions Cénomane, 2010 [2nd ed.]), annexes, 380; J.-B. Dumay, *Un fief capitaliste. Le Creusot* (Dijon: Publications de la *Revue sociale*, 1891).

50. Bellan, *Grèves et conflits sociaux au Creusot*, conclusion; note by Émile Cheysson, 2 September 1872, file SS0207, AFB.

51. Royal Trades Union Commission, *Reports of the Commissioners Appointed to Inquire into the Organisation and Rules of Trades Unions* (London: Eyre, 1867–1868); George Howell, "The Financial Condition of Trades Unions," *Nineteenth Century* 12, no 68 (1882): 481–501; G. G. Hanson, "Craft Unions, Welfare Benefits, and the Case for Trade Union Law Reform, 1867–1875," *Economic History Review* 28 (1975): 243–59.

52. Oscar Testut, *L'Internationale et le jacobinisme au ban de l'Europe* (Paris, 1872), and M. Cordillot, *La Naissance du mouvement ouvrier à Besançon. La Première Internationale, 1869–1872* (Besançon: Centre d'étude du mouvement ouvrier, 1990 [1986]), 70; J. Rougerie, *Le Procès des Communards* (Paris: Gallimard/Julliard, coll. "Archives," 1964), 242–43.

53. Dumay, *Souvenirs d'un militant ouvrier*, 126.

54. *La Marseillaise*, 7 April 1870, file SS0311-04, AFB.

55. Marc Mayné, *Eugène Hins. Une grande figure de la Première Internationale en Belgique*, Classe des Lettres, Académie royale de Belgique, 1994, 47ff.

56. *International Courier*, 20 July 1867.

57. Ad Knotter, "Transnational Cigar-Makers: Cross-Border Labor Markets, Strikes, and Solidarity at the Time of the First International (1864–1873)," *International Review of Social History* 59, no. 3 (December 2014): 409–42.

58. *La Première Internationale. Recueil de documents*, 2:114.

59. Expression borrowed from Julien Talpin, *Schools of Democracy: How Ordinary Citizens (Sometimes) Become Competent in Participatory Budgeting Institutions* (Colchester: ECPR Press, 2011).

60. *L'Égalité*, no. 2, 30 January 1869.

61. "Le capital militant," special edition of *Actes de la recherche en sciences sociales* 155 (2004).

62. Alain Plessis, *De la fête impériale au mur des Fédérés, 1852–1871* (Paris: Seuil, coll. "Nouvelle histoire de la France contemporaine," 1973), 88–89; Pierre-Cyrille Hautcœur, ed., *Le Marché financier français au XIXe siècle* (Paris: Publications de la Sorbonne, 2007), 2 vols.; Paul Lagneau-Ymonet and Angelo Riva, *Histoire de la bourse* (Paris: La Découverte, 2012), 39–42.

63. Paul Veyne, *Le Pain et le cirque. Sociologie historique d'un pluralisme politique* (Paris: Seuil, 1975).

64. Léopold Migeotte, *Les Souscriptions publiques dans les cités grecques* (Geneva: Droz, 1992).

65. Nathalie Alzas, "Don, patriotisme et sociétés populaires en l'an II," *Annales historiques de la Révolution française* 329 (2002): 41–65; Charles Walton, "Between Trust and Terror: Patriotic Giving in the French Revolution," in *Experiencing the French Revolution*, ed. David Andress (Oxford: Voltaire Foundation, 2013), 47–67.

66. Alain Corbin, *Les Cloches de la terre. Paysage sonore et culture sensible dans les campagnes au XIXe siècle* (Paris: Albin Michel, 1994), 79–87.

67. Catherine Duprat, *Usage et pratiques de la philanthropie. Pauvreté, action sociale et lien social à Paris au cours du premier XIXe siècle* (Paris: Comité d'histoire de la Sécurité sociale, 1996–1997), 2 vols.

68. Barau, *La Cause des Grecs*.

69. Elisabeth S. Clemens, *Civic Gifts: Voluntarism and the Making of the American Nation-State* (Chicago, The University of Chicago Press, 2020).

70. Emmanuel Fureix, "Souscrire pour les morts. Un don politique sous la Restauration et la monarchie de Juillet," *Hypothèses* (2002): 275–85 (here 279).

71. Emmanuel Fureix, *La France des larmes. Deuils politiques à l'âge romantique (1814–1840)* (Seyssel: Champ Vallon, 2009), 365.

72. Vincent Robert, *Le Temps des banquets. Politique et symbolique d'une génération (1818–1848)* (Paris: Publications de la Sorbonne, 2010).

73. Alain Garrigou, *Mourir pour des idées. La vie posthume d'Alphonse Baudin* (Paris: Les Belles Lettres, 2010), 123.

74. Marie Aynié, *Les Amis inconnus. Se mobiliser pour Dreyfus, 1897–1899* (Toulouse: Privat, 2011); see 332–38 on the subscription launched in 1899 by the Ligue des droits de l'homme; Stephen Wilson, "Le *Monument Henry*, la structure de l'antisémitisme en France, 1899–1899," *Annales ESC* 32, no. 2 (1977): 265–91.

75. M. Perrot, *Jeunesse de la grève, 1871–1890* (Paris: Seuil, 1984), ch. 8.

76. *La Marseillaise*, 18 and 27 April 1870.

77. Spanish Regional Federation, circular no. 23, 27 June 1873, BA 437, APP.

78. *Historique de la grève du bronze en 1867* (Paris: typographie de Gaittet, 1867), 29.

79. *L'Égalité*, no. 1, 23 January 1869.

80. *Historique de la grève du bronze en 1867*, 28.

81. Willi Krahl, *Der Verband der deutschen Buchdrucker. Fünfzig Jahre deutsche gewerkschaftliche Arbeit mit einer Vorgesichte* (Berlin: Kommissionsverlag von Radelli & Sille, 1916), vol. 1.

82. *Procès de l'Association internationale. Première et deuxième commissions*, 128, 141.

83. *Troisième procès de l'Association internationale*, op. cit., 166.

84. Report of 1 March 1867, Nord, M619/1, AD59.

85. Sacked workers, January 1870, file 0200ZZ0013-03, AFB.

86. Quoted in M. Boivin, *Le Mouvement ouvrier dans la région de Rouen, 1851–1876* (Rouen: Publications de l'université de Rouen, 1989), 1:269. Varlin's letter is reproduced in the *Troisième procès de l'Association internationale*, op. cit., 17.

3 | STRUGGLE AND MUTUAL AID

1. The number of strikes increased significantly in France, Germany, Belgium, and the United Kingdom in the late 1860s and early 1870s, reaching a peak in Germany and the United Kingdom in 1872–1873. See Knud Knudsen, "The Strike History of the First International," in Van Holthoon and Van der Linden, *Internationalism in the Labour Movement*, 1:304–22; M. Perrot, *Les Ouvriers en grève. France, 1871–1890* (Paris: Mouton et École pratique des hautes études, 1974), 1:74–80; Lothar Machtan, *Streiks und Aussperrungen im deutschen Kaiserreich. Eine sozialgeschichte Dokumentation für die Jahre 1871 bis 1875* (Berlin: Colloquium Verlag, coll. "IWK," 9, 1984); Welskopp, *Das Banner der Brüderlichkeit*, 282; Friedhelm Boll, *Arbeitskämpfe und Gewerkschaften in Deutschland, England und Frankreich. Ihre Entwicklung vom 19. Zum 20. Jahrhundert* (Bonn: Dietz, 1992).

2. In his *De la capacité politique des classes ouvrières*, published in 1865, Proudhon denounced all forms of coalition, whether of employers or workers, as obstacles in the way of commercial freedom. Proudhon, *De la capacité politique des classes ouvrières* (Paris: Éditions du Trident, 1989, 421).

3. *La Première Internationale. Recueil de documents*, 1:45, 71, 131, 242 (quotations translated from the French transcript).

4. Grimaud, *L'Âge du bronze de l'Internationale*, ch. 1.

5. E. É. Fribourg, *L'Association internationale des travailleurs*, op. cit., 141.

6. Beatrice Webb and Sidney Webb, *The History of Trade Unionism* (London: Longmans, Green, 1894), 212; *London Trades Council, 1860–1950: A History* (London: Lawrence and Wishart, 1950), 4.

7. Reid, *United We Stand*, 98–99.

8. Ibid., 86.

9. K. Marx, *Value, Price, and Profit* (New York: International, 1969 [1865]), ch. 14.

10. *Procès de l'Association internationale. Première et deuxième commissions*, 152.

11. *Troisième procès de l'Association internationale*, op. cit., 188 and 217.

12. K. Marx interview with K. Landor, published in *The World*, 18 July 1871, transcription from https://www.marxists.org/archive/marx/bio/media/marx/71_07_18.htm.

13. Report of the General Council, Congress of Geneva, September 1866, in *La Première Internationale. Recueil de documents*, 1:30.

14. Ladislas Mysyrowicz, "Karl Marx, la Première Internationale et la statistique," *Le Mouvement social* 69 (October–December 1969): 51–84.

15. Oukhow, *Documents relatifs à l'histoire de la Première Internationale en Wallonie*, appendix.

16. F. Engels to Ph. Cœnen, 5 April 1871, in *Documents relatifs aux militants belges de l'AIT*, 268.

17. Marie Bernard to Alphonse Vandenhouten, London, 21 May 1869; reply dated 27 May, in *Documents relatifs aux militants belges de l'AIT*, 157–58.

18. Hermann Jung (London), letter to J.-P. Becker (Geneva), 27 December 1868 (translated from the French), D II 29, Johann Philipp Becker papers, International Institute of Social History (IISH, Amsterdam).

19. Oukhow, *Documents relatifs à l'histoire de la Première Internationale en Wallonie*, xliii.

20. *L'Égalité*, no. 28, 31 July 1869.

21. Webb and Webb, *History of Trade Unionism*, 203.

22. The IWA Brussels section's address to the workers of Geneva in *La Tribune du peuple*, 19 April 1868, reproduced in Oukhow, *Documents relatifs à l'histoire de la Première Internationale en Wallonie*, 178–82.

23. *Minutes of the General Council*, 13 July 1869, 3:124.

24. *L'Égalité*, no. 26, 27, 28, 29, July–August 1869; Claire Auzias and Annik Houel, *La Grève des ovalistes. Lyon, juin–juillet 1869* (Paris: Payot, 1982), 119–21.

25. "Remerciements de la commission des ovalistes aux ouvriers de l'AIT de la Suisse romande," text published in *L'Égalité*, no. 29, 7 August 1869.

26. "To the people of Le Creusot, and to all those who have helped us in the struggle to lighten our burden of poverty": Address by the workers of Le Creusot, 15 April 1870, reproduced in Dumay, *Souvenirs d'un militant ouvrier*, 132.

27. Eugène Hins to Albert Richard, 16 December 1869, in *Documents relatifs aux militants belges de l'AIT*, 210.

28. H. Jung (London), letter to J.-P. Becker (Geneva), 27 December 1868, D II 29, Johann Philipp Becker archive, IISH.

29. *Minutes of the General Council*, 8 August 1871, 4:255. See also the report of 10 August 1871, BA 434, APP.

30. F. Engels to Ph. Cœnen, 4 August 1871, in *Documents relatifs aux militants belges de l'AIT*, 295.

31. Roger Morgan, *The German Social Democrats and the First International, 1864–1872* (Cambridge: Cambridge University Press, 1965), 191–92.

32. Private communication between the IWA General Council and the Conseil fédéral de la Suisse romande, late 1869, in *La Première Internationale. Recueil de documents*, 2:134.

33. Out of a total of £31 collected in 1866, £25 came from the three largest societies, the Engineers, the Carpenters and Joiners, and the Operative Bricklayers. *London Trades Council, 1860–1950*, 9.

34. London Tailors strike, 7 March 1867, Minute Book no. 2 (written report), and Rules of the London Trades Council, rule no. 9, Minute Book no. 1, both in box 1, LTC Archives, TUC Library Collections (London).

35. Léonard, *L'Émancipation des travailleurs*.

36. *Historique de la grève du bronze en 1867*, 45 (translated from the French).

37. E. É. Fribourg, *L'Association internationale des travailleurs*, op. cit., 101; Grimaud, *L'Âge du bronze de l'Internationale*; Cordillot, *Aux origines du*

socialisme moderne, 33–55; *Minutes of the General Council*, 12 March 1867, 2:101–2.

38. The sum of 20,000 francs sent by the British to the Paris bronze workers is mentioned in the minutes of the Brussels Congress of 1868. *La Première Internationale. Recueil de documents*, 1:281. Considering that each union provided between £10 and £15, the twenty unions involved contributed between £200 and £300, or something between 5,000 and 7,500 francs.

39. Marx to Engels, 2 April 1867, in K. Marx and F. Engels, *Correspondance*, 8:355 (quoted in Léonard, *L'Émancipation des travailleurs*, 99).

40. J. Guillaume, *L'Internationale. Documents et souvenirs* (Paris: Stock, 1905), vol. 1; *Procès de l'Association internationale. Première et deuxième commissions*, 139–40.

41. *Minutes of the General Council*, 7 June 1870, 3:250.

42. Collins and Abramsky, *Karl Marx and the British Labour Movement*, 172.

43. F. Engels to Ph. Cœnen, 4 August 1871, in *Documents relatifs aux militants belges de l'AIT*, 295; *Minutes of the General Council*, 13 June 1871, 4:213–14, and 20 June 1871, 4:220.

44. M. Boivin, *Le Mouvement ouvrier*, op. cit., 1:271.

45. M. Bakunin, "Lettre à la *Liberté*," *Œuvres complètes de Bakounine*, 3:148; translation available at https://theanarchistlibrary.org/library/michail-bakunin-letter-to-la-liberte.

46. William Randall Cremer speaking at the London Conference, 25 September 1865, reproduced in *Minutes of the General Council*, 1:236.

47. Letter from Graglia to Eugène Varlin, April 7, 1868, in Edmond Villetard, *History of the International*, translated by Susan M. Day, with an introduction by Henry N. Day (1874), Cornell University Library, July 8, 2009.

48. *Minutes of the General Council*, 12 July 1870, 3:265.

49. Ibid., 28 June 1870, 3:257.

50. *Minutes of the General Council.*, 2 April 1867, 2:107.

51. Ibid., 21 January 1868, 2:185.

52. "Believe us, this is the only example of a loan fully repaid in the history of strike action." E. É. Fribourg, *L'Association internationale des travailleurs*, op. cit., 101.

53. *Minutes of the General Council*, 17 August 1869, 3:142.

54. *Minutes of the General Council*, 5 January 1869, 3:58.

55. Patrick Verley, *L'Échelle du monde. Essai sur l'industrialisation de l'Occident* (Paris: Gallimard, 1997).

56. *Procès de l'Association internationale. Première et deuxième commissions*, 142.

57. See the letter of thanks from the silk workers of Lyon to the IWA's Suisse Romande section in August 1869, quoted above.

58. *London Trades Council, 1860–1950*.

59. *Minutes of the General Council*, 9 July 1867, 2:135.

60. Morgan, *German Social Democrats and the First International*, 93.

61. *L'Égalité*, no. 3, 15 January 1870.

62. *Minutes of the General Council*, 25 April 1871, 4:179.

63. Figures taken from subscription lists published in *L'Internationale* between 4 July and 10 October 1869.

64. Christian Koller, "Local Strikes as Transnational Events: Migration, Donations, and Organizational Cooperation in the Context of Strikes in Switzerland (1860–1914)," *Labour History Review* 74, no. 3 (December 2009): 311.

65. *Procès de l'Association internationale. Première et deuxième commissions*, 140.

66. R. Morgan, "The Significance of Johann Philipp Becker's Geneva Central Committee for the Development of the I.W.A. in Germany," in *La Première Internationale. L'institution, l'implantation, le rayonnement*, 209; Morgan, *German Social Democrats and the First International*, appendix 2, 245–47.

67. Vuilleumier, "À propos d'un centenaire," 7.

68. "Zur Geschichte der Internationalen Arbeiter-Assoziation," *Der Vorbote* (August 1869): 118.

69. Morgan, *German Social Democrats and the First International*, 93.

70. *L'Égalité*, no. 5, 29 January 1870.

71. *Minutes of the General Council,* 9 February 1869, 3:66; 23 February 1869, 3:71.

72. Götz Langkau, "Die deutsche Sektion in Paris," in *1871. Jalons pour une histoire de la Commune,* ed. J. Rougerie (Paris: PUF, 1973), 103–50; Mareike Koenig, ed., *Deutsche Handwerker, Arbeiter und Dienstmädchen in Paris. Eine vergessene Migration im 19. Jahrhundert* (Munich: Oldenbourg, 2003).

73. "Letter from the Naples IWA section to the Comité Fédéral de la Suisse romande," *L'Égalité,* no. 15, 1 May 1869. On the status of the IWA in Italy, see Carlo de Maria and Patrizia Dogliani, "La Première Internationale en Italie (1864–1883)," *Cahiers Jaurès* 215–16 (2015): 19–34.

74. Louis Blanc, *Organisation du travail* (Paris: Administration de librairie, 1841).

75. "Rapport de la commission sur les caisses de résistance," in *L'Égalité,* no. 6, 5 February 1870.

76. *Minutes of the General Council,* 5 January 1869, 3:57–59.

77. *Almanach de l'Internationale pour 1870* (Liège: Alliance typographique, 1870), 25.

78. *L'Égalité,* no. 38, 9 October 1869; Bernstein, *The First International in America,* 29–30.

79. K. Knudsen quotes a letter from Marx to Wilhelm Liebknecht in which he congratulates himself on the actions of the IWA in this domain. Knudsen, "The Strike History," 310.

80. *Appel des membres britanniques du Conseil général à leurs camarades travailleurs du Royaume-Uni,* January 1866, written by W. R. Cremer, reproduced in *Minutes of the General Council,* 1:313–16.

81. Collins and Abramsky, *Karl Marx and the British Labour Movement,* 69.

82. *Minutes of the General Council,* 8 August 1871, 4:254.

83. Oukhow, *Documents relatifs à l'histoire de la Première Internationale en Wallonie,* 231.

84. *L'Égalité,* no. 1, 23 January 1869.

85. Alain Supiot, ed., *La Solidarité. Enquête sur un principe juridique* (Paris: Odile Jacob/Collège de France, 2015), introduction, 7–32; Jens Beckert,

Julia Eckert, Martin Kohli, and Wolfgang Streeck, eds., *Transnationale Solidarität. Chancen und Grenzen* (Frankfurt/New York: Campus Verlag, 2004).

86. *Procès de l'Association internationale. Première et deuxième commissions*, 150.

87. Marcel van der Linden, "The Rise and Fall of the First International: An Interpretation," in Van Holthoon and Van der Linden, *Internationalism in the Labour Movement*, 1: 323–35; Van der Linden, *Workers of the World*, ch. 12, 259–83.

88. Berlin typographers' union, letter to K. Marx, 15 April 1865, in *Die Internationale in Deutschland (1864–1872). Dokumente und Materialen* (Berlin: Dietz Verlag, 1964), 50–51, and, 705n57.

89. Ulrich Engelhardt, "Zur Entwicklung der Streikbewegungen in der ersten Industrialisierungsphase und zur Funktion von Streiks bei der Konstituierung der Gewerkschaftsbewegung in Deutschland," *Internationale wissenschaftliche Korrespondenz zur Geschichte der deutschen Arbeiterbewegung* 15 (1979): 547–69 (here 564).

90. Willi Krahl, *Der Verband der deutschen Buchdrucker. Fünfzig Jahre deusche gewerkschaftliche Arbeit mit einer Vorgesichte* (Berlin: Kommissionsverlag von Radelli & Sille, 1916), b. 1, appendices.

91. General assembly of the Brussels area carpenters' union, report of 19 May 1874, BA 427, APP.

92. Christiane Eisenberg, *Deutsche und englische Gewerkschaften. Entstehung und Entwicklung bis 1878 im Vergleich* (Göttingen: Vandenhieck & Ruprecht, 1986).

93. Ad Knotter, "Transnational Cigar-Makers."

94. *Minutes of the General Council*, vol. 4, 4 April 1871, p. 167. Each worker received five francs per week, which, for a strike of from five to six weeks, required a budget of from 12,000 to 15,000 thousand francs (*Minutes of the General Council*, vol. 4, 4 April 1871, p. 168).

95. Address of the general council of the IWA, 5 April 1871, reproduced in *Minutes of the General Council*, vol. 4, p. 353.

96. *The Tobacco Workers' Union, 1834–1984*, booklet consulted at the TUC archive (London); T. Messer-Kruse, *The Yankee International: Marxism and*

the American Reform Tradition, 1848–1876 (Chapel Hill: University of North Carolina Press, 1998), 229–32.

97. Sewell, *Work and Revolution in France*; Moss, *Origins of the French Labor Movement*.

98. Collins and Abramsky, *Karl Marx and the British Labour Movement*.

99. Raymond W. Postgate, *The Builders' History* (London: The National Federation of Building Trade Operatives, 1923), 185, 205.

100. Congress of Geneva, September 1866, in *La Première Internationale. Recueil de documents*, 1:50–51; Antje Schrupp, *Nicht Marxistin und auch nicht Anarchistin. Frauen in der Ersten Internationale* (Königstein im Taunus: Ulrike Helmer Verlag, 1999); Antje Schrupp, *Virginie Barbet. Une lyonnaise dans l'Internationale* (Paris: Libertalia, 2009).

101. A. Schrupp, "Bringing Together Feminism and Socialism in the First International," in Bensimon, Deluermoz, and Moisand, *Arise Ye Wretched of the Earth*, 343–54.

102. Between 1870 and 1890, M. Perrot found 5.9 percent of "purely female coalitions" and 12.3 percent of "strikes of both sexes," while women represented 30 percent of the active industrial population. Perrot, *Les Ouvriers en grève*, 1:318.

103. *L'Égalité*, no. 27, 24 July 1869.

104. *Minutes of the General Council*, 27 July 1869, 3:135.

105. Auzias and Houel, *La Grève des ovalistes*, 122–23.

106. Perrot, *Jeunesse de la grève*, 138.

4 | THE PITFALLS OF COMPASSION

1. Paul Robin to the members of the Belgian General Council of the IWA, 9 November 1871, in *Documents relatifs aux militants belges de l'AIT*, 335–40.

2. H. Wouters, *Documenten betreffende de geschiedenis*, op. cit., 1866, 1:14–15.

3. Pièce 105, *fonds* Pierre Vésinier, IISH; *Documents relatifs aux militants belges de l'AIT*, 34n154.

4. Marx was one of the most assiduous attendees at the weekly meetings of the IWA general council. See also *Minutes of the General Council*, table of attendance, session of 20 December 1870, 4:98–100.

5. "I have piled up debts which weigh heavily on my mind and make me incapable of doing anything except the work which absorbs me. If I cannot manage to get a loan of at least 1,000 thalers, say at 5 per cent, then I can really see no way out. And in spite of the numerous letters of acknowledgement which I receive from Germany, I don't know where to turn to. I can only make use of the help of private friends, not anything public." Marx to Dr. Kugelmann, 23 August 1866, in Marx, *Letters to Dr. Kugelmann*, 37.

6. Stedman-Jones, *Karl Marx: Greatness and Illusion*, 444–46; Jonathan Sperber, *Karl Marx: A Nineteenth-Century Life* (New York: Liveright Publishing, 2013), 481–86.

7. Jean Dhondt and Catherine Oukhow, "La Première Internationale en Belgique," in *La Première Internationale. L'institution, l'implantation, le rayonnement*, 151–65.

8. Administrative committee of the International, letter to Le Frère-Orban, Minister of Justice, 20 May 1868, doc. no. 107, in H. Wouters, *Documenten betreffende de geschiedenis*, op. cit., 1:76–77; Henneaux-Depooter, *Misères et luttes sociales dans le Hainaut*.

9. *Minutes of the General Council*, 26 February 1867, 2:97.

10. Address of the Central Council of the IWA to the miners and ironworkers of Great Britain, March 1867, in *Minutes of the General Council*, 2:281.

11. Reports on the riots of 16 March 1867 in Roubaix, M619/1, AD 59.

12. Manifesto to the workers of Roubaix, Paris section of the IWA, April 1867, BA 434, APP.

13. François Jarrige, "The IWMA, Workers, and the Machinery Question (1864–1874)," in Bensimon, Deluermoz, and Moisand, *Arise Ye Wretched of the Earth*, 89–106.

14. *La Marseillaise*, 21 March 1870.

15. *L'Égalité*, no. 18, 22 May 1869; Address of the General Council on the Massacres in Belgium, written by Karl Marx, April 1869, *Minutes of the General Council*, 3: 312–18.

16. A. Herman to P. Robin, April 1869, doc. no. 262, in H. Wouters, *Documenten betreffende de geschiedenis*, op. cit., 1:183; *Die Internationale*

in Deutschland, 336–37; receipt, 22 July 1869, item 309, Hermann Jung archive, IISH.

17. Andy Croll, "Starving Strikers and the Limits of the 'Humanitarian Discovery of Hunger,' in late Victorian Britain," *International Review of Social History* 56 (2001): 103–31.

18. *Historique de la grève du bronze en 1867*, 53.

19. *La Marseillaise*, 3 April 1870.

20. *La Marseillaise*, 19 and 20 April 1870.

21. Ibid.

22. *L'Internationale*, 25 April 1869.

23. *Minutes of the General Council*, 3 January 1871, 4:103; William A. Pelz, *Wilhem Liebknecht and German Social Democracy: A Documentary History* (Wesport, CT: Greenwood, 1994), 305–11.

24. Engels to Natalie Liebknecht, 19 December 1870, in *Die Internationale in Deutschland*, 556–57.

25. *Der Leipziger Hochverratsprozess vom Jahre 1872, neu herausgegeben von Karl-Heinz Leidigkeit* (Berlin: Rütten & Loening, 1960).

26. Rougerie, "L'AIT et le mouvement ouvrier à Paris pendant les événements de 1870–1871," in Rougerie, *1871. Jalons pour une histoire de la Commune*, op. cit., 3–102; William Serman, *La Commune de Paris (1871)* (Paris: Fayard, 1986); Robert Tombs, *Paris, bivouac des révolutions. La Commune de 1871* (Paris: Libertalia, 2014); John M. Merriman, *Massacre: The Life and Death of the Paris Commune of 1871* (New Haven, CT: Yale University Press, 2014); Quentin Deluermoz, *Commune(s), 1870–1871. Une traversée des mondes au XIXe siècle* (Paris: Seuil, 2020).

27. Laure Godineau, *Retour d'exil. Les anciens communards au début de la IIIe République*, 3 vols. (doctoral thesis, directed by Jean-Louis Robert, Université de Paris I Panthéon-Sorbonne, 2000).

28. Passports at the time contained no photographs; only the written description of the bearer and his signature were there to be checked. See also Gustave Lefrançais and Arthur Arnould, *Souvenirs de deux communards réfugiés à Geneva: 1871–1873*, presented by M. Vuilleumier (Geneva: Collège

du travail, 1987), 49n1. See also John Torpey, *The Invention of the Passport: Surveillance, Citizenship, and the State* (Cambridge: Cambridge University Press, 2000).

29. Archives of the Ministère des Affaires étrangères (AMAE), 2QO/84, circular dated 26 May 1871; Georges Bourgin, "La lutte du gouvernement français contre la Première Internationale. Contribution à l'histoire de l'après-Commune," *International Review for Social History* 4 (January 1938): 39–138; Quentin Dupuis, *La Politique d'asile suisse face aux nouveaux révolutionnaires, 1871–1879* (master's thesis, Université de Lyon II, 2001).

30. Maxime Vuillaume, *Mes Cahiers rouges. Souvenirs de la Commune*, text presented and annotated by Maxime Jourdan (Paris: La Découverte, 2011 [1908–1914]), 349–51; Sylvie Aprile, Jean-Claude Caron, and Emmanuel Fureix, eds., *La Liberté guidant les peuples. Les révolutions de 1830 en Europe* (Seysell: Champ Vallon, 2013).

31. House of Commons Debates, 12 April 1872, at http://hansard .millbanksystems.com/commons/1872/apr/12/motion-for-papers.

32. Bernstein, *The First International in America*, 73–90.

33. See also Rougerie, *1871. Jalons pour une histoire de la Commune*, op. cit.; Thomas C. Jones and Robert Tombs, "The French Left in Exile: Quarante-huitards and Communards in London, 1848–1880," in *A History of the French in London: Liberty, Equality, Opportunity*, ed. Debra Kelly and Cornick Martyn (London: Institute of Historical Research, 2013).

34. Sylvie Aprile, *Le Siècle des exilés. Bannis et proscrits de 1789 à la Commune* (Paris: CNRS Éditions, 2010), ch. 12, 257–74.

35. Paul K. Martinez, *Paris Communards Refugees in Britain, 1871–1880* (PhD thesis, University of Sussex, 1981); Renaud Morieux, *Une communauté en exil. Les réfugiés de la Commune à Londres (1871–1880)* (mémoire de maîtrise d'histoire, Paris I Panthéon-Sorbonne, 1997); M. Vuilleumier, "L'exil des communeux," in C. Latta, ed., *La Commune de 1871. L'événement, les hommes et la mémoire* (Saint-Étienne: Publications de l'université de Saint-Étienne, 2004), 265–88; Cordillot, *Aux origines du socialisme moderne*, ch. "La proscription communaliste aux États-Unis," 173–93.

36. Stockholm embassy, letter, June 18, 1871, 2QO/84, AMAE.

37. *L'Internationale*, 16 April and 19 November 1871. The Belgian subscription, which was open between June and November 1871, raised a little more than 700 francs, a derisory sum for the time.

38. List of income and expenditure, July 1871 to April 1872, item 314, Hermann Jung archive, IISH.

39. Ibid.

40. Royden Harrison, ed., *The English Defence of the Commune 1871* (London: Merlin Press, 1971).

41. Collins and Abramsky, *Karl Marx and the British Labour Movement*.

42. *Minutes of the General Council*, 8 August 1871, 4:256.

43. Letter from J. Guillaume to E. Hins, 3 October 1871, in *Documents relatifs aux militants belges de l'AIT*, 326–29; Lefrançais and Arnould, *Souvenirs de deux communards*, 77–79; Charles Beslay, *La Vérité sur la Commune* (Brussels: Librairie Henri de Kistemaeckers, 1877), 159ff.

44. Documents on Louis Bologne, accused of being an undercover agent, 1878, item 134, Pierre Vésinier archives, IISH.

45. *Minutes of the General Council*, 19 December 1871, 5:61–64; Collins and Abramsky, *Karl Marx and the British Labour Movement*, 237–39.

46. London, report on the refugees, s.d., 1874, BA 429, APP.

47. *Minutes of the General Council*, 19 December 1871, 5:64.

48. Merriman, *Massacre*, ch. 4, "The Commune *vs* the Cross," 83–102.

49. London, report of 3 June 1872, BA 428, APP.

50. London, report of 6 April 1877, BA 429, APP; Geneva, session to discuss "Solidarity," 8 March 1877, BA 1516, APP.

51. *Minutes of the General Council*, 29 August 1871, 4:263–66; Marx to Dr. Kugelmann, 27 July 1871, in Marx, *Letters to Dr. Kugelmann*; Prosper-Olivier Lissagaray, *Histoire de la Commune de 1871* (Paris: La Découverte, 1996 [1876]), 444; Lucien Descaves, *Philémon, vieux de la vieille* (Paris: Les Éditions G. Crès, 1922 [1913]); M. Cordillot, *Utopistes et exilés du Nouveau Monde. Des Français aux États-Unis de 1848 à la Commune* (Paris: Vendémiaire, 2013), 268.

52. Collins and Abramsky, *Karl Marx and the British Labour Movement*, 217–18.

53. E. Hins to E. Glaser de Willebrord, 25 July 1871, in *Documents relatifs aux militants belges de l'AIT*, 287.

54. Odger and Lucraft resigned from the general council in protest, on 20 June 1871; see also Collins and Abramsky, *Karl Marx and the British Labour Movement*, 212–14.

55. *Minutes of the General Council* 29 August 1871, 4:264; Karl Marx to H. Jung, 11 October 1871, in K. Marx and F. Engels, *Correspondance*, op. cit., 11:321–22.

56. E. Glaser de Willebrord to K. Marx, 8 August 1871, doc. no. 154, in *Documents relatifs aux militants belges de l'AIT*, 300–303.

57. A. Herman to E. Hins, 9 August 1871, doc. no. 156, ibid., 307; list of incomes and outgoings, July 1871 to April 1872, item 314, Hermann Jung archive, IISH.

58. *Minutes of the General Council*, 5 February 1872, 5:95–103; F. Engels to F. Sorge, 12 September 1874, in K. Marx and F. Engels, *La Commune de 1871. Lettres et déclarations pour la plupart inédites* (Paris: Union générale d'édition, 1971), 242–43, quoted by Morieux, *Une communauté en exil*; London, report of 10 June 1872, BA 428, APP.

59. London, letter of 30 June 1873, and report of 27 January 1874, BA 428, 429, APP.

60. Project for an internal commission of inquiry into the members of the Commune in London, June 1872, item 131, P. Vésinier archive, IISH; F. Jourde, "Note concernant ma délégation aux finances et mon attitude en qualité de membre de la Commune," reproduced in J. Rougerie, *Le Procès des Communards* (Paris: Gallimard / Julliard, 1964), 80–82; Marx to the Dutch socialist Domela Nieuwenhuis, 22 February 1881, quoted by J. Rougerie, *Paris libre 1871* (Paris: Seuil, 1971), 269; J. Rougerie, "Karl Marx, l'État et la Commune," *Preuves* 212–13 (November–December 1968): 34–43, 45–56.

61. London, report of 5 September 1872, BA 428, APP.

62. Cordillot, *Utopistes et exilés*, 286.

63. London, report of 21 January 1872, BA 428, APP.

64. Brussels, report of 7 February 1874, signed "12," and London, report of 26 March 1872, BA 427, 428, APP.

65. Geneva, report of 1 February 1877, and London, report of 9 August 1874, BA 1516, 429, APP.

66. London, sale prospectus, s. d. [domiciled at the home of J. Joffrin à Londres], BA 430, APP; session of the *Solidaires*, Brussels, 8 March 1874, doc. no. 844, in H. Wouters, *Documenten betreffende de Geschiedenis*, op. cit., 2:679.

67. Jean Baronnet and Jean Chalou, *Communards en Nouvelle Calédonie. Histoire de la déportation* (Paris: Mercure de France, 1987).

68. L. Godineau, *La Commune de Paris par ceux qui l'ont vécue* (Paris: Parigramme, 2010), 243–44; Cordillot, *Utopistes et exilés*, 295; Paschal Grousset and François Jourde, *Les Condamnés politiques en Nouvelle Calédonie. Récit de deux évadés* (Geneva: Imprimerie Ziegler, 1876), 53ff.

69. London, appeal of the raffle commission to citizens of France, 1877, BA 429, APP.

70. Cordillot, *Utopistes et exilés*, 297.

71. *Tombola au profit des condamnés politiques à la Nouvelle-Calédonie. Rapport de la commission de liquidation lu à Londres en assemblée générale des anciens réfugiés de la Commune le 25 mars 1881* (Paris: Ch. Fréon, 1881).

72. London, report of 20 August 1875, BA 429, APP.

73. Ibid.

74. London, report of 3 November 1878, BA 429, APP.

75. Stéphane Gacon, *L'Amnistie. De la Commune à la guerre d'Algérie* (Paris: Seuil, 2002).

76. On these two committees, see also Godineau, *Retour d'exil. Les anciens communards*, ch. 2, "Les comités d'aide aux amnistiés," 131–75.

77. London, letter from Paul Vichard to Jean Greppo, 6 February 1877, and Greppo's reply dated 8 February, BA 429, APP.

78. The *Figaro* also objected to a subsidy of 30,000 francs that was voted by the Paris municipal council in December 1876, which it likened to a "work of hatred" rather than a "work of charity." Francis Magnard, "Trente mille francs à ne pas payer," *Le Figaro*, 31 December 1876.

79. L. Godineau, *Retour d'exil*, op. cit., 149.

80. Godineau, *Retour d'exil. Les anciens communards*, 149, 225–30; *L'Illustration*, no. 1172, 13 September 1879.

81. Appel du comité socialiste d'aide aux amnistiés et aux non amnistiés, March 1879, BA 1516, APP.

82. Report of 17 July 1879, BA 1516, APP.

5 | THE REVIVIAL OF INTERNATIONALISM

1. Maria Grazia Meriggi, *L'Internationale degli operai. Le relazioni internazionali dei lavoratori in Europa fra la caduta della Comune e gli anni '30* (Milan: FrancoAngeli, 2014); see also Constance Bantman, "Internationalism without an International? Cross-Channel Anarchist Networks, 1880–1914," *Revue belge de philologie et d'histoire* 84, no. 4 (2006): 961–81.

2. Marcel van der Linden, *Workers of the World: Essays toward a Global Labor History* (Leiden: Brill, 2008), ch. 12, "Labor internationalism," 259–83.

3. Miklós Molnár, *Le Déclin de la Première Internationale. La conférence de Londres, 1871* (Geneva: Droz, 1963).

4. Jensen, *Battle against Anarchist Terrorism.*

5. Édouard Dolléans, *Histoire du mouvement ouvrier*, vol. 2, *1871–1936* (Paris: Armand Colin, 1939), 20; Jean-Numa Ducange, *Jules Guesde. L'anti-Jaurès* (Paris: Armand Colin, 2017), 25–30.

6. Socialist workers international congress, 1878, BA 28 et 29, APP; Jules Guesde, *Le Collectivisme devant la 10e chambre (affaire du congrès ouvrier international socialiste)* (Paris: Imprimerie Adolphe Reiff, 1878).

7. Berger, *Social Democracy and the Working Class*, ch. 3.

8. Franz Mehring, *Histoire de la social-démocratie allemande, 1863–1891* (Pantin: Les Bons Caractères, 2013 [1897–1898]), 618–24, translated into French by Monique Tesseyre and Dominique Petitjean.

9. Jutta Seidel, "Internationale Solidaritätsaktionen für den Kampf der deutschen Arbeiterpartei während des Sozalistengesetzes," *Jahrbuch für Geschichte* 22 (Berlin, 1981), 139–55; Jutta Seidel, *Internationale Stellung und internationale Beziehungen der deutschen Social-demokratie, 1871–1895/96* (Berlin: Dietz Verlag, 1982); Berger, *Social Democracy and the Working Class*, 74ff.; Pelz, *Wilhem Liebknecht and German Social Democracy.*

10. L. Godineau, "Le retour d'exil de Camélinat et des communards," in *Zéphirin Camélinat (1840–1932). Une vie pour la Sociale*, ed. Michel

Cordillot, seminar organized by Adiamos-89 (Auxerre: Société des sciences historiques et naturelles de l'Yonne, 2004), 55–69.

11. Questionnaire published for the worker delegations, Boston Universal Exhibition, 1884, 291J10, AD93.

12. Questionnaire published for the worker delegations, Boston Universal Exhibition, 1884, 291J10, AD93; electoral tract of the Union des travailleurs socialistes indépendants, 20e arrondissement de Paris, August 1893, and municipal program (17e arrondissement de Paris) of the Parti ouvrier socialiste révolutionnaire, s.d., 291J8, AD93.

13. Sessions of 30 May 1879, 11 October 1881, 14 March 1882, 9 January 1883, Minute Book no. 4, box 1, LTC Archives, TUC Library Collections.

14. Brussels, report of "12," 19 October 1877, BA 427, APP.

15. Christian Borde, "La communauté des *Lace Makers* de Calais, de la contrebande maritime à l'exil australien, 1802–1848," in *Les Étrangers dans les villes-ports atlantiques. Expériences françaises et allemandes, XVᵉ–XIXᵉ siècle*, ed. Mickaël Augeron and Pascal Even (Paris: Rivages des Xantons, 2010), 333–45; Benoît Noël, "Outsiders. Petites entreprises et petits entrepreneurs anglo-calaisiens dans le marché français des tulles et dentelles mécaniques," in *Petites entreprises et petits entrepreneurs étrangers en Belgique (XIXᵉ–XXᵉ siècle)*, ed. Anne-Sophie Bruno and Claire Zalc (Paris: Publibook, 2006), 161–80; Fabrice Bensimon, "The Emigration of British Lacemakers to Continental Europe, 1816–1860s," *Continuity and Change* 34 (2019): 15–41.

16. Michel Caron, *Trois âges d'or de la dentelle. Calais, 1860–1905* (Roubaix: Le Geai bleu, 2003), 57.

17. Session of 23 October 1890, Minute Book no. 6, box 1, LTC Archives, TUC Library Collections.

18. Caron, *Trois âges d'or de la dentelle*, 59.

19. The Trades Union Congress Parliamentary Committee, *Important Circular: Urgent Appeal to the Trade Unionists of Britain on Behalf of the Lace Makers of Calais*, 2 pages, 291J10, AD93.

20. Léon de Seilhac, "La grève des tullistes de Calais," *Musée social* 4 (April 1901): 97–128; Magali Domain, "Jaurès et la grève des tullistes calaisiens (12 November 1900–7 February 1901), *Cahiers Jaurès* 211 (2014): 53–75.

On Léon de Seilhac "historiographer of strike action," see also File "Enquêter sur le monde ouvrier: autour de Léon de Seilhac," *Cahiers Jaurès* 223–24 (2017).

21. Minute Book no. 7, in box 2, Minute Book no. 10, in box 4, Annual Reports, 1873–1939, in box 15, all in LTC Archives, TUC Library Collections.

22. Annual Reports, 1891 and 1899, box 15, LTC Archives, TUC Library Collections.

23. London, "Address and General Rules of the International Labour Union," 1877, BA 430, APP; M. Cordillot, "Le congrès socialiste de Coire, ou la difficile renaissance de l'Internationale," in Cordillot, *Aux origines du socialisme moderne*, 230.

24. M. Cordillot, *La Sociale en Amérique. Dictionnaire biographique du mouvement social francophone aux États-Unis, 1848-1922* (Paris: Éditions de l'Atelier, 2002), 176.

25. Session of 11 March 1879, Minute Book no. 4, box 1, LTC Archives, TUC Library Collections.

26. Second bulletin of the London Congress, 22 June 1881, BA 30, APP.

27. Jensen, *Battle against Anarchist Terrorism*, 17; C. Bantman, *The French Anarchists in London, 1880-1914: Exile and Transnationalism in the First Globalization* (Liverpool: Liverpool University Press, 2013), 28–31, 158–59.

28. Report of the international socialist workers' congress, La Chaux-de-Fonds, July 1883, BA 30, APP.

29. David Stafford, *From Anarchism to Reformism: A Study of the Political Activities of Paul Brousse within the First International and the French Socialist Movement, 1870-1890* (London: Weidenfeld and Nicolson, 1971).

30. S. Milner, *The Dilemmas of Internationalism: French Syndicalism and the International Labour Movement, 1900-1914* (New York: Berg, 1990), 33–43; E. Jousse, *Les Hommes révoltés. Les origines intellectuelles du réformisme en France* (Paris: Fayard, 2017), 133–41; G. Haupt and Jeannine Verdès, "De la 1ère à la 2e Internationale. Les actes des congrès internationaux, 1877–1888: répertoire," *Le Mouvement social* 51 (April–June 1965): 113–26;

Leo Valiani, "Dalla Prima alla Seconda Internazionale, 1872–1889," in *Questioni di storia del socialismo* (Turin: G. Einaudi, 1958), 168–263.

31. "Rapport des délégués anglais sur la conférence internationale," published in *Justice*, 27 December 1883, BA 30, APP.

32. Voting by nationality was the rule at the congresses of the Second International until 1914, which showed that there was potential for a combination of Internationalism and ordinary nationalism. See also Pierre Alayrac, *L'Internationale au milieu du gué. De l'internationalisme socialiste au congrès de Londres (1896)* (Rennes: Presses universitaires de Rennes, 2018).

33. W. J. Davis, *The British Trades Union Congress: History and Recollections* (London: Cooperative Printing Society, 1910).

34. Ibid., 126.

35. Public Meeting, 31 October 1883, intervention by Joseph Tortelier (International Conference organized by the l'Union fédérative ouvrière in Paris), BA 30, APP.

36. Annual Reports, 1888, box 15, LTC Archives, TUC Library Collections.

37. E. Jousse, "Les traducteurs de l'Internationale," *Cahiers Jaurès* 212–13 (2014): 181–94.

38. *Report of the International Trades Union Congress, Held at Paris from August 23rd to 28th, 1886, by Adolphe Smith, Interpreter at the Congress*, 1886, 2.

39. *A Critical Essay on the International Trade Union Congress, Held in London, November 1888, by Adolphe Smith, Interpreter to the Congress* (London, 1889), 4.

40. Bantman, *French Anarchists in London*, 31.

41. One of these was Annie Besant, a leader in the matchmakers' strike, who intervened at the London Congress to denounce the marginalization of unskilled workers by the TUC. *Le Temps*, 11 November 1888.

42. Congress of 1888, article in the *Sozialdemokrat*, 20 November 1888, BA 30, APP.

43. *Histoire de la IIe Internationale*, (Geneva: Minkoff Reprint, 1976), 7:259–60.

44. Kriegel, *Les Internationales ouvrières*; Haupt, *La Deuxième Internationale, 1889-1914*; Ducange, *Jules Guesde. L'anti-Jaurès*, 58–62.

45. G. Noiriel, *Le Creuset français. Histoire de l'immigration, XIXᵉ-XXᵉ siècle* (Paris: Seuil, 1988); Berger, *Notre première mondialisation*; Laurent Dornel, *La Belgique hostile. Socio-histoire de la xénophobie (1870-1914)* (Paris: Hachette littératures, 2004); Bastien Cabot, *"À bas les Belges!" L'expulsion des mineurs borains (Lens, août-septembre 1892)* (Rennes: Presses universitaires de Rennes/Fondation Jean Jaurès, 2017).

46. The high-water marks of industrial action came at the end of the nineteenth century and the beginning of the twentieth, in "international waves." These have been well documented by quantitative historical research since the 1960s and 1970s. In most western European countries, strike activity peaked around 1870–1872, 1880–1885, 1889–1890, 1898–1899, 1904–1905, then after 1911. See also Friedhelm Boll, "International Strike Waves: A Critical Assessment," in *The Development of Trade Unionism in Great Britain and Germany, 1880-1914*, ed. Wolfgang J. Mommsen and Hans-Gerhard Husung (London: George Allen and Unwin), 1985, 78–99.

47. Webb and Webb, *History of Trade Unionism*, 330ff.

48. Aristide R. Zolberg, *A Nation by Design: Immigration Policy in the Fashioning of America* (Cambridge, MA: Harvard University Press, 2006); Adam McKeown, *Melancholy Order: Asian Migration and the Globalization of Borders* (New York: Columbia University Press, 2008); Mae Ngai, *The Chinese Question: The Gold Rushes and Global Politics* (New York: Norton, 2021).

49. The question of "blackleg" workers, rushed in from abroad to replace a local workforce on strike, will be dealt with in the next chapter.

50. Resolutions, International congress, 1883, BA 30, APP.

51. Gilles Candar, "Jaurès, les socialistes et l'immigration," *Cahiers Jaurès* 225 (July–September 2017): 109–28.

52. *Report of the International Trades Union Congress…by Adolphe Smith*, 14–16.

53. International Socialist Workers' Congress, Brussels, 18–25 August 1891, BA 30, APP.

54. Paul-André Rosental, "Géopolitique et État-providence. Le BIT et la politique mondiale des migrations dans l'entre-deux-guerres," *Annales. Histoire, sciences sociales* 61, no. 1 (2006): 99–134; Caroline Douki, "Protection sociale et mobilité transatlantique. Les migrants italiens au début du XXe siècle," *Annales. Histoire, sciences sociales* 66, no. 2 (2011): 375–410.

55. *International Socialist Workers and Trade Union Congress, London, 1896: Report of the Proceedings* (London: Twentieth Century Press, 1896), 48.

56. See also, for example, the International Metalworkers' Federation, *The Teaching of Trades in Continental Countries: The Origin and Development of Internationalism*, compiled by Charles Hobson (Birmingham: 1915), 478.

57. On the sharp differences between "cosmopolitan" Guesdists and syndicalists during the 1880s, see also Perrot, *Les Ouvriers en grève*, 1:174–77.

58. A. Thomas Lane, *Solidarity or Survival? American Labor and European Immigrants, 1830–1924* (New York: Greenwood Press, 1987).

59. Richard White, *The Republic for Which It Stands: The United States during Reconstruction and the Gilded Era, 1865–1896* (Oxford: Oxford University Press, 2017), ch. 9.

60. Philip S. Foner and Ronald L. Lewis, eds., *The Black Worker*, vol. 3, *The Black Worker during the Era of the Knights of Labor* (Philadelphia: Temple University Press, 1978).

61. For this section on the Knights of Labor, I have relied on Steven Parfitt's, "Brotherhood from a Distance: Americanization and the Internationalism of the Knights of Labor," *International Review of Social History* 58 (2013): 463–91; Steven Parfitt, *Knights across the Atlantic: The Knights of Labor in Britain and Ireland* (Liverpool: Liverpool University Press, 2016).

62. Gerald Friedman, *Reigniting the Labor Movement: Restoring Means to Ends in a Democratic Labor Movement* (London: Routledge, 2008), 93–114, for a comparative approach to the various eight-hour-day mobilizations, 1880–1890.

63. The historian Timothy Messer-Kruse recently proposed a revisionist reading of the Haymarket bombing, arguing that it was the result of a violent anarchist conspiracy. Timothy Messer-Kruse, *The Haymarket Conspiracy:*

Transatlantic Anarchist Networks (Champaign: University of Illinois, 2012). His argument has not convinced many specialists in the matter.

64. In addition to Steven Parfitt, one might quote Robert Weir, *Knights Down Under: The Knights of Labour in New Zealand* (Cambridge: Cambridge University Press, 2009); Gerald Friedman, "Success and Failure in Third Party Politics: The Knights of Labor and the Union Labor Coalition in Massachusetts, 1884–88," *International Labor and Working Class History* 62 (2002): 164–88; Leon Fink, *Workingmen's Democracy: The Knights of Labor and American Politics* (Urbana: University of Illinois Press, 1983).

65. S. Parfitt, "Brotherhood from a Distance," 465; S. Parfitt, "The First-and-a-Half International: The Knights of Labor and the History of International Labour Organization in the Nineteenth Century," *Labour History Review* 80, no. 2 (2015): 135–67.

66. S. Parfitt, "A Nexus between Labor Movement and Labor Movement: The Knights of Labor and the Financial Side of Global Labor History," *Labor History* 58, no. 3 (2017): 288–302.

67. Hubert Perrier, "De l'Internationale au 'syndicalisme pur et simple.' L'influence de l'AIT sur le mouvement ouvrier aux États-Unis," *Cahiers d'histoire de l'institut de recherches marxistes* 37 (1989): 107–23.

68. Resolution presented and adopted at the ninth session of the possibilist congress, 19 July 1889, in *Histoire de la IIe Internationale*, vol. 6, *Congrès international ouvrier socialiste. Paris, 14–21 juillet 1889* (Geneva: Minkoff Reprint, 1976), 264–65.

69. Julie Greene, *Pure and Simple Politics: The American Federation of Labor and Political Activism, 1881–1917* (Cambridge: Cambridge University Press, 1998).

70. Steven Parfitt, "Brotherhood from a Distance," op. cit. (cf. note 61 in this chapter).

71. Minutes of the International Labor Congress, 1909, in *Sixième rapport sur le mouvement syndical international, 1908* (Berlin: General Committee of German Unions, 1910); "Rapport et résolution du *Socialist Party* des États-Unis," in *Histoire de la IIe Internationale*, vol. 16, *Congrès socialiste international. Stuttgart, 18–24 Août 1907* (Geneva: Minkoff Reprint, 1978), 167–69.

72. Eric Hobsbawm, "The 'New Unionism' Reconsidered," in Mommsen and Husung, *Development of Trade Unionism in Great Britain and Germany*, 13–31.

73. Dolléans, *Histoire du mouvement ouvrier*, 2:95.

74. R. W. Postgate, *The Builder's History* (London: The National Federation of Building Trade Operatives, 1923), 340–41.

75. G. Howell, *Trade Unionism: New and Old* (Brighton: Harvester Press, 1973 [1891]).

76. Louise Raw, *Striking a Light: The Bryant and May Matchwomen and Their Place in History* (London: Bloomsbury, 2011).

77. Webb and Webb, *History of Trade Unionism*, ch. 7, 344–408.

78. H. Llewellyn Smith and Vaughan Nash, *The Story of the Dockers' Strike, Told by Two East Londoners* (London: Garland Publishing, 1984 [1890]); John Lovell, "The Significance of the Great Dock Strike of 1889 in British Labor History," in Mommsen and Husung, *Development of Trade Unionism in Great Britain and Germany*, 100–113; Terry McCarthy, *The Great Dock Strike 1889: The Story of the Labour Movement's First Great Victory* (London: George Weidenfeld and Nicolson, 1988).

79. Of the 48,736 pounds raised (1.2 million francs) during the strike, 4,473 pounds came from union aid (9 percent of the total), as opposed to 13,730 livres (28 percent) from public subscription; 30,532 livres (63 percent) was sent in from abroad, mainly Australia. So union funds were very much a minor feature, which shows how different this conflict was from previous ones, which were usually self-financed. Figures quoted from Smith and Nash, *Story of the Dockers' Strike*, appendix E, "Balance Sheet of Strike Fund."

80. John Tully, *Silvertown: The Lost Story of a Strike that Shook London and Helped Launch the Modern Labor Movement* (New York: Monthly Review Press, 2014); Melanie McGrath, *Silvertown: An East End Family Memoir* (London: Fourth Estate, 2002).

81. Neville Kirk, *Labour and Society in Britain and the USA* (London: Scolar Press, 1994), 2:63–64. The number of unionized workers reached 2.5 million in 1910, then 4 million in 1914 after the "Great Labour Unrest."

82. McCarthy, *Great Dock Strike 1889*, 149.

83. Minute Book no. 6, 24 October 1890, box 2, LTC Archives, TUC Library Collections.

84. P. F. Donovan, "Australia and the Great London Strike: 1889," *Labour History* 23 (1972): 17–26.

85. Annual Reports, 1890, box 15, LTC Archives, TUC Library Collections.

86. Jonathan Hyslop, "The Imperial Working Class Makes Itself 'White': White Labourism in Britain, Australia, and South Africa before the First World War," *Journal of Historical Sociology* 12, no. 4 (1999): 398–421; Neville Kirk, *Comrades and Cousins: Globalization, Workers, and Labour Movements in Britain, USA, and Australia, 1880–1914* (London: Merlin Press, 2003); Yann Béliard, "Imperial Internationalism? Hull Labour's Support for South African Trade-Unionism on the Eve of the Great War," *Labour History Review* 74, no. 3 (December 2009): 319–29.

87. Michael Schneider, *Kleine Geschichte der Gewerkschaften. Ihre Entwicklung in Deutschland von den Anfängen bis heute* (Bonn: Verlag J. H. W. Dietz, 1989), 74–80; Gerhard A. Ritter, ed., *Der Aufstieg der deutschen Arbeiterbewegung. Sozialdemokratie und freie Gewerkschaften im Parteiensystem und Sozialmilieu des Kaiserreichs* (Munich: R. Oldenbourg, 1990).

88. Sandrine Kott, *L'Allemagne du XIXe siècle* (Paris: Hachette, 1999), 149ff.

89. Karl-Christian Führer, *Carl Legien, 1865–1921. Ein Gewerkschafter im Kampf um ein "möglichst gutes Leben" für alle Arbeiter* (Essen: Klartext, 2009), 92ff.

90. Memberships of the free unions rose fourteenfold from 174,000 in 1889 to 2.5 million at the start of the Great War. At the same juncture the confessional unions numbered some 341,000 members, and the liberal "Hirsch-Duncker" unions, 106,000 members. The rate of unionization of the German workforce was then about 22 percent. See also S. Kott, *L'Allemagne du XIXe siècle*, 149–50.

91. Führer, *Carl Legien, 1865–1921*, 113–14.

92. Paul Louis, *Le Syndicalisme européen* (Paris: F. Alcan, 1914), 21; A. Thomas, *Le Syndicalisme allemand, résumé historique (1848–1903)*

(Paris: G. Bellais, coll. "Bibliothèque socialiste," 1903); S. Kott, *L'État social en Allemagne. Représentations et pratiques* (Paris: Belin, 1995), 42–43.

93. Michel Dreyfus, Sandrine Kott, Michel Pigenet, and Noël Whiteside, "Les bases multiples du syndicalisme au XIXe siècle en Allemagne, France et Grande-Bretagne," in Robert, Boll, and Prost, *L'Invention des syndicalismes*, 269–84, here 271.

94. Richard J. Evans, *Proletarians and Politics: Socialism, Protest and the Working Class in Germany before the First World War* (London: Harvester Wheatsheaf, 1990).

95. P. Louis, *Le Syndicalisme européen*, op. cit.

96. Peter Berkowitz et al., "Structure et organisation," in Robert, Boll, and Prost, *L'Invention des syndicalismes*, 285–302. Legien saw centralization as a "school for solidarity" (p. 299).

97. Führer, *Carl Legien, 1865–1921*, 119.

98. Dolléans, *Histoire du mouvement ouvrier*, 2:33; Jacques Julliard, *Fernand Pelloutier et les origines du syndicalisme d'action directe* (Paris: Seuil, coll. "Points. Histoire," 1985 [1971]), 230–31; Peter Schöttler, *Naissance des bourses du travail. Un appareil idéologique d'État à la fin du XIXe siècle* (Paris: PUF, 1985), in particular 146–56.

99. The number of adherents of the Bourses was between 125,000 and 250,000 people at the beginning of the century—that is, between 1.25 et 2.5 percent of the active population. This was much less than the TUC, which had over 1.2 million members at the time. Julliard, *Fernand Pelloutier*, 258.

6 | SOLIDARITY AND THE MASSES

1. Daniel Rodgers, *Atlantic Crossings: Social Politics in a Progressive Era* (Cambridge, MA: Belknap Press of Harvard University Press, 1998).

2. *Neuvième rapport international sur le mouvement syndical international, 1911* (Berlin: Éditions de la Commission générale des syndicats de la Belgique, 1912), 225.

3. Office central des associations internationales, *Organisation ouvrière internationale* (Brussels: Oscar Lamberty Éditeur, 1911–1912), 8.

4. Pierre Kropotkine, *Mutual Aid: A Factor of Evolution* (New York: McClure Philipps, 1902), ch. 8; Pichot, "Biologie et solidarité," in *La Solidarité. Enquête sur un principe juridique*, ed. A. Supiot (Paris: Odile Jacob/ Collège de Belgique, 2015), 69–91.

5. Sluga, *Internationalism in the Age of Nationalism*; Thomas Cayet, *Rationaliser le travail, organiser la production. Le Bureau international du travail et la modernisation économique durant l'entre-deux-guerres* (Rennes: Presses universitaires de Rennes, 2010).

6. Office central des associations internationales, *Organisation ouvrière internationale*, 29.

7. Louis, *Le Syndicalisme européen*, ii–iii (translated from the French).

8. Madeleine Rebérioux, "Naissance du Secrétariat typographique international," in *Syndicalisme: dimensions internationales*, ed. Guillaume Devin (La Garenne–Colombe: Éditions européennes Érasme, 1990), 37–52; Georges Lefranc, *Les expériences syndicales internationales* (Paris: Aubier, 1952).

9. J. Michel, *Le mouvement ouvrier chez les mineurs d'Europe occidentale (Grande-Bretagne, Belgique, Allemagne, France). Étude comparative des années 1880–1914* (thèse pour le doctorat en histoire, Lyon, Université de Lyon II, 1987); Peter Rütters, *Die Internationale Bergarbeiterverband 1890 bis 1993: Entwicklung und Politik* (Cologne: Bund Verlag, 1990); M. Fontaine, "Mineurs français et britanniques. Un réformisme syndical?," *Mil neuf cent. Revue d'histoire intellectuelle*, no. 30, 2012, 73–88.

10. J. Michel, "L'échec de la grève générale des mineurs européens avant 1914," *Revue d'histoire moderne & contemporaine* 29, no. 2 (April–June 1982): 214–34.

11. Chas. Hobson, *Metallurgists' International Bureau of Information: A Brief Sketch of Its History and Objects* (Sheffield: Independent Press, 1904).

12. *The Fifth International Metalworkers' Congress, August 1907 at Brussels: Official Report, Prepared and Edited at the Secretariat of the International Metallurgists' Federation* (Stuttgart: Alexander Schlicke, 1907).

13. Guillaume Courty, "*Hic et nunc*. La ressource internationale dans le secteur des transports (1878–1938)," in Devin, *Syndicalisme: dimensions*

internationales, 53–65; Michel Pigenet, ed., *Le Syndicalisme docker depuis 1945* (Mont-Saint-Aignan: Presses universitaires de Rouen, 1997).

14. Michel, "L'échec de la grève générale," 214; J. Michel, "Corporatisme et internationalisme chez les mineurs européens avant 1914," in Van Holthoon and Van der Linden, *Internationalism in the Labour Movement*, 2:440–58.

15. Ad Knotter, "From Placement Control to Control of the Unemployed: Trade Unions and Labor Market Intermediation in Western Europe in the Nineteenth and Early Twentieth Centuries," in *History of Labour Intermediation: Institutions and Finding Employment in the Nineteenth and Early Twentieth Centuries* (New York/Oxford: Berghahn Books, 2015), 117–50.

16. Rebérioux, "Naissance du Secrétariat typographique international," 47.

17. Article 25, statuts de l'Alliance, 1905, Archief van Alliance Universelle des Ouvriers Diamantaires, Archief en Museum van de Socialistische Arbeidersbeweging (AMSAB, Ghent), accessible online at http://opac.amsab .be/Record/496. Archives preserved by the La Fraternelle association at the Maison du Peuple de Saint-Claude. For the diamond cutters, see Thomas Figarol, *Les Diamants de Saint-Claude. Un district industriel à l'âge de la première mondialisation (1870-1914)* (Tours: Presses universitaires François-Rabelais, 2020).

18. Office central des associations internationales, *Organisation ouvrière internationale*, 21; *Dixième rapport international sur le mouvement syndical, 1912* (Berlin: Union syndicale internationale, 1914), 249.

19. M. Fontaine, "Mineurs français et britanniques."

20. *Deuxième congrès international des mineurs, tenu à la Bourse du Travail, Paris, le 31 mars et les 1, 2, 3 et 4 avril 1891, compte rendu* (London: Green Press, McAllan and Feilden, 1891), consulted at the IISH in Amsterdam.

21. Seidel, *Internationale Stellung und internationale Beziehungen*, 242–44.

22. Friedhelm Boll and Stéphane Sirot, "Du 'tarif' à la convention collective. Grèves et syndicats des ouvriers à Londres, Paris et Hambourg à la fin du XIXᵉ siècle," in Robert, Boll, and Prost, *L'Invention des syndicalismes*, 129–50.

23. Tom Mann, *The International Labour Movement (Socialist and Trades Unionist)* (London: "Clarion" Office, November 1897).

24. *Tom Mann's Memoirs* (Nottingham: Spokesman, 2008 [1923]), 107.

25. Joseph White, *Tom Mann* (Manchester: Manchester University Press, 1991), 111–15.

26. Seidel, *Internationale Stellung und internationale Beziehungen*, 242–44.

27. "The Hamburg Dockers' Strike (1896–1897)," article published in *The Standard*, 30 November 1896, Musée social (Paris), strike files.

28. Michael Grüttner, "The Rank-and-File Movements and the Trade Unions in the Hamburg Docks from 1896–7," in Mommsen and Husung, *Development of Trade Unionism in Great Britain and Germany*, 114–29.

29. Carl Legien, *Der Streik der Hafenarbeiter und Seeleute in Hamburg-Altona* (Hamburg: Verlag der Generalkommission der Gewerkschaften Deutschlands, 1897); see also at the Musée social, the brochure, attributed to Ferdinand Tönnies, *Les Gens de mer et les ouvriers du port de Hambourg avant et pendant la grève de 1896–1897*, circulaire no. 13, série B, September 1897, 20 pages.

30. Mann, *International Labour Movement*.

31. "Lessons from the Heroic Fight for an 8 Hours' Day Waged by the Amalgamated Society of Engineers in 1897, Showing How the Spirit of Fraternity Has Grown during Recent Years," in *Metallurgists' International Bureau of Information: A Brief Sketch of Its History and Objects*, by Chas. Hobson (Sheffield: Independent Press Limited, 1904), 21ff.

32. Amalgamated Society of Engineers, *Notes on the Engineering Trade Lock-Out 1897–1898, with List of Contributions from Trade and Labour Councils, Trade Societies, and Other Sources, and General Balance Sheet* (London: Chas Mitchell, 1898), 48.

33. "Lessons from the Heroic Fight."

34. Milner, *The Dilemmas of Internationalism*, 79–86; Michel Dreyfus, "The Emergence of an International Trade Union Organization (1902–1919)," in *The International Confederation of Free Trade Unions*, ed. Marcel van der

Linden (Berne: Peter Lang, 2000), 25–71; Bart de Wilde, ed., *The Past and Future of International Trade Unionism* (Ghent: IALHI/AMSAB Instituut, 2001); Geert van Goethem, *The Amsterdam International: The World of the International Federation of Trade Unions (IFTU), 1913–1945* (Aldershot: Ashgate, 2006).

35. Rodgers, *Atlantic Crossings*; Janet Horne, *Le Musée social. Aux origines de l'État-providence* (Paris: Belin, 2004); Davide Rodogno, Bernhard Struck, and Jakob Vogel, eds., *Shaping the Transnational Sphere: Experts, Networks, and Issues, from the 1840s to the 1930s* (New York/Oxford: Berghahn Books, 2014).

36. Eduard Bernstein, *La grève et le lock-out en Belgique. Leurs forces, leur droit et leurs résultats. Conférences faites à l'université nouvelle de Bruxelles* (Brussels: Misch & Thron; Paris: Marcel Rivière, 1908), 6 (translated in English from the French version).

37. Louis, *Le Syndicalisme européen*.

38. Führer, *Carl Legien, 1865–1921*, 156.

39. Fabrizio Loreto, "Le voyage du syndicalisme italien dans l'Europe du début du XXᵉ siècle. L'exemple allemand, le cas français, le modèle anglais," *Vingtième siècle. Revue d'histoire* 132 (2016): 3–14.

40. White, *Tom Mann*, 115.

41. Mann, *International Labour Movement*, 10.

42. Bantman, "Internationalism without an International?"; White, *Tom Mann*, ch. 6.

43. *Nouvelle histoire de la Belgique*, vol. 1 (Brussels: Complexe, 2005), 138.

44. Parti Ouvrier Belge, *Congrès scandinavique (Danemark, Suède, Norvège) tenu à Copenhague les 22, 23 et 24 août 1901 à la Maison du Peuple. Rapport suivi d'un aperçu de la situation syndicale en Belgique et de l'organisation du secrétariat général des syndicats en ce pays* (Brussels: Imp. Vve Désiré Brismée, 1901), 3.

45. Milner, *The Dilemmas of Internationalism*, 80.

46. Resolution of the Stuttgart Congress on "relations between parties and unions," *Histoire de la IIe Internationale*, vol. 17, *Congrès socialiste*

international. Stuttgart, 6–24 août 1907 (Geneva: Minkoff Reprint, 1985), 425.

47. Bernstein, *La Grève et le lock-out en Allemagne*, 74 (translated in English from the French version).

48. Perrot, *Les Ouvriers en grève*, 2:426.

49. Émile Durkheim, *De la division du travail social. Étude sur l'organisation des sociétés supérieures* (Paris: F. Alcan, 1893).

50. Mann, *International Labour Movement*, 9; *L'Ouvrier des deux mondes. Revue mensuelle d'économie sociale* 7 (1 August 1897): 111.

51. Eisenberg, *Deutsche und englische Gewerkschaften*, 217–18.

52. M. Leroy, *La Coutume ouvrière. Syndicats, bourses du travail, fédérations professionnelles, coopératives. Doctrines et institutions* (Paris: Éditions CNT, 2007 [1913]), 1:212.

53. The financial bonanza affecting the German General Committee drew the attention of the Deutsche Bank, which tried to recruit the committee as a client in 1912. Führer, *Carl Legien, 1865–1921*, 114.

54. Victor Griffuelhes, *L'Action syndicaliste* (Paris: Rivière, Bibliothèque du Mouvement socialiste, 1908), 21.

55. Louis, *Le Syndicalisme européen*, 308.

56. The progressive broadening of solidarity and its general deprofessionalization was confirmed at the end of the nineteenth century, see also Sirot, *La Grève en France*, 140.

57. This primacy of national organization and solidarity was best reaffirmed between the wars by the International Trade Union Federation (Fédération syndicale internationale). See also Johann Sassenbach, "Solidarité internationale dans les conflits de salaires," in *Compte rendu du IVe congrès ordinaire de la FSI, Paris, 1927* (Amsterdam: FSI, 1928), 170–75.

58. Mann, *International Labour Movement*, 6.

59. Tönnies, *Les Gens de mer et les ouvriers du port de Hambourg*, 394.

60. Pierre de Saint-Girons, *L'Assurance patronale contre la grève* (Paris: Sirey, 1908), 78.

61. Danièle Fraboulet, "Les organisations patronales au début du XXe siècle," in *Dictionnaire historique des patrons français*, ed. Jean-Claude

Daumas, Alain Chatriot, Danièle Fraboulet, and Patrick Fridenson (Paris: Flammarion, 2010), 1065–69; Werner Bührer, "Genèse et développement des syndicats patronaux en Belgique (XIXᵉ–début XXᵉ siècle)," in *Genèse des organisations patronales en Europe (XIXᵉ-XXᵉ siècle)*, ed. D. Fraboulet and Pierre Vernus (Rennes: Presses universitaires de Rennes, 2012), 111–21.

62. Saint-Girons, *L'Assurance patronale contre la grève*, 82–83; see also Hans-Peter Ullmann, "Unternehmerschaft, Arbeitgeberverbände und Streikbewegung 1890–1914," in *Streik. Zur Geschichte des Arbeitskampfes in Deutschland während der Industrialisierung*, ed. Klaus Tenfelde and Heinrich Volkmann (München: Beck, 1981), 194–208.

63. Saint-Girons, *L'Assurance patronale contre la grève*, 25, 194.

64. Sirot, *La Grève en France*, 206–10.

65. Jesper Hamark and Christer Thörnqvist, "Docks and Defeat: The 1909 General Strike in Sweden and the Role of Port Labor," *Historical Studies in Industrial Relations* 34 (2013): 1–27 (here 21).

66. Office central des associations internationales, *Organisation ouvrière internationale*, 40.

67. X. Vigna, "La menace de la grève," in *Dictionnaire historique des patrons français*, op. cit., 933 (see footnote 61 in this chapter).

68. Zeev Sternhell, *La Droite révolutionnaire, 1885-1914. Les origines françaises du fascisme* (Paris: Seui, 1978); Christophe Maillard, *Un syndicalisme impossible? L'histoire oubliée des Jaunes* (Paris: Vendémiaire, 2016).

69. J. Julliard, *Clemenceau briseur de grèves. L'affaire de Draveil-Villeneuve-Saint-Georges (1908)* (Paris: Julliard, coll. "Archives," 1965).

70. White, *Tom Mann*, 174–79.

71. Hamark and Thörnqvist, "Docks and Defeat."

72. "Rapport présenté au congrès de Copenhague par le Parti ouvrier social-démocrate de Suède," in *Histoire de la IIe Internationale*, vol. 20, *Congrès socialiste international. Copenhague, 28 août-3 septembre 1910* (Geneva: Minkoff Reprint, 1982), 16.

73. *Seventh International Report of the Trade Union Movement 1909*, published by the International Secretary of the National Trade Union Centers (Berlin: The General Federation of Trade Unions of Germany, 1911).

74. *The Sixth International Metalworkers' Congress, October 1910 at Birmingham: Report official, edited at the Secretary of the International Metallurgist' Federation* (Stuttgart: Alexander Schlicke, 1911).

75. Hamark and Thörnqvist, "Docks and Defeat."

76. International Metalworkers' Federation, *Teaching of Trades in Continental Countries*, 583ff.

77. Milner, *The Dilemmas of Internationalism*, 102–3.

78. Andy Croll, "Starving Strikers and the Limits of the 'Humanitarian Discovery of Hunger' in Late Victorian Britain," *International Review of Social History* 56 (2001): 103–31.

79. "Rapport du Parti ouvrier social-démocrate de Suède au congrès de Copenhague, 1910," AD93, 291J9.

80. F. Jarrige, "L'invention des soupes communistes en Belgique (1880–1914)," in *La Gamelle et l'Ooutil. Manger au travail en Belgique et en Europe de la fin du XVIIIe siècle à nos jours*, ed. Thomas Bouchet et al. (Nancy: Arbre bleu éditions, 2016), 161–78; S. Sirot, "La pauvreté comme une parenthèse. Survivre en grève du XIXe siècle à la Seconde Guerre mondiale," in *Le Syndicalisme, la politique et la grève. Belgique et Europe (XIXᵉ–XXIᵉ siècle)* (Nancy: Arbre bleu éditions, 2011), 171–88.

81. John M. Merriman, *Limoges la ville rouge. Portrait d'une ville révolutionnaire* (Paris: Belin, 1990 [1989]), 359–63.

82. Émile Vandervelde, Louis de Brouckère, and L. Vandersmissen, *La Grève générale en Belgique (avril 1913)* (Paris: Librairie F. Alcan, 1914), 265 in particular.

83. Wilfrid Harris Crook, *The General Strike: A Study of Labor's Tragic Weapon in Theory and Practice* (Chapel Hill: University of North Carolina Press, 1931), 23–24.

84. Ibid., 136.

85. Vandervelde, de Brouckère, and Vandersmissen, *La Grève générale en Belgique*, 131.

86. Michel, "L'échec de la grève générale," 224.

87. Vandervelde, de Brouckère, and Vandersmissen, *La Grève générale en Belgique*, 269.

88. Paul Lafargue called soup kitchens and "child exodus" "two new tactics in the struggle…which exalt worker solidarity." Paul Lafargue, "La confédération du travail et le parti socialiste," *L'Humanité*, 5 August 1907, quoted by F. Jarrige, "L'invention des soupes communistes," 171.

89. Louis de Brouckère, "Rapport sur les rapports entre les partis politiques socialistes et les associations professionnelles, présenté au nom du Parti ouvrier belge, 1907," in *Histoire de la IIe Internationale*, vol. 16, *Congrès socialiste international. Stuttgart, 18–24 Août 1907* (Geneva: Minkoff Reprint, 1978), 47.

7 | A REVOLUTIONARY WEAPON?

1. P. Alayrac, *L'Internationale au milieu du gué. De l'internationalisme socialiste au congrès de Londres (1896)* (Rennes: Presses universitaires de Rennes, 2018).

2. Haupt, *La Deuxième Internationale, 1889–1914*, 24. See also Moira Donald, "Workers of the World Unite? Exploring the Enigma of the Second International," in Geyer and Paulmann, *Mechanics of Internationalism*, 177–213; Patrizia Dogliani, "The Fate of Socialist Internationalism," in Clavin and Sluga, *Internationalisms: A Twentieth-Century History*, 38–60.

3. Jean Longuet, *Le Mouvement socialiste international*, reproduced in *Histoire de la IIe Internationale*, vol. 4 (Geneva: Minkoff Reprint, 1976 [1913]), 86.

4. A. Kriegel, "La IIe Internationale (1889–1914)," in *Histoire générale du socialisme*, vol. 2, *De 1875 à 1918*, ed. J. Droz (Paris: PUF, 1974), 558–60.

5. Donald Sassoon, *One Hundred Years of Socialism: The West European Left in the Twentieth Century* (London: I. B. Tauris, 1996), 10–11.

6. Van der Linden, *Workers of the World*, 272.

7. Rodgers, *Atlantic Crossings*.

8. Berger, *Social Democracy and the Working Class*, 75; Eley, *Forging Democracy*, 81, 114.

9. P. Dogliani, *Le Socialisme municipal en France et en Europe de la Commune à la Grande Guerre* (Nancy: L'Arbre bleu, 2018 [1992]).

10. Renaud Payre, *Une Science communale? Réseaux réformateurs et municipalité providence* (Paris: CNRS Éditions, 2007).

11. "Rapport du parti ouvrier social-démocrate de Suède au congrès de Copenhague, 1910," 291J9, AD93; Mary Hilson, *Political Change and the Rise of Labour in Comparative Perspective: Britain and Sweden, 1890–1920* (Lund: Nordic Academic, 2006); Hamark and Thörnqvist, "Docks and Defeat."

12. K. J. Callahan, *Demonstration Culture: European Socialism and the Second International, 1889–1914* (Leicester: Troubador, 2010), 155.

13. *Histoire de la IIe Internationale*, op. cit., 17:416.

14. Longuet, *Le Mouvement socialiste international*, 287.

15. Alexandre Courban, *L'Humanité, de Jean Jaurès à Marcel Cachin (1904–1939)* (Ivry-sur-Seine: Les Éditions de l'Atelier, 2014), 48–49.

16. Charles Kurzman, *Democracy Denied, 1905–1915: Intellectuals and the Fate of Democracy* (Cambridge, MA: Harvard University Press, 2008).

17. *Bureau socialiste international. Comptes rendus des réunions, manifestes et circulaires*, vol. 1, *1900–1907, documents recueillis et présentés par Georges Haupt* (Paris/La Haye: Mouton, 1969), 34, 39, 53, 91, for example.

18. Callahan, *Demonstration Culture*, xii.

19. Sebastian Schickl, *Universalismus und Partikularismus. Erfahrungsraum, Erwartungshorizont und Territorialdebatten in der diskursiven Praxis der II. Internationale 1889–1917* (St. Ingbert: Röhrig, 2012).

20. In 1905, the Argentinian delegate to the ISB demanded that European workers should commit to a blockade of merchandise arriving from Argentina, in solidarity with their struggle against social dumping. See also Dogliani, "Fate of Socialist Internationalism," 48n25.

21. Debates on "emigration and immigration," 20 August 1904, speech by Mr. Hillquit in *Histoire de la IIe Internationale*, vol. 14, *Congrès socialiste international. Amsterdam, 14–20 Août 1904* (Geneva: Minkoff Reprint, 1985), 396–97 (translated from the French transcript).

22. First session of the committee on emigration and immigration of workers, 19 August 1907, in *Histoire de la IIe Internationale*, op. cit., 17: 565, 568, 575 (quotations translated from the French transcript).

23. Resolution on worker emigration and immigration, in *Histoire de la IIe Internationale*, op. cit., 17: 756–59.

24. The impact of anarchism, more malleable and less institutionalized, was more "global" than that of socialism, which was still confined to Europe and the Atlantic world. This has been pointed out by Ilham Khuri-Makdisi, *The Eastern Mediterranean and the Making of Global Radicalism, 1860–1914* (Berkeley: University of California Press, 2010), and Anderson, *Under Three Flags*.

25. Circular of 18 February 1905, doc. no. 30, in *Bureau socialiste international*, op. cit., 132–33.

26. Appeal of the ISB published in *Le Peuple*, written by Émile Vandervelde, Édouard Anseele, and Camille Huysmans, 30 June 1905, art. 3/19, 8D3, Georges Haupt Papers, FMSH Archives.

27. "Circulaire transmettant une proposition du Parti socialiste italien en Suisse de verser des fonds au profit de la Révolution russe," doc. no. 55, *Bureau socialiste international*, op. cit., 194–95. On the international demonstrations organized in 1905–1906, see Callahan, *Demonstration Culture*, 227–29.

28. "Réunion du BSI 10 novembre 1906, rapport financier," art. 3/02, 8D3, G. Haupt Papers, FMSH Archives.

29. ISB report to the Stuttgart Congress, 1907, in *Bureau socialiste international*, op. cit., appendix no. XX, 437.

30. ISB report, February 1906, *Bureau socialiste international*, op. cit., appendix no. X, 365–68. The account book for the Russia Appeal is held in the Camille Huysmans Archive in Antwerp. Callahan, *Demonstration Culture*, 252n35.

31. Callahan, *Demonstration Culture*, 4n8.

32. J. Jaurès in *L'Humanité*, 15 April 1906, quoted by G. Candar, "Les socialistes français et la révolution russe de 1905," *Bulletin de la Société d'études jaurésiennes* 131 (January–March 1994): 3–10.

33. Manifesto against the Russian Loan, October 1906, doc. no. 65, *Bureau socialiste international*, op. cit., 236–39.

34. Leo Stern, ed., *Die Auswirkungen der ersten russischen Revolution von 1905–1907 auf Deutschland* (Berlin: Rütten & Loening, 1955–1956), introduction in vol. 1, and vol. 2, lviii; Longuet, *Le Mouvement socialiste international*, 288.

35. For the SPD, *Protokoll über die Verhandlungen des Parteitages der Sozialdemokratischen Partei Deutschlands. Abgehalten zu Essen vom 15. bis 21. September 1907* (Berlin: Verlag Buchhandlung Vorwärts, 1907); for the SFIO, see Frédéric Cépède, "La SFIO des années 1905–1914: construire le parti," *Cahiers Jaurès* 187–88 (2008): 29–45 (here, 35).

36. *Correspondance entre Lénine et Camille Huysmans, 1905–1914*, published by Georges Haupt (Paris/La Haye: Mouton, 1963), 50.

37. Jonathan Frankel, *Crisis, Revolution, and Russian Jews* (Cambridge: Cambridge University Press, 2009), 57–71.

38. Frank Wolff, "Eastern Europe Abroad: Exploring Actor-Networks in Transnational Movements and Migration History, the Case of the Bund," *IRSH* 57 (2012): 229–55; Frank Wolff, *Neue Welten in der Neuen Welt. Die transnationale Geschichte des Allgemeinen Jüdischen Arbeiterbundes 1897–1947* (Cologne: Böhlau Verlag, 2014), in particular ch. "Hilfsfonds als Waffen: von revolutionärem Fundraising zu transnationale Kulturarbeit," 401–54; Frank Wolff, "Revolutionary Fundraising and Global Networks: A Microeconomic Approach to the Social Meaning of Money and Mobilization before the Second World War," *History* 102, no. 351 (2017): 450–78.

39. "Rapport du *Bund* au congrès de l'Internationale socialiste à Stuttgart, 1907," in *Histoire de la IIe Internationale*, vol. 18-bis (Geneva: Minkoff Reprint, 1985), 123–24.

40. F. Wolff, "Eastern Europe Abroad."

41. Letter from San Francisco to the ISB, 11 November 1905, art. 3/23, 8D3, G. Haupt Papers, FMSH Archives (translated from the French).

42. Letter of 3 April 1905, art. 3/24, 8D3, G. Haupt Papers, FMSH Archives.

43. G. Haupt, "Lénine, les Bolsheviks et la IIe Internationale," *Cahiers du monde russe et soviétique* 7 (July–September 1966): 378–407.

44. Stern, *Die Auswirkungen der ersten russischen Revolution*, vol. 2.

45. "Circulaire soumettant au vote des partis affiliés les deux propositions pour le partage des fonds russes," 1 June 1905 (14,184 francs received by that date).

46. ISB note, 23 February 1907, art. 4, 8D3, G. Haupt Papers, FMSH Archives.

47. Letter dated 3 April 1905, art. 3/24, 8D3, G. Haupt Papers, FMSH Archives.

48. *Correspondance entre Lénine et Camille Huysmans.*

49. Letter of 28 November 1913, art. 136, 8D3, G. Haupt Papers, FMSH Archives.

50. Letter of 6 February 1914, art. 7/18, 8D3, G. Haupt Papers, FMSH Archives.

51. Dolléans, *Histoire du mouvement ouvrier*, vol. 2, "Internationale politique ou syndicale? 1889–1900–1909," 89–116.

52. Robert Brécy, *La Grève générale en France* (Paris: Études et documentation internationales, 1969); Julliard, *Fernand Pelloutier*, ch. 2, "La grève générale (1892–1895)," 61–89.

53. Quoted in Julliard, *Fernand Pelloutier*, 87.

54. CGT committee for strikes and general strikes, *Grève générale réformiste et grève générale révolutionnaire* (Paris: Imprimerie économique [Association ouvrière], 1903 [2nd ed.]), 2.

55. Report on the general strike and political strike, compiled by the Dutch Social Democratic Party, in *Histoire de la IIe Internationale*, vol. 14, *Congrès socialiste international. Amsterdam, 14–20 août 1904* (Geneva: Minkoff Reprint, 1978), 127–46.

56. É. Vandervelde, *La Grève générale* (Gandz: Société coopérative "Volksdrukkerij," 1908).

57. See also introduction by Irène Petit in Rosa Luxemburg, *Réforme sociale ou révolution? Grève de masse, parti et syndicats* (Paris: La Découverte, 2001), 5–14.

58. R. Luxemburg and F. Mehring, *L'expérience belge de grève générale. Grèves sauvages. Spontanéité des massess* (Paris: Spartacus, 1969), 17–22.

59. R. Luxemburg, *The Mass Strike, the Political Party, and the Trade Unions* (Detroit: Marxist Educational Society of Detroit, 1925 [1906]), 48.

60. Helge Döhrin, ed., *Generalstreik! Abwehrstreik . . . Proteststreik . . . Massenstreik? Streiktheorien und diskussionen innerhalb der deutschen Sozialdemokratie vor 1914. Grundlagen zum Generalstreik mit Ausblick* (Lich, Germany: Edition AV, 2009); Wilfrid Harris Crook, *The General*

Strike: A Study of Labor's Tragic Weapon in Theory and Practice (Chapel Hill: University of North Carolina Press, 1931); Phil H. Goodstein, *The Theory of the General Strike from the French Revolution to Poland* (New York: Columbia University Press, 1984).

61. Berger, *Social Democracy and the Working Class*, 69ff., 84.

62. Ibid., 85; Führer, *Carl Legien, 1865–1921*, 157ff.

63. Herbert Hill, "The Problem of Race in American Labor History," *Reviews in American History* 24, no. 2 (1996): 189–208.

64. Patrick Renshaw, *The Wobblies: The Story of Syndicalism in the United States* (London: Eyre and Spottiswoode, 1967).

65. Emma Goldman, *Living My Life*, 2 vols. (New York: Alfred Knopf, 1931–1934).

66. Peter Cole, David Struthers, and Kenyon Zimmer, eds., *Wobblies of the World: A Global History of the IWW* (London: Pluto Press, 2017).

67. Kenyon Zimmer, *Red Exiles: America's Political Deportees in a Revolutionary World, 1917–1939*, manuscript in preparation.

68. *The Fifth International Metalworkers' Congress, August 12–15, 1907 in the House of People at Brussels: Official Report, Prepared and Edited by the Secretary of the International Metallurgists' Federation* (Stuttgart: Alexander Schlicke, 1907).

69. Legien's speech to the Stuttgart Congress, second session of the committee on relations between political parties and trade unions, 21 August 1917, in *Histoire de la IIe Internationale*, op. cit., 17:532–33 (translated in English from the French transcript). See also Führer, *Carl Legien, 1865–1921*.

70. First session of the committee on "militarism and international conflict," 19 August 1907, in *Histoire de la IIe Internationale*, op. cit., 17:440–513.

71. Ibid., 442 (translated from the French transcript).

72. Second session of the committee on "militarism and international conflicts," 20 August 1907, ibid., 472 (translated from the French transcript).

73. Gerd Krumeich, "Internationalisme, patriotisme et social-démocratie allemande," *Cahiers Jaurès* 212–13 (2014): 53–63.

74. First session of the committee on "militarism and international conflict," 19 August 1907, in *Histoire de la IIe Internationale,* op. cit. 17:453 (translated from the French transcript).

75. Third session of the "committee on militarism and international conflicts," 21 August 1907, ibid., 487–88 (translated from the French transcript).

76. Vincent Robert, "'La protestation universelle' lors de l'exécution de Ferrer. Les manifestations d'octobre 1909," *Revue d'histoire moderne et contemporaine* 36 (1989): 247–65; Daniel Laqua, "Freethinkers, Anarchists and Francisco Ferrer: The Making of a Transnational Solidarity Campaign," *European Review of History — Revue européenne d'histoire* 21, no. 4 (2014): 467–84.

77. Michel, "L'échec de la grève générale," 220.

78. Édouard Vaillant, letter dated 25 March 1912, in Camélinat archive 291J9, AD93.

79. Dolléans, *Histoire du mouvement ouvrier,* vol. 2, *L'Internationale ouvrière et la guerre (1914–1915–1916),* 206–40; G. Haupt, *Le Congrès manqué. L'Internationale à la veille de la Première Guerre mondiale* (Paris: F. Maspero, 1965), 278.

80. Christopher Clark, *The Sleepwalkers: How Europe Went to War in 1914* (London: Allen Lane, 2012).

81. Kriegel, "La IIe Internationale (1889–1914)," 578; Madeleine Rebérioux, "Le socialisme et la Première Guerre mondiale (1914–1918)," in Droz, *Histoire générale du socialisme,* 2:585–642; Romain Ducoulombier, ed., *Les Socialistes dans l'Europe en guerre. Réseaux, parcours, expériences, 1914–1918* (Paris: L'Harmattan, 2010); R. Ducoulombier, *Camarades! La naissance du parti communiste en France* (Paris: Perrin, 2010), chs. 1–2.

8 | FOOTPRINTS AND LEGACIES

1. "La justice sociale dans un monde global. L'organisation internationale du travail (1919–2019)," special edition of *Mouvement social* 263 (2018).

2. Dogliani, "Fate of Socialist Internationalism," 50–55; Talbot C. Imlay, "Socialist Internationalism after 1914," in Clavin and Sluga, *Internationalisms: A Twentieth-Century History,* 213–41.

3. Reiner Tosstorff, *The Red International of Labour Unions (RILU) 1920-1937* (Leiden: Brill, 2016). For Edo Fimmen, see Van Goethem, *Amsterdam International*, 32.

4. *L'Œuvre de la Fédération syndicale internationale dans les années 1922-1924* (Amsterdam: Fédération syndicale internationale, 1924), 255.

5. Kriegel, *Les Internationales ouvrières*; Brigitte Studer, *The Transnational World of the Cominternians* (London: Palgrave MacMillan, 2015), 6 (quotation).

6. Claude Pennetier and Bernard Pudal, eds., *Autobiographies, autocritiques, aveux dans le monde communiste* (Paris: Belin, 2002).

7. Quoted by Gleb J. Albert, "To Help the Republicans Not Just by Donations and Rallies, but with the Rifle: Militant Solidarity with the Spanish Republic in the Soviet Union, 1936-1937," *European Review of History/ Revue européenne d'histoire* 21, no. 4 (2014): 501-18 (here, 501). This quote is drawn from an article "The Crisis Has Matured," published on 29 September 1917. Vladimir Illitch Lénine, *Œuvres* (Paris: Éditions sociales, 1958), 26:68–79, consulted online on 12 May 2022, https://www.marxists.org/archive/lenin/works/1917/oct/20.htm.

8. Daniel Laqua, "Democratic Politics and the League of Nations: The Labour and Socialist International as a Protagonist of Interwar Internationalism," *Contemporary European History* 24, no. 2 (2015): 175–92; Talbot C. Imlay, *The Practice of Socialist Internationalism: European Socialists and International Politics, 1914-1960* (Oxford: Oxford University Press, 2018).

9. Sabine Hering and Kurt Schilde, eds., *Die Rote Hilfe. Die Geschichte der internationalen kommunistischen "Wohlfahrtorganisation" und ihrer sozialen Aktivitäten in Deutschland (1921-1941)* (Opladen: Leske and Budrich, 2003); Holger Weiss, ed., *International Communism and Transnational Solidarity: Radical Networks, Mass Movements, and Global Politics, 1919-1939* (Leiden: Brill, 2017). On Red Aid in France between the wars, see Axelle Brodiez, *Le Secours populaire français, 1945-2000. Du communisme à l'humanitaire* (Paris: Presses de Sciences Po, 2006), ch. 1.

10. Claudio Natoli, "Pour une histoire comparée des organisations communistes de solidarité. Le Secours ouvrier international et le Secours rouge

international," in Gotovitch and Morelli, *Les Solidarités internationales*, 17–42 (here 27).

11. Sean McMeekin, *The Red Millionaire: A Political Biography of Willi Münzenberg, Moscow's Secret Propaganda Tsar in the West* (New Haven, CT: Yale University Press, 2003), 106.

12. Matthew Lloyd Adams, "Herbert Hoover and the Organization of the American Relief Effort in Poland (1919–1923)," *European Journal of American Studies* 4, no. 2 (2009), online at https://ejas.revues.org/7627; Bruno Cabanes, *The Great War and the Origins of Humanitarianism, 1918–1924* (New York: Cambridge University Press, 2014), ch. 4, "The Hungry and the Sick: Herbert Hoover, the Russian Famine, and the Professionalization of Humanitarian Aid," 189–247.

13. Kasper Braskén, *The International Workers' Relief, Communism, and Transnational Solidarity: Willi Münzenberg in Weimar Germany* (London: Palgrave MacMillan, 2015), 56; Cabanes, *The Great War and the Origins of Humanitarianism*, 215; Olivier Zunz, *Philanthropy in America: A History* (Princeton, NJ: Princeton University Press, 2011).

14. Gotovitch and Morelli, *Les Solidarités internationales*, 8.

15. *L'Œuvre de la Fédération syndicale internationale*, 68, 74. The IFTU also participated in the effort to help workers hit by the great inflation. The total raised by this action of solidarity was 494,000 florins (3.8 million francs).

16. *Rapport sur l'activité de la Fédération syndicale internationale en 1924, 1925 et 1926, présenté au quatrième congrès ordinaire, Paris, août 1927* (Amsterdam: FSI, 1927), 4.

17. B. M. Zabarko, "Die internationale solidarität mit dem Bergarbeiterstreik 1926 in Grossbritannien," *Beiträge zur Geschichte der Arbeiterbewegung* 28 (1986): 630–34; Larry Peterson, "Internationalism and the British Coal Miners Strike of 1926: The Solidarity Campaign of the KPD among Ruhr Coal Miners," in van Holthoon and van der Linden, *Internationalism in the Labour Movement*, 2:459–88; K. Brasken, "The British Miners' and General Strike of 1926: Problems and Practices of Radical International Solidarity," in Weiss, *International Communism and Transnational Solidarity*, 168–90.

18. Patricia Clavin, "The Austrian Hunger Crisis and the Genesis of International Organization after the First World War," *International Affairs* 90, no. 2 (2014): 265–78.

19. "Pour secourir les travailleurs viennois," 6 April 1920, circulaire no. 43, boîte 20, Fonds CGT avant 1940, Institut CGT d'histoire sociale, Montreuil.

20. Gotovitch and Morelli, *Les Solidarités internationales*, 51.

21. Cabanes, *The Great War and the Origins of Humanitarianism*, ch. 5, "Humanitarianism Old and New: Eglantyne Jebb and Children's Rights," 248–313.

22. *Le Mouvement syndical international* 1 (1921): 25; "Premier rapport sur l'activité de la Fédération syndicale internationale, 1919–1921," *Le Mouvement syndical international*, supplément 5 (April 1922): 53–54. These figures look small when compared to the nearly one hundred thousand Austrian children sent abroad through the efforts of Save the Children Fund and American Quakers. Tara Zahra, *The Lost Children: Reconstructing Europe's Families after World War II* (Cambridge, MA: Harvard University Press, 2011), 37, quoted in Cabanes, *The Great War and the Origins of Humanitarianism*, 287.

23. Gotovitch and Morelli, *Les Solidarités internationales*, 51.

24. *Le Mouvement syndical international* 1 (1921): 17–18; Edo Fimmen, "Le boycottage de la Hongrie," *Le Mouvement syndical international*, no. 4, 1921, 105–11.

25. Van Goethem, *Amsterdam International*, 208.

26. On the links of solidarity maintained by members of the Bund after the First World War, see Mark Mazower, *What You Did Not Tell: The Russian Past and the Journey Home* (New York: Other Press, 2017).

27. Erez Manela, *The Wilsonian Moment: Self-Determination and the International Origins of Anticolonial Nationalism* (Oxford: Oxford University Press, 2009); Michael Goebel, *Anti-Imperial Metropolis: Interwar Paris and the Seeds of Third World Nationalism* (Cambridge: Cambridge University Press, 2015).

28. Sabine Dullin and Brigitte Studer, "Communisme + transnational. L'équation retrouvée de l'internationalisme (premier XXe siècle)," *Monde(s)* 10 (November 2016): 9–32.

29. Conference by Charles Rappoport at the propaganda school, Seine Federation of the Socialist Party, 10 May 1920, art. 54, 8D3, G. Haupt Papers, FMSH Archives.

30. Anderson, *Under Three Flags*.

31. Lisa McGirr, "The Passion of Sacco and Vanzetti: A Global History," *Journal of American History* 93, no. 4 (2007): 1085–115; Moshik Temkin, *The Sacco-Vanzetti Affair: America on Trial* (New Haven, CT: Yale University Press, 2009).

32. S. Dullin, B. Studer, "Communisme + transnational," 13; M. Goebel, "Geopolitics, Transnational Solidarity or Diaspora Nationalism? The Global Career of M. N. Roy, 1915–1930," *European Review of History/Revue européenne d'histoire* 21, no. 4 (2014): 485–99.

33. Holger Weiss, "Between Moscow and the African Atlantic: The Comintern Network of Negro Workers," *Monde(s)* 10 (November 2016): 89–108.

34. D. Featherstone, *Solidarity, Hidden Histories and Geographies of Internationalism*, ch. 3, 69–98; H. Weiss, "The International of Seamen and Harbour Workers: A Radical Global Labor Union of the Waterfront or a Subversive World-Wide Web?," in Weiss, *International Communism and Transnational Solidarity*, 256–317.

35. Hakim Adi, "The Comintern and the Black Workers in Britain and France, 1919–1937," *Immigrants and Minorities* 28, no. 2–3 (2010): 224–45.

36. Lisa A. Kirchenbaum, *International Communism and the Spanish Civil War: Solidarity and Suspicion* (Cambridge: Cambridge University Press, 2015), 84.

37. Jim Fyrth, *The Signal Was Spain: The Spanish Aid Movement in Britain, 1936–1939* (London: Lawrence and Wishart, 1986); Denis Smyth, "'We Are with You': Solidarity and Self-Interest in Soviet Policy towards Republican Spain, 1936–1939," in *The Republic Besieged: Civil War in Spain, 1936–1939*, ed. Paul Preston and Ann L. Mackenzie (Edinburgh: Edinburgh University Press, 1996), 53–86; Albert, "To Help the Republicans Not Just by Donations and Rallies."

38. Claudio Natoli, "Pour une histoire comparée des organisations communistes de solidarité," 39.

39. Célia Keren, *L'Évacuation et l'accueil des enfants espagnols en France. Cartographie d'une mobilisation transnationale (1936-1940)* (thèse d'histoire, EHESS, 2014); Célia Keren, "Les défis de la solidarité internationale. La collaboration entre la Ligue des droits de l'homme et la Confédération générale du travail au sein du Comité d'accueil aux enfants d'Espagne (1936-1939)," in *Le Phénomène ligueur en Europe et aux Amériques*, ed. Olivier Dard and Nathalie Sévilla (Metz: Presses universitaires de Metz, 2011), 269-86.

40. Harold D. James, *The End of Globalization: Lessons from the Great Depression* (Cambridge, MA: Harvard University Press, 2001).

41. John Gerard Ruggie, "International Regimes, Transactions, and Change: Embedded Liberalism in the Postwar Economic Order," *International Organization* 36, no. 2 (1982): 379-415.

42. Van der Linden, *International Confederation of Free Trade Unions.*

43. Adom Getachew, *Worldmaking after Empire: The Rise and Fall of Self-Determination* (Princeton, NJ: Princeton University Press, 2019).

44. First meeting, International Solidarity Fund, Tunis, July1957, item 844, ICFTU Archive, IISH.

45. Waters and van Goethem, *American Labor's Global Ambassadors.* For money dispensed, particularly in South America, see Robert Anthony Waters Jr. and Geert van Goethem, eds., *American Labor's Global Ambassadors* (London: Palgrave MacMillan, 2013), esp. ch. 7 by Dustin Walcher, "Reforming Latin American Labor: The AFL-CIO and Latin America's Cold War," 123-35.

46. Caroline Moine, "La RDA à l'heure de la 'Solidarité internationale.' Berlin-Est, August 1973," in *La République démocratique allemande. La vitrine du socialisme et l'envers du miroir (1949-1989-2009)*, ed. Chantal Metzger (Brussels: P.I.E. Peter Lang, 2010), 289-300.

47. Caroline Moine, "'Votre combat est le nôtre.' Les mouvements de solidarité avec le Chili dans l'Europe de la guerre froide," *Monde(s)* 8 (2015): 83-104.

48. Kim Christiaens, "The Difficult Quest for Chilean Allies: International Labor Solidarity Campaigns for Chile in the 1970s and 1980s," in

European Solidarity with Chile, 1970s–1980s, ed. Kim Christiaens, Idesbald Goddeeris, and Magaly Rodríguez García (Frankfurt: Peter Lang, 2014), 93–123.

49. Shirin Hirsch, "The United Kingdom: Competing Conceptions of Internationalism," in Christiaens, Goddeeris, and Rodríguez García, *European Solidarity*, 145–62; Samuel Moyn, *The Last Utopia: Human Rights in History* (Cambridge, MA: Belknap Press of Harvard University Press, 2010).

50. Idesbald Goddeeris, ed., *Solidarity with Solidarity: Western European Trade Unions and the Polish Crisis, 1980–1982* (Plymouth: Lexington Books, 2012); Eric Chenoweth, "AFL-CIO Support for Solidarity: Moral, Political, Financial," in Waters and van Goethem, *American Labor's Global Ambassadors*, 103–19.

51. Robert Castel, *Les Métamorphoses de la question sociale. Une chronique du salariat* (Paris: Fayard, 1995); Thomas Piketty, *Capital in the Twenty-First Century* (Cambridge, MA: Harvard University Press, 2014).

CONCLUSION

1. Samuel Moyn, *Not Enough: Human Rights in an Unequal World* (Cambridge, MA: Belknap Press of Harvard University Press, 2018).

2. A distinction drawn by Pierre Rosanvallon in the conclusion of his book *La Démocratie inachevée. Histoire de la souveraineté du peuple en France* (Paris: Gallimard, 2000).

3. Geoffrey Pleyers, *Alter-Globalization: Becoming Actors in the Global Age* (Cambridge: Polity, 2010).

4. Anne-Catherine Wagner, *Vers une Europe syndicale. Une enquête sur la Confédération européenne des syndicats* (Bellecombe-en-Bauges: Éditions du Croquant, 2005); Hélène Michel, ed., *Représenter le patronat européen. Formes d'organisation patronale et modes d'action européenne* (Brussels: P.I.E. Peter Lang, 2013); Sylvain Laurens, *Les Courtiers du capitalisme. Milieux d'affaires et bureaucrates à Bruxelles* (Marseille: Agone, 2015).

Archives and Sources

The main source material for this book was drawn from public and private archives, correspondences, brochures, and workers' newspapers held in the IISH (International Institute of Social History) (Amsterdam), the Friedrich Ebert Foundation (Bonn), the AMSAB-Institut d'histoire sociale (Ghent), as well as in the collections of the Trades Union Congress Library and the British Library (both in London), and of the Institut d'histoire sociale de la CGT (IHS-CGT, Montreuil). Other information was mined from the archives of the Préfecture de Police de Paris (APP, Pré-Saint-Gervais), the Centre des archives diplomatiques du ministère des Affaires Étrangères (AMAE, La Courneuve), the departmental archives of the Nord and Seine-Saint-Denis departments (respectively, AD59, Lille, and AD93, Bobigny, *fonds* Zéphirin Camélinat), as well as from the collections of the Musée social (Paris) and the Académie François Bourdon (Le Creusot). Details of all documents consulted are recorded here in endnotes, page by page as they occur.

Very many pertinent documents and materials were reprinted and re-examined in critical studies between 1960 and 1970. Among these, the most useful references for the history of the European worker internationals are the minutes of the General Council of the First International (Institute of Marxism-Leninism, *The General Council of the First International: Minutes*, 1864–1872, 5 vols., Moscow: Progress Publishers, 1964), the correspondence between Marx, Engels, and other members of the International (Germany, Belgium, Spain, France, Italy, and the Netherlands), and the many volumes of the *Histoire de la IIeme Internationale* (Geneva, Minkoff Reprint, 1976–1985, 23 vols.).

Select Bibliography

Solidarities, Money, and Philanthropy

Barau, Denys. *La Cause des Grecs. Une histoire du mouvement philhellène (1821–1829)*. Paris: Honoré Champion, 2009.

Blais, Marie-Claude. *La Solidarité. Histoire d'une idée*. Paris: Gallimard, 2007.

Beckert, Jens, Julia Eckert, Martin Kohli, and Wolfgang Streeck, eds. *Transnationale Solidarität. Chancen und Grenzen*. Frankfurt–New York: Campus Verlag, 2004.

Blic, Damien de, and Jeanne Lazarus. *Sociologie de l'argent*. Paris: La Découverte, coll. "Repères," 2007.

Boltanski, Luc. *Distant Suffering: Morality, Media, and Politics*. Cambridge: Cambridge University Press, 1999 [1993].

Castel, Robert. *Les Métamorphoses de la question sociale. Une chronique du salariat*. Paris: Fayard, 1995.

Fassin, Didier. "Les économies morales revisitées." *Annales. Histoire, sciences sociales* 64, no. 6 (2009): 1237–66.

Featherstone, David. *Solidarity: Hidden Histories and Geographies of Internationalism*. London: Zed Books, 2012.

Fontaine, Laurence. *Moral Economy: Poverty, Credit, and Trust in Early Modern Europe*. Cambridge: Cambridge University Press, 2014 [2008].

Jonsson, Pernilla, and Silke Neunsinger. *Gendered Money: Financial Organization in Women's Movements, 1880–1933.* New York: Berghahn Books, 2012.

Lemercier, Claire, and Claire Zalc. "Pour une nouvelle approche de la relation de crédit en histoire contemporaine." *Annales. Histoire, sciences sociales* 67 no. (2012): 979–1009.

Prochasson, Christophe. "La gauche et l'argent." In *La Gauche est-elle morale?*, 115–58. Paris: Flammarion, 2010.

Rosanvallon, Pierre. *L'État en France, de 1789 à nos jours.* Paris: Seuil, 1990.

———. *The Society of Equals.* Cambridge, MA: Harvard University Press, 2013 [2011].

Scott, James C. *The Moral Economy of the Peasant: Rebellion and Subsistence in Southeast Asia.* New Haven, CT: Yale University Press, 1976.

Stjernø, Steinar. *Solidarity in Europe: The History of an Idea.* Cambridge: Cambridge University Press, 2004.

Supiot, Alain, ed. *La Solidarité. Enquête sur un principe juridique.* Paris: Odile Jacob, coll. "Travaux du Collège de France," 2015.

Thompson, Edward P. *The Making of the English Working Class.* London: Victor Gollancz Ltd., 1963.

———. *Customs in Common: Studies in Traditional Popular Culture.* New York: New Press, 1993.

Veyne, Paul. *Le Pain et le cirque. Sociologie historique d'un pluralisme politique.* Paris: Seuil, 1975.

Zelizer, Viviana A. *The Social Meaning of Money*, Princeton, NJ: Princeton University Press, 1995.

Globalization and Internationalisms at the Turn of the Twentieth Century

Anceau, Éric, Jacques-Olivier Boudon, and Olivier Dard, eds. *Histoire des internationales. Europe, XIXe–XXe siècle.* Paris: Nouveau Monde éditions, 2017.

Bayly, Christopher A. *The Birth of the Modern World (1780–1914).* Malden, MA: Blackwell Publishing, 2004.

Berger, Suzanne. *Notre première mondialisation. Leçons d'un échec oublié.* Paris: Seuil/République des idées, 2003.

Clavin, Patricia, and Glenda Sluga, eds. *Internationalisms: A Twentieth-Century History.* Cambridge: Cambridge University Press, 2017.

Geyer, Martin H., and Johannes Paulmann, eds. *The Mechanics of Internationalism: Culture, Society, and Politics from the 1840s to the First World War.* Oxford: Oxford University Press, 2001.

Herren, Madeleine. *Internationale Organisationen seit 1865. Eine Globalgeschichte der internationalen Ordnung.* Darmstadt: Wissenschaftliche Buchgesellschaft, 2009.

Jensen, Richard Bach. *The Battle against Anarchist Terrorism: An International History, 1878-1934.* Cambridge: Cambridge University Press, 2013.

Kott, Sandrine. "Les organisations internationales, terrains d'étude de la globalisation. Jalons pour une approche socio-historique." *Critique internationale* 52 (2011): 11–16.

Kott, Sandrine, and Joëlle Droux, eds. *Globalizing Social Rights: The International Labour Organization and Beyond.* London: Palgrave MacMillan, 2013.

O'Rourke, Kevin H., and Jeffrey G. Williamson. *Globalization and History. The Evolution of a Nineteenth-Century Atlantic Economy.* Cambridge, MA: MIT Press, 1999.

Osterhammel, Jürgen. *The Transformation of the World: A Global History of the Nineteenth Century.* Princeton, NJ: Princeton University Press, 2014 [2009].

Rosenberg, Emily, ed. *A World Connecting, 1870-1945.* Cambridge, MA: Harvard University Press, 2012.

Rosental, Paul-André. "Géopolitique et État-providence. Le BIT et la politique mondiale des migrations dans l'entre-deux-guerres." *Annales. Histoire, sciences sociales* 61, no. 1 (2006): 99–134.

Singaravélou, Pierre, and Sylvain Venayre, eds. *Histoire du monde au XIXᵉ siècle.* Paris: Fayard, 2017.

Sluga, Glenda. *Internationalism in the Age of Nationalism.* Philadelphia: University of Pennsylvania Press, 2013.

Socialist, Anarchist, and Communist Internationalisms

La Première Internationale. L'institution, l'implantation, le rayonnement. Paris: Éditions du CNRS, 1968.

Alayrac, Pierre. *L'Internationale au milieu du gué. De l'internationalisme socialiste au congrès de Londres (1896).* Rennes: Presses universitaires de Rennes, 2018.

Anderson, Benedict. *Under Three Flags: Anarchism and the Anticolonial Imagination.* London: Verso, 2006.

Archer, Julian P. W. *The First International in France, 1864–1872: Its Origins, Theories, and Impact.* New York: University Press of America, 1997.

Bantman, Constance. *The French Anarchists in London, 1880–1914: Exile and Transnationalism in the First Globalisation.* Liverpool: Liverpool University Press, 2013.

Bensimon, Fabrice, Quentin Deluermoz, and Jeanne Moisand, eds. "Arise Ye Wretched of the Earth." In *The First International in a Global Perspective.* Leiden: Brill, 2018.

Berger, Stefan. *Social Democracy and the Working Class in Nineteenth and Twentieth Century Germany.* Harlow: Longman, 2000.

Callahan, Kevin J. *Demonstration Culture: European Socialism and the Second International, 1889–1914.* Leicester: Troubadour Publishing, 2010.

Candar, Gilles, and Jean-Jacques Becker, eds. *Histoire des gauches en France.* 2 vols. Paris: La Découverte, 2004.

Collins, Henry, and Chimen Abramsky. *Karl Marx and the British Labour Movement: Years of the First International.* London: Macmillan, 1965.

Cordillot, Michel. *La Naissance du mouvement ouvrier à Besançon. La Première Internationale, 1869–1872.* Besançon: Centre d'étude du mouvement ouvrier, 1990 [1986].

———. *Aux origines du socialisme moderne. La Première Internationale, la Commune de Paris, l'exil.* Paris: Éditions de l'Atelier, 2010.

———. *Utopistes et exilés du Nouveau Monde. Des Français aux États-Unis de 1848 à la Commune.* Paris: Vendémiaire, 2013.

———. *Eugène Varlin, internationaliste et communard.* Paris: Spartacus, 2016 [1991].

Dogliani, Patrizia. "The Fate of Socialist Internationalism." In *International-isms: A Twentieth-Century History*, edited by Patricia Clavin and Glenda Sluga, 38–60. Cambridge: Cambridge University Press, 2017.

Donald, Moira. "Workers of the World Unite? Exploring the Enigma of the Second International." In *The Mechanics of Internationalism: Culture, Society, and Politics from the 1840s to the First World War*, edited by M. H. Geyer and J. Paulmann, 177–213. Oxford: Oxford University Press, 2001.

Ducange, Jean-Numa. *Jules Guesde. L'anti-Jaurès*. Paris: Armand Colin, 2017.

Dullin, Sabine, and Brigitte Studer. "Communisme + transnational. L'équa-tion retrouvée de l'internationalisme (premier XXe siècle)." *Monde(s)* 10 (November 2016): 9–32.

Evans, Richard J. *Proletarians and Politics: Socialism, Protest and the Work-ing Class in Germany before the First World War*. London: Harvester Wheatsheaf, 1990.

Haupt, Georges. *La Deuxième Internationale, 1889–1914*. Paris–La Haye: Mouton, 1964.

Holthoon, Frits van, and Marcel van der Linden, eds. *Internationalism in the Labour Movement, 1830–1940*. 2 vols. Leiden–New York: Brill, 1988.

Hostetter, Richard. *The Italian Socialist Movement*. 2 vols. Princeton, NJ: Princeton University Press, 1958.

Imlay, Talbot C. *The Practice of Socialist Internationalism: European Social-ists and International Politics, 1914–1960*. Oxford: Oxford University Press, 2018.

Jousse, Emmanuel. "Une histoire de l'Internationale." *Cahiers Jaurès*, nos. 212–13 (2014): 11–25.

——. *Les Hommes révoltés. Les origines intellectuelles du réformisme en France*. Paris: Fayard, 2017.

Kirchenbaum, Lisa A. *International Communism and the Spanish Civil War: Solidarity and Suspicion*. Cambridge: Cambridge University Press, 2015.

Kriegel, Annie. *Les Internationales ouvrières (1864–1943)*. Paris: PUF, 1964.

Léonard, Mathieu. *L'Émancipation des travailleurs. Une histoire de la Première Internationale*. Paris: La Fabrique, 2011.

Linden, Marcel van der. *Workers of the World: Essays toward a Global Labor History*. Leiden: Brill, 2008.

Meriggi, Maria Grazia. *L'Internazionale degli operai. Le relazioni internazionali dei lavoratori in Europa fra la caduta della Comune e gli anni'30*. Milan: FrancoAngeli, 2014.

Morgan, Roger. *The German Social Democrats and the First International, 1864–1872*. Cambridge: Cambridge University Press, 1965.

Puissant, Jean. *L'Évolution du mouvement ouvrier socialiste dans le Borinage*. Brussels: Académie royale de Belgique, 1982.

Schickl, Sebastian. *Universalismus und Partikularismus. Erfahrungsraum, Erwartungshorizont und Territorialdebatten in der diskursiven Praxis der II. Internationale 1889–1917*. St. Ingbert: Röhrig, 2012.

Sperber, Jonathan. *Karl Marx: A Nineteenth-Century Life*. New York: Liveright Publishing, 2013.

Stedman-Jones, Gareth. *Karl Marx: Greatness and Illusion*. Cambridge, MA: Belknap Press of Harvard University Press, 2016.

Studer, Brigitte. *The Transnational World of the Cominternians*. London: Palgrave Macmillan, 2015.

Welskopp, Thomas. *Das Banner der Brüderlichkeit. Die deutsche Sozialdemokratie vom Vormärz bis zum Sozialistengesetz*. Bonn: Dietz, 2000.

Workers, Strikes, and Unions

Boll, Friedhelm. *Arbeitskämpfe und Gewerkschaften in Deutschland, England und Frankreich. Ihre Entwicklung vom 19. zum 20. Jahrhundert*. Bonn: Dietz, 1992.

Cabot, Bastien. *"À bas les Belges!" L'expulsion des mineurs borains (Lens, août–septembre 1892)*. Rennes: Presses universitaires de Rennes–Fondation Jean-Jaurès, 2017.

Devin, Guillaume, ed. *Syndicalisme. Dimensions internationales*. La Garenne–Colombes: Éditions européennes Érasme, 1990.

Dolléans, Édouard. *Histoire du mouvement ouvrier.* Vol. 2, *1871–1936.* Paris: Armand Colin, 1939.

Dreyfus, Michel. "The Emergence of an International Trade Union Organization (1902–1919)." In *The International Confederation of Free Trade Unions,* edited by Marcel van der Linden, 25–71. Bern–New York: Peter Lang, 2000.

Goethem, Geert van. *The Amsterdam International: The World of the International Federation of Trade Unions (IFTU), 1913–1945.* Aldershot: Ashgate, 2006.

Hatzfeld, Nicolas, Michel Pigenet, and Xavier Vigna, eds. *Travail, travailleurs et ouvriers d'Europe au XXe siècle.* Dijon: Éditions universitaires de Dijon, 2016.

Knotter, Ad. "Transnational Cigar-Makers: Cross-Border Labour Markets, Strikes, and Solidarity at the Time of the First International (1864–1873)." *International Review of Social History* 59, no. 3 (December 2014): 409–42.

Julliard, Jacques. *L'Autonomie ouvrière. Études sur le syndicalisme d'action edecte.* Paris: Gallimard-Seuil, coll. "Hautes Études," 1988.

Machtan, Lothar. *Streiks und Aussperrungen im Deutschen Kaiserreich. Eine sozialgeschichte Dokumentation für die Jahre 1871 bis 1875.* Berlin: Colloquium Verlag, coll. "IWK," 9, 1984.

Mommsen, Wolfgang J., and Hans-Gerhard Husung, eds. *The Development of Trade Unionism in Great Britain and Germany, 1880–1914.* London: George Allen and Unwin, 1985.

Moss, Bernard. *The Origins of the French Labor Movement: The Socialism of Skilled Workers, 1830–1914.* Berkeley and Los Angeles: University of California Press, 1984.

Noiriel, Gérard. *Les Ouvriers dans la société française (XIXe–XXe siècle).* Paris: Seuil, 1986.

Perrot, Michelle. *Jeunesse de la grève. France, 1871–1890.* Paris: Seuil, 1984.

———. *Workers on Strike: France, 1871–1890.* New Haven, CT: Yale University Press, 1987.

Rancière, Jacques. *Proletarian Nights: The Workers' Dream in Nineteenth-Century France.* London: Verso, 1992 [1981].

Reid, Alastair J. *United We Stand: A History of Britain's Trade Unions.* London: Allen Lane, 2004.

Ritter, Gerhard A., ed. *Der Aufstieg der deutschen Arbeiterbewegung. Sozialdemokratie und freie Gewerkschaften im Parteiensystem und Sozialmilieu des Kaiserreichs.* Munich: R. Oldenbourg, 1990.

Robert, Jean-Louis, Friedhelm Boll, and Antoine Prost, eds. *L'Invention des syndicalismes. Le syndicalisme en Europe occidentale à la fi n du XIXe siècle.* Paris: Publications de la Sorbonne, 1997.

Rosanvallon, Pierre. *La Nouvelle Question syndicale.* Paris: Seuil, 1988.

Sewell, William. *Work and Revolution in France: The Language of Labor from the Old Regime to 1848.* Cambridge: Cambridge University Press, 1980.

Sirot, Stéphane. *La Grève en France. Une histoire sociale, XIXe–XXe siècle.* Paris: Odile Jacob, 2002.

———. *Le Syndicalisme, la politique et la grève. France et Europe (XIXe–XXIe siècle).* Nancy: Arbre bleu éditions, 2011.

Vigna, Xavier. *Histoire des ouvriers en France au XXe siècle.* Paris: Perrin, 2012.

Vinel, Jean-Christian, ed. *La Grève en exil? Syndicalisme et démocratie aux États-Unis et en Europe de l'Ouest (XIXe–XXIe siècle).* Nancy: Arbre bleu éditions, 2014.

Wagner, Anne-Catherine. *Vers l'Europe sociale? Une enquête sur la Confédération européenne des syndicats.* Bellecombe-en-Bauges: Éditions du Croquant, 2005.

Wilde, Bart de, ed. *The Past and Future of International Trade Unionism,* Ghent: IALHI-AMSAB Instituut, 2001.

Zancarini-Fournel, Michelle. *Les Luttes et les rêves. Une histoire populaire de la France de 1685 à nos jours.* Paris: Zones, 2016.

Index of Names

Abramsky, Chimen, 41

Adler, Victor, 291

Allemane, Jean, 185

Allende, Salvador, 313

Andrieu, Jules, 175

Anseele, Édouard, 210

Applegarth, Robert, 85, 102, 116, 120–24

Assi, Adolphe, 78, 83

Aubry, Émile, 110, 120

Bailey, Alfred, 203

Bakunin, Mikhail, 4, 6, 27–8, 37, 43, 56–8, 85, 121, 143, 187

Barbet, Virginie, 142–43

Bastelica, André, 174

Bastiat, Frédéric, 62

Baudin, Alphonse, 90

Bebel, August, 113–14, 131, 154, 159, 193, 272, 290–91

Becker, Johann Philipp, 99, 107, 130–31, 195

Beesly, Edward Spencer, 165

Benbow, William, 264

Berger, Stefan, 285

Bernard, Marie, 106

Bernstein, Eduard, 244, 249, 283

Beslay, Charles, 166, 174

Biétry, Pierre, 258

Bismarck, Otto von, 2, 57, 146, 194–95, 222, 225, 251

Blanc, Louis, 133, 184

Bologne, Louis, 166, 181

Boltanski, Luc, 8–9

Boon, Martin, 49, 52, 67

Bowen, Paul T., 215

Bradlaugh, Charles, 167

Briand, Aristide, 280

Brismée, Désiré, 151, 169, 194

Broadhurst, Henry, 203, 218

Brouckère, Louis de, 265

Brousse, Paul, 185

Bruce, Henry, 162

Burnett, John, 203

Burns, John, 217–19

Callahan, Kevin, 273

Camélinat, Zéphirin, 62, 99, 117, 168, 172, 174, 196–98, 304, 395

Caporusso, Stefano, 55–56
Chemalé, Félix, 41–42, 65
Choiseul, Étienne-François (duc de), 88
Christenert, Constant, 169
Cockerill, John, 153
Cohn, James, 49–50, 66, 136, 140, 197
Collet, Joseph, 67
Collins, Henry, 41
Combatz, Lucien, 172
Compère-Morel, Adéodat, 275
Coullery, Pierre, 100
Coulson, Edwin, 116
Courbet, Gustave, 181
Cremer, William Randal, 45, 53, 121

De Paepe, César, 50, 53, 63, 194,
    209–10
Dilke, Charles, 166
Dodot, Émile, 174
Dogliani, Patrizia, 325
Drury, Victor, 213
Dumay, Jean-Baptiste, 78–80, 83, 161
Dupont, Eugène, 29, 46, 82, 201
Durand, Gustave, 174

Eccarius, Johann, 29, 34, 36, 50, 64, 66,
    152, 194, 201
Engels, Friedrich, 4, 27–28, 31, 34, 37,
    44, 46, 52, 55, 58, 60–61, 85, 113, 149,
    159, 166, 172, 175, 187, 269
Esquiros, Alphonse, 79
Eudes, Émile, 175

Farga i Pellicer, Rafael, 43
Favre, Jules, 161–62
Featherstone, David, 7
Ferré, Théophile, 179
Ferrer, Francisco, 291, 305

Fimmen, Edo, 294
Foy, Maximilien Sébastien (General),
    90
Frankel, Léo, 33, 103, 174
Fribourg, Ernest Édouard, 31, 41,
    99–101, 117, 123, 148
Fureix, Emmanuel, 89–90

Gambetta, Léon, 79
Garibaldi, Giuseppe, 2, 78
Gladstone, William Ewart, 64, 141
Glaser de Willebrord, Édouard, 44
Godeau, 54
Gompers, Samuel, 215–16
Gould, Jay, 213
Graglia, François, 119, 122, 130
Greppo, Jean, 184
Griffuelhes, Victor, 251
Grousset, Paschal, 179
Guesde, Jules, 185, 193–94, 206, 211,
    280, 289
Guillaume, James, 50–51, 85, 166, 187

Hales, John, 33–36, 167, 194, 201
Hardie, Keir, 218, 291
Harris, George, 34
Harrison, Frederic, 165, 172
Haupt, Georges, 268
Hazeldine, Georges, 198
Henry, Hubert-Joseph (Colonel), 91
Hepner, Adolf, 159
Herman, Alfred, 154, 171
Hervé, Gustave, 286, 288–90
Herzig, Georges, 202
Hillquit, Morris, 274
Hins, Eugène, 84, 111, 158
Hoover, Herbert, 298, 300
Howell, George, 116, 218

Hugo, Victor, 184
Huysmans, Camille, 269, 278
Hyndman, Henry, 206, 217

Jamar, Alexandre, 76
Jarrige, François, 153, 263
Jaruzelski, Wojciech, 314
Jaurès, Jean, 198, 211, 272, 276, 280,
    289–91, 320
Jebb, Eglantyne, 301
Joffrin, Jules, 202
Johannard, Jules, 51, 124
Jourde, François, 174, 179, 182
Jung, Hermann, 30, 33–34, 40, 46, 50,
    100, 107, 112, 119, 164–65, 169–72, 201

Kamenev, Lev Borisovich, 279
Kato, Tokijiro, 274
Kautsky, Karl, 38
Kin, Arsène, 117
Klein, Nicholas, 274
Kollwitz, Käthe, 302
Kroemer, Victor, 274
Kropotkine, Pierre, 202, 231

Lafargue, Paul, 211
Lagardelle, Hubert, 280
Landeck, Bernard, 178, 182
Lassalle, Ferdinand, 56, 103, 131, 149,
    194
Law, Harriet, 142
Lawrence, Matthew, 41
Legien, Carl, 222–25, 141, 143, 145, 148,
    284, 288
Le Lubez, Victor, 167
Lenin, Vladimir Ilyich (Ulyanov), 279,
    296, 298
Lessner, Friedrich, 34, 50, 64

Liebknecht, Wilhelm, 113–114, 131, 159,
    181, 193, 195, 273
Limousin, Charles, 62
Linden, Marcel van der, 138
Lissagaray, Prosper-Olivier, 169
Louis, Paul, 232
Lucraft, Benjamin, 34
Luxemburg, Rosa, 279, 283–84, 289, 299

Malatesta, Errico, 202
Malon, Benoît, 79, 85, 185, 202
Mann, Tom, 217–19, 234, 239–40,
    246–47, 250, 254–55
Marx, Jenny, 164, 169, 172
Marx, Karl, 3–6, 27–28, 29–30, 32–35,
    37, 42–44, 46, 48–51, 57–58, 60–62,
    66, 82, 85–86, 97, 103–105, 113–116,
    119–120, 124, 134, 143, 149, 154, 159,
    164–165, 169–172, 175, 187, 211, 317
Matteotti, Giacomo, 302
May, Gustave and Elie, 175
Melotte, Georges, 171
Meriggi, Maria Grazia, 191
Michel, Louise, 202
Migeotte, Léopold, 88
Milner, George, 33, 36, 40
Moss, Bernard, 141
Most, Johann, 213
Mottershead, Thomas, 34, 49, 201
Münzenberg, Willi, 296–298, 301,
    307–8
Mussolini, Benito, 303, 307

Napoleon III, 2, 29, 57, 77, 146, 148
Nieuwenhuis, Ferdinand Domela, 288

O'Brien, James Bronterre, 67
Octors, Alphonse, 247

Odger, George, 116–18
Owen, Robert, 46, 99

Parfitt, Steven, 214
Pelloutier, Fernand, 226, 280
Perrot, Michelle, 92, 143, 249
Pinochet, Augusto, 312–13
Pouget, Émile, 280
Proudhon, Pierre-Joseph, 14, 61–64, 99

Rappoport, Charles, 304, 336
Razoua, Eugène, 162
Richard, Albert, 110–11, 143
Robin, Paul, 148, 154
Rochefort, Henri, 92, 155, 179
Rothschild (family), 168
Roy, Manabendra Nath, 306
Rozan, Philomène, 143

Sacco, Nicola, 305–6
Schneider (family), 77–80, 83, 156
Schulze-Delitzsch, Hermann, 69
Schweitzer, Johann Baptist von, 130
Seilhac, Léon de, 199–200, 264
Serwy, Victor, 269
Smith Headingley, Adolphe (aka
    Adolphe Smith), 167, 205
Sorel, Georges, 280, 286
Sorge, Friedrich, 201
Steens, Eugène, 194

Teulière, Ernest, 172

Theisz, Albert, 103
Thomas, Albert, 295
Thompson, Edward Palmer, 6, 12
Tillett, Ben, 217, 219, 239
Tolain, Henri, 62, 65, 99, 101, 117, 148
Tortelier, Joseph, 204

Uhry, Jules, 275

Vaillant, Édouard, 269, 289, 291
Valdun, 117
Vandenhouten, Alphonse, 53, 106
Vandervelde, Émile, 272, 282
Vanzetti, Bartolomeo, 305–6
Varlin, Eugène, 79, 95, 97, 103, 126,
    129–30, 138, 142, 179
Vésinier, Pierre, 148, 155, 174
Veyne, Paul, 88
Viard, Auguste, 175
Vollmar, Georg von, 289

Walentynowicz, Anna, 314
Walesa, Lech, 314
Weston, John, 103
Williams, Hugh, 166
Wilson, Woodrow, 298
Wolff, Frank, 278

Yvetot, Georges, 280

Zelizer, Viviana, 13
Zetkin, Clara, 270, 297

NICOLAS DELALANDE is an associate professor of history at the Centre d'Histoire de Sciences Po and editor in chief of *La Vie des Idées*, an online magazine. He is the author of *Les Batailles de l'impôt: Consentement et résistances de 1789 à nos jours* (2011) and a coeditor, with Patrick Boucheron, et al, of *Histoire mondiale de la France* (published in English in 2019 as *France in the World*) and, with Nicolas Barreyre, of *A World of Public Debts: A Political History* (2020).

ANTHONY ROBERTS is a freelance writer, journalist, poet, and prize-winning translator. He currently lives in France.